On Revolt

ON REVOLT

Strategies of National Liberation

J. Bowyer Bell

Harvard University Press
Cambridge, Massachusetts, and London, England
1976

Library of Congress Cataloging in Publication Data

Bell J   Bowyer, 1931-
   On revolt: strategies of national liberation.

   Bibliography: p.
   Includes index.
   1. Revolutions—Case studies. 2. Violence—
Case studies. 3. Guerrillas—Case studies.
4. Great Britain—Colonies—Case studies. I.
Title
JC491.B36   322.4'2   75-44026
ISBN 0-674-63655-4

This book was written under
the auspices of the
Center for International Affairs,
Harvard University

This is for my wife, Charlotte, who in various countries and sundry climates has coped with our four daughters and my four previous books, in hopes that she will prefer five of the latter instead of another of the former.

Preface

This study, the latest in a lengthening list of academic ventures into violence, has had a long and often uncertain gestation. Some years ago, in the course of various academic misadventures, I became intrigued with the similarities between various Irish revolts and that undertaken by the Irgun Zvai Leumi in what was to be Israel. While there might to the perceptive eye be no striking similarities between the green island of clouds and ancient dreams and the hot, dry desert polis between a blue sea and an Arab one, or between the Irish of legend and the Zionists of deed, I found that with little or no elaboration there was a curious parallel between the struggles, only partly successful, of the IRA and those, also only partly successful, of the Irgun. While it is perhaps true—as all revolutionaries, past and present, retired and active, have assured me—that each armed struggle is unique, I was troubled and then fascinated with the proposition that at least in revolts against the British there might be more common scarlet threads to the tapestry of violence than had at first been visible. If the British remained largely British, at least over a control period of a single generation, reacting relatively consistently to provocation and political violence, then it might be possible to examine a fair number of revolts in hopes of at least a few generalizations.

One all but insurmountable obstacle faces any comparative study of contemporary revolutions—and for most of those involved, the last generation is still quite contemporary: the sources are people. True, there was a rather substantial literature of British reactions to revolution and even a heartening group of primary memoirs, not to mention a small library of solid scholarly work on the period—but, alas, almost nothing that I wanted to know. I was most concerned with the slow unfolding of revolutionary strategy, the calculated response to repression, and the shift of tactics under pressure—and much, if not all, of that remained in individual memories. Why did you launch that operation? What did you expect to happen? And then what? A few revolutionaries *had* written their memoirs but often to set down a tale of valor or an apologia pro bella mea, not to answer my as-yet-unasked questions. To seek out and question at length an entire generation of rebels scattered from one end of the world to the other, to trace the old dragons to their pleasant palaces, was a project to boggle the mind of the most enthusiastic potential patron. Fortunately in Professor Thomas C. Schelling of the Center for International Affairs at Harvard, I found a boggleproof scholar possessed of massive patience and quiet enthusiasm. Because of his aid and comfort, it became possible to venture forth, if not to interview *every* rebel against the crown at least a startling number, and if not into *every* corner of the world at least into some very strange nooks and crannies. Tom Schelling's quiet confidence and long-lasting encouragement, despite the problems—including my decision to write another, quite different book first—made all the difference, made possible not just the book and whatever merits it may have, but insured that for three years I would have support proffered to few, the freedom of my convictions, and the opportunity to travel my own way through the revolts against the crown.

There are pitfalls and problems with oral history, but in the case of many revolutionary movements the alternative is no history at all. Man's memory is a fallible and often tricky guide; but if there are few and faulty written records, the only hope of amassing sufficient material for analysis is through interviews. Many memories for one reason or another proved pliable or faulty; some men were reticient; but few for any reason were malicious or patently mendacious. Not all saw the past as their fellows did or as I did, but seldom did men adjust the past solely to present usage. There were exaggerations and failed recollections, postdated motives and veiled recriminations. Some had over the years altered the past to buttress the future, unknowingly, perhaps even unconsciously, tinkering with their shifting fortunes. Still, with all the problems and all the lurking dangers of the interviews, the basis of the book had to be largely the human memory, checked and balanced by cross-reference and recourse to the printed word, but still and always open to doubt.

And so, with my family settled overlooking the gardens of Ennismore Square in Knightsbridge, I began over a year of voyages out of London's Heathrow into the recent past, commuting to the old battlegrounds of revolution in Africa and the Middle East—and some were not all that old nor were the revolutionary battles always quite finished. There were all the anticipated interviews, of course, the gradually heightening pile of five-by-eight cards, the raw ore; but there were also massive secondary returns. I sat at the great bars of the Emergencies—the Ledra Palace, in Nicosia, surely the most charming site to wait out a revolution, saw the forests of the Aberdares, the Canal

Zone (then a front line position for the Egyptians), the former safe houses in Cyprus, and the King David in Jerusalem, and talked to the old legends, Grivas and Begin, and to the new men in Zambia and Malawi. I walked the Murder Mile in Aden, and in London I journeyed to the House of Lords more often than most Lords, in Nairobi lunched at the Parliament, in Lahej up-country from Aden was feasted at a picture-book oasis, in Beirut spent an abortive revolution in the St. George bar. And everywhere I talked at length with the anonymous of the unmentionable: the arms smuggler out of the Congo, the old missionary from the Zambezi Valley, the mercenary looking for a comfortable slot, the pundits of the bar, the traveling salesmen of chemical goods or tomorrow's revolution, the journalists, the diplomats on leave, the cousins of sultans and the friends of the famous. Atmosphere and ambience are hard to footnote and, perhaps, of dubious academic value; but I, if not the book, am richer for the opportunity of the thousands of hours spent on wars and rumors of wars.

I did not of course get everywhere—Malaya was a bit out of the way—nor talk to everyone on my list, a list that grew to appalling proportions. And there were unforeseen difficulties. I was forbidden entry into three countries, prohibited from working in another, questioned by various authorities, followed twice, and bugged not too efficiently once. Then with the book in draft I had an opportunity three times to return to the Troubles in Northern Ireland to test my tentative conclusions against Celtic reality—and was on occasion shot at for my trouble, field work a bit too near the center of the field.

And still I found courteous, open-hearted cooperation nearly everywhere for an academic purpose that must have, at best, seemed passing strange to most. The names of all those who aided me with their recollections and sometimes later in correspondence are included in the sources. They are responsible for nothing but whatever virtues the book may have; all the egregious errors remain my own. There is no really effective way to thank so many people who in troubled and uncertain times were willing to help a strange man with a suspect mission—a search in alien fields for the rebellious heart—but it is a comfort to know that in far places the vocation of the scholar, the chronicler of past history, in a suspicious world still has some validity for many very different men. And there were many whose kindness will have no reward in the printed text, those who bought me too much beer or took me home to dinner or mailed clippings or sent me to see for myself or in some way took pity on the transient—from Mike Rowbotham and the untiring Mac McGuiness far to the south in Salisbury to the gentle and kind Sir John and Lady Shaw on the green in Winchelsea, thousands of miles north in Sussex.

I have included below those kind souls who in some way—and often at some expense, much time, and great patience—eased my path. In London: Dorothy Harnetton (Royal Institute of International Affairs, Library), Tom Little (Regional News Service), Patsy Robertson (Commonwealth Institute), Chaim Bermant, Professor Michael Foot (University of Manchester), Sir Derek Riches and Miles Hudson (Conservative Party Research Office), William B. King and my former professor, the late Edward D. Myers (the United States Embassy), Tom McNally (Labour Party Overseas Department), Dr. Roger Morgan (Royal Institute of International Affairs), Justin Nason and Henry Brian Shepherd (the Foreign Office), Professor Panayiotis J. Vatikiotis (University of London), Pavlos Hadjitofis (High Commission of Cyprus), M. Arad, Lieut-Colonel Yoseph Offer, and Yehuda Taggar (Embassy of Israel), F. C. Makoza (High Commission of Malawi), A. E. Smith and Christopher Rossow (Rhodesia House), Zafer Hassan (Embassy of Jordan), Faridon Hikmat and Peter Salah (Embassy of Lebanon), Taheen M. Basheer, M. Samir Ahmed, and Dr. Hussein Amin Fawzi (Embassy of the United Arab Republic), Saeed Ali Khubara (Embassy of the People's Republic of Southern Yemen), and S. L. Muhanji (High Commission of Kenya).

In Paris, Constantin Chryssostalis (Embassy of Cyprus); in Athens, Christopoulus Papadopoulos (Hellenic Red Cross) and Harris Vovides (Embassy of Cyprus); in Cyprus, Christopoulos Papachrysostomous (Cypriot Struggle Museum), Peter Stylianakis (Public Information Office), Dr. T. W. Adams, Dr. George Georgallides, and Alex Efthyvoulos (Associated Press); in Israel, David Niv, Meir (Marc) Kahan (*Hayom Daily*), Edna Zamir and Dr. Yehuda Benari (Jabotinsky Institute), Professor David Vital (Bar Ilan University), L. Pyetan (Public Information Office); in Beirut, Professor Walid Khalidi (American University Beirut), Ibrahim Noori (Regional News Service), Ghossan Tueni and Michele Abi-Jawdeh (*Al-Nahar*); in Amman, Riad Batchon, Burham Jayoussi, and Ghazi Saudi (Ministry of National Guidance), Faris Glubb, Hamad Farhan; in Cairo, Dr. Salah El-Addad, Ismail Imam Issa (Department of Foreign Cultural Relations), Dr. Osama El Baz (Director of Diplomatic Institute), Ahmad Baheaddin (*Al-Musawwar*), Dr. Louis Awad (*Al-Ahram*), Ahmed Anis, Dr. Metwally Shehata, Kemalba Bakr, and Mounir Hafez (Ministry of National Guidance); in Aden, Gawad M. A. Ghabary and Mohammad Abdel Wahad Chowdery (Tourism Office), Munawar Hazmi, Khalid Muheiraz, and Ali Ba-Dib (Ministry of Culture and National Guidance), Mohammed Abdo Ali (NLF) Foreign Relations Committee), Hemza Luqman (formerly the United States Consulate), Farouq Luqman (Reuters), and Mahmoud Arasi (later Director of Civil Aviation), William L. Eagleton, Edward Keller, and Steven Buck (Consulate of the United States); in Khartoum,

Dr. Fareed A. Atabani and Mohamed Omer Beshir (University of Khartoum); in Asmara, Murray Jackson (Consulate of the United States); in Nairobi, Professor James Coleman (Ford Foundation), Frank Ferrari (Afro-American Institute), S. Owens and the late Howard V. Funk (Embassy of the United States), Larry Fellows (*New York Times*), Stanley D. Moss (United States Information Service), Edmund Matu and Philip Wangwala (Ministry of Information), F. H. Mayieka (Office of the President), Professor Bethwell Alan Ogot (University College, Nairobi), John Nottingham (East Africa Publishing House); in Dar el Salaam, Tom Pickering and George Roberts (United States Embassy); in Lusaka, B. Chabafimbi and George Chipampata (Ministry of Foreign Affairs), L. J. Mwansmshiku (Ministry of Finance), Milimo Punabantu (Ministry of Information), Hillary Cunningham and Art Tienken (Embassy of the United States); in Salisbury, Harry Graham Jolly (High Commission of Malawi), Douglas Garner (Ministry of Information, Immigration and Tourism), T. V. R. Barbour (Office of the Officer Administering the Government), John Williamson (Public Information Office), Paul O'Neill and Irl Smith (Consulate of the United States); and in the United States, Kenneth Towsey (Rhodesian Information Service), Ambassador Ismail Al-Nouman (People's Republic of Southern Yemen), Mahmoud El Okdah (Arab League Office), Frank Crump and Don Tice (State Department).

Some of those offering aid and comfort fell into a middle ground, for they took a part in the events under question and their names also appear in the sources. Despite the risk of invidious distinctions, several names must be singled out for special thanks: Mahmoud El Okdah, who probably knows more important Arabs—or at least Arabs I should like to meet—than anyone else in America and remains through the years patiently on call. He is in fact a private Middle Eastern referral agency. In Nicosia, Peter Stylianakis, who brought an artist's touch to the Public Information Office, and all the Loizou clan, kind beyond measure. Dr. Yehuda Benari of the Jabotinsky Institute in Tel Aviv, a scholar, and a diplomat, is an intermediary par excellence. In Cairo there was Ismail Imam Issa as well as Dr. Osama El Baz, who knows everyone worth knowing. In Aden, Mahmoud Arasi shepherded me through weeks of interviews with great courage and undying patience. In Salisbury, Doug Garner, along with his wife and family, adopted the exhausted traveler.

Once the manuscript finally reached a legible draft, I received considerable advice and not a little comfort from a vast number of my academic collegues. Three desire special thanks: Dr. Barton Whaley, lately Center for International Studies, Massachusetts Institute of Technology; Professor Gil AlRoy of Hunter College, City University of New York; and Professor David Rapoport, University of California, Los Angeles.

Several institutions, with their, alas, anonymous staffs, deserve more than simple mention: The Cypriot Struggle Museum, the Jabotinsky Institute, the Royal Institute of International Affairs, and the Royal Commonwealth Society; also Harvard University in general and the Center for International Affairs in particular, especially the Library of Maury D. Feld and the patience of first Zoltan Tomory, Administrative Officer, and then Dr. Lawrence S. Finkelstein, Secretary to the Center. The Center, hardly an ivory tower with the contemporary vandals at the ivied gates and bombs in the attic, provided a most congenial atmosphere and all those involved, from the Director Robert R. Bowie down to the straggly yellow cat, displayed superb grace under pressure. In the process of producing the first draft, the editorial advice of the late Marina A. Finkelstein was crucial, assured that there would be other and far superior drafts. Then using the strategy of Fabian the Delayer, Martin Kessler succeeded in encouraging me to convert my script into a more general analysis of the strategies of national liberation. And during my time at Harvard, the enthusiasm and dedication of my secretary Jeannett Asdourian was heartening. Finally, at the end of the course at Columbia's Institute of War and Peace Studies, my research assistant Stephen Marsh was always on call, and at Harvard University Press, Aida DiPace Donald and Ann Louise McLaughlin were both keen, impressively efficient, inevitably prompt, and in all most elegant editors indeed.

The rebels are at last between these covers. Without it, they would still be out there in men's memories, where, perhaps, they might have preferred to remain, remnants of history that escaped the scholar's pen. Still I have, at last, finished my course.

Knightsbridge, London   J.B.B.
Cambridge, Massachusetts   Autumn 1975
New York, New York

It has been said that though God cannot alter the past, historians can; it is perhaps because they can be useful to Him in this respect that He tolerates their existence.—Samuel Butler

Contents

Part I.   **Revolts and Strategies of National Liberation**   **1**
1. The Nature of Revolt   3
2. The British Imperial Stage   19

Part Two.   **Revolts against the Crown**   **31**
3. The Palestinian Archetype: Irgun and the Strategy of Leverage   33
4. Two Alternative Strategies: Agitation in the Gold Coast and Communism in Malaya   71
5. Two Flawed Strategies: The Mau Mau in Kenya and the Egyptian Fedayeen in the Suez Canal Zone   92
6. Two Classical Confrontations: Containment of EOKA in Cyprus and Concession to the NLF in South Arabia   115

Part Three.   **On Revolt: Matrix, Models, and a Template**   **165**
7. A Generation of Violent Dialogue: The Evolving British Matrix   167
8. The Rebel Models   179
9. An Irish Template   192

Part Four.   **The Rebel Vocation**   **207**
10. The Lethal Dialogue   209

Sources   241
Notes   255
Index   265

Illustrations

page 2. A Provisional IRA volunteer of the Belfast Brigade explains the working of a rifle. (Photograph by David Gifford)

page 32. Jomo Kenyatta under arrest for Mau Mau activities. (United Press International photo)

following page 70:

Sinn Feiner held at pistol point by British Auxiliaries, November 1920. (Radio Times Hulton Picture Library)

A British soldier maintains his lonely vigil overlooking the Old City of Jerusalem. (Associated Press photo)

Barbed wire in the streets of Jerusalem, 1947-1949. (Photograph courtesy of Zionist Archives and Library)

The bodies of kidnapped British Sergeants Clifford Martin and Mervyn Paice, Palestine, July 1947. (World Wide Photos)

Shepheard's Hotel in Cairo, a crumbled ruin in the wake of anti-British rioting, February 1952. (United Press International photo)

Mahatma Gandhi with Nehru and Maulana Azad. (Photograph courtesy of Information Service of India)

following page 114:

Commonwealth troops on patrol deep in the Malayan jungle, August 1957. (Keystone photo)

Five women MLRA members on the day of their surrender, 1953. (Photograph courtesy of Federal Department of Information, Malaysia)

Detainees at a rehabilitation camp near Penang, Malaya, 1950. (Radio Times Hulton Picture Library)

The Duchess of Kent and Prime Minister Nkrumah dancing (Photograph courtesy of Information Services Department, Ghana)

General George Grivas on his arrival at Athens airport. (W. Byford-Jones, *Grivas and the Story of EOKA* [London, 1959])

Gamal Abdul Nasser addressing an Egyptian crowd. (Photograph courtesy of Arab Information Center) *page 166.* Anti-British banners held by angry Egyptians in Ismailia Square, November 1951. (United Press International photo)

following page 178:

Qahatan Ashaabi, leader of the National Liberation Front, 1967. (United Press International photo)

British soldiers stand guard over a suspect in Aden, March 1967. (United Press International photo)

The first car bomb being constructed in Derry, Northern Ireland, March 1972. (David Gifford photo)

A bomb being concealed in a woman's cosmetic case. (David Gifford photo)

A camouflaged British soldier in Northern Ireland. (David Gifford photo)

An Arab Fedayeen on the balcony of the captured Israeli team quarters at the Munich Olympic Village, September 1972. (World Wide Photos)

A BOAC VC-10 dynamited by the PFLP at Dawson Field, Jordan, September 1970. (United Press International photo)

page 208. A Palestinian Fedayeen at the Munich 1972 Olympics. (World Wide Photos)

PART ONE

Revolts and Strategies of National Liberation

Without a revolutionary theory there is no revolutionary practice.

—*V. I. Lenin*

Face concealed to protect his identity, a Provisional IRA volunteer of the Belfast Brigade
explains the working of a rifle.

1 The Nature of Revolt

C'est une revolte
                        —Louis XVI, July 14, 1789
Non, Sire, c'est une revolution
                        —Duc de La Rochefoucauld-Liancourt

The vocation of the rebel has been a long if not always honorable one in Western history. The centuries have been littered with fallen angels, with romantic exiles across the water and wild geese fled from failure, with the faithful few waiting for the shift in the tides of fortune to rise in arms, just as the reins of power have been held by those rebels more ruthless or more fortunate. At the very beginning Cain slew Abel, Antigone denied authority and the gods, and Spartacus rose against Rome. In the West, Cromwell would come to power, a regicide in puritan garb, and the Young Pretender would die uncrowned. Excluding legends and myths, the rebel Robins in Sherwood Forest, and the clash of dynasties, there could be no revolt under the banner of national liberation until the men of the eighteenth century took to the streets to fashion republics of virtue. The long litany of revolt, however comforting to the rebel, forms no real prologue to the armed struggle for national liberation, offers few effective strategies of action beyond the dictum of a Machiavelli or the example of Greece. In the long course of violent opposition to authority, the banner of national liberation has only recently been raised.

Revolution

Frustrated or oppressed, denied justice or inalienable rights, the enlightened rebel rose to replace the alien or illegitimate authority by resort to an armed struggle. Some few revolts, more carefully led or more fortunate, swept new men into old chairs. Even the French sons of the revolution were driven from Haiti by L'Ouverture, a more faithful disciple than they. Most attempts aborted. And not all rebels had an elegant motive or a rigorous rationale: enraged peasants sacked the manor and slaughtered the sheep and servants, roaring mobs burned their way through the city. These uprisings flickered out in ashes and executions, narrow pogroms of the spirit, lances for ancient boils of oppression. Endemic rebels on the boundaries of civilization, red Indians or black slaves repelled with primitive tools the exertion of appropriate authority. Neither the noble savage nor the simple peasant, fighting under strange devices, played a relevant role in the repeated staging of revolts for national liberation by the children of the enlightenment. Even they, before the creation of republics of virtue and the emergence of nations from geographic expression, found others on the road to the future bearing similar banners but acting in the name of the proletariat and the peasant. The barricades had grown crowded.

Most of those rushing toward the barricades—Mazzini, Garibaldi, Wagner, Bakunin, or Marx—sought not simply to revolt but to launch the revolution, their revolution. On the night of July 14, 1789, Louis XVI responded to the news of the fall of the Bastille with *"C'est une révolte."* The bearer of bad tidings, the Duc de La Rochefoucauld-Liancourt replied, *"Non, Sire, c'est une révolution."*[1] And of course it was; but the distinction, so clear at the moment of the Bastille and so obvious in the mind of Marx or Bakunin, has become blurred in the wealth of ensuing examples. Is revolution simply a change in regime—the government—as most dictionaries would have us believe? Surely there can not have been that many revolutions in a single Syrian generation? Is something more fundamental involved? No one seems to be certain of the exact nature of an insurrection, of the difference between rebellion and revolt or between a rebel and an insurgent or when, if ever, a revolt becomes a revolution. In the course of academic and activist analysis, a variety of terms have become either interchangeable or defined in contradictory ways; standard British military practice differs from the usage at revolutionary conferences. No general agreement is likely on appropriate definitions or accepted distinctions.

For most people revolution at least implies substantial change, a most serious transformation of an existing society beyond the arrival of a new elite concerned solely with the accumulation of assets or uninterested or unable to effect the tenor of life. A revolution seeks to transform or transpose basic values. Old ways are ridiculed, entrenched power expropriated, and old classes destroyed. New men are admired or created, former habits and attitudes, even those held by men distant from the center, decay or are warped in the service of new ideals. A revolution may, must, take time to fashion the new, and the heritage of the past can not be easily discarded. It took Stalin a decade to create socialism in one country, and that country was demonstrably very Russian indeed but equally demonstrably not Tsarist Russia either. Revolutions may come in many ways—on the wake of riot in France or in the course of an armed struggle in China—but the crucial factor is the change in attitudes, not postures, in values, not offices.

Initiated and directed by a talented and zealous elite, a revolution establishes a new vision, compelling in logic and effective in practice, that converts the many to changed values, establishing a new legitimacy not entirely unrelated to the heritage of the past but alien to the displaced. In a political revolution such a transformation is almost inevitably associated with violence during the seizure of power or in the protection of the new. This is not necessarily true with revolutions of the mind or eye, although violence may well be done to the spirit by the implications of Max Plank's postulation of quantum theory or Picasso's first cubist painting. In all cases the momentum for change appears to expand from a nodal point, whether 1776 or 1917, increasingly irreversible and demonstrably different: all is utterly changed or to contemporaries appears to be. Thus, the almost annual changes in physical theory after 1900 or painterly practice after 1909 left the former orthodoxies in shambles; only the most determined could maintain the pace in an era of intense creativity, and sufficient change occurred in a decade to require almost fifty years of elaboration and refinement. Yet in retrospect it is clear that Plank and Picasso, like Jefferson or Lenin, stood on the shoulders of giants; they fulfilled a potential as well as imposed the novel. Revolutions, in physics as in politics, are not quick bright flashes, but a matter of a decade or a generation, for men are not so easily converted from the comfortable habits of the past either by the exertion of coercion or the appeal of right reason.

Revolt

A revolt is a quite different matter, and a much less complex one. A revolt is narrower than a revolution. It is a violent, continuing reaction to centralized authority that may lead to revolution, an early grave, or despotic power. Revolts have been described in terms of goals, wars of separation; or of means, guerrilla war; or in light of the opponent, civil war. But for the self-serving, *our* revolution, the distinction is clear. Essentially, in a revolt the rebel abrogates previous authority by recourse to armed force in an effort to seize power in the name of a denied legitimacy. Although the aims of a revolt may in large part determine the orchestration of rebel resources, no new vision nor any intention of fashioning a new society is necessary. A revolt is a means to an end, or varying ends, a determined and coherent response with violence to the intolerable. Simple violence, the decay of order and bombs in the street does not indicate a revolt.

It is no easy matter to distinguish between sporadic disorder and spontaneous violence (that is, low-intensity violence exploited by rebels) and rational violence carefully used not to subvert but to influence authority. Violence, no matter its level or potential, is an inadequate gauge to define a revolt. The following examples of low intensity violence occurred in various parts of the world almost simultaneously. On May 22, 1973, in Srinagar, Kashmir, police fired into a crowd, killing two members of an anti-British demonstration. By the end of the day, over one hundred people had been injured, including more than fifty police, because the British publishers of the *Book of Knowledge* had included an "insulting" reference to Islam—the inclusion of a photograph of Mohammed. On the same day, in the Indian state of Uttar Pradesh, during widespread disorder, thirty people were killed in a heavy gunfire exchange between the army and the Provincial Armed Constabulary. The local police had formed an alliance with protesting students at Lucknow University, a protest that had extended to riot and arson, forcing the intervention of the army. In Srinagar the protest, grounded in the changing values of a modernizing society and the images of a colonial past, may have revealed to the cunning the prospects of subsequent revolt, but on May 22 the incident could be defined only as a sporadic disorder. In Lucknow the alienation of the students and the armed police in a nation torn by ethnic, religious, linguistic, and regional divisions led from the burning of the university to a situation that the central government in New Delhi might well view as a rebellion—spontaneous violence that if escalated might lead to a regional revolt.[2] On May 23, in Derry, Northern Ireland, a young man was mortally wounded by the British security forces during one of the endless confrontations and incidents concomitant to the armed struggle of the Provisional Irish Republican Army. In retaliation, young men hijacked buses and cars, creating barricades that in turn attracted British military, who in turn were fired on by snipers. This riot, undoubtedly largely spontaneous, formed an integral tactical part of the IRA campaign—analytically a quite different matter from the events in Asia a day earlier. On the other hand, in Argentina, on May 22, a conservative Peronist labor leader was assassinated in La Plata, in a continuing radical campaign to coerce the Peronist government-elect into pursuing a radical course. Superficially, a campaign of assassination would appear a revolt, but in Argentina this was not the case.[3]

In Angola in 1960 the declining earning power of the African worker coupled with growing Portuguese repression produced a volatile situation. Generations of colonial injustice and the slow but inevitable decay of traditional social institutions left the African population largely disoriented and in despair. The specifically and therefore abrupt worsening of the situation led to a sequential explosion—widespread, unrelated, almost always spontaneous outbreaks that culminated on March 15 in bloody attacks on white settlers throughout the areas on the Congo border and deep into the interior. Swift, indiscriminate, and ruthless reprisals by the Portuguese drove still other Africans into rebellion. At the time two major Angolan liberation movements were attempting, in one way or another, to subvert Portuguese authority and prepare the way for an armed struggle if need be. Neither foresaw the events of March 1961, but both exploited the opportunity.[4] By the end of the year two coherent rebel movements directed a guerrilla campaign that a decade later the Portuguese had been unable to frustrate. In Ireland the Provisional IRA had in a quite different way exploited a civil rights campaign that had sparked violent Protestant resistance, necessitating the intervention of the British army, to begin one more campaign for a united Ireland. Fearful of the Protestants, the Irish Catholic population had tolerated or encouraged IRA provocation of the British army, not a popular institution with Irish nationalists; this in time led to a continuing round of incidents and outrages that wedded the IRA and the nationalist community still further and engendered violent and self-defeating retaliation on the part of British security forces.[5] Increasingly during 1971 it was clear that the IRA had gone over from a defensive posture to open revolt.

A revolt is also neither a coup nor a mutiny—or at least there seems little point in draining quite satisfactory meaning from either.[6] If arbitrarily an insurgency implies less orderly rebel control, such as the rising of the wretched, angry tribes in the bush, the disorganized resistance of the natives and the pillage of peasants can be put aside in the present analysis. Here a revolt implies neither swift success (the king hustled out of the country and the junta in power) nor simple resistance (by Red sailors to reactionary admirals) nor the undirected brutality of spontaneous risings. A revolt may be immediately transformed by failure or success, at least for analytical purposes. The Egyptian Free Officers "rose," only to find a vacuum; the Spanish generals in July 1936 sought a coup, but initiated not so much a revolt as a civil war. For there to be a revolt the rebels must meet resistance, not so efficiently that they win immediately or so effective that they can create a recognizable, legitimate alternative to the existing regime. When Lenin found power in the streets of Petrograd in November 1917, there was no revolt; he simply picked it up and defended the new revolutionary communist center during a complicated civil war. The incapacity of centralized authority to respond effectively to a disorderly challenge may permit riot and arson to evolve into coherent revolt in the streets of Budapest or the steppes of the Ukraine or may encourage the continuation of endemic violence, an ill-directed insurrection not a revolt. For present purposes, a revolt is a coherent, armed rising of sufficient proportion to challenge seriously the existing central authority, but without the capacity to create an alternative authority: a lethal dialogue between rebel aspirants to power and the forces of authority.[7]

Increasingly over the last generation rebels have launched their armed struggle under the banner of national liberation, however apt this may appear to the distant. Earlier, and throughout much of the nineteenth century, the revolutionary age of heroes, there were two parallel paths to the barricades, often indistinguishable tactically but directed at different goals: The Nation, descendent of Republics of Virtue; and Communism, The Triumph of the New Class. Not until the collapse of Trotsky's exercise in permanent revolution and the triumph of Stalin's Revolution in One Country did the communist theorists, albeit reluctantly, contemplate a revolution limned mainly in national terms. By then the repeated betrayal by socialists choosing national loyalty rather than class duty had underlined the appeal of the old patriotism. To a degree, Mazzini's vision of a stable democratic world founded on satisfied nations living in harmony began to be adapted for communist usage: Socialism in Many Countries just as there were many Socialist Republics in Communist Russia. And, of course, both the nationalists and communists opposed imperialism—others' imperialism.

In the 1930s three major schools of revolution contemplated revolt. The communists, addicted to the barricade, anticipated the triumph of the urban proletariat and one more socialist nation. The rebels of redemption, fascists by and large, sought to liberate their nation from alien institutions such as parliamentary democracy or universal education. There also were the nationalists, who had not completed their nation's liberation—a united Ireland, an independent Egypt—or, like the Zionists or Filipinos, as yet had no nation. Almost until World War II the colonial target did not seem promising. Until 1945 the prime ideological and theoretical interests of poetential rebels remained focused on the old examples analyzed with orthodox terminology. With the sapping of imperial vitality by 1945, the targets of rebel opportunity suddenly became more numerous and more promising. After 1945, the rebels of redemption largely disappeared and communists of varying flavors and nationalists of different hues sought to dismantle the old empires. The new banner of national liberation began to be borrowed by rebels who sought to overturn seemingly indigenous regimes. No matter that the target nation had a long and independent history, generally accepted legitimacy, membership in the United Nations, a flag, postage stamps, and an army, the rebels contended that the tyrannical regime, often imposed or encouraged from abroad, oppressed the real nation. Just as the rebels of redemption in the twenties and thirties sought to release the ancient nation from new and alien institutions, the new rebel wanted to liberate his nation from old and corrupt institutions and made off with the banner of national liberation. And Castro won in Cuba under the new device just as Ché lost in Bolivia.

Most of the postwar rebels have seldom collaborated in projects to further world revolution or envisaged a future without national boundaries. In Latin America the new rebels cooperated with each other and were often sponsored from revolutionary centers—Havana in particular —but structured their struggle in a national context: many were revolts against the many pawns of imperialism. In Africa the rebels often had to build nations within old colonial boundaries during the course of the armed struggle. All attempts to do otherwise have aborted—Biafra, Katanga, South Sudan, or Eritrea. In Asia only Bangladesh adjusted old colonial boundaries. There have been some rebel definitions of the target nation that vary in not unimportant ways from historical inheritance. Some rebels seek national boundaries that embarrass an existing, relatively contented regime. The IRA wants a thirty-two-county united Ireland,[8] the followers of Grivas a Greek Cyprus. Others, as have their ideological ancestors, seek a nation submerged beyond all memory —a Basque state. Some few rebels seek to go far beyond the old and irrelevant cartography: the fedayeen hope to liberate not just an inchoate Palestine from Zionism but the entire Arab nation from sloth, imperialism, the legacy of the past, and the tyranny of the existing establishment. No matter whether the focus of the rebel is narrowed to an irredentist scrap in the Tyrol or includes the liberation of all workers and peasants, the revolt is legitimized under the new national banner.

Often the banner has been stolen by driven or dreadful men seeking authority for violence. Tribal warfare, riotous confrontation, endemic murder along old ethnic fault lines, pathological bombers, snipers out of the urban ghettos, lone assassins, arson in low vengeance—all the dreadful results of laxity at the center, the slippages of order, the frustration of the wretched are hardly liberation struggles. A revolt in the name of national liberation may be fashioned out of random violence and chaos or from old hatreds, but by rational if desperate men, who impose a coherence and continuity. With rare exceptions these rebels, like those who have long conspired to subvert authority, do so in the name of national liberation.[9]

Ideological Models for National Liberation

The great ideological strategists of revolution, Marx or Mao, Mazzini or Bakunin or Sorel, Jefferson or Lenin, prepared the rebel to rise, defined the cause and the opponent, indicated the future, detailed the obstacles; but their grand strategy has remained, as is the

wont of philosophy, difficult to apply in the field. Those historic coun-
sels to rebels on the eve of the armed struggle always insisted on flexibility, imagination, a grasp of the unexpected, a creative use of the manual
of tactics—admonitions profoundly true but difficult to apply. Yet the
worth of the world view, the grand strategy, may be of inestimable value,
if not practical use, permitting an effective mix of ideological legitimacy
with the vicious tactics of the bush, producing real tactical gains, deep
psychic comfort, and movement toward power. Toussaint L'Ouverture
under the banner of Revolution in the name of a Republic of Virtue
swept away his former French masters in the name of the Rights of Man.

The most prevalent of contemporary ideological strategies is that
great current of scientific socialism arising in Marx and his immediate
predecessors, cresting in Lenin, diverted and exploited for differing purposes and with varying emphases by Trotsky and Stalin, renewed by Mao
and Giap in Asia, and refined beyond reality in the *focos* of Latin American jungles or the rhetoric of Parisian students. Always the foundation
has been Marx, who gave to the cause of revolution a philosophy, an
explanation of history, a program of action, and an outline of the future.
For much of the Left the rigor of his analysis had and has an overpowering logic, but for many there was more than one road to revolution. The
orthodox disciples of the Master, including Lenin, who proved far more
flexible in both analysis and practice than most Leninists, foresaw an
urban proletariat insurrection that would sweep away the old regimes
sapped by internal contradictions. As Lenin pointed out, before that
moment there would be many revolts at different times, in different
places, and of different kinds; all would fail until at last the mass was
mobilized. At that moment the rush to the barricades would result in the
triumph of the proletariat: the Paris Commune writ large. To achieve
that end, Lenin advised a variety of tactics but concentrated on the role
of the party to orchestrate the class struggle. Others, less orthodox,
placed their dependence on the peasants or parliaments as an alternative
to the proletariat and the party. Some of the heretics of the Left, in particular the anarchists, advocated terror and practiced assassination.
Others sought power through subversion or conspiracy, a general strike,
or an alliance with the bourgeois. The attraction, however, of the urban
rising remained, even for many anarchists. The collapse of Russia into
chaos in 1905 seemed to augur well for the common revolutionary wisdom fashioned thereafter by Lenin. The triumph of 1917 in the streets of
Petrograd came without the final onslaught. While Trotsky and Stalin
differed, among other matters, on persistence and timing, the major
hope for revolution remained attuned to Lenin's vision: escalating urban
proletariat insurrection.

While Stalin concentrated on Socialism in One Country and Trotsky on exile polemics, Mao Tse-Tung in China was in the process of fusing the tactics and strategy of a classical guerrilla war with a new revolutionary theory based on the peasant masses. Beginning with the disastrous Autumn Harvest Uprising in 1927, and continuing until the collapse of Chiang Kai-shek in 1949, Mao evolved his new theory out of practice in the field, mobilizing the masses and refining his theoretical explanation of objective reality simultaneously. As the Chinese masses were mobilized, the revolution would move through three stages—strategic defense, equilibrium, and strategic offense—each furthered by a special method of warfare—guerrilla-war, positional-war, and mobile-war. On each level Mao analyzed the problems, tactics, and strategy and tested his concepts in practice. To a degree he minimized certain factors—the impact of the Japanese invasion, for example—and in retrospect adjusted events to buttress theory; but the end result was a theory of guerrilla-revolution so intensive, so closely reasoned, and so effective in Chinese practice that an ideological alternative to The Barricades existed in The Long March. A new and potent strategy of national liberation had been fashioned in the Chinese cauldron.[10]

While Ho Chi Minh and Vo Nguyên Giap tried to apply Mao's dictum with varying success in Indochina over the next generation, another option for revolutionaries was proposed, based in part on the success of Fidel Castro in 1959 and in large part on the impatience of the dedicated who could not create and did not want to wait for the elusive optimum conditions that would guarantee the success of the general onslaught. In Cuba, Castro began his campaign with a dozen guerrillas in the Sierra Maestra—hardly optimum conditions. Yet he won; for his guerrillas had vitalized the masses. Or so said his advocates, who did not realize the carefully orchestrated campaign Castro had conducted against a brutal and inefficient opponent. The bearded men in the mountains were very important but not all-important—as believed Castro's aide Ché Guevara, who remained convinced that the injection of a small guerrilla foco in the countryside could begin the chain reaction of revolution. Ché became a myth in his own time, and his death in Bolivia an example to a generation of potential rebels. Some more pragmatic drew back from the illusion of the isolated foco; others turned to the opportunities of urban guerrilla war that shatter the fragile tyrannies in the capitals; but many in far places accepted Ché dictum. Daniel Cohn-Bendit insisted that the Paris "Revolution" of 1968 proved that "small revolutionary groups can, at the right time and place, rupture the system decisively and irreversibly."[11] And, throughout the Third World, scores of revolutionary-guerrillas in small movements and large sought to apply the theories of Ché or Mao in some variant of the new revolutionary orthodoxy. Many of these new revolts are launched not just to liberate the nation but also in the process to create that nation. Many rebels have accepted and elaborated the ideas of Frantz Fanon, based on his experience during the Algerian war, that a "native" could—must—be transformed into a free man by means of the armed struggle. Violence would be the midwife to new nations created out of wrangling tribes and historic enemies smelted in the guerrilla oven. Other contemporary rebels with similar aims and comparable tactics wanted no part of that atheistic, materialistic, heretical heritage. For a man like General George Grivas in Cyprus, his EOKA and his struggle had nothing to do with Mao, nor did any real campaign for national liberation; communism under whatever guise, offering any variety of alluring tactics, was a means to oppress not to liberate. For Grivas "the liberation struggle of the Algerian people has nothing in common with Mao's Chinese social revolution."[12] Colonel Muammar el-Qaddafi, leader of Libya's ruling council, responded in much the same way to the ideological postures of the more radical Palestinian fedayeen groups: their leaders like George Habash and Naref Hawatmeh would subvert the traditional Islamic basis of the Arab nation or any future Palestinian nation. In the case of Grivas and el-Qaddafi, both pious men, the key component of the spurned strategy is atheism. Others have rejected the current out of fear of manipulation by self-interested "strategists" in Moscow or Peking or Havana. For them Fanon may well be right that violence has a creative function, Ché's bravery may be worthy of emulation, and Mao's tactics of use in the field; but the new men and new nations their struggle seeks to create are quite different. As a result, there are those, alienated from the socialist strain, who are representatives of national egotism, who see an ideological basis of self-determination coupled with social justice as ample for their needs. Grivas assumed that his own Hellenic tradition would be sufficient ideological grounding, as his selection of a cover name, *Dighenis,* out of that heritage indicated. For him, as for others, tactics were tactics, guerrilla or otherwise, ideologically neutral, and national liberation meant just that. Ideologically, this is a minority position. Most rebels no longer feel the dreams of Jefferson or Wilson sufficient, a Republic of Virtue or a Bill of Rights the ultimate goal. On the other hand, most believe their struggle has a special egotism, a particular history, and a unique future. And the current theories of guerrilla-revolution are a comfort in troubled times.

It is possible to draw back from the ideological content of various strategies of national revolt and apply a different typological matrix. By and large, the division of strategies into ideological camps is useful in explaining why a rebel goes to the barricades, what he anticipates will there occur, and what he seeks to win. How he fashions the means to win may relate only marginally to the vast generalizations of ideological strategic strictures or those means may be parsed rigidly from the authorized manual. If the focus remains on the means, remarkable similarities between a George Washington and a Mao Tse-Tung could be observed. Both started from military scratch with considerable political support, and substantial domestic opposition. Both over a considerable period of time created irregular armies capable of fighting and winning major battles. Both evaded battle more often than not, depended on flexibility, stealth, and surprise, relied on the political convictions of their soldiers and the internal contradictions of their enemies. Both fought for a revolutionary cause, using unorthodox tactics familiar to their troops but alien to the enemy. Both exploited to the best of their isolated ability the existing world situation to their opponent's disadvantage, using pragmatism or ideology to win friends and subvert enemies.

Nonideological Models for National Liberation

Although striking differences exist, it is possible to suggest a nonideological model for strategies of national liberation. First, the men of the Optimum Moment go to the barricades convinced that no one is on the other side. Considerable time and effort have been spent during the last century, particularly in orthodox communist circles, in setting out the objective conditions that guarantee inevitable, almost immediate success. To some degree all rebels believe that if the people would just come out—even with knives and forks, as one Irish rebel noted—all would be well. Certainly a large number of men have not so much gone to the barricades but come out of the barracks to fill what, as some suspected, turns out to be a vacuum. Nasser's Free Officer "Revolt on the Nile" turned out to be a long evening filled with compensating errors and threats followed by immediate power. A second major strategy is that of the Instant Alternative: the rebel legitimized and able to employ force proportional to the authority of the center at once. Thus, after July 1776 the American rebels hoped to maintain an alternative legitimacy: a regular army, a Continental Congress, the Articles of Confederation, and emissaries abroad. In this George Washington and Mao Tse-Tung followed different courses. The Chinese, assuming history's legitimacy and isolated by war and distance, made little effort to produce a recognizable alternative in a great leap forward. Obviously an unoccupied base is of great help in this stratagem and often produces, as it did with the Confederate States of America in 1861, a conflict best analyzed as civil war. Even without a firm base possibilities remain, as the Spanish generals found when their coup collapsed, in July 1936, but not before the weakness of the Republicans permitted the army to coalesce into an alternative regime. In both cases the strategies of the Optimum Opponent and the Instant Alternative must fail to produce the necessity for a more orthodox revolt. This was true of Ho Chi Minh, when on September 2, 1945, he set up a Democratic Republic of Vietnam. The French were an ideal opponent for they had been expelled by the Japanese and presumably would recognize reality. For many reasons the French did not accept the role of Optimum Opponent, thus forcing Ho to opt for his Republic as an Alternate Legitimacy, a legitimacy defended in 1946 with conventional military forces that the French defeated. Only then did Ho have recourse to a strategy of revolt.

At the moment of truth or the call to the barricades—in Ho's case the return to the jungle—the strategist has decided on one of several scenarios. Ho and Mao projected an Incremental Strategy, and assumed that from the given base a careful mix of tactics would produce additional assets that in the fullness of time would be comparable to and then superior to those of the opponent in the field. There might be retrogression, or errors in the application of tactics suited to a level not yet reached or a shift of opponents, but the assumption was that every day in every way the rebels would get better and better and become first a viable alternative and then the inevitable victor. In an incremental strategy the accumulating strength may be geographically secured—an ink blot moving out of the revolt-center—or demographically secured—an increasing number of the population subverted to the new authority. Obviously a judicious mix of both would accelerate an incremental revolt, but most observers have suspected that a populated free-zone, isolated by distance or terrain, may be vital, that is, that an incremental strategy might have little chance in a smaller, less rugged country.

A second scenario depends on a discrete and violent event—the Foco Flash—to transform objective conditions to rebel advantage. The Irish in 1916 until nearly the last minute hoped that a mass rising in Dublin, followed by risings elsewhere in the island plus some aid from Germany, would face the British Empire, deeply engaged in a world war, with quite unpleasant options. With the island nearly entirely liberated, or at least with the security forces severely pressed, the British government might well come to terms; if they did not the basis for conventional resistance had been created. When in April it became clear that the Dublin Rising would largely be isolated and little could be expected from the country, the rebels decided to go ahead, and fashion a Blood Sacrifice that would inspire the next generation to rise, a delayed flash. In essence, the Irish had first planned a detonation that would explode British authority to rebel advantage. They had settled on lighting a fuse that would do so in the future. A second variant of the Foco Flash is a discrete event that sets off an escalating chain reaction, a sequential destruction of authority. The most elegant, though disastrous in practice, so far, formulation of this strategy is described in the work of Regís Debray, *Revolution in the*

Revolution.[13] The basic idea is that the small core of armed rebels, injected as a foco of revolution, by their activity and example will mobilize the masses and create sympathy for further focos. There would not be a single detonation, as the Irish had planned for Dublin; instead the foco would light a string of firecrackers. Founded on a misinterpretation of the Cuban revolution and the dreams of Guevara, the foco strategy, urban or rural, has had only the most limited success. The concept, however, is neither recent nor novel; many desperate and frustrated men have felt that someone some place must strike the first blow—even if that blow seemed to be futile. Those rebels dead in an Irish ditch or hanged on an Egyptian gallows may well have lit long and smouldering fuses.

A third stategist places his faith in a particular technique or tactic—the Magic Means—that alone will achieve the rebel purpose. As in the case of the Foco Flash, a single means appropriately applied can have vast effect, will prove to be a special key heretofore ignored by more conventional leaders. The two most attractive techniques in the course of modern revolts have been assassination and guerrilla warfare. Most impressive theoretical castles have been cunningly constructed on single murders and the men in the far bush. An entire generation of anarchists, acting in small groups or often even alone, sought repeatedly to transform the entire Western world—in fact the very nature of Western man —by killing those in the pinnacle of power. Tsars are bombed, presidents gunned down. Executed by individuals not in the name of vengeance, rarely in relation to a subversive conspiracy to snatch power, always with great moral conviction, the victims had been sacrifices to the Magic Means that would topple a system of institutional oppression that warped the real soul of man and release a new free race. Some anarchists and some assassins may have been motivated by vengeance or more pragmatic in their expectations, but for others the means not only justify the end—the idyllic society of the future—but guarantee it. There have, of course, been subsequent recourses to assassination by men who assumed that the single act would change history—who would deny that a Germany without Hitler would have produced different end results—but assassination has tended to be either an individual act (thus raised to strategic importance by men without other resources as the Stern Group did when they shot Lord Moyne in Cairo in 1944) or an integral part of a terrorist campaign (thus not a Magic Means but a useful technique). On the other hand, those who have elevated the tactics of the guerrilla to a strategy of revolt work on quite different principles. The Palestinian fedayeen insisted that guerrilla warfare alone would lead to an Arab Palestine, that after 1967 the way of the guerrilla was not the last Arab alternative once all else had failed but the true road long ignored by the conventional strategists. Guerrilla action would lead to the mobilization of the masses, the expulsion of the Zionists, and the transformation of the entire Arab nation. Guerrilla action led instead to a series of defeats, Jordanian suppression, a decay of the entire movement, and in time recourse to spectacular terror as a last option. There was no more magic in the way of the guerrilla for the Palestinians than there had been in the assassin's option for the anarchists.

A final scenario, the strategy of the fulcrum, proposes that, if an opponent is too powerful *ever* to be matched, no matter what the means, a revolt must seek a weakness of will. One approach is to maintain a certain level of rebel violence until the opponent decides to concede. In Algeria the FLN, or at least some of its cadres, at first hoped to be able in time to match French strength. When it became increasingly apparent that such a hope was ill-founded, the FLN resorted to attrition: "The guerrilla fighters have never looked for a military victory over the French army. We know that a great nation can exterminate a little people. But the guerrillas remain invincible and in existence so long as their political objectives are not reached."[14] In time the French will to make war did erode and the guerrillas, all but defeated in the field, achieved their political objectives. Another approach is to confront an opponent with a level of violence or a provocation that can be eradicated only by means that are morally objectionable to the opponent. The use of torture in Algeria, effective or not, had serious repercussions in Paris. In Ireland in 1920 and 1921, fighting murder from a ditch, the British security forces' repressive measures alienated British public opinion. If murder and arson were the only means to hold Ireland, then it was not worth holding. Depending on the decency and morality of an opponent entails certain risks. There will always be those who insist on bombing a village in order to save it, that civilians shot in the street were gunmen, that information gained by torture saves innocent lives. And there are of course opponents who have historically been untroubled by the moral dilemmas of repression and those whose vital interests required continuing resistance to rebel violence.

Beyond the rigorously argued, ideologically elegant strategy of Mao or the expectations of those dedicated to an urban guerrilla foco, looms the true test of the rebel strategists: the application of tactics and techniques, the mix of art and science, politics and car bombs, leaflets and ambush in the lane—all to the given end. As anyone involved in a revolt knows only too well, the view from the midst of the melee tends to be confused: simultaneous operations and constant recriminations; lapses of concentration and unexpected disaster; brilliant feats engineered by muddle; misdirection and compensating errors; and little time for reflection. Subsequently, after victory or defeat, in jail or an ivory tower, all becomes clear or at least explicable: here Mao missed; there Giap overleaped; and once more the British blundered or the French struck to the core. A certain inherent skepticism should always be associated with later analysis. The scholar is apt to see structure where none existed, cause and effect where only confusion reigned, canny wisdom instead of desperate grappling for elusive straws. The ideologue finds the elegance of theory where only rough practice existed. And the old activist finds honor and vindication, for time has edited his more unfortunate manuevers and cloaked his egregious errors with retrospective wisdom. The acts and intentions of men under severe pressure, with lives at risk and cause at stake, must be evaluated with caution. There can rarely be elegant and rigorous dissections into neat categories—Magic Means or Maoist guerrilla-revolution without warping the rebel woof—any more than there can be a value-free ideological or personal explanation of a campaign that even at the time appeared confusing. Still, pitfalls and hurdles have never long prevented analysis, for at least certain pertinent questions may be posed about applied strategy, even given the state of the evidence.

Rebels against the British Crown

For a very long time men have sought to understand the nature of the rebel, applying the tools of factor analysis or the intuition of the philosopher or the experience of the historian. What is the etiology of revolt or the comparative anatomy of revolution? Who revolts and why? When does the rebel resort to arms and with what expectations? How is the struggle organized and adjusted to reality? How does it all end and to whose advantage? What has really changed? As yet, certainly in the academic world, there is no common wisdom, no general agreement, not even an acceptance of the boundaries of inquiry and the limits of speculation. The intention is to focus on the application of strategy, the orchestration of revolt in the name of national liberation, particularly of a special group of rebels who rose against the British Empire after World War II. These rebels against the crown—seven very different movements motivated by the most diverse ambitions—applied a remarkably wide spectrum of strategies, however defined, against an equally remarkably consistent opponent. This existence of a single British stage, the twilight empire, permits a greater degree of comparative analysis than might a different mix of case studies, but it by no means limits the results to an isolated sub-genre. The revolts against the crown were special, but not so special that broader conclusions are merely speculative. The intention is to follow in seven revolts the application of strategy that led to diverse and largely unforeseen results—and not always to the barricade. In each case, the British presence aside, those elusive objective conditions, the long train of abuse or the cause of the moment, were quite disparate, the rebels came from very different backgrounds, organized in varying ways, pursued their campaign under varying assumptions, and reached the end of the road with mixed results. Yet in retrospect the lethal dialogue between the Crown and the rebel reveals a remarkable consistency, a pattern not inapplicable elsewhere and repeated as if on cue in Northern Ireland after 1969.

The rebels generally selected a national liberation strategy designed for the British opponent, waged a campaign on the basis of certain, often unstated, assumptions concerning the nature of the British response, and came to grief or to power in remarkably similar ways for remarkably similar reasons. Each revolt was unique, but the profiles have much in common—and not just because the British constant proved over the generation in question to be remarkably constant, for the experience of the rebels against the crown proved not unlike that of rebels everywhere. Instead of a simple series of isolated, independent case studies of anti-colonial revolts, where rebels succeed or fail in the mountains or in the back alleys, what evolves from the postwar generation, tentatively if not clearly, is an anatomy of revolt that can with some profit be compared to other rebels.

2 The British Imperial Stage

Land of hope and glory, mother of the free.
How shall we extol thee, who are born of
thee? Wider still and wider shall thy bounds
be set; God who made thee mighty, make
thee mightier yet.
—Arthur Christopher Benson

On the eve of World War II the British Empire remained an institution for all times and seasons, the pride of the past, the school of virtue, the conduit for civilization, capable of evolution, the foundation of the future, the force that generated both prosperity at home and enlightenment abroad. For a century no British political party had lacked an imperialist wing; no critic, however mean, could deny the Empire some virtue. This great imperial machine was largely a Victorian invention erected on the foundations of the eighteenth-century mercantile possessions. The construction had been undirected by a master plan, a coherent ideology, or a single mission. From the first Victorian acquisition, Aden in January 1839, until the end of the halcyon days of accumulation that the Boer war brought, like Topsy, the Empire just grew. The process was aided by the expansion of the British economy, the idealism that an imperial mission awakened, and the lack of serious competitors. In time there would be imperial rivals, but for most of the century Britain faced the opposition only of native levies, savage tribes, and horsemen on the hill. The major imperial mission became that of ruling the hundreds of millions of subjects, often sunk in poverty and superstition, previously outside the protection of law or civil order, now an imperial responsibility.

In this responsibility, as tutor to the underdeveloped and guide to the immature, Britain shared the attitudes and assumptions of the other imperial powers. Each shaped their tutelage in particular ways but all assumed the right to rule. Britain, however, had simultaneously with the haphazard accumulation of Empire also developed a policy of devolution, of ceding power from the center to those advanced and developed imperial areas grown restive under centralized control. There were no British overseas provinces; instead there was the assumption that the maturing and able within the Empire would follow the route from colony to Dominion and to a place at the new Commonwealth table, established in 1931 by the Statute of Westminster. Some colonies might not stay the course for one reason or another—size, resources, strategic importance —but the idea of colonial political development had a long and honorable history in British political thought.

The loss of the North American colonies underlined the danger of playing the absentee British parent. In 1839 Lord Durham produced his famous Report favoring a united Canada with responsible Cabinet Government. This Report laid the foundation for subsequent Canadian constitutional developments that led step by step to a Canadian nation. Following similar courses, Australia, New Zealand, Newfoundland, and the Union of South Africa had by the eve of World War I emerged as nations, the original members of a still inchoate Commonwealth. As early as 1884 Lord Roseberry noted that the Empire was a Commonwealth of Nations and the constitutional developments of the ensuing years culminating in the Statute of Westminster appeared to bear him out. Beyond the five founder Dominions, however, no colonial candidate appeared to have the basic requisites for rapid, indeed deliberate, constitutional development that would lead to equality with the existing Commonwealth Dominions, much less complete independence. Consequently, there were and remained in effect two imperial responsibilities: to rule and to resign.

The necessity to rule had long been obvious. The underdeveloped, unstructured, disordered areas of the Empire stood in need of capital, settlers, guidance, and protection. It was the British responsibility to continue to supply these, thereby assuring law, order, justice, development, and the welfare of the colonial population. Naturally few of the British involved in these colonial ventures could conceive of any time in the immediate or in some cases distant future when their services would no longer be needed, when the moment to resign would come. The idea that India, perhaps the next candidate, could within one's lifetime be transformed into a viable, modern democratic nation state, was not so much anathema as inconceivable. "The nation of a parliamentary representation of so vast a country—almost as large as Europe—containing so large a number of different races is one of the wildest imaginations that ever entered the minds of men."[1] The organization of the Indian National Congress by Mahatma Gandhi, Jawaharlal Nehru, and other nationalists that launched a vast civil disobedience campaign convinced few of the skeptics of Indian political maturity. In 1935 to Winston Churchill,

Gandhi was still a half-naked fakir. The concessions won by the disobedience campaign, incorporated in the Government of India Act of the same year, in most imperialist eyes were considered premature. Still Britain was pledged to seek "responsible government in India as an integral part of the British Empire" and, in time, the Commonwealth would most certainly be enlarged with the entry of India and perhaps Ceylon.[2]

Thus, the idea of imperial devolution and an institution of devolution existed, but only for certain areas. The idea that tribal African "states" could ever evolve into Dominions was unthinkable. The same was true for those tiny bits and pieces, the islands and rocks accumulated for strategic reasons or as the residue of various enthusiasms and individuals' contributions in Asia or the Americas or along the crucial imperial lifelines. Since most of the British Middle East was ruled by treaty or under terms of the League of Nations Mandates, the Commonwealth option seemed inapplicable. There spheres of influence could be maintained or ceded by traditional means. What should stay or what might go usually seemed a matter of definition. What still had not become fully apparent, even by 1939, was that no longer would all the definitions be issued out of London with the Crown's imprimatur. Times had begun to change even before the impact of World War II fractured the imperial core.

Even in such areas of unpromising "devolution," the simple process of maintaining the imperial machine had vastly accelerated the supposedly distant day of autonomy. With colonial law and order came commercial development and capital investment. With peace in the countryside and the introduction of modern public health facilities the population spiraled, diluting the benefits of colonial investment and development. Exposure to the new standards and possibilities created an anticipation of future gain beyond the parochial desires of the past. One of the most attractive prospects was a Western education; for idealistic as well as pragmatic reasons colonial policy encouraged education. The newly educated not only helped to run the colonial and commercial institutions but also found the opportunity to criticize their shortcomings. Often just where Britain invested the most, instituted great change at great cost, labored and taught, were "native" aspirations most frustrated and "native" ambitions most visible. Thus, at the very moment British imperialism appeared most expansive and most effective, developing the colony and co-opting the educated leadership, conditions had usually matured sufficiently for people to feel that the process of devolution should begin.

The idea, on the other hand, usually had *not* ripened in the minds of the British. Only the colonial subjects seemed to perceive that their "rights" were being denied. Having benefited from the impact of British-imposed law and order, British-sponsored education, British standards, and most of all British ideals, they wanted no more than justice. When their frustration led to violence or protest the British tended to define away their grievances. In 1931 disorders in Cyprus favoring union with Greece were clearly the work of agitators. In 1936 a general strike followed by nearly three years of insurrection in the Palestine Mandate was a result of special conditions that were corrected in 1939 with the publication of a White Paper. Trouble in Jamaica was economic, and the meetings and conferences of African nationalists were better left to the radical fringe of the Labour Party.

By the Second World War, throughout the Empire an increasing number of articulate and dedicated men did not appreciate the rule of law and order maintained all too often by British bayonets. Although many had admired, even if briefly, the imperial virtues, accepted the advantages of law and order, taken the opportunity to learn cricket or economics, and grown fond of Grey's Inn or the London School of Economics, they felt that in the postwar world the time for acquiescence would have passed. This was often true even for colonies still sunk in the past, hampered by tribalism fostered by the British, exploited by an economy contrived by the British. Many agreed that the process of self-determination would be slow and certainly be postponed until after the war, but all wanted a start to be made. Some saw a pattern of development not unlike that in India; others suspected that only violence would prove effective. A few placed their hopes in Britain's enemies, and many in their demonstrable loyalty and service during time of war. A few Marxists anticipated the promised revolution, and many nationalists hoped for opportunities as a result of the dislocations of war.

In 1942 the perceptions of the nationalists were transformed by two extremely important events. First, on February 16, in the worst single imperial defeat, General Arthur Percival surrendered Singapore to the Japanese General Tomoyuki Yamashita. In a brilliantly conceived, whirl-wind campaign, at the cost of a few thousand casualties, Yamashita defeated a force superior in all aspects but aircraft and competence. Percival surrendered not only 130,000 men and the Crown Jewel of the Empire but also British prestige in Asia. The fortress had been "impregnable," the British garrison keen, the outcome certain—and no one believed that more than the British. But Yamashita had cut away the bland face of British superiority and revealed the tired muscles and frail tissues of a decaying empire. Later victories never made up for the debacle at Singapore, and prestige was never regained.

Later in the year Gandhi scored one more coup, revealing again British impotence. Sir Stafford Cripps had rushed to India to offer the most extensive compromise: India would be a Dominion, with the right to secede. Gandhi refused to accept the "compromise" and continued his

Quit-India campaign. The writing was on the wall, and even Churchill admitted that after the war India would be independent. And, if India, why not Burma or Malaya or the Gold Coast? The rising powers—Russia and the United States—were anti-imperialist. Anything might happen.

The Indian Example

In India, the Congress Party had perfected one of the classic strategies to force political change. Embodied in Mahatma Gandhi, a huge mass organization had been fashioned that could, if not persuade, then coerce the British Raj into concessions demanded in the name of British principles. This was an incredible feat in a vast and disorganized country, inhabited largely by illiterate peasants, divided by religion, distance, language, history, and habit. The struggle, which took three generations, was not so much against the British as against lethargy, doubt, suspicion, and narrow self-interest—the limitations of the wretched. Gandhi called not only to those with hope for the future, the educated and ambitious, but also by relying on the habits and attitudes of the past involved the millions without faith or future. The long campaign years rather than concessions were intended to fashion the Congress. Once the movement had reached critical mass, had become disciplined, determined, capable of bringing to bear a coherent strategy of disobedience and the implicit threat of anarchy, the British had to come to terms. If tens of millions of people fail to obey the most innocuous regulations, there is no alternative but to maintain order by force or cede control.

By the thirties, Gandhi had come close enough to his goal to convince the shrewd that the Dominion of India was the only means of maintaining British presence in India. If the Indian National Congress were to manage a full-scale campaign of civil disobedience—and indications were that Gandhi could and would—the British position would decay rapidly. Even if the spirit of coercion had been willing, the capacity did not exist. A massacre in hot blood might be accepted or a pacification campaign against unruly tribes undertaken, but Gandhi offered the British Raj the alternatives of ruling by murder or not ruling at all. The first grudging British recognition of the dilemma, the Government of India Act of 1935, although too short a step for the Congress, which repudiated it, was clear indication that the Raj would chose concession over coercion.

The British still doubted Indian capacity to rule and were disheartened that the provincial elections under the new Act apparently provided the Congress with a base for further agitation rather than the practice of governmental responsibility. The fakir wanted more, when many thought he already had too much. By 1940 the Moslems were going off in one direction, demanding a "Pakistan," and the Congress was holding out for unity—one India—while demanding that Britain quit, even with a world war and after 1941 the Japanese on the borders. Omens for a peaceful, responsible Indian move toward self-determination hardly seemed propitious to the British. Yet, from 1942 there were really no alternatives. Whether the British thought the Indians quite ready or considered the various "problems" of devolution too severe was immaterial. The Indian National Congress in 1942 had arrived at the point that willy-nilly, partition or not, long practice or not, the British after the war could not afford to impose a solution unsatisfactory to India—and India wanted independence. Gandhi's strategy had proved effective and the prestige of his means soared throughout the British colonies.

Gandhi's strategy of nonviolence based on firm moral principles and dependent on the discipline and dedication of the masses had for other nationalists several attractive features. First, it placed the British in a peculiarly British dilemma: if they reacted to the nonviolent provocation with coercion, the imperial purpose would be undermined; if they did not, the imperial order would decay. The British could not "win" except by concession—a zero-sum game, with the British getting the zero. (As an anti-British strategy it had great appeal; as a general anti-imperialist strategy it had somewhat less, since not all imperial powers were as dedicated to fair play as the British.) Equally important, such a strategy was cheap, requiring only time and vast patience, qualities most subject peoples had in abundance. Armed rebellion could be crushed and the British not only had long practice but also would view rebellion as unsporting; on the other hand, disobedience on a mass scale could not be suppressed. Moreover, it had worked in India, where the British had seemed at a loss when the Indians refused to play the game according to the old rules. Finally, the Indian strategy allowed a gradual process of politicization and offered the prospect of temporary concessions. In the most backward colonial areas it was also a means to educate the masses as well as a strategy that might lead to ultimate independence, an exercise in nation-building as well as a campaign of liberation. If not the Magic Means, the Indian Strategy had much to offer.

With the odd exception, the India Act of 1935 and the Cripps mission in 1942 were the first major imperial concessions since the Anglo-Irish Treaty of 1921—and that was the only real rebel success since the American Revolution. Consequently, for most nationalists the obvious alternative to the Indian Strategy was recourse to the gun: the Irish route. In point of fact, revolts against the Crown had never been a novelty within the British Empire. The British government had generally regarded revolts, rebellions, as mere tribal agitation or the result of border marauders; insurrection, or localized eruptions led by mesmeric leaders as riot. And usually the government had been right. In 1915 in Nyasaland,

John Chilembwe, isolated and alone, had struck a blow and died without his example meaning anything to anyone—then. The Mad Mullah sweeping through the bleak Somali deserts or the brigands on the Northwest frontier did not seem alternatives to Empire, only distractions. Even the Arab revolt in Palestine between 1936 and 1939 could be classified as an eruption of suppressed indignation based on nostalgia for the past and fear of the future. Only when an alternative to the existing imperial system could be perceived would London consider accommodation—and neither Chilembwe, the Mad Mullah or the Mufti of Jerusalem appeared adequate alternatives. There could be no accommodation. Thus, rebels without potential legitimacy in British eyes might seek to accelerate a process of concession through the Indian Strategy or, disheartened by British adamancy, seek to coerce by countervailing force—take up arms as had the Irish and the Americans before them.

The Irish Alternative

The American Revolution, a one-time affair and long in the past, had almost no real effect; but the Irish experience was another matter. For hundreds of years the Irish risings, as predictable as the weather, had been put down if not with ease at least with severity. The Irish had simply lacked compelling force. Generation after generation they could strike, wound, but not kill. Yet the Irish revolts, so bold in courage and so futile in execution, had by their very numbers fashioned a revolutionary tradition. Decade after decade, the Irish perfected new stratagems that time after time had to be discarded after disaster on the field of battle. After the final blood sacrifice during the Easter Rising of 1916 they at last constructed an appropriate strategy and by 1921 had won a partial victory. Between the Treaty of Paris of 1782 and that of London in 1921 no other revolt managed as much in the face of imperial power. The example and the strategy did not go unnoticed. No matter that many insisted that democratic politics and nonviolence might have worked in Ireland, the Irish had gone to the gun and the alternative to India was Ireland.

The Irish Strategy evolved not out of theoretical studies of revolutionary options but out of Irish experience, particularly the failings of the Easter Rising, and the elaboration of a specific political tactic—abstentionism, the boycott of British institutions long advocated by certain radicals. The new strategy after 1916 was an effective amalgamation of diverse Irish political techniques and the use of historical tested guerrilla-terror tactics. Combined with the existing balance in British politics and the pressure of a British society exhausted by war, this combination rather than one more Glorious Rising forced far-reaching compromise on a reluctant British Cabinet. Quite simply, the Irish wanted to make Ireland ungovernable by British institutions, no matter what the level of repression London brought to bear, while those institutions would be replaced with Irish ones. Thus, the Irish would deny their consent to the ruler and abstain from the old system, while constructing an alternative and parallel system of rule that would be defended by an irregular guerrilla-army—an Irish Republican Army that would also terrorize the British garrison and administration. The major task was to persist until the British accepted the facts that the alternative to repression was concession and that to be effective repression would have to be on a scale unpalatable to British opinion and perhaps even British capacities.

By the time of the British General Election of December 1918 the first major thrust, the political, had been prepared. Ireland would support only Irish Republican institutions. The new Irish members of the Parliament at Westminster would meet instead in Dublin and form an Irish Dáil to rule the Irish Republic declared in 1916. And so there evolved a set of shadow Irish institutions, cabinet ministers in attics and courts in basements. To protect these institutions and to prevent the official British ones from working, the Irish Republican Army carried on a hit-and-run guerrilla war in the countryside—"murder from a ditch"—and a terror-sabotage campaign in the towns—"a nest of assassins." Neither was terribly costly in terms of lives, but combined they prevented the British from ruling without recourse to force and at last without adopting tactics abhorrent to British opinion. By 1921 British security forces had prevented the effective "working" of Irish Republican institutions but had not been able to crush the armed resistance. Abroad the Irish had not been able to acquire any significant diplomatic support; the Irish Republic was not a viable alternative nor capable of waging a conventional civil war. In Britain there was strong sentiment to continue the repression, not to abandon in Ireland those loyalists, particularly in the North, who had sacrificed so dearly during the war. For emotional as well as strategic reasons, the total separation of Ireland from the United Kingdom remained inconceivable to the British cabinet. The revolt must, and could, be crushed. Yet, as the resistance continued month by month, many in Britain felt the moral justification for rule was being lost by the means used. And Britain was tired of war, gripped by economic depression, sullen in poverty, disillusioned, restive at more sacrifice.

The British government could not succeed through the military means permitted by public opinion, could not ignore the rising public clamor for an end to the war, and yet could not envision a "normal" political solution that would not deny vital British interests. The only hope was an "abnormal" political solution. Prime Minister David Lloyd George's task was to persuade the Irish to accept a formula short of the

Republic, as nearly normal as British draftsmen could devise. The solution, the Anglo-Irish treaty of 1921, partitioned off a six-county Protestant-dominated enclave in the North, the loyalists' reward, assured Britain of several naval bases, and incorporated the newly fashioned Irish Free State as a Dominion, of sorts, grudging devolution. Dedicated Irish Republicans once more took up arms—this time against the Free Staters—rather than accept less than their Republic. They still held to the dream of the founder of Irish Republicanism, Wolfe Tone: "to assert the independence of the country, to break the connection with England, to unite the whole people of Ireland, to abolish the memory of all past dissensions, and to substitute the common name of Irishmen in place of denomination of Protestant, Catholic, and Dissenter."[3] The purists, organized as the IRA, lost the civil war and Tone's dream faded but was not forgotten. His dictum has remained the ideological base of Irish Republicanism, and, by and large, efforts to move the faithful off dead center toward the Left and the array of more fashionable liberation strategies have failed. For two centuries Tone has been sufficient and physical force, often alone, the most cherished lever. Still, the Irish Strategy had in three years won more than all the other risings and revolts had won in eight hundred years. If there was no Republic at least there was a prospect of achieving it through the new Irish Free State. The example was not missed by other distant nationalists, yearning to break the imperial connection.

The Marxist Matrix

Within the British Empire, the Indian or Irish Strategy loomed large; but the world stage was dominated by the Communist Strategy, based on Marx, elaborated by Lenin, and later to be transformed by Mao Tse-tung. Thus, one set of potential rebels, the Marxist-Leninist, foresaw the end of the British Empire as the climactic moment in the struggle against imperialist capitalism. They assumed that Britain and the Empire would disappear into a new and totally different communist world—revolution not devolution. The Communist Strategy did not anticipate and could not seek an accommodation, a compromise, could not imagine a community of interests between imperial Britain and the emerging colonial proletariat aligned with world communism and dedicated to the destruction of capitalism. By the eve of the Second World War, there was still at best only a small colonial proletariat, apparently uninterested in either world communism or the destruction of capitalism. The potential of the peasant lay in the ideological future. For the colonial communists, the problem of their revolutionary strategy was simply that there were too few communists and that in any case orthodox

Marxist-Leninist strategy seldom was applicable to local conditions. In large areas of the British Empire the communists were thin on the ground indeed; only in Asia and in parts of the Middle East Treaty Empire could one find much more that the odd study group, a cell or two, and some trade union influence. There seemed to be more advocates of the Communist Strategy in London than in Singapore or Accra. Even the better communist structures were primitive, hardly a match for the local nationalists. In any case, the potential of orthodox communist tactics seemed inappropriate in a colonial context—except perhaps for those new maneuvers of Mao, which were still imperfectly understood.

Many radicals were attracted to socialist ideas, particularly after exposure in British classrooms or tea seminars. A few of the emerging elite became dedicated communists but most remained concerned with the liberation of their nation first and the transformation of its society second. Either the Indian or the Irish Strategy seemed to offer far more as a national liberation strategy than the means offered by Moscow, though Moscow's example might prove of use later. The "contamination" of the national struggle with a communist connection—a Red Scare—could only persuade the British to maintain control rather than concede to rebels aligned with Moscow. Within the Empire the Communist Strategy usually seemed alien and restrictive, an exotic intellectual import with little appeal to the masses and no pragmatic advantages, in contrast to the attractions of the Indian Strategy, a means that far outshone any alternative, or of the Irish Strategy, a proven winner under difficult conditions.

The only other revolt, that of the Palestinian Arabs, produced not really a strategy but an experience in insurrection that apparently taught no one, least of all the Arabs, anything of great moment. In April 1936, after riots in Jaffa had resulted in twenty Jewish deaths, the Arabs in the Mandate formed the Arab National Committee under the presidency of the Mufti of Jerusalem, al-Hajj Amin al-Huseini. The Mufti was determined to force the British to halt Jewish immigration by calling a general strike. Although the strike sputtered out in October, for over two years endemic low-level violence tied down British security forces and troubled civic order. The Arab leadership was bitterly divided and there was little control from the center; the campaign relied on traditional brigandage and random violence. Eventually in 1939, for a variety of purposes and not unmindful of the drain of the Arab "revolt," the British issued a White Paper that in part satisfied Arab aspirations. Subsequently the Arabs apparently ignored the period, continued their feuds, and ultimately decided to depend on the conventional armies of the Arab states rather than another revolt to achieve an Arab Palestine. The Palestine experience of 1936-1939 became an unread text—and has remained unopened even during the Arab return to fedayeen tactics in 1967.

Before the Second World War the idea of various, supposedly effective revolutionary strategies would have appeared to the British not simply alien but slightly ridiculous. No rebels, even the Arabs in Palestine, appeared a *serious* threat. Since the devolution of power to the Dominions had been largely voluntary, the cost of suppressing mature colonial aspirations was not clear: Palestine was a parochial, little-understood event, and as usual the British had learned nothing from their exposure to the Irish. In any case, the challenges to British authority—in India, Ireland, and Palestine—had been met with concessions. With minimum re-editing of reality it was possible to consider these concessions—the Anglo-Irish Treaty, the Government of India Act, the White Paper—as freely given to ameliorate real grievances. And so the British had assumed that the dialogue between ruler and ruled within the Empire continued. If the demands had been irresponsible or endangered crucial interests, London had no doubt that the will and means to enforce British order existed.

By 1945, however, many observers suspected that neither the will nor the means existed. Again the British would have disagreed. Britain had after all been victorious; the territory controlled by British troops was more extensive than in 1939. In the rush to triumph, those in positions of power had forgotten the trauma of Singapore and the implications of the Cripps mission to India. Because to the naive the Empire seemed the same, because Britain *had* won the war, because the trappings of glory still existed, the advocates of Empire did not foresee the need, or possibility, of rapid devolution. The Labour Party, triumphant in the 1945 general elections, assumed that simply to scuttle from the colonies was out of the question: India as a Dominion of course but Togo or Aden was, even for the Labour Left, another matter. The evolution of the Commonwealth would make possible over time the gradual and responsible dissolution of the old Empire. That imperial institutions would have to be changed was accepted, but that these changes might have to be swift and drastic was not realized. If the dialogue of ruler and ruled broke down, as it had in India, Britain might lack both the will and power to maintain order, for victorious or no, the British were stretched very thin.

British resources to resist sudden change had been drained, physically by the losses of war, emotionally by the long years of sacrifice, and intellectually by the decline of the imperial idea. Yet Britain had by no means become a minor power nor alien to empire. Much of the Empire had been acquired specifically to protect the routes to and from India. After 1942 British interests in India would be transformed. British perception of what areas of the Empire retained strategic value in a period of radically changing responsibilities was unclear. The nation was prepared to defend imperial positions that no longer had any relevance to its needs. Britain had to balance a limited capacity to enforce order with the shifting security needs of a reduced Empire and the legitimacy of the advocates of rapid self-determination. The equation seldom balanced; consequently, the postwar road to devolution was often rutted and pitted with surprises.

By 1945, the new British Labour government had been painfully surprised. Bogged down in pressing domestic crises and partly responsible for devising a postwar settlement, the Cabinet had given little thought to imperial matters. Labour had a long record of anti-imperialism. Many individual members treasured their friendship with nationalist colleagues in India or Africa. The party was pledged to extensive concessions based on self-determination. And yet there was another revolt in Palestine: Labour's old friends, the Zionists, had not even waited until the common enemy had been defeated to begin an armed struggle. The revolt in Palestine increasingly appeared immune to compromise or conciliation, indicating that the smooth devolution of power—the Commonwealth Strategy—faced a severe challenge. In Palestine men with guns had rushed onto the British imperial stage under a new banner of national liberation, unwilling to continue a reasoned dialogue with the "alien oppressor—the occupying power." They would not be the last, for in Palestine the archetype of revolts against the Crown would be fashioned. During the next generation the British would find that they had much to learn about bringing freedom to emerging people.

PART TWO

Revolts against the Crown

To subvert the tyranny of our execrable government, to break the connection with England, the never-failing source of all our political evils, and to assert the independence of my country—these were my objects.
—Wolfe Tone

Jomo Kenyatta under arrest for Mau Mau activities.

3 The Palestinian Archetype: Irgun and the Strategy of Leverage

History and our observation persuaded us that if we could succeed in destroying the government's prestige in Eretz Israel, the removal of its rule would follow automatically. Thenceforward we gave no peace to this weak spot. Throughout all the years of our uprising, we hit at the British Government's prestige, deliberately, tirelessly, unceasingly.

—*Menachem Begin*

Drift

For twenty-five years after the establishment of the League of Nations Mandate, Britain's ultimate intentions in Palestine drifted from one extreme to the other. They ranged from enthusiastic support for the creation of a Jewish National Home, promised in the Balfour Declaration and written into the Mandate, to the White Paper of 1939 that proposed halting Jewish immigration, the limitation of Jewish land purchases, and ultimate independence for Palestine with an Arab majority.[1] By the end of 1942 there was evidence that the White Paper, in turn, might be replaced, but no one in Palestine knew by what. While out of office, Prime Minister Winston Churchill became a known advocate of Zionism, but several members of his Coalition War Cabinet supported an Arabist policy in the name of British strategic interests. No matter what Britain actually intended, neither Arab nor Jewish supplicant was in a position to follow an active policy of persuasion inside or outside the Mandate.

The Arab case had been to a considerable degree contaminated by the Arabs' ambivalent response or, sometimes, open opposition to the British war effort when an Axis victory seemed probable. There were plots in Egypt, a coup in Iraq, and the Mufti of Jerusalem in Germany. Consequently, the Arabs had perforce to maintain a low profile and wait for concessions that few had done much to earn. Their hope was that, despite their lack of help during the war, Arab friendship in the postwar world would be vital to British interests. The Zionists of Palestine, on the other hand, had no leverage because their bitterest enemy, Hitler, was also Britain's major foe. Because the British knew that the Zionists must ally themselves with the anti-Nazi front, concession to induce cooperation was unnecessary. The Jewish contribution to the war effort—thirty thousand Palestinian Jews mobilized in contrast to nine thousand Arabs —was far more important to Jewish purpose than to British advantage and, therefore, could be meanly rewarded. The Zionists, too, realized that to antagonize the British prematurely by querulous demands might only lose the ear of the ultimate arbitrator of their destiny.

That Britain would be the ultimate arbitrator was accepted by almost everyone. As the paramount power, the British could look forward to ordering the Middle East largely at their pleasure. The British government was by no means sanguine about the prospects of complete acquiescence to its wishes, particularly in the case of the Palestine Mandate, where Arab and Zionist aspirations had repeatedly clashed, often to British disadvantage. In 1941, in the midst of the most pressing priorities, the British Minister of State in Cairo, Oliver Lyttleton, had to spare time for the persistent Palestine problem.

> Our dealings with the Jewish Agency were uneasy and our general security in Palestine rested more upon military strength than upon any consent of the inhabitants to the existing regime.
> The great controversies about the extent and nature of the Zionist state were always hanging over us, though kept in the background.[2]

For the Arabs the question of ultimate devolution of the Mandate, once the 1936-1939 revolt had flickered out, seemed insoluble. Some hoped the Arab states would act, others that Britain would prove reasonable, many that justice alone would serve. Few depended on their own efforts and none thought of open revolt, much less of the optimal strategy for an armed struggle. For the Zionists the future was clouded by the ambiguous position of Palestine: a League of Nations' Mandate but an integral part of Britain's Middle East treaty empire; not a colony and not really a Commonwealth candidate; promised to the Zionists but filled with Arabs; a Palestinian majority whose aspirations were difficult to reconcile with a Jewish National Home. For a generation orthodox Zionist strategy had been to persuade Britain, and to a lesser degree the international community, of the wisdom of supporting a Jewish National Home, while simultaneously the settlers in the Mandate were creating Zionist facts, orange grove by orange grove expanding the Jewish presence. Both prongs—diplomatic and practical—of Zionist strategy were largely aimed at Britain, the authority with the ultimate power of decision. After the White Paper of 1939 Zionist anxiety increased, but the analysis of the problem remained the same: the Zionists would never consent to the British discarding the National Home but the means to protest remained diplomatic.

Then, in the autumn of 1942, a new and desperately compelling factor began to emerge. In April 1942 the mass deportations of Hitler's final solution had begun. By the time the conference of delegates from the World Zionist Organization met on May 9-11, 1942, in New York, information out of occupied Europe indicated that only 25 percent of the endangered Jews might survive. In Palestine on July 18 the newspaper *Davar* first published the probable fate of European Jewry. On December 17 the Big Three Allied Powers announced the transportation of the Jews, "in conditions of appalling horror and brutality," to Eastern Europe. "None of those taken away are ever heard of again. The able-bodied are slowly worked to death in labour camps. The infirm are left to die of exposure and starvation or are deliberately massacred in mass executions . . . The number of the victims of these bloody cruelties is reckoned in many hundreds of thousands."[3] No one could yet think in terms of millions. Even with information made available by the Polish government-in-exile in London and the arrival in the Mandate in November of Palestinians detained in Poland who could verify the other reports, the scope of the disaster was beyond comprehension.

Despite reluctance to accept the reality of genocide, the reaction of the Palestine Jews—the Yishuv—was rage, first directed mainly at their own inability to help, then gradually toward the complacent powers that could help but did not. Those Zionists who had wanted to create the Jewish Homeland, trusting to the good faith of the British, began an agonizing reappraisal. There seemed no ready means either to save European Jewry or to strike at Hitler. Many Palestine Jews had enlisted in the British army and others had served in special operations or commando forays, but there was no Jewish Legion fighting Hitler similar to that organized by Vladimir Jabotinsky with British aid during World War I. Even if the British in late 1942 had permitted the mass enlistment of Jews, such a new wave of volunteers could not have acted on events immediately, if at all. What most of the Yishuv wanted was action. What they began to find was Allied reluctance to act solely in the cause of European Jewry against various "strategic" interests.

There was growing evidence that Britain placed strategic interests not only above its supposed commitment to the Jewish National Home but even above the fate of Jewish refugees. Operating under the provisions of the White Paper, the British continued to impose stringent restrictions on visas and made a concerted effort to halt "illegal" immigration. When the "illegals" succeeded in evading the blockade, the series of expulsions, exiles, and denials created deep anxiety and bitterness. In November 1940 the *S.S. Patria,* sailing from the Mandate for Mauritius with over 1,500 illegal and expelled immigrants, blew up and sank with a loss of 252 lives. The Haganah, the militia-army dedicated to settlement defense, had exploded a protest bomb on board. On February 23, 1942, the *S.S. Struma,* forced to sail from Istanbul when the British refused to grant all the refugees entry permits, foundered and sank; there was only one survivor out of the 769 refugees. Also, the British had enacted the restrictions on Jewish land acquisition embodied in the White Paper, had postponed consideration of proposals for a Jewish Army, and had continued to treat the Haganah with great suspicion.

Britain's anti-Zionist policy might have been reasonable, even possibly excusable, before news of the holocaust; but to continue to close the gates of Palestine was not only inexplicable, but indefensible, in Jewish eyes. The British apparently did not feel the same sense of urgency; they even indicated that if an exodus to Palestine from Eastern Europe was technically feasible—and they had much evidence that it was not—the flood of Jews would create more problems (for the British not the Jews) than it would solve. This complacency—increasingly some charged cold-blooded collusion in genocide—created grave strains within the Jewish community in Palestine. The formal Zionist institutions, recognized by the Mandate authorities, were impotent in the darkening night of European Jewry. Not only the British but also the Americans seemed unwilling or unable to act on suggestions that they ransom Jews or accept refugees, even in temporary camps, or bomb the rail lines to the death camps. And the news from the camps continued to trickle into Palestine. Then came word of the rising in the Warsaw Ghetto in 1943. The Jewish Agency and the Yishuv could do nothing and could persuade no one to act.

The Emergence of the Irgun

In 1942 nearly all Zionist opinion in Palestine was prepared to wait out the war in hope of a British return to a pro-Zionist solution. Only a little band of fanatics led by Avraham Stern, a dissident Zionist, attempted armed struggle. By the end of the year the charismatic Stern was shot down "trying to escape" and most of his followers were scattered, in hiding, or in prison. In 1943 an increasing number of Jews felt that they should not wait to open the gates to the refugees, should not wait on the slow change of British opinion. During 1943 the British began to suspect that the pressure of the refugees might lead to serious trouble in the Mandate. Zionist efforts to cooperate in the British war effort ended abruptly. Theft of arms from the British military establishment became commonplace. There was a boom in the illicit arms trade. In response, the British instituted stricter arms searches, leading, in August 1943, to a show trial of two British deserters for illegal possession of arms. This was followed by accusations that the Yishuv and its institutions were deeply involved in illicit arms deals, which of course they were and which of course the British had known for years. By late autumn resistance to military and police arms searches was so bitter that one Jew had been killed and many injured. The Jewish Agency by January 1944 seemed to be defying the Mandate Government "to the extent rebellion could be said to exist."[4]

Many Jews realized that an overt rebellion—and trying to protect secret arms caches was hardly open rebellion, no matter what the authorities might think—would hamper the Allied effort against Hitler. It would also be a hopeless gesture that would antagonize the Allies and throw away the minimal chance that Palestine might yet become a refuge for European Jewry. A few, however, decided someone must strike a blow, that the essential Zionist duty was to take arms and seek a state. These former comrades of the martyred Stern, who in 1942 felt his struggle premature, in 1943 believed the time to revolt had come. Such a revolt against Hitler's foe with the war far from over, a revolt with few arms and faint prospects, a revolt that might negate all the quiet years of diplomatic gain, to most Zionists seemed a mad act. Stern's gesture had been futile, and a more serious gesture would have more serious results for the Yishuv. Consequently, few outside the ranks of the militant Revisionist underground contemplated an armed struggle—even in the shadow of the holocaust.

In January 1944 an illicit proclamation pasted on the walls of the Mandate announced that a revolt had begun, directed by the small Irgun Zvai Leumi, the National Military Organization which had evolved out of Jabotinsky's Revisionist movement. The decision had been secretly made without recourse to the opinions and policies of the legitimate institutions of the Yishuv. The High Command of the Irgun believed that the Jews had to rise or else must accept the intolerable burden of a complacency different only in degree from that of the British. Death, they felt, was more desirable than a life lived in shame, than a life after the final destruction of Judaism. If a Jewish haven in Palestine could not be achieved, the Irgun had absolutely no doubt that death awaited a substantial proportion of European Jewry and the slow death of assimilation, absorption, and dispersion the remainder. In the shadows of Treblinka and Dachau, the Jewish alternatives appeared stark. There was no time to wait on the considered opinion of the men of the legitimate institutions, the intricate ideological analyses, the intricate theories of irrelevant men. The Jewish Agency's twin strategy of international pressure, diplomatic Zionism, and the campaign of illicit immigration, practical Zionism, was as outdated as the orange-grove philosophy or the radical theories imported from Eastern Europe half a century before. The Irgun did not want to convert the British by diplomatic means or evade British law to bring in more Jews but to coerce the "foreign occupier" into accepting Zionist aspirations. Resistance to arms searches was well and good, but the use of those husbanded arms in open revolt was, it felt, the only logical course; only in revolt was there hope for Jews. Even if the revolt failed, the sacrifice might at least turn the Yishuv from reliance on the old doctrine of self-restraint (havlaga), so long urged as the proper posture by "legitimate" institutions.

The Irgun considered itself specially fitted for a revolutionary task, for armed struggle, since its history had been a long, militant opposition to the Jewish Agency's complacency and British hypocrisy. The organization more than once had responded to provocation, Arab or British, with the gun and a minimum of self-restraint. Not only did the Irgun have a military tradition; by the end of 1943 a commander had appeared with a promising strategy of national liberation to exploit the organization's tradition of armed resistance. In the spring of 1942 Menachem Begin, the former commander of Betar, the Revisionist youth movement, in Poland, arrived in Palestine to find that the Irgun had fallen on difficult days. His presence revitalized the movement.

The Irgun had its origins in the inability of the Haganah to defend the Jewish community during the Arab massacres in Hebron in 1929. Dissatisfied with the official Jewish Agency policy of havlaga and deeply disturbed by the lack of arms and military training, some of the more militant members of the Haganah split off and formed the Irgun, or Haganah-Bet. Under the leadership of Avraham T'homi and former Haganah officers, the new force was open to all but members of the Communist Party. By 1936 it had grown from a few hundred men with a hundred revolvers to a force of three thousand men with substantial if still insufficient arms. The Jewish Agency and the Haganah regarded the Irgun as an unwelcome and unnecessary competitor at best, and a military Trojan Horse dominated by members of Jabotinsky's Revisionist movement at worst.

Jabotinsky had long infuriated the legitimate institutions of world Zionism. He had founded his own party in 1925, urging in place of practical Zionism a political Zionism putting pressure on the Mandate authority. In 1935 he withdrew from the World Zionist Organization and founded the New Zionist Organization, which had tremendous appeal in Eastern Europe, especially in Poland. There, as leader of the Betar, Begin had been Revisionism's most potent figure. By the mid-thirties the Revisionists looked forward to organizing, training, and arming the Betar in Poland, with Polish cooperation, and descending on the Mandate, presenting the British with a de facto coup.

Chaim Weizmann, David Ben Gurion, and the rest had no time for Jabotinsky and his plots or his repeated warnings that the rise of Hitler threatened the existence of European Jewry. For them the man was a charismatic charlatan, a romantic, a dangerous plunger into matters better left to prudence and wisdom; besides his political credentials were insufficiently socialist for most Palestinian Zionists. His followers, on the other hand, were awed by his vision, his charm, his analytical and incisive mind. Revisionism largely polarized Zionism. Anything Jabotinsky touched or tolerated, advised or accepted, almost inevitably became anathema to his Zionist opponents. This included the Irgun in Palestine.

In 1936, as Begin was deeply involved in preparations for the Betar expedition to be launched from Poland, in Palestine the Irgun had more immediate problems. The Arabs had again grown militant. The adamantly anti-Zionist Mufti of Jerusalem was stirring up trouble, mostly for the British, but with enough sporadic violence to alarm the Jews. Negotiations to reunite the Irgun and Haganah began in the autumn and continued until the spring of 1937. Mistrustful of the legitimate authorities dominated by his old Zionist enemies, Jabotinsky vetoed the final unity pact; but T'homi and somewhat less than half of the Irgun returned to the Haganah in defiance of him. The Irgun became in effect the military arm of the Revisionist movement. Instead of havlaga, in response to repeated Arab attacks on Jews, the Irgun instituted a policy of retaliation. First under Robert Bitker, then briefly Moshe Rosenberg, and finally David Raziel, and despite stringent British security measures, it fought a hit-and-run campaign against the Arabs. The Irgun became the subject of regular and bitter criticism by the Jewish Agency, which insisted that the outlawed, dissident terrorists endangered the Yishuv and the gains of the past. It was certainly true that the Irgun brought down British wrath on themselves: many members were jailed or detained, and one, Ben-Yosef, was hanged for firing on an Arab bus. The main threat to law and order remained the Arabs, but the Irgun gained invaluable experience in the underground. And, just as important, certain attitudes and responses were reinforced.

The partisanship of the British had for some time been clear to the Irgun; the Arab "revolt" often appeared a quarrel between friends. The British White Paper of 1939 was only the last act of betrayal. The Revisionist leadership no longer believed that British interest in Zionism had been a moral commitment; all but a few individuals felt it had been a means to further British strategic interests, interests that by 1939 could best be served by an Arabist policy. Any future Jewish state would have to depend on force rather than persuasion. Weizmann and the rest had been duped. Havlaga and the orange-grove philosophy of the orthodox Zionists was a disaster. The Irgun invasion of the Mandate with Begin's Betarim was set for April 1940. But in September 1939 Hitler overran Poland and Britain went to war.

There could no longer be any "invasion" of the Mandate; the Polish Revisionist movement had been destroyed in a month, all contact with Palestine lost. Nor would there be a revolt in Palestine, for hurting Britain would only help Hitler. Jabotinsky instructed the Irgun to refrain from anti-British operations. In September 1939 the possibility of any Irgun military activity was slight, for both Raziel and his deputy Stern, along with most of the High Command, were in British jails. Raziel was released in 1939 and the rest by spring 1940. After a period of confusion, in June 1940 the leadership split over Jabotinsky's order. Stern would not accept a "truce," took his people out of the Irgun, and went down the road that led to gun battles in the streets of Tel Aviv and his death.

As a result of the split and the self-imposed truce, the Irgun as a revolutionary organization remained quiescent. Some members joined the British army. After Jabotinsky's death in New York in 1940, the Revisionist movement was in complete disarray. The sources of strength in Eastern Europe were gone. The loss of Jabotinsky snuffed out the spiritual flame. Raziel was killed in 1941 while on a commando mission into Iraq. Irgun activities seemed largely irrelevant, a holding operation. By 1943, despite the untiring efforts of the new commander, Yaakov Meridor, the Irgun was a husk without a sense of mission. Some militants despaired. An indication of the rising frustration was the beginning of independent operations, at least one of which, the burning of buses, almost certainly carried out by impatient Irgun members. The need to revolt was intense; but to take up arms when there were none, to challenge the British Empire with a few hundred men without authorization and with the risk of massive retaliation, to fight against Hitler's foe was another matter.

Begin's Strategy of Leverage

Begin offered a solution. He was a leader and he had a strategy. Hardly the romantic image of a flaming rebel, he was physically unprepossessing. (He was described unkindly in the *Jewish Terrorist Index* by the British as having a long, hooked nose, bad teeth, and horn-rim glasses.) Nor had he the tongue of prophets or the skills of war.[5] What Begin did have was a remarkable presence, which created an atmosphere of contained power and immense moral authority, and a keen analytical mind, cleared of the dense undergrowth of past Zionist strategy and assumption. He appeared at the optimum moment for he knew what he—and the Irgun—wanted and how to get it.[6] Meridor was exhausted by the long holding action and uncertain of the future. He was more than willing to take the unusual step of resigning as Irgun commander so Begin's ideas could find expression. For Begin the "impossible" revolt had a logical base: first, no military targets until Hitler was defeated (that satisfied lingering qualms of conscience); and, second, use Irgun weakness and British strength to advantage in a strategy of leverage. British prestige in Palestine could be eroded by spectacular operations that humiliated the authorities. With two anti-imperialist allies, Russia and the United States, a Britain drained by the long war would be unable to recoup the loss of prestige by naked force—world opinion would oppose such coercion. Once the revolt began, the Mandate would resemble, Begin believed, "a glass house . . . the world was looking into with ever increasing interest and could see most of what was happening inside . . . the transparency of the glass was our shield of defense."[7] Essentially Begin was adjusting the Irish Strategy to take advantage of the Irgun's assets and the attitudes of the British opponent—but many of the Irish assets did not exist. He felt, nevertheless, that as long as the Irgun could carry out military operations—guerrilla-terror forays—British prestige would ebb, and with it British capacity to order the Mandate as they saw fit.

An important component of Begin's analysis was the projection of the British response to provocation. Under certain conditions, in the face of specific Irgun attack, Begin assumed they would act in predictable ways. The first, most important assumption was that, unlike the Russians or Germans the British would not run amok and slaughter the Jewish community in Palestine, either as a policy or spontaneously in reaction to provocation. World opinion, if not their own character, would prevent such a policy. Begin stressed that even if the British Palestinian commanders *wanted* to turn to murder as a method of governing they could not do so. Any lapse from Britain's self-avowed ideals—and as in Ireland there would surely be sufficient for Irgun's purpose—would engender a level of protest too great for the British government, dependent on the American ally, to ignore. Although members of the Irgun might run the ultimate risk of all rebels, the Jews of Palestine would not be in jeopardy.

This was Begin's strategy of leverage. Once the Irgun had raised the level of violence—destroyed British prestige through humiliation—to the point where the only choice was between counterviolence and withdrawal, it was a matter of persistence. Begin wanted to give Attlee and Bevin the same choices Lloyd George faced in 1921. As in Ireland, Britain had crucial interests involved, but the Irgun was determined that no non-Zionist solution could be imposed on Palestine. If the British attempted to do so, they would do so at a cost, not in blood and gold, but in decency and self-respect, not to mention international obloquy, that would not be worth the price. The war Begin proposed to fight was largely psychological. His tactics would be those of the weak, of the underground, the means of the guerrilla, the techniques of terror. His strategy would be one of leverage, using revolutionary jujitsu to turn British strength into weakness, British virtue into an Irgun asset. His authorization came, not from the legitimate institutions, but from the needs of Jewry under the shadow of the holocaust. And his victory, if there were to be such, would surely be to the advantage of his Zionist rivals.

One imponderable that did not trouble Begin was the Arab variable. That was largely ignored or, rather, assumed. As had many Zionists before them, the Irgun felt that there need be no fatal confrontation between Arab and Zionist aspirations and that the Arabs should and would recognize the anti-imperialist nature of a revolt so akin to their own struggle for independence.[8] Anyway Jewish need was greater than that of the Arabs. Actually, nobody thought much about the Arabs: the battle would be against the British. Far more important to the future would be the response of the Yishuv. If the revolt were to succeed, the Jews of Palestine had to realize that they could control their own destinies, that they were taking arms to determine the future. The Jews had to realize that they could *fight,* that Jews *had* fought—as in the Warsaw Ghetto. They had to be persuaded by the example of the Irgun that to risk something was not to lose all. With this realization would come toleration of the Irgun revolt. The greatest danger lay in the refusal of the Yishuv to permit others to risk British vengeance. The official institutions would of course oppose the revolt, as a challenge to legitimacy and a threat to the future. Begin hoped the Yishuv would find the courage of his convictions, would not oppose in deed the revolt, would tolerate his struggle in their name.

The Irgun did not simply launch a "revolt" without at least an attempt to involve others. Many in the Haganah felt the time had come to take action. The White Paper, the closed gates, the Warsaw Ghetto had caused second and third thoughts within the legitimate institutions. In the autumn of 1943 the Irgun sponsored an anti-British front, Am Lohem, that included Palmach commandos and Haganah members. The various programs remained proposals. On December 7, 1943, the Haganah General Staff warned its members that all Am Lohem activities must cease within seventy-two hours. The Haganah members withdrew, Am Lohem collapsed, and a united-front policy ended. The Haganah refusal to cooperate was no surprise. Ben Gurion and the Jewish Agency believed any wild "revolt" might destroy all that had been so laboriously won over the past generation. The Irgun believed nothing had been won but scornful toleration. Neither side trusted the other; neither respected the other. The scars of past political maulings had not healed. Whatever the advantages of reconciliation, there was insufficient trust on both sides, even by men of good will—and over the years within Zionist politics few had been able to keep their tempers much less their good-will. Thus, the Irgun opened the revolt in January 1944 certain of the opposition of the legitimate authorities and with no evidence but their own faith in the character of the Yishuv that their "illegal" operations would be tolerated.

Begin had made very few changes in the structure of the Irgun, and though organization may not have the romance of the bomb or the intellectual attraction of grand strategy, there can be no revolt without one. In order to operate in the British Mandate, the Irgun had evolved, not so much as a military organization as its name implied, but as an underground, secret, conspiratorial, and largely part-time. The link with the Revisionist movement had become tenuous; in January 1944 Begin broke it to keep the party from acting on or suffering from the revolt. This reduced the Irgun's options to underground operations and propaganda. At the top of the Irgun was a small High Command, including Begin, whose members, often replaced under the attrition of arrest or by missions abroad, had responsibility for specific areas. Under them a small General Staff was divided into a support (finance, intelligence, propaganda, and communications) and a military (operations, training, armament, first-aid, and planning) function. The staff never met jointly and maintained liaison through the High Command. Under this centralized, although often geographically dispersed, control were six basic geographical commands, shifting in size and importance under the pressure of arrests and the efficiency of recruiting. Each had an O/C, a small staff, and a core of members. Few were really strong and several were quite weak indeed. With only six hundred activists in 1944, there were never enough men to fill the slots on the organizational table. Everyone had to double up, performing two or three jobs, shifting about the country. For all purposes, the Irgun really had two varieties of volunteers: the propaganda squads that also fed new recruits into the assault forces; and the fighters.

With the exception of as few as twenty, and never more than forty, all the Irgunists remained "aboveground"—holding jobs, living at home, and going underground only for operations. Beginning with two hundred members in the fighting unit and four hundred actives elsewhere—plus five hundred supporters contacted weekly—the Irgun was never an army, even a mini-army, until the threat of the Arab irregulars swelled its ranks to nearly ten thousand in May 1948. Because of the small size of the operational areas and the capacity to move freely, the Irgun did not need and probably could not have used too many more operational people. To strike psychological blows of humiliation by military means it had fashioned, only in part by intention, an ideal structure, one that could be expanded with the task. In any case, to have increased the numbers involved in the revolt would have risked an overload. The men lost in the small organization could readily be replaced. A larger organization with all the pigeonholes filled would have been no more efficient for the purposes intended but also far harder to maintain. The entire Irgun was in actuality a dedicated band of brothers, with the same intimate loyalties and deep mutual trust. At times, under stress, they might have wished for more brothers but not better.

In the beginning there had to be a great deal of trust and dedication for there was little else. In January 1944 the Irgun had on call only four submachine guns, sixty pistols of various and dubious makes, thirty rifles, and less than a ton of explosives. Additional arms were purchased or stolen from the British or acquired as a result of private initiative, but there were never nearly enough to go around. Later, various arms manufacturing centers were developed to produce grenades, Sten guns, a variety of mines, and even mortars that, however, had more psychological than military impact. Even by November 1947, with an overall Irgun strength of two thousand and four years in the field there were arms for only seven hundred.

The vital question of money, more important to a revolutionary movement than arms, was never satisfactorily solved. Money from abroad was cut off during the war, and even after 1946 only the Revisionist movement in South Africa contributed much to the struggle in Palestine. Other funds were channeled into Europe to prepare for a massive influx of armed and trained men who would flip the balance against the Anglo-Arab alliance. In the meantime, the High Command had to make do with Palestinian contributions volunteered with enthusiasm or paid for fear of retribution and funds stolen from the British.[9] In 1944 the normal monthly cost of the revolt ranged between £1,000 and £1,500— no small sum for the times. By 1945 the cost had risen to £2,500 and it continued to grow. And there were always unexpected expenses: special operations could not be financed out of the monthly budget—a spectacular escape might cost £ 3,000—and special operations often were crucial. Personal expenses could not be reduced since most Irgun members took no money and the full-time people lived on a pittance.

Even with few arms and less money, the staff had in 1943 undertaken an extensive program of covert military training. The Irgun turned out to be an army with members rather than soldiers. Camps were set up and regular but not continuous sessions were held. There was evening training, test-firing by the sea or in the desert, regular two-hour classes for recruits. Later a volunteer might attend a camp training session and a desert test-firing. There were also special heavy-weapons training camps —in the fullness of time when heavy weapons were acquired—and a year-long explosives course. The camps and programs did not, of course, produce an "army" in any real military sense but a body of men who knew the use and maintenance of their weapons and the principles of guerrilla operations. This was all that could be done and all that was necessary. In a campaign of hit-and-run or bomb-and disappear, ingenuity, secrecy, intelligence, and daring were more important than military training.

The capacity of the Irgun to disorganize the British administration, even to attract international attention, was very limited; but Begin's strategy did not call for *vast* operations, only visible ones. There was no intention of creating parallel structures as in Ireland or liberated zones and only some vague hope of using the tactics of civil disobedience. The major thrust—in truth the only thrust possible—was to create chaos, forcing the British into repressive actions that would prove self-defeating.

The Proclamation of Revolt

In January 1944 the Proclamation of Revolt was issued. The Irgun's organization, armament, and training, if not finances, had reached a level that permitted limited operations. No matter what the problems, it was necessary to begin. The first series of strikes were planned to hit vulnerable, symbolic targets: immigration offices—the closed gates; income tax offices—the foreign occupier; and CID (Criminal Investigation Division) offices—the imperialist oppressor. None were military targets and all, according to the local commanders and operational-planning staff, could be hit with what the Irgun had on hand. On the night of February 12 Irgun incendiary bombs went off almost simultaneously in the offices of the Department of Migration in Jerusalem, Tel Aviv, and Haifa. On February 27 income tax offices in the same three cities were hit, and on March 23 the CID offices.[10] The attack on the police and CID offices did not go off smoothly. In Jerusalem there was a serious fire fight; one of the Irgun commanders was killed and a volunteer captured, a captain of the CID was killed and several British policemen wounded. There were casualties in the Jaffa and Haifa attacks as well. These CID operations, in part because of the losses to both sides, caused consternation. Bombs in migration offices was one thing, but dead policemen and shooting in the street was another, was open rebellion. The British, despite years of anxiety, were unprepared. Their security was lax and their intelligence nonexistent.

For the High Command, the fact that the Irgun could carry out the operation was less important than the impact of the attacks. The reaction of the Yishuv, of the British, and the ramifications on the international plane were more important than the details of the operations. And the response of the Yishuv was, at first, most vital. Thus, an unending stream of Irgun proclamations, posters, pamphlets, and position-papers were distributed so Jews would know what the revolt was and why it had been undertaken and what the results would be. This was not always easier than the military operations; for until the autumn of 1944, there was no printing press, the vulnerability to arrest of people pasting up *Herut* wall-posters was high, and the only radio transmitter was captured after only a few broadcasts. But the propaganda campaign was vital. "We disseminated the declaration of revolt through the length and breadth of the country, posting it up on the walls . . . We published leaflets, appeals and communiques on military operations. At least once every two or three days, at times every day or every night, our message was proclaimed. We never tired of explaining."[11]

At best the response was ambiguous. As the High Command had anticipated, the "common reader" of the wall-newspapers was not convinced that the British would not identify all Jews with the Irgunists and act accordingly. The British reaction to the operations of February and March did not indicate such a policy, but as yet there was no firm proof that the Irgun was not risking the existence of the Yishuv. The general reaction was consternation and anxiety in general and bitter criticism by the official institutions in particular. The Jewish Agency felt that the legitimate, democratic leadership of the Yishuv had been betrayed by men of narrow vision, dubious motives, and cold arrogance. There was no question of permitting the dissidents' "revolt" to continue.

The first attempt to persuade the Irgun to call off the armed struggle was an approach to the Revisionist Party. Beginning on February 18, Dov Joseph for the Agency met with the Revisionists five times. Only during the last meeting, on March 3, did he find out that the Revisionist Party no longer controlled the Irgun. The Jewish Agency then sought to construct a program of opposition. That a program was necessary was obvious: the revolt was a challenge to legitimate authority, a fearful gamble, and might even lead to defections from the ranks of Haganah. On April 2, 1944, after long debate an official policy of opposition was accepted: efforts to stop extortion and terror, increased propaganda, isolation of the separatists, and the activation of a special force to put an end to the Irgun if need be. The program appeared on paper to be a very strong response. Most of it remained on paper. Anti-Irgun propaganda was increased and help to those whose contributions had been extorted was offered, but there was no resort to physical force and no cooperation with the British. The Irgun had passed the first hurdle: the institutions had not killed the asp in the egg.

By August 1944, with Irgun operations continuing to mount, both the British and the Jewish Agency's reaction hardened. The British intelligence files were of little use. There were few informers to open a way into the Irgun, and conventional sweeps, intensive searches, and random arrests had proved minimally productive. Obviously the easiest and most efficacious solution would be to let the Jewish Agency, the legitimate authority, crush revolt from the inside. Logically in this particular case British and Agency interest ran parallel. The Agency, however, still had hopes that the Irgun could be brought to see reason. Various contacts had been set up that might lead to a Begin-Ben Gurion meeting. The Irgun hoped that Begin's offer to continue the resistance under Ben Gurion's leadership might be accepted. Ben Gurion, however, saw only the challenge to the Agency's authority by men he had never trusted. Agency leaders felt Begin must be made to see that the British might soon be alienated and all the promised gains lost. In the end not Ben Gurion but Dr. Moshe Sneh and Eliahu Golomb of the Haganah met with Begin and Eliahu Lankin of the High Command on August 10. Sneh could not convince Begin that the British intended to grant the Zionists "the biggest plum in the pudding" after the war. Begin felt that nations were created by struggle not by accepting dubious plums. Essentially, Sneh and Begin talked at cross-purposes, for their basic assumptions differed totally. The "negotiations" ended with the one meeting. The Jewish Agency was still not ready to consider cooperation with the British, but the time for more stringent measures was surely coming.

On September 27 a raid on the Katra police station brought the first Bren into the Irgun arsenal, an indication of just how much a shoestring operation the revolt remained after nine months. The High Command felt that what mattered was not so much the scale of operations but that they could be mounted at all. What the Irgun sought, however, was a dramatic coup that would simultaneously weaken British prestige and encourage the Yishuv that there would be no massacre in retaliation. For fourteen years the British had in the name of security forbidden the sounding of the Shofar on the Day of Atonement at the Wailing Wall. The Irgun began a Yom Kippur campaign of intimidation, threatening disaster if the British continued the prohibition. If the Mandate authorities maintained their position in the name of order, they almost assured a situation in which the Irgun would feel "justified" in the use of the violence the ban was suppose to avoid. "Any British policemen who on the Day of Atonement dares to burst into the area of the Wailing Wall and to disturb the traditional service—will be regarded as a criminal and will be punished accordingly."[12]

To a degree the Irgun was bluffing, since the High Command had no intention of risking an operation in the midst of the crowd at the Wailing Wall, but the Yom Kippur ploy was not all bluff because a series of operations against Tegart police fortresses had been planned to coincide with the Day of Atonement. These would be either the Irgun's "answer" to the continuation of the ban or, if the ban were rescinded, simply further offensive operations unrelated to the Wailing Wall. In any case, the British security forces did not enter the area around the Wailing Wall but stood at a distance and heard the Shofar being blown. The forces of authority had been levered just that wee bit.

Up to September 27, the day of the Shofar, the Irgun had cost the British administration little but anxiety. The Jewish Agency opposed the revolt and apparently so did the mass of the Yishuv. The mini-raids had no military importance. Lives had been lost but not British credibility. Everyone waited for the Irgun's challenge to authority to end not to escalate. The British Yom Kippur withdrawal in the face of Irgun coercion was a disaster for them, small as yet but a harbinger of other errors. Psychologically it was a significant victory for the Irgun. The British had been intimidated. They had preferred not to pay the Irgun's asking price. They had, for whatever very good and logical reasons, taken a step backward. Most important of all, even after the Irgun hit the three police stations that same night, the British did not seek "revenge" from the Yishuv. The Irgun was certain that the Yishuv would now realize that fears of extensive British retaliation were groundless. Two days later a senior British police officer was shot and killed in a Jerusalem street by the Stern Group.

The Agency was convinced that it was but a matter of time before the continuing Irgun stunts produced disastrous results in the Mandate. The newspaper *Davar* condemned "this lunacy" as crimes that could bring calamity upon Jewish Palestine. Just as the White Paper logjam seemed to be breaking up to Zionist advantage, the British were being shot down in the streets of Jerusalem. In the United States the Republican and Democratic parties had both passed pro-Zionist planks at their national conventions. In Britain in April the Labour Party had renewed a position on Palestine more Zionist, if possible, than that of the Jewish Agency. Churchill had indicated that the Yishuv would not be disappointed with a postwar settlement and that a good partition was under discussion. No matter who decided the future of the Mandate, Labour or Conservative, both were shifting to sympathy—and there was always America. All this might be lost if the Irgun continued their murder campaign. On October 6 the Irgun looted a government textile warehouse, selling the contents for funds or distributing them as charity. No admonitions seemed to have any effect as the dissidents went from one outrage to another. Worse they seemed to be gaining momentum and sympathy.

The British were far from satisfied with the Jewish Agency's response to the revolt; something more than admonitions was required. On October 10 an official announcement called for active collaboration with the forces of law and order. By mid-October, fifteen members of the Palestine police had been killed. Pressure on the Agency to take effective steps to break the Irgun grew. Within the Agency the only point in dispute was whether to cooperate with the British in breaking the Irgun—a most dangerous tactic since in reprisal the Irgun might denounce the secret Haganah leadership. At last, on October 25, the Inner Zionist Council announced that drastic steps would be taken to counter the terrorists—but without collaborating with the British. On October 20 the Haganah had already opened a training course for 170 men to wage the anti-Irgun campaign, subsequently labeled the Season. The British too had lost patience with half-measures; on October 21, 251 suspected terrorists were exiled to Africa.[13] The Jewish Agency, deep in plans for the Season, protested the exile of any Jew from Palestine and made one last attempt to reason with Begin. Again Golomb and Sneh met Begin and Lankin. Golomb demanded the cessation of Irgun activities. Begin replied as expected. Finally, well after midnight, the streetcorner conference broke up, with Golomb warning Begin, "we shall step in and finish you."[14] The Season had opened.

The Haganah versus the Irgun

The Haganah faced a difficult problem. It would not be hard to close down the sources of Irgun funds—conventional police work within the capacity of the Haganah—but to remove Irgun people from circulation without turning them over to the British or executing them was far more difficult, for as an underground army the Haganah had no jails. The Haganah, nevertheless, intended to seize and hold the Irgunists in safe houses—a secret campaign of internment. Even as the seizures and "internments" began, it was clear that the policy was a stopgap. If the spirit and resiliency of the Irgun could be broken swiftly, the tactic might work; if not, the Haganah would run out of safe houses. To back down and free the "internees" would bring about a disastrous loss of prestige; to turn to executions would shake the moral position of the legitimate institutions. This left the only avenue collaboration with the British, with the moral and physical risks that implied. Unless the Irgun cracked quickly, the Agency Executive would have to resort to most unpalatable alternatives or dismantle the Season, and with it much of their own authority. Yet the tactics of the Season as pursued during October and into November were half-measures. No one wanted to go too far. Developments in November convinced the Agency that half-measures were insufficient.

During 1944 the revived Stern Group entered into negotiations with the Irgun that led not to a merger but to a working agreement. The Sternists, with even fewer assets than the Irgun, pursued a quite different course, one that produced a major crisis. On November 6 in Cairo two young men assassinated Lord Moyne, British Minister of State in the Middle East. Both were captured and it became clear that the operation was officially authorized by the Stern Group—a step in the strategy to change history through resort to personal terror. Moyne's assassination was almost universally condemned. Weizmann called at 10 Downing Street to express his deep moral indignation and horror. The British were outraged at the senselessness of the deed. The Mandate authorities had already indicated all Jews might be tarred by the terrorist brush, and the Irgun, completely ignorant of the Stern Group's plans, would be the first. Killing Palestine police was one thing, and bad enough, but killing a British Minister of State, a personal friend of the Prime Minister, was quite another. Stern Group or Irgun made little difference; the madmen were about to ruin a good postwar settlement. The White Paper was finished. New men were taking over and the old ones coming around. On November 1 Lord Gort had arrived as the new High Commissioner with, reportedly, an open mind. On November 4 Weizmann had lunched with Churchill and come away convinced that the Zionists would get a good partition. Churchill had assured Weizmann that his demands for a large immigration and speedy decisions would be taken into consideration. Weizmann, the Jewish Agency, and the Zionists could have asked for little more. Instead they received the fateful blunder of the assassination of Moyne, a man whose death could change history, but in ways hurtful to Zionism. When Churchill spoke before the Commons on November 17, his voice shocked by emotion, their very worst fears became reality.

> If our dreams for Zionism should be dissolved in the smoke of the revolvers of assassins and if our efforts for its future should provoke a new wave of banditry worthy of the Nazi Germans, many persons like myself will have to reconsider the position that we have maintained so firmly for such a long time. In order to hold out a possibility for future peace, these harmful activities must cease and those responsible for them must be radically destroyed and eliminated.[15]

On the elimination of the dissidents the Agency and Churchill were of one mind. The Season was intensified and accelerated. A policy of cooperation with the British was accepted. For the Irgun the obvious options seemed violent resistance or surrender. In the High Command and the ranks there was no interest in surrender and near unanimity for hitting back. The impact of accelerated kidnappings, physical beatings, expulsions from schools and jobs, the denunciations and deliveries to the British created an atmosphere of crisis within the Irgun. The Agency appeared determined to destroy Revisionism once and for all. The excuse of the Moyne assassination was only that, for the Season remained focused on the Irgun, not on the Stern Group. Operations became impossible. Unless action were taken, the Irgun would be destroyed. The British already had hundreds of names and the police were making daily round-ups, picking up long-secret members. The obvious step, the desirable step, the natural step was to retaliate. That step was not taken because Begin imposed his will first on the High Command and then on the Irgun: "Not logic, but instinct said imperatively: 'No; not civil war. Not that any price.' And who knows: perhaps instinct is the very heart of logic."[16]

Pragmatic logic was replaced with emotional logic and, as Begin noted, the latter turned out to be more profitable in the long run. Retaliation would have led inevitably to gun battles in the streets, reminiscent of the disastrous Sternist tactics of 1942, and could ultimately have had but one victor, the British. Given time and will, the far larger Haganah would surely win any extended shoot-out, breaking the Irgun in a miniature civil war but at the cost of undermining the legitimate authorities and the future capacity of the Haganah. Begin insisted successfully that this time the Jews would not shed each other's blood as they had so often in Biblical days, that even at the cost of the Irgun there would be no civil war. With luck, with persistence in the face of provocation, the time would surely come when the Haganah leaders would recognize that the Season was against their own interests: it could only be distasteful to the Yishuv, and would label them as collaborators in an occupied country. The Irgun would burrow down, eschew revenge, and wait. It was the most difficult and certainly the most important decision of the revolt, and the one most adamantly resisted by his colleagues.

Several hundred Irgunists were arrested or detained. The commanders, often well known to the Haganah, were swept up by the British. Funds dried up. Communication became difficult and training almost impossible. No operation could be considered. Yet, despite the attrition of hundreds of arrests its basic strength remained the same. Moreover, the new replacements were often unknown to the Haganah and the new commanders too young to have a reputation that would endanger them. After a couple of months the Irgun still had not been crushed, merely contained. The urgency of the Season seemed to fade rapidly. The initial enthusiasm of the Palmach-Haganah evaporated after the decision to cooperate with the British had been taken. There were fewer volunteers for the Season and growing defections. It began to resemble a collaborationist campaign instigated for special political interests within Zionism. The rank and file began to express serious reservations. In March 1945 a meeting of the Season leaders heard Sneh and Golomb announce that activities against the separatists would soon cease. In June the Season finally ended—a disaster for everyone but the Irgun.

The Haganah assumed that the Irgun has sustained grave injury. This was undeniably true, but no one could suggest that the Irgun no longer existed or was incapable of launching operations, that it had been "finished." In the spring of 1945 at the end of the Season, the alternatives that had existed the previous October were still present: cooperate, tolerate, destroy. Failure to destroy the Irgun in cooperation with the British was surely the worst possible policy. Six months of pressure had steeled the Irgun, improved its capacity to act under coercion, and, most important, adorned its leadership with a mantle of national responsibility. The Irgun had prevented a civil war and attracted the sympathy and understanding of many who previously had abhorred their politics, suspected their motives, and even doubted their sanity. The Haganah's Season had maimed without killing, created sympathy where none had existed, and assured the Irgun that the great divide had been safely if painfully passed. The revolt would have the toleration of the Yishuv.

Until the spring of 1945 British response to the revolt within the Palestine Mandate had been, both consciously and often unwittingly, most astute. With a little bit of luck, a degree of cunning, and more conscious leadership from London, they might have scraped through. By waving the carrot of a "good" partition and immediate immigration, the British had persuaded the legitimate authorities to wield the stick against the rebels. If the stick had been, as seemed only likely, replaced by the gun, the Haganah would have simultaneously rid the Mandate of the terrorists, contaminated itself and the Zionist authorities in most Jewish eyes, and compromised its own security by collaboration. With any luck, the divisions between the three covert military forces—Haganah, Irgun, and Stern Group—could have led to their mutual destruction. At the same time, if the cooperation of the Agency could have been rewarded, even with promises—especially with promises—then the long-awaited postwar solution could have been withdrawn farther into the future.

The refusal of the Irgunists to break discipline under provocation, and the end of the policy of collaboration, a policy that did not pay the

Jewish Agency sufficient political dividends, meant that the British still had to contend with a revolt. To retrieve the situation, Britain would have to continue to depend on coercion without collaboration. Unless such repression proved swiftly successful all of the Yishuv might be antagonized and Britain's Arab friends alienated at half-measures. By the middle of 1945 the British still did not feel seriously challenged. There was still hope that the general distaste for Begin's revolt could be exploited and that the residue of the Season would prevent intra-Zionist cooperation. And the Irgun was really only a few hundred fanatics—or perhaps more, British intelligence was never quite sure. It seemed only logical that for the British to come down hard with the boot would be sufficient to maintain order. Apparently the capacity of London to decide the fate of the Mandate to London's satisfaction, hand out big plums or small, albeit with a *pro forma* bow to Washington, still existed. The essential point for Britain was to maintain law and order in the Mandate, reveal the Irgun's "revolt" as little more than low-level brigandage.

By June 1945, however, when the Season closed, London had lost the safest, most profitable means to end the revolt within the law, quietly and with clean hands. With the end of the war in Europe, Britain had lost invisibility; henceforth many eyes would be watching through the glass walls of the Mandate. Then, before more hints and guesses concerning a postwar settlement, the entire Middle Eastern kaleidoscope unexpectedly shifted. In May, Churchill had dissolved the coalition War Cabinet and called for a general election, certain that his wartime leadership would be rewarded at the polls. The result was quite the reverse. On July 27 the new Labour government, with Clement Attlee as Prime Minister and Ernest Bevin as Foreign Secretary, formally took office. As recently as April 25, the Labour Executive Committee had proclaimed a pro-Zionist policy. The Jewish Agency hoped for a positive response to requests for an immediate decision to establish a Jewish state, authority to bring in Jews, an international load to transfer one million emigrants with international cooperation, and reparations from Germany. The problem of Begin's revolt had been settled for both the Jewish Agency and the British by the Labour Party victory. Outside the ranks of the Irgun, Zionist optimism ran rampant. The Irgun decision to wait weeks not months for a satisfactory British initiative was regarded as no more than a refusal to accept the fact that the whole structure of Irgun strategy had been based on error and miscalculation. A calm settled over Palestine, while all eyes, Arab and Zionist, Agency and Irgun, focused on London.

Nothing happened. There was no decision in favor of the Zionists, only disquieting rumors and vague postponements. The Labour Cabinet faced a massive array of problems. The war in Asia had ended only in September, and the future of Palestine had a relatively low Labour priority. The real interest of most of the Party and much of the Cabinet was the transformation of British society. Imperial interests had long been covered by well-meant and high-sounding resolutions, usually against the excesses of colonialism. The Party had seldom given much thought to the use of British power abroad or the advantages ensuing from such power to those other than the "bosses." A Zionist solution in Palestine had long been Labour policy; but once in office it became clear that if such a "solution" were imposed the Arab Middle East would be alienated. British hegemony would be threatened and British economic interests curtailed. Such a course could have a damaging effect on the Western alliance and, more important, on the pay packets of British workers and on the capital needed to transform British society. Complete alienation of the Arabs could not be contemplated without danger to policies and programs even more dear to Labour hearts than the triumph of Zionism. Amid constant crisis in Westminster, there was no time for serious reappraisal. Bevin had to construct a Palestine program that would protect British interest, even those long-despised imperial interests now recognized as vital to the future of the British worker.

The nature of that policy in substance, if not in detail, became increasingly clear to Zionist advocates in London. Instead of intimate consultation they discovered closed doors, and instead of firm promises, received uncertain hints of future policy. On August 25 the Colonial Office informed Weizmann that the emigrant quota of fifteen hundred would not be increased. By the time Bevin presented his Palestine policy in the House of Commons on November 13, nearly all Zionist opinion had been alienated, driven willingly or unwillingly into an activism only slightly less extreme than that of the Irgun. Bevin announced that the United States had accepted an invitation to join in an Anglo-American investigating committee. This was the only "good" news. The monthly quotas would continue. An immediate Jewish state, unlimited immigration, and territorial expansion were out of the question. Only the old White Paper, ill-disguised by the proposed Anglo-American Committee, remained. The gates would stay closed. This above all else was intolerable to the Zionists, aware of the agony and expectations of Jews who had barely escaped the ovens. It seemed that Britain's Zionist friends had for years believed Labour's promises—only to be rewarded with the same old imperial interests.

Bevin's policy was to maintain a British presence in the Middle East that would be to Britain's interest first and foremost, that would involve America and thereby mute trans-Atlantic criticism, that would not alienate the Arabs, and, therefore, could not placate the Zionists. The fate of Jewish refugees in Europe could be considered later. British policy was what the Revisionists had always contended, policy fashioned for British interests, and such interests ultimately were not compatible with Zionist ambitions. This was made abundantly clear when, in a press conference after his Commons speech, Bevin indicated that Britain had never undertaken to establish a Jewish state, only a Jewish Home. It was clear in the autumn of 1945 that such a British-built Home would have few rooms and those mean.

The United Resistance Movement

From late August the Jewish Agency had to reconsider the prospects. Increasingly the militants within Haganah urged a policy of pressure—a "demonstration"—so Bevin and the British could not continue to ignore Zionist demands. A truce with the Irgun was arranged and consideration of joint action begun. The Agency, still uncertain as to the proper strategy, tried to persuade the Irgun to merge with Haganah. Although the Irgun was not necessarily adverse to the closest possible cooperation and Begin had already offered to operate under Ben Gurion, grave doubts remained about the havlaga mentality. Once absorbed and dispersed, the Irgun would be in no position to renew the revolt if the Jewish Agency and Haganah lost their nerve or revised their strategy. The Irgun, however, was willing to operate under the command of a united resistance that would in effect through Haganah give the Agency a veto over all Irgun operations except arms raids. The Sternists also accepted the united command. The result was the Tenuat Hameri, the United Resistance Movement.

The Tenuat Hameri pursued two parallel but by no means identical strategies. The Jewish Agency originally contemplated not a "military" campaign but one or more "demonstrations." Sneh, who saw Britain not so much an enemy as a bad partner, wanted to create one serious incident, "as a warning and an indication of much more serious incidents that would threaten the safety of all British interests in the country if the Government did not grant the Zionist requests."[17] The Haganah wanted the incidents to relate directly to the major grievance, the closed gates, and not be integrated into a full-scale attack on British personnel and institutions. Stern-Irgun simply wanted to pursue their revolt under the umbrella of the Tenuat Hameri unhampered by the rationalizations necessary to relate each operation directly to the emigration problem. The Irgun believed, and so it proved, that the artificiality of the Haganah restraint would erode under the pressure of maintaining momentum. The Haganah felt that retaliation would placate the Zionist Left and still let them have a piece of the action. Everyone was satisfied, if still somewhat suspicious; the Season remained in the background, an unburied skeleton.[18]

In October, Kol Israel, the illegal Haganah radio station, began broadcasting. On October 10 the Haganah raided a clearance camp for immigrants south of Haifa and released 208 Jews. Kol Israel began to call for an active resistance movement to assist the immigration of Jews into the Mandate. Sneh's "demonstration" took place on the night of October 31/November 1. The Palmach commandos sank three small naval vessels and destroyed the tracks of the Palestine Railway in fifty localities: 135 blown breaks and 500 explosions. The Irgun attacked Lydda Railway Station and the Sternists attempted to hit the Haifa oil refinery.

By that time the situation in the Mandate had slipped out of British control. In the early spring Britain might have been able to impose a "bad" partition on the Zionists by permitting relatively easy immigration into the enclave and withdrawing to secure military bases, letting the Arabs, preferably Emir Abdullah of Transjordan, have the remainder of the Mandate. Such a *fait accompli* might have eased Britain out. A few months later, with Zionist opposition hardening, the war in Europe over, and the glass house too transparent for a *coup de main,* Britain might have tried the reverse, offering a relatively good partition, state included, and hope that the Arab dismay would not harden into intractable opposition. Subsequent events indicate that probably neither would have produced a "solution" satisfactory or even tolerable to either side. But a British decision in mid-1945 would have been preferable to drift—and drift compounded by muddle became British policy.

The time lost could not be made up. Both the Arabs and the Zionists became too strong to be imposed upon without Britain's paying increasingly high costs in prestige, in strategic advantage, in good faith. This was most assuredly not apparent to the new government in 1945. Until June things had largely gone Britain's way. After that nothing again went Britain's way. On every level, tactical and strategic, diplomatic and political, British policy foundered in a welter of errors. For eighteen months there was no indication that anyone in authority had a reasoned policy—or even a sense of the possible.

Despite an increasing investment of time and consideration no conclusion was reached on the value to Britain of the Mandate. All the options—to stay in Egypt or just in the Suez Canal Zone; to use Cyprus as an alternative; to upgrade Aden or fall back on Kenya; to renegotiate the Arab treaties or turn to private investment instead of treaty alliances —were weighed but no decision was reached as to what were Britain's future interests in Palestine and how they could be achieved. Many wanted to stay for strategic reasons, others to withdraw for political ones. The arguments might as well have taken place in a vacuum. The Labour government had neither time nor energy to expend on any but the most urgent or the most recent dilemma. The social revolution needed constant tending as did the decay of American-Russian relations and the collapse of order in India. Western Europe appeared on the verge of collapse into penury, and Britain often seemed not far behind. There was little time for Palestine.

The result was that without firm central direction those responsible for the Mandate had to make do. A firm case could be made that British policy was following any one of several, often contradictory, directions. Statements, declarations, overt acts, and covert plots were summoned up as evidence that Britain intended to placate the United States by offering concessions to the Zionists or intended to create an Arab empire, controlled by London through the new Arab League. There was undeniable proof that Britain intended to stay in the Mandate[19]—why else continue to build elaborate military installations?—and that Britain intended to withdraw—why else organize the Anglo-American Committee that would suggest some form of Arab and/or Zionist independence? Labour spokesmen seemed to feel that the enumeration of British responsibilities, not to mention the long roster of failed "solutions," was the equivalent of a policy.

No one felt the absence of direction more than those on the spot in the Mandate with the responsibility of maintaining law and order and holding together the painstakingly constructed structure of government. The lack not only of direction but also of communication meant that within the Mandate British authorities were reduced to tactics; there was no strategy, Commonwealth or otherwise. Any hypothetical list of tactical errors to be avoided in the Mandate would reveal few items that the British did not put into practice. Both the Arabs and the Zionists, all the Zionists, were alienated, and a universal lack of support for Britain abroad resulted. All the tools to repress violent opposition were used in such a way as to encourage further and more violent opposition. Every attempt to punish the terrorists produced more terror. At every turn and at every stage, the British were outmaneuvered, often if not always by their own incapacities, their own blunders. Perhaps without a central strategy and the stern pressures of the existing international alignment, any roster of tactics would have failed; but no matter how difficult the situation was, the British tactics made it worse than even their most adamant opponents could have dared to wish.

For the Irgun the British errors were unanticipated gifts in some cases and the expected results of the strategy of leverage in others. The alliance with Haganah had not changed its plans; no one believed Britain would yield to a "demonstration." The main task was to persist, with as many operations as possible, fraying British tempers and eroding British prestige.[20] The alliance with the Haganah at worst meant sharply increased pressure against the British. From November 1945 until June

1946 there were over fifty separate incidents: constant minor operations, bombing or arson, shots in the streets and mines on the roads, coupled with large-scale strikes. Although all major operations were directed or authorized by the joint command of Tenuat Hameri, dominated by the Haganah, there was remarkably little friction; almost everyone wanted to get on with the campaign.

On the night of December 27 the Irgun hit the Central Headquarters of the Police and CID in Jerusalem and Jaffa. In Jerusalem seven British officers and soldiers were killed and fourteen wounded; the Jaffa attack was a success without casualties. That same night an Irgun raiding party held forty British soldiers captive in a camp in Tel Aviv until the arms had been cleared. On the night of February 25, 1946, there was a massive Haganah action against police stations and radar installations. An Irgun-Stern strike against three RAF airdromes caused, according to the official estimate, losses of £ 2,000,000—thirty-five planes destroyed; others damaged. At midday on March 7 the Irgun raided the British army camp at Sarafand for arms and hit the Tel Aviv radio station. The Anglo-American Committee arrived the next day, but there was no "diplomatic" pause. At the beginning of April three heavy attacks were carried out on the railway system; this time the Irgun lost thirty-one men, captured on the way back to their base. On April 23 the Irgun hit the police station at Ramat Gan. On April 25 the Stern Group attacked a British army car park in Tel Aviv, killing seven of the eight paratroopers.

In November 1945 the potentially moderate Lord Gort was replaced as High Commissioner by General Sir Alan Gordon Cunningham, who instituted a policy of stern retaliation. In December pressure was put on the Jewish Agency. Its members denied responsibility, pointing out that the closed gates had sparked the violence. There was to be no new Season; the rising level of violence in 1946 was to Zionist advantage. Britain had no policy option in the Mandate but to maintain order. The twenty thousand men of the Sixth Airborne Division had been moved to the Mandate; and as the resistance continued British troop strength rose to eighty thousand regulars, plus thousands of police and units of the Transjordanian Arab Legion.[21] There were two cruisers, three destroyers and other naval units off the coast. The ratio of British security forces to the Jewish population was approximately one to five. The Mandate had been turned into an armed camp, the countryside studded with huge, concrete Tegart fortresses, British army bases, and roadblocks. Cities were constantly patrolled and government buildings protected by barbed wire and sentry blocs. The British withdrew into wired and protected ghettos, the largest in Jerusalem known as Bevingrad. Extensive security regulations and restrictions were issued and enforced, insofar as possible. There were curfews, confiscations, searches, sweeps through the countryside, collective fines, detentions, and arrests. The newspapers were censored and travel restricted.

Locked in their barbed wire ghettos and devoid of adequate, often any, intelligence, the authorities faced a Jewish population alienated by not only the British policy of the closed gates but also by the day-to-day indignities that repression required. When the Sternists shot—murdered in cold blood in British, and many Jewish eyes— the soldiers in the Tel Aviv carpark on April 25, the local commander Major General A. F. H. Cassel's justifiable response was horror and disgust, his immediate response rash. He accused the Jewish Mayor of Tel Aviv of complicity: "There is no doubt whatsoever in my mind that many members either knew of this project or could have given some warning before it happened . . . you could produce the criminals."[22] British troops, again victims of murder from a ditch, rioted in the Jewish towns of Natanyah and Be'er Tuveyah, smashing stores and manhandling anyone on the streets. Antisemitic slogans were daubed on walls, searches were cruder, insults freer. All was grist to the Zionist propaganda mills, to the outrage of the British authorities who felt that under the most extreme provocation the troops had and were showing remarkable restraint.

On the night of June 16, there was another massive strike on the Palestine railway system. Nine bridges crossing the Palestine border were sabotaged and rails broken throughout the Mandate. The damage was estimated at £ 250,000. The British struck back at what they felt was the core of the resistance: the Jewish Agency.[23] British forces occupied the Agency's offices in Jerusalem and Tel Aviv. There were 2,700 arrests, including most of the significant political figures in the Mandate with the exception of Weizmann, and a substantial portion of suspected Haganah and Palmach men were picked up. More arrests followed. The suspects were moved to internment camps at Latrun or Rafah on the Egyptian border. On June 29, "Black Saturday," a massive search-and-seizure operation was carried out against the Jewish kibbutzim. This pressure had an effect. Ben Gurion in Paris feared the entire structure of the Jewish institutions was going to be dismantled. Until June the Agency believed that "demonstrations" would pressure London and gain international sympathy at low cost. Now the British had swept up the political leadership—the military being out of reach. If the united resistance ceased, the Irgun and the Stern Group would keep up the pressure in any case, leaving the Agency free to negotiate with clear hands. If the Haganah wanted action, it could concentrate on illegal immigration. In July these tentative considerations became final.

On July 1 Tenuat Hameri authorized the Irgun's Operation "Chick." The Irgun operations officer Amihai "Gideon" Paglin had devised a means to place a huge explosive charge in the basement of the

King David Hotel in Jerusalem, the British administrative headquarters, heavily protected by wire and patrols. At 12:36 P.M. on July 22, Jerusalem was rocked by the impact of the huge explosion that dumped the entire southwest wing of the hotel into a heap of rubble under a billowing cloud of smoke. Eighty-eight Jews, Arabs, and British were killed, forty-three injured. The Irgun claimed that the British had not reacted to their warning, the British that there had been no warning. Wherever the ultimate responsibility lay, the reaction to the King David operation was horror and indignation. Ben Gurion told a reporter from *France Soir* that "The Irgun is the enemy of the Jewish people." The Tenuat Hameri policy was a shambles and the opportunity for the British to drive in the opening wedge in a divide-and-rule gambit seemed clear.

The British not only failed to exploit their opportunity, but bungled again. Lieutenant-General Sir Evelyn Barker issued a secret order, vituperative in tone and language, to the British army, banning Anglo-Jewish fraternization and attacking in scathing terms the whole of the Yishuv.

> I am determined that they should be punished and made aware of our feelings of contempt and disgust at their behavior . . . I understand that these measures will create difficulties for the troops, but I am certain that if my reasons are explained to them, they will understand their duty and will punish the Jews in the manner this race dislikes the most: by hitting them in the pocket, which will demonstrate our disgust for them.[24]

Even Barker should have known that in Palestine nothing could be kept secret for long. Within a week the order was being pasted up on walls by the Irgun. But nothing could put Tenuat Hameri back together again. Haganah carried out only one operation in July and two in August. On August 23 Tenuat Hameri was formally dissolved.

By the time of its dissolution neither Ben Gurion nor Begin needed Tenuat Hameri. The Irgun had enough momentum to continue alone, while Ben Gurion, above the struggle, could hold firm as the British produced one unsatisfactory "solution" after another. So the proposals for accommodation continued: an altered Anglo-American plan that would not open the gates as President Truman had suggested; a revised canton scheme, the Morrison-Grady Play; a Palestine Round Table Conference; and in September a London Conference. Nothing worked. Haganah concentrated on "illegals" and the Jewish Agency on propaganda, while, as expected, the Irgun pursued their revolt. Steps had already been considered that would widen the revolt and, exploiting changing European conditions, take the struggle beyond the Mandate. In

September 1945 the High Command decided to send a mission to Europe authorized to rescue refugees and bring them back to Palestine, to recruit, train, and arm volunteers, and to carry out missions against the British. Until then, because of the war and the divisions within the world Revisionist movement, operations and activities abroad, even fund-raising, had played little part in the revolt. Unlike Ben Gurion and the World Zionist organizations, the Irgun still intended to concentrate on military matters: propaganda by deed.

The Irgun mission which arrived in Italy in January 1946 initiated extensive diaspora activities. Wide semiofficial contacts were made to acquire arms. Men, mostly refugees, were recruited, armed, and trained, until eventually 25 percent of the Irgun was abroad. Efforts to move these men and arms into the Mandate failed until June 1948. Some of the activities abroad, public propaganda and the collection of funds, followed the conventional route of exile-rebels; others did not. The diaspora Irgun also carried out military operations against the British—notably a bomb that damaged the British Embassy in Rome on October 31, 1946. Strikes against British targets extended the atmosphere of crisis, first into Western Europe where British soldiers in occupied Germany were harassed by the very people they had in part supposedly fought a war to save, and then in Britain itself where journalists reported that Irgun assassins were stalking the streets of London.[25] Thus, the Palestine problem became far more urgent and far more visible to the British public, the pressure on the government to "do something" far greater.

In Palestine, meanwhile, the Irgun persisted in mounting operations, uninterested in various British initiatives, except insofar as they might tempt Ben Gurion to compromise what was well on the way to being won. The prime responsibility of the High Command was to keep up the pace. Operations were authorized because they were feasible and their timing related directly to the demands of the mission. Only rarely could a spectacular demonstration be organized for specific strategic purpose. In the case of Chick, no one had foreseen the impact since no one had planned on the deaths. The Haganah requested the operation solely to destroy their records, taken there by the British after the raid on Jewish Agency headquarters. Thus, the destruction of the King David was for operational not "political" reasons. Some operations, however, were far more subtle, intended to coerce the British into a course of action costly to their prestige. On December 27 two Irgun volunteers were sentenced to flogging. One, Binyamin Kimchi, received eighteen lashes. In response, on December 29, the Irgun kidnapped three British NCO's and a Major and gave them each eighteen lashes. The second Irgun prisoner was not flogged nor were any subsequent prisoners. The British "reversal" was commented on in London as well as in Palestine.

The same tactic was used when two Irgun men captured during the Sarafand arms raid in March 1945 were sentenced to death. Five British officers were kidnapped in Tel Aviv and one in Jerusalem (the latter escaped) and were held during complicated negotiations through intermediaries that led in June to the remission of the sentences. When Dov Gruener, captured during the raid on the Ramat Gan police station in April 1945, had his death sentence confirmed on January 25, 1947, the Irgun kidnapped Judge Ralph Wyndham and a Major Collins, holding them until the execution of the sentence was postponed for an appeal to the Privy Council. In neither case was bluff involved. When the Irgun threatened a gallows for a gallows, authorities assumed that, if possible, it would make good the threat.

The British refusal to recognize a state of war in the Mandate meant that murder was not taking place on a battlefield but in a criminal context and thus *had* to be punished by normal judicial means. Yet to do so would create martyrs, as it had in Ireland, and might well lead to an endless round of vendetta murders. So the authorities chose the worst road, sentencing the "killers" and under threat failing to execute them. More prestige was lost, more credibility gone. For those within the Mandate the existence of British double standards had long been accepted: an illegal Haganah that produced a Moshe Dayan sentenced to ten years in prison one year and leading a commando raid into Syria the next, or a Raziel in jail in 1939 and buried with British military honors in 1941. Now with the new glass-house Mandate, British credibility began to be eroded in more distant places. No one seemed to understand British purpose or sympathize with British responsibilities, and in London the government increasingly felt misunderstood and ill-used, even by old allies.

In Britain the winter of 1946-47 was as bad a time as the country had suffered since the 1940 blitz. The weather was appalling . The economy seemed to be grinding to a halt. There were innumerable shortages and no surpluses. British resiliency after the two years of peacetime austerity and six years of war seemed broken. Britain informed the United States that the cost of defending Greece could no longer be borne. India hovered on the brink of civil war. Everywhere were problems—always more urgent and more crucial than Palestine. London insisted that the only solution there must be satisfactory to the Arabs and the Jews, a posture that would surely permit continued British occupation. The delay simply alienated both groups and their friends, all of whom were agreed only on the necessity for British departure. The delay irritated, then disgusted many in Britain who saw a bad situation becoming worse.

On February 14, 1947, the British announced that in September the problem would be referred to the United Nations General Assembly. To the suspicious, and they were legion, the gambit seemed to be that the United Nations would be given the responsibility of negotiating a settlement while the British maintained the privileges of occupation freed of the onus of "deciding." The Colonial Secretary, Arthur Creech Jones, made this clear on February 25, when he told the House of Commons, "We are not going to the United Nations to surrender the Mandate."[26] The Irgun had not thought they were, but felt that the level of revolt was such that the British would soon recognize that few "privileges" were to be gained from staying on. In February there were forty-eight incidents. On March 1, for the first time striking on the Sabbath, the Irgun attacked Goldsmith House, a British officers' club inside the Bevingrad security compound, and a car park in Haifa. The next day the British declared martial law.

The Irgun had anticipated martial law, were eager to see the threat realized, and instigated a series of operations to challenge the declaration. The British responded with two massive search-and-question screenings—huge, clumsy, mass interrogations that once more antagonized the Jewish community. The Irgun strikes continued, sixty-eight within a week, including attacks within Bevingrad on Citrus House on March 7, and on March 12 on the Schneller Building in the center of Jerusalem. On March 16 martial law was lifted—a badly broken reed. In the Commons, Churchill demanded to know how long this squalid warfare would continue, and the Conservatives urged that the appeal to the United Nations be expedited. The *Sunday Express* headlines read "Govern or Get Out." The British finally had recognized the horns of the dilemma so long in the Irgun's making.

The demand to govern or get out placed the British authorities in a most uncomfortable position. The only means to govern in the Mandate was by compelling force, and there was doubt whether that was possible. Yet to get out in a mad scramble might destroy Britain's credibility in the Middle East. On April 2 the British government called for a special session of the United Nations General Assembly to consider the Palestine question. This at least gave the illusion of movement and indicated that the government understood the urgency of the matter. Yet, the British position still was that *only* a solution acceptable, more or less, to both Arabs and Jews would be acceptable. Since there was little hope of any such solution emerging, the decision to go to the United Nations solved nothing. In Palestine the Mandate authorities no more than anyone else could determine what the Cabinet intended. Their only logical course was to attempt to govern by even more stringent repressive measures and hope for the best—or at least a bit of guidance.

On April 16, without prior announcement and in an atmosphere of considerable secrecy, four Irgun prisoners, including Dov Gruener, were hanged in the Acre prison. On April 28 the United Nations General Assembly met in Special Session and appointed a Special Committee on Palestine (UNSCOP). On May 4 the Irgun broke into Acre prison and freed a carefully selected forty-one of the eighty-nine Jewish prisoners. (In the confusion two hundred and fourteen Arabs also escaped.) Nine Jews were killed and one Arab. Thirteen of the Jewish prisoners, eight of whom had been wounded, were recaptured; the rest evaded the widespread British searches. Three captured members of the rescue party were later executed. The British had only eight men wounded, but the loss in prestige was vast. The Acre attack seemed a direct reply to the four executions, not exactly answering a gallows with a gallows, but revealing that nothing so far devised by the British could crush the revolt, that even "impregnable" Acre was vulnerable, even there the British could not rule. The specific timing of the Acre operation had been fortuitous, but the impact on British public opinion and most particularly on the UNSCOP had been as great as if the attack had been turned on by Begin shrewdly pushing the appropriate button at the ideal moment.

Neither the Irgun nor the British had any intention of easing up on their efforts simply because the UNSCOP would arrive to investigate "conditions." The Irgunists involved in the Acre raid were swiftly tried. On June 16, the day that the UNSCOP arrived in Palestine, the British with an elegant sense of timing handed down three death sentences. The Irgun warned that the gallows would answer the gallows, and on July 13 kidnapped Sergeants Martin and Paice. Neither British searches nor threats against Jewish officials produced any results. To compound British difficulties, on July 17 the illegal immigrant ship *Exodus 1947* appeared off the coast, trailed by British naval vessels. Early on the morning of July 18 a British boarding party fought its way on deck; three Jews were killed and more than one hundred injured; the events were relayed by radio to Palestine. When the *Exodus* under British escort reached Haifa later that day, Justice Sandstrom, Chairman of UNSCOP, was watching from shore. The authorities decided to return the *Exodus* and its illegal immigrants to their port of origin in Germany rather than to the internment camps of Cyprus as was the usual practice. Instead of making the ship an example, this decision turned the *Exodus* into a symbol, dragging out the agony over a period of two months. Even the normally mild and optimistic *Ha'aretz* announced that faith in Britain had been lost. The High Commissioner, Sir Alan Cunningham, accepted the fact: "Time has shown a constantly accelerated deterioration of conditions in this country. The sands are running out."[27]

No matter how little time was left, there was always margin for accelerated deterioration. Despite the continued absence of the two sergeants, on July 29 the British hanged the three Irgun prisoners. On

July 30 the Irgun hanged the sergeants. At the news of their deaths British soldiers ran wild, shooting into cars and cafes, killing seven Jews and wounding others. In Liverpool and Glasgow Jewish shop windows were broken. Once again sane and reasonable men were appalled, horrified with Irgun terror. Creech Jones in the Commons spoke of the "deep feelings of horror and revulsion shared by all of us here at this barbarous crime."[28] The wave of revulsion was as much directed against the necessity for the British presence and British tactics: the exhausted refugees of the *Exodus* dragged screaming back onto German soil, the death of two innocent young men trapped in a humiliating struggle for vague purpose against a persecuted people. Instead of a cry for vengeance, as might have been expected, the demand was for evacuation. In a very real sense the British had at last been levered into position after three and one half years of revolt.

Although it was by no means clear in July 1947, in many ways the death of the two sergeants was the culmination of the revolt. A great many Zionists had grave doubts about the United Nations' capacity to make a just, that is, satisfactory, decision and implement it. The Irgun remained convinced that the British had too great a stake in the Middle East simply to withdraw from the Mandate. There was a constant paper chase through British statements and proclamations to find the means by which the British would maneuver to stay. They might feel "obligated" to remain in order to prevent open war between Arabs and Jews—a less than remote possibility given the communal fighting along the border between Tel Aviv and Jaffa that broke out in August. They might "accept" a new mandate from the United Nations when no satisfactory solution could be found. They might actually "withdraw," only to return on the backs of their Arab allies. Consequently, the Irgun kept up the pressure in the Mandate, but with a widening purpose: the revolt would not be over until the last British soldier had been evacuated and the state declared. The Irgun simply did not, and on adequate evidence, trust the British. The number of investigatory commissions before the UNSCOP boggled the imagination—and the British were still in Palestine.

Even if the United Nations did produce a Palestine formula—which was unlikely—and attempted to impose it—more unlikely—and the British did withdraw—quite unlikely indeed—the Irgun's revolt would have fallen short of the announced goal of a Jewish state on both sides of the Jordan, a state that would incorporate the East Bank, originally included in the Mandate and subsequently given by Britain to Emir Abdullah. Whatever in their hearts the leadership of the Irgun in Palestine and Europe thought that they *could* get, their diplomats and agents relentlessly pursued a strategy of the whole loaf. Such an extreme stand might improve the ultimate United Nations' decision, might raise an alternative magnetic pole to the Arabs' insistence on not one inch. In any case, the necessity to continue the armed struggle was clear; without that there would be no leverage, without that there would be no telling what doves like Ben Gurion would do.

What the Irgun feared as much as British perfidy was compromise by the Jewish Agency, for in the end the legitimate institutions would accept or reject the United Nations' decision, would declare the state. And the Irgun put little faith in the Agency's staying power. After the end of the united resistance, the institutions had even tried a mini-Season, half-heartedly to be sure, and given evidence of too great a willingness to accept solutions the Irgun felt would be betrayals. An un-compromising Irgun position, and the continuing armed struggle, might stiffen the Agency; it certainly antagonized orthodox Zionist diplomats. At last on November 29, 1947, the United Nations General Assembly passed a resolution partitioning the Mandate and, thereby, authorizing a Jewish state. The Irgun was hardly surprised at the jigsaw partition that created "a tiny little state . . . a mutilated Eretz Yisrael without Jerusalem and without Haifa, without land and without water, without freedom and without a future."[29] The Irgun faced a variety of new and challenging tasks: first, to see that the Zionist "diplomats" did not bargain away in panic even the nugget granted and did establish the state as soon as possible; second, to bring in arms and men from the diaspora to extend the boundaries of the state; third, to begin to switch resources to meet the incursions of irregular Arab bands and consider the prospect of a real invasion by the Arab armies in the not too distant future; and of course to keep up the pressure against the British.

The last was not necessarily the least. As a result of apparent British partisanship in Palestine and London's equivocal attitude toward the United Nations' "solution," the British threat did not simply fade away but, if anything, grew more ominous in Irgun eyes. A policy of unofficial counterterror against the Yishuv seemed under way. The *Palestine Post* was bombed and an explosion in Ben Yehuda Street in Jerusalem killed fifty-two people. The British investigation did not appear very intensive. Nothing was done about the growing irregular Arab army. Restrictions on Jewish defense remained in force. Consequently, the Irgun operations against the British, open allies of the Arabs, continued until the last moment. The operations after November 1947, however, were efforts to consolidate and expand an inchoate Eretz Israel against Anglo-Arab opposition rather than a continuation of the revolt begun in January 1944. By 1948 the revolt imperceptibly had turned into a war for independence during the twilight months of the Mandate. By May, and the declaration of the state, the Irgun would be largely integrated into the national defense, not without subsequent crisis, and the revolt a matter for historians.

Analysis

The revolt of the Irgun was a remarkable effort because the national liberation strategy employed by Begin appeared to have achieved a success quite disproportionate to the numbers involved.[30] In the beginning there were so few and their aspirations so improbable. Before, usually long before, there can be a revolt there must be that dedicated core of zealots whose deepest aspirations and dearest dreams have long been denied. They are impatient, inflexible, caught in the grip of an idea before its time. There had been an emotional Zionism for two thousand years—next year in Jerusalem—and a modern nationalist Zionism since 1897. The men of the Irgun had been brought up, had lived their lives, within the militant Revisionist movement, converts to the absolute. For over a decade all had anticipated the use of the gun in Palestine politics— either the descent from Poland under Begin or a rising within the Mandate—a rising that Stern began somewhat prematurely. In Palestine the organization for revolt, the Irgun Zvai Leumi, had existed for a decade, and only thus, through armed struggle, would the goal of a state be reached. Their plans and postures had been thwarted by the war against Hitler that eliminated the Betar route on the fall of Poland and eliminated the British target by turning the occupying power into an ally.

What in 1943 drove the zealots to rise with only faint prospects and few arms was the trauma of the holocaust. No longer was the timing of a Zionist state at stake but the existence of Jewry. A revolt might not establish a Palestine refuge in time but at the very least would prevent a shameful acquiescence in genocide. A revolt, if for no other reason than as a message of armed defiance—a witness that only thus could freedom be won—had become essential. Even if the Irgun failed, the Yishuv would still have the Haganah as defenders and their honor as Irgun's heirs. Begin and the Irgun, inheritors of a militant ideology, a military tradition, and an overwhelming need to act, rose as much against the holocaust as the British, against the culminating horror of two thousand years, against the ultimate betrayal of caution, against history. Begin's strategy, however, was specific, pointed, narrowly directed, and pragmatic to the core.

By avoiding British military targets until after the war Begin allowed those with qualms to strike and created the precipitant condition necessary to begin. Even without Begin there were those already waiting in the wings, less organized, less experienced, but equally determined. What the Irgun had—all it had in those darkest days—was an organization, an underground, conspiratorial "army" in-being, directed by determined and experienced men dedicated to the gun as a means and emboldened by a luminous vision of the future. More than the militia-Haganah, the Irgun was fitted to the task Begin envisaged, not just because of its size, structure, and assumptions, but because of internal attitudes—a band of brothers dependent on cunning and improvisation, prepared for any sacrifice. Begin's strategy thus made optimum use of his limited assets: maximum leverage would have to be gained from minimal means. Had he possessed the resources and, more important, the responsibilities of the Haganah, his task would have been more complicated. In Palestine between 1944 and 1947 less was more. His anticipation that the destruction of British prestige by a series of spectacular operations would create the old Irish dilemma, responding with self-defeating repression or withdrawing, proved justified.

The Irgun revolt differed in significant ways from the Irish example. The Jews were a minority in the Mandate, whereas IRA leadership counted on the support of a considerable majority. Moreover, Begin's dissidents were a distrusted minority—the Revisionists—amid the Zionist minority. Two assumptions were made: the Arabs would not matter, and the Yishuv would tolerate the revolt. The first assumption proved largely correct; the second was more difficult and required Begin's refusal to respond in kind to the Season. The Irgun could not create parallel institutions as had the Irish—after all, these existed and were recognized by the authorities—or call into play the whole range of diplomatic, propaganda, and political resources available to the Irish. At the beginning the war isolated the revolt, and toward the end diaspora activities could not be brought to bear in the Mandate in time. It was as if Begin could control only one IRA brigade, yet by keeping up the pressure provoke the British and push the Jewish Agency into more radical positions.

The Irgun concentrated almost entirely on the armed struggle. Begin was willing to cooperate with the other Zionists in pursuing the struggle but not limiting it. Nor could the Irgun, seeking a state on both sides of the Jordan, heed any of the accommodations suggested by Britain and the others. The armed struggle would have to continue until the state had been secured; and the legitimate institutions would be dragged along, reaping all the political advantages of the Irgun's violent sowing. And that crop was planted with urban terror, guerrilla techniques most fitted to the strategy of leverage. "All" the Irgun need do was continue until the British were hoist on their own petard—if only their Zionist "allies" did not weaken. So the only flexibility necessary was to appease or threaten the other Zionists—join a united resistance, offer to serve under Ben Gurion, later promise to disband on the declaration of the state. And in this area the great decision was to suffer the Season. Elsewhere tactically the only difference between 1944 and 1947 was the number and size of operations. After 1947, with the revolt all but over, the Irgun shifted rapidly toward a more orthodox structure and more conventional tasks. The revolt did not so much end as merge with a different struggle, a blurred slide into conventional war as the British moved to the sidelines and then out of Palestine and the immediate picture.

Whether or not Begin's strategy worked depends on one's analysis of what actually happened in the Palestine Mandate between 1944 and 1948. Everyone admits to most of the facts—the two sergeants, Acre, the King David, and the lot—but not to the meaning. The orthodox Zionist position is that without the Irgun the result would have been the same: the British out and a state established. The revolt had hampered more than it helped. The real victory had been won through the efforts of thousands of orthodox Zionists, the contributions of millions, the winds of history, and the manuevers of the Jewish Agency. The Irgun simply caused trouble.

The Irgun caused trouble, and it also created facts that would not have existed in the same manner or at the same time. In retrospect several of these Zionist facts appear very nearly crucial. First, the revolt increased the pressure on the British earlier and harder than the Agency or the Haganah intended or liked. Pressure for concessions to Zionist demands certainly did exist and would have continued to exist, but without the Irgun, ruthless, violent, and uncompromising, the British would have had less room to maneuver. What this might have meant remains problematical but, as the Irgun pointed out, after 1945 British interests in the Middle East were not converging on those of the Zionists. And if the Agency-Haganah had decided to exert pressure, the means would not have been as ruthless as those of the Irgun and, therefore, less effective or at least less immediate. At worst, the Irgun revolt accelerated events, and at best it determined which options and at what cost the British and later the United Nations might practically select.

If the Irgun played the central role in the armed struggle against Britain, and there can be only limited doubt that this was the case, it must be recognized that alone or even in conjunction with other forces the Irgun did not simply determine the course of events. A few thousand men, no matter how dedicated or how violent, could not alone transform the policies and intentions of the Empire. The Irgun acted within a context, largely beyond its control to alter, dependent on the direction, ambitions, and limitations of many powerful players to insure that the revolt would have maximum effect. Only in small ways and often inadvertently could the Irgun alter major political and international factors that in the long run would determine the outcome of the revolt. The Irgun ran a poor second, often a very poor second, in matters of diplomacy, propaganda, and influence, yet it benefited from the spinoff of the efforts of the World Zionist Organization. The Irgun was not even a close match for the Haganah as a military organization. What Begin and the Irgun *did* was to weigh the factors involved, estimate the impact of an open revolt, and then single-mindedly pursue the armed struggle.

That the Irgun felt compelled to revolt in the first place and managed to persevere in the second was largely because of an international situation they had not created, because of an opponent they had not selected, because of the diplomatic and political skills of a Zionist rival they could not deny, and because of the actions of a Nazi Germany they would have given anything to have prevented. Yet the Irgun did revolt, did persevere, and did see an Israel created. No matter what *might* have happened if the Irgun had followed the cautious, well-reasoned, eminently rational strategy of the legitimate institutions, what *did* happen was that the revolt forced the pace of events, albeit at grave risks, forced "solutions," even if ones the Irgun could not control, and therefore played a central role in the destinies of many who would have preferred a quieter and less violent pace. The Irgun played a major role in a drama that many sought to end before the final curtain. If it did not dominate the play, at least the men of the underground, after all those nights black with despair, could rest assured that they had done more to the final script than their detractors in Jerusalem as well as in London have been willing to concede.

Sinn Feiner held at pistol point by British Auxiliaries, November 23, 1920.

A British soldier maintains his lonely vigil overlooking the Old City of Jerusalem.

Barbed wire in the streets of Jerusalem, 1947-1949.

The bodies of kidnapped British Sergeants Clifford Martin and Mervyn Paice, Palestine, July 1947.

Internationally famous Shepheard's Hotel in Cairo, a crumbled ruin in the wake of anti-British rioting, February 12, 1952.

Information Service of India

Mahatma Gandhi with Nehru and Maulana Azad.

4 Two Alternative Strategies: Agitation in the Gold Coast and Communism in Malaya

To fight relentlessly by all constitutional means for the achievement of full Self-Government NOW for the chiefs and people of the Gold Coast
       —Convention Peoples' Party programme

Don't be afraid. We're only out for Europeans and running dogs. . . . We are going to shoot all Europeans.
       —Communist guerrilla, before shooting two British planters, June 16, 1948

For the Labour Party the Palestine affair was an almost unmitigated disaster, an inexplicable apparition that should not have arisen to bedevil the sane, closely reasoned foreign policy of British socialism. Labour had wandered into Palestine equipped with the Party's long-standing Zionist policy, an often professed friendship for colonial peoples, including the Arabs, deep suspicion of "traditional" British interests in the Middle East, and a considerable reservoir of goodwill. Unable to jettison the Zionists and grasp the Arabs, lumbered by responsibilities, unappreciated and slandered, the Labour leadership muddled on from one blunder to another. Not since the Irish Troubles had an "imperial" problem so divided the British, left so bitter an aftertaste of frustration and disappointment.

The essential question for anti-imperialist strategists in London and out was whether the Irgun option was a generally applicable revolutionary strategy. The Irish-Irgun parallel might simply be the result of quite different forces. The Irgun revolt evolved out of the impact of the holocaust that literally drove men to arms in anguish. Nowhere else within the Empire did such pressures exist. Thus, Palestine, the nexus of contradictory and exclusive aspirations, might be without parallel. Consequently, conventional British thinking, particularly within the Labour Party, remained that the Commonwealth Strategy could and would work without recourse to violence. Many of even the most extreme nationalists scattered throughout the Empire were willing at least to adopt a policy of watchful waiting. Many lacked a long revolutionary tradition or an effective political structure or even a sense of urgency. Most had sufficient time to wait and see, build and plot. Many trusted the British, kept faith in the Labour Party's ideals, and anticipated that the Indian Strategy, judiciously applied, would prove effective.

Yet in India the transfer of sovereignty over hundreds of millions of divided people engendered riots, massacre, and revenge. The British spread thin on the ground could not maintain order. By April 1947 they had at least persuaded the reluctant Nehru to accept partition rather than certain civil war. The old Hindu-Moslem hatred was beyond the scope of the Commonwealth Strategy, and instead of smooth devolution there was chaos at the creation of the two new states. In London the Labour Cabinet felt Britain could not be blamed; despite flaws, the Commonwealth Strategy had appeared to work. Yet the entire Indian political establishment knew Britain no longer had any option but to accede to Indian wishes. The Indian, not the Commonwealth, Strategy had been vindicated. Graciously, the gift of independence had been received and not snatched—as valid one way as the other. The Indians played, perhaps partly believing, the Commonwealth game.

The Empire had changed out of all recognition. The independence of India and Pakistan had liberated three-quarters of the imperial population, incorporated them into two hostile states with republican institutions, and had transformed thereby British security requirements and responsibilities. On February 4, 1948, Ceylon became a Dominion, and on January 4, 1948, Burma became an independent republic—outside the Commonwealth.

African Agitation: Gold Coast into Ghana

The first and one of the most effective adaptations of the Indian Strategy in the postwar world came in a colony that few British observers had ever considered as a potential Commonwealth candidate.

It was not that the objective factors for rapid self-determination were particularly lacking in the Gold Coast, but rather that the idea of Black African independence was by no means ripe. Except for the specialist, Africa was still the romantic sphere of lions and white hunters. Yet, though relatively small, the Gold Coast was relatively rich, producing most of the world's cocoa and possessing a substantial middle class. There were African judges, barristers, and doctors—and a dearth of white hunters. The Gold Coast was, all things considered, hardly less developed than Portugal or Albania. It was in fact a model colony, so considered by the Colonial Office. To that point in 1946 a new constitution had been arranged that increased the unity of the colony and offered a central legislature with a majority of unofficial members. Despite the narrow franchise, the various qualifications and safeguards, and the substantive power that remained in British hands, London felt considerable progress had been made—for Africa.

The Africans did not. With the Indian example very much in the news, the war over, and the prerequisites for self-determination present, many in the Gold Coast wanted more than the 1946 constitution offered. One of the British arguments for the independence of Ceylon had been the long training in responsibility made possible by the 1931 constitution; yet, with an equally talented citizenry, the 1946 Gold Coast constitution would offer only limited opportunities in African responsibilities. There was not a different "law" for Africans, of course, but there was surely a flawed British vision. And the closer to the Gold Coast, the more limited African potential seemed to become in British eyes. There were those who, while sympathetic to a degree with the British blindness and enthusiastic concerning British principles and politics, like Oliver Twist, wanted more. In April 1947 Dr. Joseph B. Danquah, a barrister, a London Ph.D., and an advocate who wanted greater self-government for "Ghana," formed the United Gold Coast Convention. At fifty-two, he was neither an angry young man nor a wild-eyed agitator and most certainly not the voice of the inarticulate African masses. He simply wanted more responsibility for his middle-class Anglophile colleagues than the British seemed willing to give.

In 1947 Danquah invited Kwame Nkrumah home from London to become organizing secretary of the United Gold Coast Convention Party. Nkrumah was everything Danquah was not: politically ambitious, a first-rate agitator, a seeker of power, and a tireless organizer. He had both a sense of the possible and for the jugular. Nkrumah turned the theoretical ideas of Danquah and the barristers into slogans to attract and inspire the masses. Co-opting World War II veterans, he undertook a campaign of protest and parades that eventually forced the British to take notice. In February 1948 his nonviolent campaign collapsed, not altogether unexpectedly, into riots that lasted three days. Lives were lost, buildings burned, and stores looted. The riots could not be seen solely as the results of outside agitators and hooligans—verandah boys—or an expression of criminal violence. Some found an economic motive in the postwar inflation, but none could deny the political message. Nkrumah without the patience to fashion a highly disciplined nonviolent (à la India) congress party had almost by sheer will created a mass party and a volatile atmosphere of expectation. There was no need to contrive disorder; recourse to violence by the mass, limited violence to be sure, could almost be guaranteed. In this model colony, peaceful, stable, and prosperous, in a single year one man had exploited a discontent that the British still could scarcely credit. The open hostility to British colonialism with all its attendant benefits appalled the knowledgeable and frightened the innocent. What did the Africans want?

What they wanted—political power—seemed incongruous, the gift of a gun to a child, in Nkrumah's case a childish "communist." But to hew to the 1946 constitution after the events of February 1948 would be a foolish tactic. A commission under the British barrister A. A. Watson in its report to the governor on August 17, 1949, emphasized the political frustration of the Africans and the need for further African self-government. The Watson Commission was followed by the Coussey Commission, which would in turn recommend the changes necessary to implement the Watson proposals. Liberation by commission had begun, for this new body's all-African composition was quite revolutionary and the proposals only slightly less so, implying as they did very wide self-government, far beyond anything conceived of by Whitehall. During the quiet deliberations of the commissions Nkrumah broke with the United Gold Coast Convention. Given his style and ambition and the party elders' qualms and disclaimers, this was hardly surprising. In June 1949 he formed the Convention People's Party. Nkrumah campaigned not for more but for self-government at once, a proposal the British viewed with alarm. To British eyes Nkrumah seemed a shrewd and articulate politician and an overly ambitious, irresponsible demagogue. He was in that gray area of British perception between the half-naked fakir and the sound statesman. Whatever else, Nkrumah was a clear and present danger to a constitutional process that many felt was going much too rapidly as it was.

The proposals for the new constitution were for Nkrumah quite insufficient. On January 8, 1950, he opened a campaign of "Positive Action." Although it was based directly on Gandhian principles, to the British his campaign appeared suspiciously like a replay of the February 1948 riots. When Nkrumah spoke to the masses, the authorities simply did not take him at his own evaluation.

I went on to discuss the aims of self-government and affirmed that the next step was a question of strategy; that although the British government and the British people (with the die-hard imperialists) acknowledged the legitimacy of our demand for self-government, it was only by our own exertions that we would succeed.

I pointed out that there were two ways of achieving self-government, one by armed revolution and the other by constitutional and legitimate nonviolent methods. I gave the repulsion by British armed might of two German attempts at invasion and the victory over British imperialism in India by moral pressure. We advocated the latter method. Freedom, however, had never been handed over to any colonial country on a silver platter; it had been won only after bitter and vigorous struggles.[1]

The Governor of the Gold Coast, Sir Charles Noble Arden-Clarke, declared a state of emergency and locked up Nkrumah, hoping thereby to avert violence and perhaps open rebellion. With Nkrumah out of the way, the British organized a general election under the new, liberal constitution. If the British, or at least some of those within the colony, anticipated a rejection of Nkrumah's all-or-jail program, they were sorely disappointed. Nkrumah out of jail might be a serious problem; in jail he became a martyr and a household name. The Convention People's Party carried forty-eight of the eighty-four seats and all the municipal constituencies. The British were caught in a dilemma: give way or dismantle the untrustworthy "democratic" system, to rule instead by decree and coercion, insist on London's responsibilities and native incapacity and face the inevitable descent into violence. The new Colonial Secretary, James Griffiths, and the Labour Cabinet, whatever their private doubts about native incapacity and Nkrumah's intentions, had no doubts about the proper course: the people had spoken, whether wisely or well was not the essential issue. Nkrumah came out of prison as Leader of Government Business.

I desire for the Gold Coast dominion status within the Commonwealth. I am a Marxian socialist and an undenominational Christian. The places I know in Europe are London and Paris. I am no communist and have never been one. I come out of gaol and into the assembly without the slightest feeling of bitterness to Britain. I stand for no racialism, no discrimination against any race or individual, but I am unalterably opposed to imperialism in any form.[2]

The writing was on the wall. The Gold Coast was going to be transformed into Ghana decades before wiser heads would have considered it possible or prudent. And once the direction became apparent, the wise discovered the inherent potential of the colony to be far greater than they had imagined: the Africans more trained and talented; their leadership, even Nkrumah, more responsible and competent; the economy sounder; the exotic animals less visible and the roads and schools and marketing boards more apparent.

Nkrumah had discovered the key to "constitutional" advance on the Indian road. Danquah had demanded self-government in the shortest possible time, a program open to interpretation and adjustment and keyed to varying explanations of "shortest." Nkrumah had demanded "self-government now"; there was no need to interpret. *Nothing* that the British might offer in the way of constitutional advance was sufficient. With Danquah compromise on British terms was possible, but with Nkrumah the concession would come from the nationalists, an acceptance of less-than-fair in the name of goodwill. And no matter *what* was granted by the British, except full and immediate independence, the form of the concession was by definition unsatisfactory to Nkrumah: this year's "constitution" to be replaced as rapidly as possible by next year's. Nkrumah's demands were by no means non-negotiable. He was willing and ready to accept less than the best; but the constitutional game at which so many of Britain's legal experts exerted their talents and time was a nationalist means, never an end. The new complex and highly balanced provisions were for the nationalists not basic law, not the structure nor even the description of governing, but a formal recognition in a somewhat curious and often irrelevant form by the British of their own changed perception of reality.

In the Gold Coast the new Burns Constitution included a Legislative Council that had an African majority. What that African majority did or did not do, how well they governed or how much they absorbed of parliamentary practice, how relevant they were to the needs of the colony simply did not matter as much as what an African majority *meant*—particularly to the British. It meant that Britain would have to give more, perhaps not self-government, but more. To keep the process underway there were always new commissions that led to more constitutional changes and still another committee to recommend still further constitutional changes. In India such constitutional change often had been measured in decades; but in West Africa the processes became almost continuous, a continuity each incremental constitutional concession accelerated. In 1954 there was another new constitution; in 1956 another general election; and then the request by the Gold Coast Parliament for independence in the name of Ghana. That, too, came the following year, in March 1957.

It had taken the Gold Coast just about a decade to complete a process which brought not only independence but some considerable practice in governing. In view of what the Labour Cabinet had anticipated in 1946, the pace had been accelerated beyond all measure. In 1946 it had seemed beyond reason that any African colony, even the Gold Coast, could possibly contemplate broad self-government for a very long time. Once into the bargaining process, particularly after the arrival of Nkrumah, the logic of concession—of course they can't have *that* but surely we can give a bit *here*—always tied to safeguards that ultimately meant nothing if the Africans refused to cooperate, pushed the British rapidly down the road of liberation. Even to stop, which had been part of the response to Nkrumah's Positive Action, was difficult and, given the progress already made and obviously to be made, pointless.

London began to realize that not only was Nkrumah a shrewd and capable negotiator—everyone had recognized from the start that he was a highly talented agitator—but that he was also surrounded by able men, or at least men who often got their way in disputes with the British, who had been trained at the same colleges or inns of court, who black or no spoke sound sense, often with appropriate accents. Even later, with the advent of the Conservatives, when there had been doctrinaire doubts, too much had been won, too many in the Colonial Office, including those conservative if not Conservative, felt the die had been long cast. Just when that die was in fact cast is difficult to determine. Once the Gold Coast had been seen as an evolving entity and not a guarded zoo, then devolution was possible.

Those who could spare a thought to this eventuality seldom worried about a time schedule. They did not realize that the consideration of the eventuality of independence at some later date assured that it would be the case at a much earlier date. Labour, stressing imperial self-determination, eager to aid in colonial development and fulfill socialism's colonial responsibility, even while still working to a schedule little different from the Tory's, made sufficient concessions by 1951 that only a brutal and unnecessary program of coercion and repression could have reversed the process. Such a program was not only barren but futile—even in Conservative eyes. The fact that the British had no overriding security interest in the Gold Coast meant the imperial strategic posture would not be threatened by declining British control. The astute estimated that British economic interests would not be ill-served with the end of colonial tutelage and the drain on British sterling reserves might even be less. Once the idea of African devolution took root in London, the advantages became more obvious and the costs, physical and moral, of postponing the inevitable higher.

The Strategy of Agitation

There had of course been no revolt in the Gold Coast nor even serious contemplation of the possibility, yet in a way the example of the Irgun had as much to do with the ultimate creation of Ghana as did that of India. In essence Nkrumah had used moral pressure, as had Gandhi, and Begin as well, to "persuade" Britain to grant what their own principles demanded. In India, Gandhi's strategy rested firmly on the moral issue, on nonviolence, noncompliance, on suffering the most, on a discipline that related to India's own past and her peoples' own inclinations. That route was alien to Nkrumah, a rebel at heart, who would have been as comfortable with the gun as in the leadership of a protest march. Nkrumah foresaw a bitter, vigorous struggle that could not rest on a disciplined mass party that did not exist when he arrived in the Gold Coast nor on a nonviolent tactic alone that was alien to his countrymen's heritage. Nkrumah had to fashion a congenial application of the techniques of nonviolence and the tactics of uproarious agitation. His Convention People's Party proved an adequate vehicle, sufficiently clamorous to be heard, sufficiently coherent, eventually, to be regarded as legitimate. Nkrumah thus appeared with a simple slogan, a charismatic appeal, and a congenial opponent. His triumph, largely a personal one and made possible by the considered reaction of the British, appeared to offer all nationalists, certainly those within the British Empire, a means to liberation that required neither the Irgun's gun nor the Indian Congress' moral discipline.

The Strategy of Agitation appeared an ideal means to liberation of the underdeveloped colony. All that was needed was an educated and zealous elite, the slogan of freedom now, the talent to organize a mass party that would respond to appropriate keys with a variety of "nonviolent" but disruptive campaigns—and the British. There was no need of revolt; the odd riot would do. Not unexpectedly the formula did not always work, and certain rebels felt it quite inappropriate—none more so than those with a heritage quite different and aspirations for their nation beyond a new flag and a seat at the Commonwealth table. These rebels until too late often remained unknown, invisible to those in London watching colonial developments. At the center of the rapidly evolving Empire, devolution appeared to be proceeding apace and peacefully.

The pace had to be slow for in many of the colonies, particularly in Africa, little outside of a few cities had changed. There had been only scant investment; few educated native leaders appeared, and those often were in exile; visible economic development was rare. The political or economic activity that did exist was the result of British settlement and investment. The Labour Party felt that much of the African Empire needed massive inoculations of aid and development, rapid construction of the basic infra-structure of schools, roads, and sewers, and the expansion of marginal and barter economies. Investment would speed the transformation from tribal existence to participation in the contemporary world as something more than a ward of Empire. And what was true for Africa was also true for the remainder of the Empire, perhaps not filled with Commonwealth candidates but certainly capable of measured governmental responsibility and further economic development. As Colonial Secretary Arthur Creech Jones noted, Labour had opened the gates to the liberation road.

> The Colonial people are set on the road; we have helped to build for them the machines for their progress; we have given them the technical and financial aid necessary and brought more of their recourses into their control and possession: the beginnings in education, better social living, improved economic standards are being made and the old ways are passing as the people advance to responsibility. It is a good beginning—but it is only a beginning and we shall press on with the work with pride in our hearts that we are extending the boundaries of freedom and enlightenment and in so doing are winning goodwill and friendship.[3]

The basic premise was that the devolution of power would be a long and relatively slow process that would not be accelerated by recourse to violence. Events in the Gold Coast had adjusted the timetable, not the basic principle. And there could be no doubt, in London at least, that the Cabinet and the Colonial Office were working with more than deliberate speed to create the necessary foundation for self-government: revolt was still out and devolution in.

> The Labour Government put Ghana on the road to independence, made constitutional advance possible in Nigeria and laid the basis of a united Malaya after the collapse of the Japanese invaders. The Montego Bay Conference was summoned and launched the discussions for a Federation of the British Caribbean Colonies. Internal self-government, with a substantial financial settlement, was bestowed on Malta; Chartered Company status in North Borneo was ended, and new constitutions were given to Mauritius, Singapore, Gibraltar and Trinidad. A liberal constitution was offered to Cyprus in the place of official direct rule; Africans were brought into the political life of Kenya, N. Rhodesia and Nyassaland, and Sarawak was transferred from private sovereignty and set on the road for its development. Transjordan and Palestine were released from the Mandate; independence was granted to Ceylon; political changes were made in Uganda, and European ascendancy and federation opposed in Central Africa. The East African High Commission was set up without conceding political fusion, and an Assembly based on principles of race equality and public control for developing the common economic services of the three territories concerned was established.[4]

Asian Communism, A Twelve-Year Revolt

There were those who marched to a distant, nonimperial drummer, who were not for the quiet life or concerned with the ripple of commissions and constitutions. For their purposes, the Nkrumah route march of riots and reform was irrelevant. In fact on the other side of the world, in Malaya, Nkrumah was unknown for it was there that the second revolt against the Crown occurred. Although not a tiny island nor an underdeveloped enclave, Malaya, in British eyes, was not a candidate for rapid self-government. The British, however, had been away from Malaya during the vital war years and politics had changed, ambitions had been whetted, and the Asian balance of power had shifted.

Scattered through Malaya were the cadres of the Malayan Communist Party (MCP), principal benefactor of the Japanese occupation, who had no intention of a quiet return to the old days. Emboldened by Stalin's triumphs in Europe and Mao's in China and their own experience as a resistance army in the jungle, the MCP aspired to power. Their ideology offered two traditional routes: conspiracy and subversion until mature revolutionary conditions existed, the way of Moscow; or the initiation of revolutionary-guerrilla war as had been done in China, the way of Mao. In the immediate postwar period, the MCP began to suspect their situation might be unique, that the mature revolutionary conditions actually existed and that the means to exploit them had been discovered by Mao. For the first time the British were to face the thrust of the Communist option—and in a most unlikely arena.

Malaya had been acquired haphazardly and ruled or guided in diverse ways. There had been little unity of purpose and no particular urgency. Some Sultans had British advisers; some did not. The population was compartmentalized into ethnic blocs, dominated by the native Malay, deeply suspicious of the Chinese immigrants who had become the largest ethnic segment. In 1946 the British created the Malayan Union minus Singapore, a step that in varying degrees pleased no one but the Colonial Office. Additions, corrections, and changes to the Union resulted in the Federation of Malaya, which combined unity with diversity and opened the door to more rapid constitutional development. No Nkrumah appeared. The constitutional future appeared assured: a long and busy span devising formulas to satisfy conflicting political and ethnic aspirations as Malaya moved slowly toward a seat at the Commonwealth table.

Up to 1948 the Malayan Communist Party apparently had not been considered a serious factor and British plans had moved forward with little thought of its intentions or capacities. The MCP, uninterested in the Indian Strategy and hardly aware of the Irish example, had determined to play a significant role in what appeared as a rapidly accelerating world revolution. British-instituted constitutional change would do little for MCP aspirations; revolt would. Although the MCP revolt against the Crown would by necessity be anti-British, the leaders assumed they would enter the lists as one regiment of an international army in arms against capitalistic imperialism. Yet much of their motivation and direction, many of their aspirations and expectations, were not even as broad as Malaya, much less the British Empire, but were grounded in the peculiar nature of the Malayan Chinese community and the direction of the Malayan Communist Party.

The Party had long been isolated and parochial, the recipient of handed-down information, hampered by an ideology parsed from books that might have appeared relevant in Moscow but not in Kuala Lumpur or in Penang. The leadership had remained often directionless and uncertain, advised from time to time by Comintern agents usually from China, for the membership had become not merely predominately but overwhelmingly Chinese. Until December 1941 the MCP, despite occasional exaggerated British fears, was a curiosity in the communist spectrum and irrelevant in Malaya. Once the Japanese seized the Malaya peninsula, the Chinese were vulnerable. Between 1942 and 1945 the Japanese executed approximately five thousand; many others were imprisoned, detained, or fined. Most were fearful of the future. One of the few effective organizations that offered even the prospect of protection was the mysterious Malayan People's Anti-Japanese Army (MPAJA), dominated by the MCP. Supported by a civilian network of agents experienced in the labor union movement, aligned with the anti-Japanese struggle everywhere, and exuding an aura of growing strength and competence, the MCP controlled the resistance, extended its underground net throughout the peninsula, and put together the foundation of an alternative means of control. What the MCP most certainly did not do was fight an irregular, guerrilla war against the Japanese. Such a course would have endangered the organization, reduced the security and protection that could be given to the uncertain recruits, and jeopardized the entire operation. During the jungle years the Japanese lost at most a few hundred men to the guerrillas; the Malayans, mostly Chinese, suffered the execution of 2,542 "traitors" by the MPAJA. Thus, the jungle army of something over five thousand volunteers was the hard but militarily quiescent core of a rapidly expanding communist-dominated political structure. The Japanese could afford to tolerate the "guerrillas" in order to maintain peace and may have had an arrangement to that effect with the MCP. When the Japanese surrendered and withdrew (in Malaya they were not driven out or defeated in the field), approximately seven thousand members of the MPAJA emerged to claim credit for the triumph.

After all, no one else was in the field; no one else had carried on the struggle; no one else had maintained the power through the war years to punish and reward.

The British persuaded the MPAJA to disarm and disband, partly at least by the offer of rewards for weapons. In case of a rainy day, the MCP leadership saw that sufficient weapons were held back and that few commanders of significance appeared publicly. In 1945 the leadership of the MCP returned hopefully to conspiracy and subversion with a large and influential organization, attractive to many of the ambitious Chinese youths who were no longer certain of traditional values. The period of peaceful agitation between 1945 and 1948 eventually reached a plateau. To grow still further the MCP would have to deliver on part of the program. That could be managed only with the use of force, thereby reducing the size of the party as reluctant and prudent members left it. Action, particularly violent action, would hamper recruitment. But without action—and because of the very success of the MCP, violent action was all that offered much by 1948—recruitment would decline. Something more was needed. Ideologically there was an obvious answer: revolution. But to discard peaceful agitation and take up arms entailed very grave risks.

The decision to do so was gradual, a result of not only the decline in the Communist momentum in Malaya but also the MCP perception of the world situation, where imperialism seemed to be in retreat and communism in arms. Soviet Russia had emerged from the war victorious. The Communist Chinese appeared well on the road to victory. The Dutch were under pressure in Indonesia, the French in Indochina. And the British, clearly a paper lion, had evacuated India. MCP people traveling in Asia in 1947 found communist circles optimistic and ambitious. At the Asia Youth Conference, in Calcutta in February 1948, speakers urged militancy on the group. The course of the MCP toward open revolt became more apparent. Its leadership realized that such a switch traditionally began with a political cleansing of the existent, and mistaken, leadership. Lai Teck did not wait for his comrades to move; he disappeared along with the party treasury, a fact carefully concealed from the lesser membership for a year. With Lai Teck gone, his senior aide, Chin Peng, took over control, assisted by the first native generation of Malayan Chinese communists, determined to resort to armed struggle.[5]

The MCP secretly organized the Malayan People's Anti-British Army (MPABA) and, as during the jungle days, set up a feeder network, the Min Yuen or People's Movement. A crucial error was the use of intimidation. The MCP Blood and Steel Corps often acquired "support" by indiscriminate terror. This alienated many in the Chinese community, and even the subservient were doubtful converts. This campaign of extortion for funds and coercion for cooperation at first went on largely under unsuspecting British eyes. By the middle of June 1948, however, there had been 298 murders or abductions, 107 in the first six months of the year. The decay of order had passed beyond Chinese "crime."

The purpose of the coercion was to weed out the party doubtfuls, guarantee party acceptance of the new line, expand the underground support network, and assure acquiescence if not enthusiasm from the Chinese population. Little attention was paid to other ethnic groups. The MCP leadership was entirely Chinese; the membership 90 percent so; and the attractions of the Party to non-Chinese seemed minimal. Reliance on the Chinese population, a minority, proved an error worse than the use of terror: the armed struggle would be based on a Chinese infra-structure, achieved in part by intimidation. The MCP was unconcerned; by mid-June it was ready. Some three or four thousand members had been by one means or another brought into the jungles and some ten thousand Min Yuen members tied into the net. By the end of the year, there would be nearly five thousand volunteers in the jungle as guerrillas of the MPABA, at least twice that number in Min Yuen, and perhaps a further fifty thousand others willing to aid the revolt.[6]

The basic strategy of Chin Peng was to employ Mao Tse-tung's principles of guerrilla warfare. The campaign would have three stages: first, liberate base areas; second, expand these in mobile warfare; finally, join the areas for the stage of confrontation. Many of Mao's tactical and operational lessons were taught the recruits, including rules of conduct. Lau Yew, former Chairman of the Central Military Committee of the MPAJA felt that by applying Mao's tactics, the British could be worn down. He anticipated that the base areas could be won by September 1948; then, buttressed by international communist support and world opinion, the MPABA would drive the British from the colony. Lau Yew assumed that the "protracted" war would follow the Chinese pattern, but at such a rapid pace that the "revolution" would not be long protracted. Even the reluctance of his old comrades to return to the jungle, the lack of enthusiasm of the Chinese population, and the failures to attract either Malaya or Indian nationalists did not diminish his optimism.

By June, with the entire MCP leadership in the jungle, the armed revolt began in earnest with widespread sabotage, terror attacks on isolated camps and mines, bombs and grenades in the towns, and assassination attempts on Europeans. On June 6 British Commissioner-General Malcolm MacDonald spoke of the rule of knife and gun. On June 12 three Chinese Kuomintang leaders were assassinated. High Commissioner Sir Edward Gent the next day noted that ten murders and three attacks on European estate managers had already occurred. On June 16 three planters in Perak were killed. The following day a state of emergency was declared in Johore and Perak. Then—at long last many European planters felt—on June 18 a state of emergency for the entire Federation was declared. On June 21 the police arrested six hundred suspects. The revolt was officially on.

The British had inherent advantages as well as inherited disabilities. Because the Malaya states were not far advanced toward internal self-government, the British could operate an anti-insurgency campaign without being limited by an indigenous allied government with differing interests, desires, and opinions. The differing interests of the various ethnic communities was a complication, but at least Britain could fulfill, visibly, promised political reforms, granting increased political participation with its various material, emotional, and psychic rewards, in contrast to the communists who could only make promises or threaten vengeance. If the British anti-insurgency campaign could effectively limit the communists' ability to carry out promised vengeance, there would be little appeal in the revolution except to those specifically attracted to communist ideology. And even within the Chinese community these were clearly a minority, probably a small one.

On the rebel side, first, the MCP had accepted a direction and created an organization that could not appeal to the majority of the people in the Federation, and at best might attract substantial support only among the Chinese. Unlike the goal of the Irgun, the MCP's intentions and aspirations were anathema to a substantial portion of the Chinese minority. Admittedly this minority was 45 percent of the population, but unless an MCP victory was assured, the strong anti-communist elements, and the cautious, would deny or delay support if possible. Second, there were many uncertain and reluctant guerrillas, many who had been intimidated. Many Chinese "converts" were motivated by self-interest and a desire for the easy life, the fruits of successful revolt not the sacrifices of armed struggle. Many, attracted to the Party for reasons of security and advancement, faced the violent future with reluctance. Third, to keep the Party and through it the Army disciplined, a highly authoritarian command structure was devised, control being diluted only by distance or faulty communication. The traumatic disappearance of Lai Teck created an atmosphere of suspicion and confidence only in the very orthodox, along with stringent control and security measures. Because the guerrilla regiments were scattered throughout the Federation and communication, although swift, was not instant, the new intraparty regulations, made in the name of purity and discipline, narrowed the scope for initiative and independent action so necessary in a guerrilla war. Finally, a disquieting factor for the pessimists was the optimistic application of Mao's grand strategy to Malaya.

Apparently Lau Yew and Chin Peng organized under the impression that to begin was sufficient, that afterward the guerrilla war would follow the anticipated course, international comrades would help, and the British would slink off, bested almost without battle. In other words, the MCP perception of their own value to international communism was grossly inflated, while at the same time the reactions of the British were analyzed in fantasy terms from used Mao texts. Ideological postures and slogans became imbued with reality. The MCP saw a Malaya that did not exist.

The MCP did have solid assets: real experience in the jungle as well as in agitation and subversion, great staying power, considerable talent, a faith in the future, and a lack of visible alternatives. The MCP could not really see an option as attractive as revolt. Even if the war were protracted, international communism cool, and the volunteers reluctant, much of the MCP in 1948 believed that hard work, persistence, and the forces of history would bring them through.

By the end of August 1948, Lau Yew's original date for the shift into the second and perhaps third stage, it was becoming clear that adherence to Mao's strategy did not automatically bring Mao's victories. In fact, the MCP had entirely miscalculated the British reaction to their armed struggle. The MPABA had not even managed to create a single, liberated base area, the first stage. Almost symbolically, Lau Yew, despite his optimism the most talented MCP military leader, had been killed on July 16, a month after the declaration of the Emergency. The first decisions taken by the British security officials proved in the long run to be crucial: all Malaya would be held; there would be no withdrawal from terror, no matter how isolated the area. Equally important, the British counterstriking force was not broken up into small units to defend everywhere, thereby assuring that security would everywhere be weak. While the military launched offensive strikes, keeping the MPABA off balance and on the move, special constables and additional police were hastily recruited and moved into threatened and endangered areas.

The British troops on constant patrol harried the guerrillas, forcing them to seek security in the jungles, which many new volunteers and recruits still found alien. Without Lau Yew, without solid jungle experience, without a single base area, and perhaps most of all without the comfortable illusion of a "protracted" war won in three months, the MPABA had by August fallen on evil days. So had the British security forces, who were exhausted, bitter that promised reinforcements and equipment had not arrived, and without effective civilian direction following the death of High Commissioner Sir Edward Gent in an airplane accident in Britain. The result was a pause that lasted two months while both sides regrouped and reconsidered. The MPABA groups, often four hundred strong, kept up the campaign of terror and sabotage and incorporated new volunteers. The British attempted to seal off the Thailand border in the north in September, and in October mounted various large anti-guerrilla sweeps, and released a Ferret Force of trackers and fighters to infiltrate the jungle in small groups—a most promising experiment discarded in a few months for policy reasons.

Despite the steady stream of incidents, arson, murder, sabotage, and robbery, the MPABA, transformed in February 1949 to the Malayan Races' Liberation Army (MRLA), came up with few new answers. Mobilization was complete with a total of approximately four thousand men in the jungle under control of the MCP Politburo and a few regional guerrilla officers. Combat units were still far too large. Large operations usually produced heavy losses and few results. The ten MRLA regiments were in jungle camps, often engaged in a sterile round of training and indoctrination, increasingly tied into nearby Chinese squatter settlements for food and information. Despite the losses to the security force, Chin Peng assumed that the protracted stage was well underway and that liberated areas could still be won by attacks on isolated villages and posts.

Throughout 1949 MRLA attacks aborted. No liberated areas could be fashioned, but neither could British security sweep up the guerrillas in the jungle or break the Min Yuen organization, by then over thirty thousand strong. The guerrillas, sustained by Chinese squatters and Min Yuen, existed in a gray-zone on the fringes of the jungle. They could hack at the edges of British power but not move beyond the jungles onto another stage without being wiped out by the waiting security forces. To stay in the fringe was a constant drain on MRLA strength and returned no significant military victories, but to withdraw deeper into the jungle to stay the attrition meant risking starvation and stagnation. The long years that followed saw an effort by the British to devise means to force the MRLA back into the jungle and keep the guerrillas on the run, defensive, desperate, and futile, and on the part of the MCP leadership to prevent just such a course while seeking a means out of the jungle and into the liberated areas. For a considerable length of time, either goal seemed impossible to achieve, and the struggle dragged on and on. The MRLA tenaciously held on, waiting for the British to tire or international communism to intervene, while the security forces whittled away at MRLA strength and support system.

MCP strategy and reaction to adversity is far simpler to recount because, despite several ideological shifts, the guerrilla command simply persisted with the old routines. Mounting a declining number of military operations, the commanders nearly always used too large formations for the terrain. They undertook centralized terror and sabotage operations under an often irrelevant quota system that demanded a certain number and variety of operations no matter what local conditions might be. Increasingly after 1949 the MRLA simply reacted to British pressure. After Britain won the struggle over the fringes, the guerrillas sought only to evade jungle patrols while finding sufficient supplies to avoid surrender. The British, on the other hand, evolved a collection of often novel anti-insurgency tactics and, more important, an anti-insurgency strategy that the tactical operations supplemented. To a very real extent, the key British decisions were made early. These led inevitably, though often clumsily, to further elaboration and refinement that often took a great deal of time before results could be seen.

The basic British aim was to maintain order. This was not purely and perhaps not mainly a military matter but rather one of creating an environment that would not support the guerrilla system, a system dependent on a supply and information net that in turn depended on the existing Malayan social and political structure. If that structure could be manipulated and adjusted so that the guerrilla-support system withered away, so too would the guerrilla threat. The military thrust at the jungle fringe was to push the guerrillas away from Min Yuen and the support system, while the sociopolitical policy was intended to reduce the attractions, and thereby the success, of Min Yuen in Malaya.

The military harried the guerrillas in the jungle. The Chinese squatters moved from the fringe to the New Villages. The police and home guard were vastly expanded to protect the civilian population. As soon as possible, rapid constitutional changes were instituted to lead Malaya toward independence and immunity to the nationalistic claims of the guerrillas. Despite all this, by 1951, Labour's last year, the situation to most of the British looked quite bleak. The Emergency was three years old, the number of incidents seemed to be no less, the guerrillas no fewer, the future no brighter. Each year the various guerrilla indicators had given no sign of a turning point: for example, British weapons lost: 1948, 100; 1949, 214; 1950, 551; 1951, 770. During 1951 there were 6,100 incidents, with 636 civilians killed and 135 missing; in June alone there had been 606 incidents.[7] All intelligence reported that the MRLA remained at the normal peak strength, 5,000, and obviously Min Yuen had been hampered but not halted. The New Village operations had often been bungled, further alienating the Chinese squatters. Even the jungle aborigines seemed to be opting for the guerrillas, and there was no sign of a sudden flood of Malaya support. The low point came on October 6, 1951, when High Commissioner Sir Henry Gurney was ambushed and killed. British morale plummeted. The prospects for 1952 looked bleak indeed.

In December, soon after taking office, the new Conservative Colonial Secretary Oliver Lyttleton flew out to see what could be done.

After three months there still was no new High Commissioner, no rise in morale, and no sign of either political or military progress. The police were divided, the civil administration still leisurely, and intelligence uncoordinated. Lyttleton was appalled.

> Our weapons were not fitted to the task; there was a serious shortage of armoured or protected cars. Morale amongst planters, tin miners, and amongst Chinese loyalists and Malaya was at its lowest. The grip of the terrorists was tightening, and the feelings of the loyalists could be summed up in one word, despair.[8]

Even before his return to London, he had a string of suggestions for reforms and changes.

His first and perhaps most important decision was to choose a man to pacify Malaya: Sir Gerald Templer, General Officer Commander-in-Chief Eastern Command. Templer had a mystique: he dominated his colleagues, impressed his subordinates, intimidated his foes, and ultimately convinced the wavering. Although his approach was essentially an elaboration of aspects of earlier ideas, his plan incorporating a variety of techniques, a central control, and a general confidence put new life into not only the loyalist planters but also the entire anti-communist force. Templer, a vastly talented man with almost complete control in Malaya and the total backing of the Cabinet, made the people, at least those involved, believe that he had the key to success, that he would isolate the guerrillas. More important, he was believed even when there was limited evidence that the ebb tide of the revolt had begun. When Lyttleton arrived the MRLA was hungry and hunted. No single attack under the MCP new strategy had succeeded in 1951. Min Yuen was in trouble. The squatters were almost gone. Still there was loyalist despair and exhaustion. Templer's arrival injected hope and confidence.

Templer's tenure was the turning point in Malaya. Militarily the battle of the fringes was won, the MRLA driven into the jungle away from politics. The Min Yuen was crippled if not eradicated, and large subversion-free sections "White Areas" were freed of Emergency regulations. Politically, Malaya moved steadily toward independence, a process that increasingly incorporated the Chinese population into constitutional politics, immunizing them from the lures of jungle communism. In both spheres highly innovative, often harsh measures produced results. Pacification was not a continuous process. MCP morale rose and fell with shifts in communist strength elsewhere. Their one real hope was that international communism would come to the rescue if the MRLA kept up the good fight. But except for one or two early visits by Chinese Communist agents, apparently unimpressed with the MCP's reading of Mao, no help came. As the years passed, all but the dedicated hard core lost hope that it would. At the time of Templer's departure in July 1954 there was a last brief period of hope, followed by a steady, irreversible decline into starving banditry, with the Politburo seeking a way out of annihilation through negotiations to legalize the MCP.

The new Malaya government of Tengku Abdul Rahman took office after the July 1955 elections to prepare the way for independence. After the amnesty it offered was largely ignored, it agreed to negotiations. Chin Peng actually met Tengku Abdul Rahman late in December 1955 to see if he could maneuver a return for the MCP, but after seven years of terror he convinced no one that he had been converted to Malayan democracy. Later initiatives by Chin Peng also failed and the war of attrition continued. By January 1956 the MRLA had lost 5,933 killed, 1,752 wounded, and 1,173 captured; but it had renewed itself three times and still had over 2,000 men in the jungles. By the end of the year coherence had been lost. The leadership was in Thailand and most of the "regiments" were hunted bands, desperate, starving, prey to disease, persisting in the jungle from fear of retribution or for lack of alternatives. In August 1957 Malaya became independent, joining the Commonwealth. There were still 1,500 MRLA in the jungles and still British troops ferreting them out. The southern part of the country was nearly cleared. By mid-1958 perhaps a thousand guerrillas remained—a bandit problem. On July 31, 1960, almost as an afterthought, twelve years after the armed revolt in the name of national liberation began, the Emergency was legally ended. Somewhere in the depths of the jungles 500 MRLA survivors still survived, wandering on to die unnoted or emerge to an almost indifferent world. The security forces had won a clear-cut victory, not without agony and not with remarkable speed but ultimately with assurance.

British response to open revolt in Malaya, not simply armed revolt but a communist armed revolt, was quite different from what it had been in Palestine. The British could more easily recognize the enemy, Asian communism, and the priorities, maintain a Western presence and aid Malaya friends. In spite of muddle and delay, there was always an overriding purpose: to win, to win on the ground, and to win with a political-military mix so that a Commonwealth solution would be possible. More than anyone else Templer made the mix, fashioned the plan, and led the effort with *élan*. Tactically in the jungle war the British devised elaborate and effective techniques of counterinsurgency—aerial reconnaissance, river patrols, paratroop drops, tracker squads, ferret patrols—to harry and erode the guerrillas, while at the same time offering an out to the MRLA by various ingenious means—loudspeaker aircraft, millions of air-dropped pamphlets, safe-conduct passes, and huge monetary rewards for surrender or capture of important individuals. Beyond the fringe the sources of supply were intimidated or rewarded for proper conduct by mass collective fines and curfews or substantial rewards for information delivered in a variety of leakproof schemes. Strategically, the population was isolated from the guerrillas, physically at great cost in the case of the Chinese squatters, or politically by the move toward self-government increasingly involving the population, particularly its Chinese segment, in opposition to the guerrillas.

Year by year the MCP watched their resources wither away, their Chinese support evaporate, their capacity to strike erode. Yet, although hampered by early errors and continuing misperceptions, they put up a good show. The MRLA soldiered on for twelve years, inflicting substantial casualties (2,947 Malaya Police, 1,478 Military, and 4,668 civilians) and absorbing vast revenues.[9] (At peak strength there were 350,000 security forces deployed in Malaya.) If nothing more, they left as their legacy an example of guerrilla-revolution that despite minority backing, international communist indifference, and grave strategic error had for the British been a near run thing.

The Irgun and MCP

As in Palestine a cause—Communism instead of Zionism—convinced potential rebels that the future was theirs. In Malaya, however, the future was more important than the past: the MCP opted for the armed struggle because it assumed victory was not only possible but, once the revolt was underway, imminent. Like the Irgun the MCP had been involved in a previous campaign; unlike the Irgun, they had learned all the wrong lessons. The MCP seemed to believe their own propaganda, that they had fought a guerrilla war in the jungle against the Japanese and could do as well against the British. The Irgun always had some idea just how limited were their options and capacities. The MCP seemed to believe they could combine their "experience" with Mao's dictum and win in a walk. In fact they did better than might have been expected, for as usual the British were unprepared, reacted slowly, and, given the nature of Malaya politics, had to build a counterforce with vast investment in time and patience. Yet the Malayan communists never did exploit their advantages and continued to see the British as a capitalist empire reacting in textbook fashion to textbook tactics.

For the British the two revolts had proven quite different in the field and in their perceptions. In Palestine the British had faced an Irgun resistance operating as the focus for intense international interest, applying a specially designed anti-British strategy. In Malaya there had been a guerrilla war in the jungle, a direction chosen by the MCP because of ideological considerations and previous experience. The full-time nature of the party, in any case, made it difficult to create an above-ground resistance. A further handicap was that the leadership was not only minority-based but also communist, impossible as a legitimate successor and dangerous to British security interests. In Palestine the Irgun, in cooperation with the Haganah, at least might be perceived as possible successors in part of the Mandate, and the threat of Zionism as a partial challenge to British Middle Eastern interests. There probably could not be a deal with Begin, perhaps not even with Ben Gurion, but a Zionist "victory" could be accommodated. In Malaya the MCP was, for the British, illegitimate and dangerous. Both Labour and Tory felt that the British responsibilities to the Malayan people could not be easily discarded nor could Asian communism be easily conceded a victory. There could be a grudging withdrawal in Palestine where it had become abundantly clear that neither Jew nor Arab any longer wanted Britain to be "responsible," and thus British interests could best be served at a distance; there could not easily be such a withdrawal from Malaya where even, where especially, the Chinese community depended on Britain to save them from disaster, where British interest ran so absolutely counter to MCP aspirations.

The two revolts had been rather special cases led by men imbued by strange ideologies, Zionism and Communism, driven by desperate fears or unwarranted ambitions. The British could not adjust the aspirations of the Malayan communists to the responsibilities of the imperial mission or the requirements of national security. The only option open to either side was to win on the field of battle or deny their aspirations and responsibilities. For the MCP there could be no levering the British into a dilemma of rule or retire because of the British perceptions of what retire might mean. In Palestine there had been the hope that the Commonwealth and Zionism could find common ground, that British and Zionist aspirations were complementary. Increasingly British policymakers had realized that this was not the case and the commitment to the terms of the Mandate had eroded. Although a Zionist state was not absolutely to British disadvantage, there could be little doubt that within the Arab Middle East an anti-Zionist posture by Britain would be advantageous. In any case, the cost of remaining in Palestine, no matter what the priorities, had by 1947 grown far too great; and withdrawal was not necessarily a disaster any more than had been the granting of greater responsibilities in the Gold Coast. A victory for the MCP, however, would have been disastrous. So the British persisted and the MCP found no means of applying their strategy of national liberation with effective results. They fought the good fight according to the proper rules and refused to admit defeat even in the last dreadful months in the jungle. The impact of their struggle, even coupled with the Palestine experience, did not convince the British that the Commonwealth Strategy of devolution could not be universally applied.

5 Two Flawed Strategies: The Mau Mau in Kenya and the Egyptian Fedayeen in the Suez Canal Zone

By driving him off his ancestorial lands, the Europeans have robbed him of the material foundations of his culture, and reduced him to a state of serfdom incompatible with human happiness. The African . . . must fight unceasingly for his own complete emancipation.

—Jomo Kenyatta

Every British Prime Minister seems to imagine that he is Disraeli.

—Anwar el-Sadat

On their return to power in 1951 the Conservatives discovered that their Labour predecessors had left several painful, imperial crises without visible solutions, as well as a network of colonial initiatives that could not, even if advisable, be readily undone. The Indian subcontinent had been transformed and the Commonwealth broadened. Although, supposedly, the Conservatives had given the Empire considerable thought, colonial matters had not been a pressing political issue, and responsibility was soon scattered. British strategic interests often became the concern of Defense or Foreign Affairs. The Commonwealth Office had absorbed much of the Colonial Office's former territory, and economic matters were often the province of the Treasury. Without a single, overall imperial policy, colonial decisions had to be made piecemeal, often hurriedly without reference to a grand plan. No Colonial Secretary could do more than keep up with the immediate crises, and soon there were far more crises than anticipated. The Conservatives were by no means conservative in their institutional initiatives, but most did not see revolutionary changes in the immediate future.

In 1951, despite events in the Gold Coast, the concept of African independence was still a revolutionary idea. This was particularly true in East Africa, where political progress had been slow and economic development halting. Signs of change should have indicated to the wary that time was running out but did not. The Sudan had been promised self-determination as early as 1946. Once an agreement could be reached with Cairo, British control would be phased out. Northeast of British East Africa, the United Nations had granted Italy a ten-year trusteeship to prepare Somalia for independence, in conjunction, it was assumed, with British Somaliland. Thus to the north in the immediate future would be three independent African states: Somalia, Ethiopia, and the Sudan. Independence was clearly the wave of the future.

These events appeared to make little impression on the European settlers in Kenya, those most likely to feel threatened, or on colonial authorities. No one could discover any significant African "nationalist" agitation. There was simply no expectation of a current toward independence. The disagreement between London and Nairobi focused on the best formula to protect all racial interests. Actually, Kenya's European settlers, though a tiny minority, had always hoped for a formula giving them control of the colony. They had long doubted the motives of the Colonial Office, officially dedicated to African paramountcy, and regularly denied the African capacity or desire to enter politics. The settlers claimed to know their natives and assumed that no matter what happened to the north the virus of African nationalism had not and would not reach Kenya.

In point of fact, African nationalism had surfaced several years previously in Kenya, but in forms and expressions the settlers and Colonial Office refused to credit as legitimate. If there were no African nationalism, obviously "agitators" attempting to employ tactics similar to those of Nkrumah or Gandhi must be up to something else. Consequently, no matter what the Africans said, informed opinion denied that it had been said or that the Africans meant it or that it was important. The result was that in Kenya, African nationalism, still fragile, tribally based, poorly led, and wavering of purpose, faced an appallingly difficult problem. There was no dialogue. All the African requests, programs, suggestions, and aspirations, no matter what their form, fell on deaf ears. Peaceful protest or nonviolent confrontation could not be used because the authorities saw no purpose in any protest and considered all confrontation potentially violent. Attempts by African leaders to employ the tactics of agitation created deep and abiding anxiety in the settler community.

With far less organizational talent than existed in the Gold Coast, the Africans, particularly the dominant Kikuyu tribe, had to make do. They haltingly tried to piece together a parallel strategy of political agitation and tribal violence carried out by an oath-bound conspiracy. The opportunity to allow tribal militants to play the part of the Irgun, while the Western leadership of the tribe negotiated or agitated as had Ben Gurion, never arose. In Kenya the revolt against the Crown was to grind on for seven years almost without direction.

The Kenya Emergency

By 1952 the central problem for Kenya's authorities was the accelerated alienation of the Kikuyu. Of the forty tribes and out of the 5,500,000 Africans, the Kikuyu, though the largest and most advanced, were the least appealing to Europeans. The warrior Masai with their pigtails, arrogance, and cattle raids, the seventeenth-century Scots of Kenya, won the settlers' admiration and affection. The Kikuyu were different: impossible to understand, impossible to like. Collectively they seemed bound into some sort of vast secret society, communicating in protracted parables. They were exclusive, isolated, without humor or grace, ambitious, scheming. Endowed with magnificent cunning and the political acumen of Byzantine emperors, the tribe was dedicated to trickery, concealment, and profit—or so went the common wisdom at the bar of the Norfolk Hotel.

Increasingly after World War II the Kikuyu became a source of serious concern. In 1946, after years in Europe, Jomo Kenyatta had returned to Kenya. In June of the following year, he was elected President of the Kenya African Union (KAU), for the settlers a band of fanatical agitators exploiting the ignorant Africans. And the KAU did agitate. The Kikuyu refrain "You Stole Our Lands" continued, despite elaborate explanations that only a small encroachment on Kikuyu tribal lands had been made by error and that the settlers had turned the Highlands into lush agricultural land where none had existed before. In any case there were only 16,000 square miles of White Highlands, 4,000 of them forest, in contrast to 52,000 square miles of rich African land, improperly farmed, not to mention another 148,000 square miles, admittedly less rich and impossible of serious cultivation.

The Kikuyu paid no attention and the KAU grew. There appeared to be ample grievances: ten thousand Africans without a place to sleep on any given night in Nairobi; domination of the Legislative Council by Europeans, the first African admitted only in 1944; a disproportionate investment in European education, while not all Africans received the benefit of even crude primary education. There was almost no access to secondary and university education for Africans. There was a color bar. There was insufficient investment in African agriculture. The White Highlands were barred to Africans, even as managers on white farms. Colonial agricultural policies favored the settlers. There was serious overcrowding on the Kikuyu reserves; too many young men and too little land. There was no legislation facilitating African trade unions. Any attempt at African organization with a political or economic goal brought harassment if not suppression. The settlers viewed the demands as often irrational, emotional, and largely inspired by either the peculiarities of the Kikuyu character or the personal ambitions of the KAU leaders. Their postwar fear was that a Labour government might prove soft, not understand Kenya reality. Thus there was some concern when Colonial Secretary James Griffiths arrived in Kenya in May 1951 and received a KAU delegation demanding twelve elected African seats in the Legislative Council, an end to the color bar, and financial aid for the African farmers. This was considered outrageously radical.

The 1951 election results, though they removed any prospect of Labour "concessions," did not indicate the direction of Conservative policy for East Africa. Discussions about an East African Federation had not been hopeful; however, the size of the Kenya settler community was too small to make multiracial, equal partnership for the whole of East Africa a viable proposition. In fact, with only 40,000 whites and 150,000 Asians to counterbalance 5,500,000 Africans, even a Kenya multiracial society would present certain problems of unbalance. Although the settlers were concerned about the future, they seemed less determined to come to terms with African nationalism than were the Europeans in Central Africa. Yet Kenyatta's troublesome presence created settler anxiety even if the Africans seemed to blame their estate on the Asian merchants and even if the Kikuyu appeared incapable of seriously challenging the authorities.

The difficulty for Kenyatta and the KAU was that ordinary political means to challenge settler and colonial policies were largely denied them. The Colonial authorities and certainly the settler community could not conceive of legitimate African political opposition to policies accepted by the whites as beneficial. There could be no effective application of the Indian Strategy if the imperialists defined all African political activity as rank subversion or latent vandalism. Most of the British could not accept the reality of African aspirations and, therefore, could not accommodate those aspirations. Africans were children beyond the political arena except for a few educated agitators. The KAU could only warn in exasperated tones of serious trouble unless the British paid attention. The British did not. No reforms were forthcoming, only lectures or arrests. Consequently, the foundation for a movement was laid by the more militant, already involved in the highly emotional world of oathing, who began to foresee an escalation into real resistance. Arson, sabotage, the mutilation of livestock, intimidation, and threat became more common. Some incidents were clearly criminal; more were highly political; few if any could be traced to a master plot. The Kikuyu were simmering, and Kenyatta and the KAU were at best only partially responsible for lighting the fires. In 1952 the killing oath was introduced and the possibility of open revolt, no matter how futile in practical terms, became a reality.

As the months passed, settler anxiety in Kenya grew. The first reports of oathing and a new cult—called Mau Mau—had appeared as far back as 1948 and 1949. Catholic priests were the first to be seriously concerned about the new anti-Christian sentiment that divided the Kikuyu into Christians and Mau Mau converts. Mau Mau and the oaths began to loom larger and larger, a black cloud over the White Highlands. The authorities did not seem concerned. The settlers had grave doubts that the Governor, Sir Philip Mitchell, had any intention of viewing with alarm a cult that might cost him a peerage at the end of his term.[1] The settlers, in any case, had little use for Sir Philip, despite his intention of settling in the colony on retirement. Although there had been a decline in the division between the settlers and the colonial civil servants when the latter had been permitted to buy land and remain on retirement, the old suspicions lingered. The District Commissioner or the Chief Accountant in Nairobi would go home in five years or ten, but the settler went home every night. Their priorities were different. The civil servant had to worry about African paramountcy and Treasury policy, the settler about rains and competent labor. The settlers did not trust London, did not trust the Colonial government, and often did not trust each other.

For all the bucolic beauty, lush farms, lovely mountains and open space, the Kenya settlers were a society long on the narrow edge of anxiety. Whatever stresses the massive numbers of Africans surrounding their rural paradise might have had on them psychologically, the fragility of the Kenya economy and the fear that change almost certainly would tip a precarious balance and lead to ruin was very real. Many of the settlers had invested not just years of work in their farms, but their future, even to the extent of using government pensions as collateral. So far, the decade after the war had been glorious—boom times for Kenya agriculture—but few were out of the woods, few could rest easy. There was an air of brittle glamour, false gaity, and deep uncertainty. So the settlers worried about the oathing, worried about the return of Kenyatta and his seemingly ambivalent speeches.

On July 10, 1952, Michael Blundell introduced a motion in the Legislative Council, noting the increasing disregard for law and order and requesting that the government take the necessary measures. The Colonial administration, or much of it, had long suffered under the criticism of outraged settlers. The colonial authorities could discover no new wave of crime. Beginning in January there had been a series of arson incidents. Grass fires had been set in the Nyeri area when Princess Elizabeth came to the Treetops game resort on February 5 (and left as Queen Elizabeth on February 6). There had been scattered incidents and more than scattered reports of oathing by the Mau Mau, but Sir Philip foresaw no emergency and he departed on his terminal three-month leave. The settlers, even some of the police, began to feel there was or would be a general revolt of the Kikuyu. On July 26 Jomo Kenyatta spoke to twenty thousand wildly enthusiastic people at Nyeri and insisted that "We do not know this thing Mau Mau." The settlers knew his audience did not believe him and they suspected that the Kikuyu did not either.

The oathing grew more impressive, often eight hundred at a time. Finally, on August 17, in the first report of the situation to reach London, the Acting Governor indicated to the Colonial Office that there might soon be major trouble. During ten days in mid-September fourteen Kikuyu were killed for reasons apparently related to the Mau Mau oathing. The Kikuyu were divided, with Christians resisting the pagan Mau Mau. On September 25 there were extensive reports of arson and brutal mutilation of livestock. On September 29 Sir Evelyn Baring, the new Governor, arrived and immediately embarked on an investigation tour. The settlers poured out their grievances and anxieties. Then, on October 7, 1952, Senior Chief Waruhiu, a prominent government spokesman in the Kikuyu areas and a devout Christian, was assassinated just outside Nairobi. The Governor decided that a declaration of an Emergency was inevitable. The Mau Mau had contaminated the Kikuyu, who were on the verge of insurrection. At best Kenyatta and the KAU were no more than the front for rebellion.

At five P.M. on October 20, 1952, the Governor signed a proclamation declaring that a State of Emergency existed which made it necessary to confer special powers on the authorities. A British battalion was airlifted by the RAF into Nairobi from the Suez Canal Zone. That night the police arrested eighty-three known KAU leaders, including Kenyatta. British troops patrolled the streets of Nairobi. Within a week, nearly two hundred Kikuyu were detained, and the number grew until over ninety thousand passed through either prison or detention camps.

At first, however, the security forces lacked visible rebels. There was no jungle insurgency as there had been in Malaya and no Mau Mau "military" operations. There was simply a high level of intra-Kikuyu violence and mysterious cases of arson and stock mutilation. Mau Mau rebels were rumored to be in the forests of the slopes of Mount Kenya and the Aberdares, but neither the police nor the army had enough men to launch broad sweeps. Instead, security forces concentrated on searches and interrogations in the Kikuyu Tribal Reserve areas. With the rising number of arrests and detentions, young Kikuyu men began drifting into the forests.

For several months the authorities lacked the resources to control the Reserves, patrol Nairobi, and also go into the forests. The reinforced Kenya African Rifles were largely African, hence not necessarily trustworthy. The troops from the Suez Canal Zone knew nothing of Kenya and nothing of the Kikuyu. There was no settler paramilitary force nor loyal African home guard. The police had no Special Branch worth the name and no real intelligence on the Mau Mau and the KAU.

In time, further regular troops were moved in, until at peak they numbered eleven battalions. These, with the help of the expanded police and African home guard, carried out an extensive anti-insurgency campaign. In the meantime the settlers formed volunteer commandos. But relatively few settlers could volunteer without abandoning their White Highland farms to rapid decay, so early anti-Kikuyu efforts were on a small scale. I-Force under Nev Cooper did move directly into the forests swarming with Kikuyu gangs of youths. Later D-Force, first under David Dobie and then Mike Rowbotham, continued the sweeps. In the early days the Kikuyu, without arms or leaders, suffered appalling casualties, forty to fifty killed each day. The fittest survived and moved higher into the mountains.

The Kenya problem had mushroomed so swiftly after the arrival of the new Governor that London was uncertain of the situation. Once more Colonial Secretary Lyttelton flew out to inspect a colonial emergency. His impressions in late October were not unlike those of the new Governor. Lyttelton's insistence that law and order would be imposed was comforting to the settlers. Kenyatta would be tried, and the rogue Kikuyu brought to heel. Then, with reimposed domestic tranquility, the prospects for Kenya and East Africa would again be promising. Lyttelton felt that in the long run Britain could not govern Kenya by force alone, either as a practical proposition or as a morally justifiable policy. The confidence of the African had to be gained and a share of government gradually given them. Meanwhile, the Mau Mau had to be eradicated.

The Kikuyu and the Mau Mau

By the time of the Colonial Secretary's departure, or soon thereafter, nearly everyone even remotely interested in the Emergency had reached contradictory conclusions as to exactly what was happening in Kenya.[2] The view originally proposed and subsequently defended by Governor Sir Philip Mitchell was that the Mau Mau was nothing new. There had always been trouble between the government and the Kikuyu; Mau Mau was simply a new cult, not unlike previous Kenya cults. The implication was that not only was the Mau Mau not novel but also its dangers had been overplayed. This view was not shared by most of the settlers who felt that the Mau Mau was a savage and secret descent into barbarism that lurked below the black African surface. The obscene rites were the dark side of Africa not yet eliminated through the benefits of European guidance. This Kikuyu savagery was not simply another cult but a very serious pathological condition that threatened European civilization in Kenya. Both the cultists and the pathologists, however, agreed that there was very little "civilized" content to the Mau Mau. Lyttelton and most Conservative British opinion disagreed to a degree suggesting that the savagery and brutalism—nostalgia for barbarism—was in effect a perverted form of Kikuyu nationalism, pathological, dangerous, brutal, and not susceptible to traditional forms of accommodation. Adjustments of the existing political and economic structure in Kenya, though desirable in themselves, would not rectify the situation. The key problem was the conversion of the Kikuyu to brutalism, and this could not be rectified by "political" means.

The opposing view was that the Kikuyu had ample economic grievances and had responded to them violently, often with insensate brutality. The Mau Mau was a peculiarly African response to obvious European exploitation and the "rebellion," though it might often seem savage and brutal, was not without reason. For those of this persuasion, most members of the Labour party, the Mau Mau problem could best be met with vast economic reforms.

Finally, some felt that the Mau Mau spearheaded not simply a Kikuyu but rather a Kenyan struggle of national liberation. The oathings were no more than the use of a traditional tactic for modern purposes. The predominance of the Kikuyu resulted from the level of tribal talent available in Kenya. All Kenyan Africans might not be in rebellion or sympathetic to Kikuyu tactics, but all understood their motives and aspirations: political power. A solution to Kenya's problem could only in the long run be political. In time, even to the settlers, it became clear that this view was held by most Africans.

Neither economic reforms nor political concessions could affect "pathological" conditions in 1952, so neither Nairobi nor London gave them serious consideration. Naturally a continued policy of agricultural reform would be to African advantage and a deliberate broadening of African political participation, whenever possible, would be desirable; but such enlightenment could hardly have any effect on the mad society created by the Mau Mau. Some of the harmlessly mad may be humored but a homicidal maniac can only be killed or caged. Once caged, a cure might be sought; but until then the major effort must be to prevent further mayhem.

In Palestine, the British had recognized that the Zionists had legitimate, if extreme—and undesirable for British purposes—aspirations. In Malaya, the British accepted the fact that the Malayan Communists, Chinese Communists in effect, had a rational if unacceptable political goal. In Kenya, the British authorities assumed that the Mau Mau represented neither legitimate nor illegitimate interests, had no rational goal, offered no alternative except anarchy. The Mau Mau was collective hysteria and must be brought to heel without compromise, without delay, but if possible with compassion. The clamor from the Left that the Mau Mau was a national liberation movement was viewed as either the foolishness of the ignorant or a political maneuver by callous men.

During the remainder of 1952 and into 1953 British strategy continued to stress coercion. Jomo Kenyatta was tried and, in April 1953, convicted as the director of the Mau Mau. The settlers and authorities decided that the KAU was merely a front for a revolt by primitive savages.

On January 24, the Mau Mau ambushed and massacred a young settler family. Apparently two trusted Kikuyu employees set up the slaughter of Michael Ruck, his pregnant wife, and their six-year-old son. The European community was shattered, not simply by the brutal crime, hardly the first Mau Mau outrage, nor the victims, a young family who seemed to symbolize the best of Kenya, but by the implications: no Kikuyu could be trusted, no matter how loyal in the past, no matter how devoted in the present. Subsequent murders of settlers intensified this fear, although some settlers refused to send "their" Kikuyus back to the Reserves. On a deeper and more profound level, the fragility of the settler presence was uncovered, a few thousand civilized white men in a vast black jungle of mysterious and malevolent Africans.

On March 26, nearly a thousand Mau Mau in bands of thirty to one hundred descended on the village of Lari, a center of loyalist Kikuyu-Christian opposition to them. They massacred every man, woman, and child they could find, burned down huts, and slaughtered cattle. The carnage was dreadful. Eighty-four people were killed, many slashed and ripped with pangas; another thirty-one were horribly mutilated but might live; two hundred huts were burned, and a thousand cattle slashed and torn. In every sense of the word, Lari was a bloody and brutal massacre, a savagery that fulfilled the authorities' worst expectations about the nature of the Mau Mau. On the same day, an even more ominous Mau Mau incursion occurred. A band of eighty Mau Mau attacked the police station at Naivasha, released one hundred seventy three prisoners, kept the police pinned down by infiltrating fire, and made off with a truck load of arms and ammunition. The twenty-minute operation had the precision and order of orthodox guerrilla tactics and seemed to indicate that the authorities were faced not only with brutal savages capable of massacre but with shrewd irregular fighters equally capable of effective military organization. There could no longer be any doubt that Kenya did, indeed, face an emergency that could not be ended by volunteer commandos or arrests in the native reserves. In March military reinforcements arrived; and on June 27, 1953, General Sir George Erskine flew in as Commander-in-Chief of East Africa.

Throughout 1953 the Kikuyu continued to drift into the forest. By conviction or by geography they became members of the Mau Mau. The forest sanctuaries of Kenya were on the upper slopes of Mount Kenya and the Aberdares. At the seven-thousand-foot level began the dense growth of podo, cedar, and wild fig, rising to heights of sixty or eighty feet and protecting a heavy undergrowth. Two miles farther up the slopes, a thousand feet higher, began the bamboo, with giant stalks three to four inches thick or almost impenetrable clumps of one-inch clusters: both grew out of a heavy carpet of waist-height dead stalks. Sounds carried only a few yards and sight was limited to the end of the panga. This bamboo band was four miles thick and rose to eleven thousand feet. There in a strange high altitude world of mist and marsh, bleak moors, covered with heather and giant lobelia, undulated on up to the steep final slopes of the two great peaks of the Aberdares to the east and Mount Kenya to the west. The two impenetrable forests were almost ideal guerrilla sanctuaries as long as contact could be maintained with the Passive Wings, supporters living in the Reserves. If that contact were broken, the forests, bitterly cold at night, filled with wild animals, and devoid of food, were not so much sanctuary as prison. At first the Mau Mau bands had no difficulty in maintaining supply links with the Reserves despite British efforts to seal off the forests with ditches and fences and isolate the Reserves by relocation and loyal home guards. In mid-1953 estimates of Kikuyu in the forest ran as high as twelve thousand, with thirty thousand outside in the supply and administrative nets. By the end of the year the number was down sharply, and continued to drop although even a decade later some "Mau Mau" still lived in the forests.

Because most of the militant Kikuyu leadership had been picked up in the early sweeps or were detained at one time or another in 1953 and 1954, the forest bands had 'o depend largely on self-appointed or self-elected commanders. The Mau Mau in the forests were an almost uncoordinated collection of independent bands allied to face a common enemy but incapable of joint action. Without traditional legitimacy, leaders increasingly depended on more and more extreme oaths along with the adoption of European titles. The forests abounded with Generals and Field Marshals. One of the most charismatic and successful of the forest leaders, Dedan Kimathi, at one time or another was Knight Commander of the African Empire, Prime Minister Sir Dedan Kimathi, and Popular Prime Minister of the Southern Hemisphere. The grandiose titles and the fearful oaths could not conceal, however, that the Kenya Land and Freedom Army was a collection of fugitive bands, rarely in contact with Nairobi or the urban areas, increasingly isolated from the Kikuyu Reserves, and by the end of 1953 almost incapable of any action but flight.

The technical advances in the anti-insurgency campaign in Kenya were slight. Simply because the Mau Mau were incapable of responding to propaganda on the same level as the MCP in Malaya the British made less effort in this direction. No vast rewards were offered for the leadership, or what there was of it, nor high prices paid for weapons. The level of force, often the rumor of murder and torture, and the number of executions, heretofore unheard of in a colonial situation, evoked bitter criticism by the Labour opposition.[3] There can be no doubt that the authorities were ruthless, although less so than the settlers, who repeatedly urged summary executions and an end to technical "niceties" when on the track of murderers.

After 1952 the settler community passed through several years of great fear and anxiety, trusting no one, particularly not the British government and often not the security forces, living lives of shrilly articulated dread, gripped by near hysteria that little could calm. Most could do nothing but wait it out and demand action at any cost. Their escalating demands, the bestiality of the Mau Mau oath as reported by informers, and the trauma of massacres and murder, particularly when the victims were European, certainly played a considerable part in the atypical repressive measures undertaken as policy. In Nairobi, the White Highlands, and Lyttelton's Colonial Office, the British felt these stringent measures were necessary in a struggle between the Forces of Evil and Those of Western, Christian Civilization.

> I can recall no instance when I have felt the forces of evil to be so near and so strong. As I wrote memoranda or instructions, I would suddenly see a shadow fall across the page—the honored shadow of the Devil himself.[4]

It was the sense of dread rather than the actual casualty list that made the Kenya Emergency so visible. Because of the brutality of the Mau Mau attacks and the difficulty of coping with the forest bands, the authorities tended to overestimate the actual threat. Those in greatest danger were the loyal Kikuyu, but by the end of the first year of the Emergency most could be protected. The authorities soon had 3,500 British troops, 3,500 Africans, 21,000 police, and 25,000 Kikuyu Home Guards to contain the gangs. By the end of 1953 the Mau Mau losses were officially estimated at 3,064 killed and 1,000 captured. The constant sweeps, ambushes, and deep patrols in the first half of 1954 kept eroding the gangs' strength. Beginning on April 24, 1954, Operation Anvil, a massive cordon-and-search in Nairobi, screened 30,000 Kikuyu; some 16,538 were detained and 2,416 of their relatives returned to the Reserves. Anvil and intensified screening in the Reserves crippled what remained of the Passive Wing. After the spring of 1954, although the Emergency would continue for years, the major security problem was to eliminate the elusive bands in the mountain forests.

The Emergency in Kenya lasted a considerably shorter time than that in Malaya—approximately seven years instead of twelve—for the simple reason that the Land and Freedom Army was not an army at all but bands of hunted men. Cattle mutilation, arson, and murder in the night of the unprepared and undefended was their limit. They had few firearms (and many of those pathetic, homemade copies of the real thing), no coherence, little effective leadership, only the faintest idea of tactics and none of strategy. Once the settlers and the army had cropped out the thousands of young Kikuyu, the rest could only hope to evade capture and on rare occasions strike at Kikuyu loyalists or settler livestock. The British anti-insurgency campaign in the wilds of the forests within a year resembled a big game hunt against a dangerous and devious beast, but a game hunt nevertheless. The relative losses of the hunted and hunter were as might be expected in such an exercise. British tactics were to isolate the free-fire zones[5] physically, by ditches and fences as well as resettlement, and then sweep back and forth through the forest. Only the fittest, most elusive Kikuyu survived, shrewder and shyer than traditional game. The confirmed kills gradually declined. Hard intelligence was difficult to acquire. The technique of counter-gangs, using converted Mau Mau to infiltrate under the leadership of disguised security men, further cut into Mau Mau strength in the forest. The aborting of an amnesty agreement with the major Mau Mau group in February 1954 postponed the end of the Emergency; but by mid-1954, the Mau Mau had no momentum and no hope. The last flicker was the capture of Dedan Kimathi late in 1956.

In the forest the sweeps went on for years. Occasionally, for psychological effect, the forests were bombed. The only really successful method of hitting the declining number of hidden gangs was hard intelligence. Sir Percy Sillitoe, Director General of the Security Service in Britain, had come to Kenya in April 1953 and outlined the nature of a

Special Branch and the direction such a force should take. The police soon built up a vast file of cross-checks, constantly revised by intelligence from informers. Questioning techniques that often coupled threats of exposure and physical force produced a stream of information. The realization that simply taking the Mau Mau oath was a capital crime opened even more mouths. Perhaps as many as five out of six forest contacts were the result of hard information gained through interrogation. And even those contacts seldom resulted in inflicting more than minor losses on the Mau Mau: long hours of creeping through the bamboo maze in total silence, the fire in the clearing, a single burst of automatic fire at scrambling shadows, a body, a smashed cook-pot, and silence. Then the major effort shifted away from anti-insurgency to the rehabilitation of the Kikuyu—a strategy of therapy.

The first efforts to discover an antidote to the allure of the Mau Mau had taken place before the declaration of the Emergency. In an effort to bring sanity to the mad, Colonial authorities devised a counter-Mau Mau oath to be administered by trustworthy Kikuyu—His Majesty's Witchdoctors. This oath proved ineffectual. After the Emergency declaration one of the settlers, Ronnie Fellows, devised a process of screening Mau Mau suspects that produced not only information but apparently rehabilitation. His method kept the suspect under loose guard, unwillingness to escape being the first step, then led him through a series of symbolic acts and confessions until the power of the oaths had been dissipated and the cleansed man could return to normal life. The Department of Community Development and Rehabilitation pursued a mass program to rid the Kikuyu of the poison of Mau Mau. To that end, thousands of detainees and prisoners were put through a rehabilitation course, moving through a pipeline of camps and ultimately out into normal Kikuyu society. By the end of 1956, 20,016 Kikuyu were detained in thirty-nine camps and 7,825 Mau Mau convicts were in twenty-one prisons. Few were dedicated Mau Mau, but there were several thousand hard-core cases who even under compelling force had no intention of playing the British game. In contrast to the vast majority, approximately 77,000 released by February 1959, the final hard core refused to confess and were consequently isolated in the remote Hola Camp. By 1959, however, the African situation had changed, the view from Westminster was different, and the inmates inadvertently caused an "incident" destroying the last official conviction that Kenya's problem had been solely the result of a tribal psychosis. By then, African politics had come to Kenya.

In 1952 the arrest and detention of Kenyatta and much of the leadership of the KAU, followed over the months by further arrests and detentions, largely removed the literate, Westernized Kikuyu leadership.

African political activity was prohibited or severely restricted, thereby assuring no alternative tribal leadership. Those who opposed the tenor of British policies were either in prison, in detention camps, prohibited from any activity, or in open revolt. With one or two exceptions, the rebels in the forests had neither the talent nor the experience to fashion a national liberation movement, to create a real Land and Freedom Army, or to open a dialogue with the British at any but the most primitive and most violent of levels.

Consequently, while anti-insurgency operations and the pipeline cleansing camps whittled away at the Mau Mau infestation, constitutional developments in Kenya went on almost in a vacuum. In 1954 the principles of multiracialism were incorporated into what was known as the Lyttelton Constitution, providing a complex variety of checks and balances with a Legislative Council on racial lines. This scheme was to run until 1960 before revision. Since the colony supposedly was moving toward greater order, in June 1955 African political association on a district level was permitted. With the Kikuyu still largely barred from political activity, leadership fell to other tribes and young men. This leadership was exercised in the name of all Kenya and with the understanding that the KAU, Kenyatta, and certain of the men in the forest were not the victims of a mass delusion but of British persecution. The African nationalists did not buy the madness thesis.

> Many times during the Emergency we said categorically that Mau Mau was the child of economic and social problems which had accumulated over the years which had not found any solution through constitutional channels. They were nearly all problems of discrimination against Africans in different forms; discrimination in employment and in salaries . . . refusal by the Government to let Africans grow cash crops like coffee, tea, sisal and pyrethrum . . . discrimination in post offices, hotels and restaurants . . . in giving aid to schools and hospitals established on a racial basis; the absence of African representation in the Legislature of any voice at all in the Government; the indirect rule of African people through chiefs and administration officers who did not reflect any local African opinion. All these irritations went together to create frustrations which accumulate over the years.[6]

There was also the sensitive land problem. The British were by no means blind to these grievances, although the settlers were, but assumed that legitimate complaints could be accommodated within the new multiracial system. In the elections of March 1957, six of the eight Africans returned to the Legislative Council were opposed to the "racist" 1954 Constitution. Henceforth African political agitation was carried out openly à la Nkrumah. The results were similar: a new constitution three years later, early in 1957. The Africans were delighted, for though still opposed to the multiracial nature of the new document, it could be used as a lever to pry greater concessions from London. Sufficient political ground had been cleared in Kenya to permit the positioning of the fulcrum, the opening of the dialogue that the Africans felt certain after the independence of Ghana in 1957 could have only one end. In the high forest a few hunted men were all that remained of the forces of evil and darkness. Whatever their original intentions and hopes, their talents had been insufficient to fashion an effective strategy of national liberation. But they had focused British attention on Kenya, created a sense of urgency, and in part made possible the opening of the dialogue in East Africa that led to the application of the Commonwealth Strategy.

The Egyptian Fedayeen: The Gesture of Revolt

On his return to office on October 26, 1951, Churchill inherited not only the Malayan Emergency and the Kenya crisis but also an Egyptian problem. This was hardly a novel situation; Egypt had long been a problem, only this time the crisis was of distressing proportions. From the assassination of Premier Ahmed Maher on February 24, 1945, after his announcement that Egypt would declare war on Germany, until the autumn of 1951, Egyptian politics had descended through various circles of disorder, riot, and murder in the streets, each succeeding government apparently incapable of maintaining order or instigating reform. The King, ever corrupt, grew increasingly capricious. The old parties were venal. The new parties were often violent. The Muslim Brothers sought Egypt's future in the Koran, the Young Egypt movement in fascism, and the Communists in Marx and Lenin. The discourse of politics was frequently argued with bullets. Three times Prime Minister Mustafa el-Nahas had escaped assassination. His rival, Mahmud Fahmi Nokrashy, who dissolved the Muslim Brothers on December 8, 1948, evaded Brethren vengeance for less than three weeks. He was shot dead on December 28. The Supreme Guide of the Brethren, Hassan el-Banah, in turn fell on February 12, 1949. The Jews of Cairo were attacked, culminating in a slaughter in September 1948 that cost twenty lives. General Selim Zaki of the police was killed on December 4, 1949. No representative of the old parties or the new, the palace or the British, the police or the Jews, was immune. All authority decayed.

The Wafd Party, so long a majority, so long kept from power by the palace and the parties of great wealth, had lost the lust to reform and appealed to an ever-diminishing constituency. The attractions of the old nationalist leadership, corrupt in soul if not pocket, had nearly vanished when the defeat in Palestine gave the invisible death blow to all who had held power or office, all who shared in the defeat, all who had dishonored Egypt if not out of knavery then because they had grown foolish.

Real power was draining away to new men and new parties. The Brethren, Ahmad Hussein's Green Shirts of Young Egypt (renamed the Socialist Party in 1946), and the Communists appealed to a new generation. Only a few radicals hoped to transform the Wafd; increasing numbers despaired of conventional politics. Frustrated in their efforts to achieve meaningful independence, responsible in part for the Palestine debacle, the older nationalists had grown secure. Pudgy, sun-glassed elders in fez and limousines, they could engender popular righteous indignation, manipulate mobs in the streets of Cairo to howl for vengeance or British withdrawal from the Canal Zone—while, in elaborate drawing rooms, they waited for the fall of their rivals and the call of the Palace offering the fruits of office. The game had become a ritual, the politics of interchangeable elites, with the palace coteries and Cairo mobs running on schedule, while millions of ignorant, uninterested fellahin worked the land, as had their ancestors for little and without hope. By 1950, however, the old game had just about run its course.

Egypt was filled with men of no property, caught between the old ways and the new, who through talent and skill had left the comfortable poverty of the village but not yet captured affluence or position in the city. They had won entrance to the military academy or a place at the university or a seat on the bench of a new factory but not peace of mind nor pride of place. The Egypt of the politicians was no more theirs than that of the peasant. Each of the competitors—the Brethren, Young Egypt, and the Communists—offered an ideology, a community of believers in a changing world, a direction that related to the fragmented and disoriented lives of the men who held commissions or diplomas or union cards but not the keys to the future. The new leaders, charismatic, conspirators, men of vision, who could weld the village to the city, offered their followers a challenge instead of simply a sinecure. The shrewd knew that the sinecure would come later; the idealist cared not. On January 3, 1950, in a general election the Wafd won a majority of seats, though with only 40 percent of the votes. It was the Wafd's last chance and the reformists hurriedly attempted to pass a broad social and economic program while the more conservative wing of Interior Minister Faud Serag el-Din grumbled. The situation was impossible. A combination of rapid population growth and maldistribution of income meant that not only was inflation rampant but the real average annual income had dropped.[7] There were masses of urban poor beyond the reach of Wafdist reforms, huge reservoirs of clerks, workers, and partially employed living in sullen desperation. And all the while the life of the Pashas, splendid, elegant, luxurious beyond comprehension, went on under the amused eye of the King, more venal than any. But the Wafd tried. And as always the National Issue, the British presence, the diplomatic circus, might attract attention from a real lack of bread. Negotiations had been opened with the British Labour government, but Attlee and Bevin seemed convinced of the need to stay in Egypt and lacked a sense of urgency.

Finally, on October 8, 1951, the Wafd lost patience and unilaterally abrogated the Anglo-Egyptian Treaty of 1936. The next day Egyptians rioted in Ismailia and attempted to loot a storehouse of the British NAAFI. The British army moved in armored cars and fired on the crowd. These were the opening shots in a most peculiar Revolt against the Crown by fedayeen guerrillas operating out of "independent" Egypt. Without official support, and often with the opposition of both the Palace and the Premier, the fedayeen moved into the "occupied" Suez Canal Zone against the forces that held sway by privileges granted by a treaty abrogated by the same Egyptian government. Surely only in Egypt could rebels rise against one Crown, despite the opposition of another, in order to liberate an already independent nation. For Egypt, bound to Britain within the Treaty Empire of the Middle East, it seemed quite appropriate to rise against a treaty, not actually rise, of course, for such a capacity did not exist.

Before the abrogation of the Treaty, attacks on the British in the Zone had been independent forays, more concerned with painting slogans or indulging in patriotic theft than with guerrilla operations. Immediately following the Wafd government's October 8 gesture, a spontaneous wave of enthusiasm swept through Egyptian schools and universities and on to the cells and branches of the various militant political organizations. Everyone, high or low, student or worker, Brethren or Comrade, seemed convinced that something more than the street circus was going to take place, that this time the gesture would be followed by action. This response was channeled by the existing organization, including the more militant wing of the Wafd and the more nationalist officers of the army, into the creation of paramilitary guerrilla units. These fedayeen were trained, if not well at least rapidly, for the task of harassing the British in the Zone. Although the government had not foreseen and did not regard with any great enthusiasm the sudden birth of the fedayeen, the Minister of the Interior, Faud Serag el-Din, no friend even to his own party's reform wing, realized that if he could not disband the fedayeen at least he could hope to control them by cooperating. The problem was that no single center controlled the fedayeen organizations.

Every segment of Egyptian national opinion seemed to have fostered a guerrilla organization.[8] The Brethren already had the Jawwala vigilantes as the basis of a rapidly expanding paramilitary force, trained by sympathetic officers—and there were many officers sympathetic to the Brethren—armed by purchase and theft. Ahmad Hussein was delighted to combine the self-interest of his Young Egypt program with the idealism of the national issue. The Communists, dragged willy-nilly into the fedayeen campaign by their militant young, felt that the real battle was in Cairo not the Zone; but for the moment nothing could be done without risking wholesale defection.[9] Even the most secret of all political organizations, the nebulous Free Officers Movement inside the Army, felt the pressure. The young officers were fearful of prematurely becoming involved in an overt act that might reveal their identities. Their leadership dithered, supporting the anti-imperialist fedayeen secretly but fearful of the consequences. Several officers, such as Wagih Abaza, resigned from the Army to help the untrained young men; others gave assistance covertly. For several years the Egyptian Army intelligence, first under Amin Hilmy and then Kamal Rifaat, had built up an underground network inside the Zone that proved most useful to the fedayeen.

By November 1951 the amorphous fedayeen movement had taken some shape. The volunteers had been trained, briefly, with Lee Enfield rifles, Sten guns, and grenades. The introduction of explosives classes, often with instructors less than expert, had led to accidents; but most of the trainees were satisfied. The time had come for action. Each organization was alloted separate zones of operation in a loose agreement. The first minor raids, however, composed of tiny units each with one "officer" and four student volunteers, attracted only the very militant. The idea of assaulting the power of Britain, with its tens of thousands of troops, rows of tanks, ranks of aircraft, and the Royal Navy offshore, intimidated many. The early intrusions proved the British fallible, or so it seemed. The theft and display of British stores as war booty in Cairo turned the ebbing tides of enthusiasm. Fedayeen raids suddenly became feasible as well as fashionable. Operations increased in number, although not really in effectiveness. As the number of raids climbed during November and December, eighty thousand Egyptian workers, clerks, sweepers, and stevedores in the Zone withdrew. British goods were boycotted. Water and supplies into the Zone were cut off.

The raids continued, with small bands snatching supplies, firing on the British guards, and stealing off into the night. The British response, however, became increasingly effective, and the fedayeen often found themselves in a deadly ambush. The British pushed out of the Zone, extending their area of control and thereby protecting the Zone as a staging base. Militarily of course the fedayeen proved no threat, nor did the boycott or disruption of services do more than irritate the British troops locked in behind barbed wire without prospect of leave or the comforts of Cairo. The circus that had so often been played in the streets of Cairo had simply been sent on the road to the Zone. The fedayeen violence uniting the Egyptians in the national cause was not unlike the riots of previous crises. Just as the crisis of 1951 had far exceeded previous bounds, so too did the ambitions of those who directed the fedayeen. Their ultimate aim was not to fill a place for a while in the game of musical chairs but to change the rules of the game altogether. Thus, all were agreed that the *visible* purpose of the fedayeen was to drive out the British imperialist, as all were divided on the results such action would bring. Many knew that the fedayeen campaign would not drive out the British; evidence indicated that the British intended to expand rather than narrow their control of Egypt.

The British forces were expelling Egyptians from positions of control, moving closer to Cairo by building a wider and wider buffer zone. For all but the comfortable Wafdists, whose only official action had been the withdrawal of the Egyptian Ambassador from the Court of Saint James's, the feeling was that no matter what the British did, stay or go, normal order decayed daily to the advantage of the militant. The government could neither control nor channel the fedayeen. Increasingly the career officers of the Army felt that neither the Palace nor the government was responding effectively to the national issue, making use of the Army's talents or pursuing a sufficiently active course. Increasingly the leaders of the Brethren, Communists, Young Egypt, and radical Wafdists felt the ground of Egyptian politics tremble. No one could bring back the old rules when order had so far decayed that independent armies fought pitched battles without benefit of government legitimacy, without the prospect of interference by King and Cabinet.

Actually, the fedayeen campaign into the Suez Canal Zone was a tactic in a hidden revolt against the Egyptian Crown, the system of millionaire Pashas with jobs for cousins and contracts for cronies, but crumbs for the people. It only appeared to be a revolt against the British Crown and the British Treaty Empire. For three months the major rivals for the future competed in the intensity of their sacrifice. The struggle against the British was essentially one long riot—a prolonged and elegant gesture. What exactly this gesture meant, or would mean, what real role the fedayeen played in the Egypt drama was hidden until a later act.

Then, in January 1952, came the climax—and still no clear revelation of the fedayeen role. Until that time, the direction of events was a matter of considerable interpretation by the ambitious. Only the Palace seemed remarkably unconcerned. The King as usual played out his hand, crude, capricious, without regard for the opinions of the people or his Pashas, with little interest in the prudence so often offered by Mortada el-Maraghi, head of police and security. Farouk lacked caution, lacked discretion, lacked the decency or even the cunning to hide his whims under the guise of patriotism. Being corrupt, the Palace could only corrupt, and apparently the King without shame intended to do so. The Wafd were increasingly desperate, unable to ride the rampaging tiger of nationalism, horribly fearful of ending inside. Party coherence disappeared in plotting and panic. Some made deals with the students, with the Brethren, with the Palace, with any tree taller than the tiger. The old trusted policy of creating a sense of national momentum without dangerous motion—the Strategy of the Stationary Epicenter—would not do. Recalling the Ambassador at the Court of Saint James's, a daring and significant act in former days, meant little to the ambitious who each morning rushed to the window expecting to find power in the streets. So the Wafd clung to office, evaded the wiles of the Palace, wove nets and threw out lines, aided the fedayeen and showed a face of calm and reason to the British—and waited for the pause that surely must come.

None but the Wafd foresaw a pause in what appeared to be the first act of the national revolution. Each of the competing factions, including the apolitical and unambitious in the army or the civil service, concentrated on the struggle for the Zone as a lever to power. All continued to use the idealism and energy of the fedayeen, thereby building a base for the morrow. The reasonable men—and often none were more reasonable than the returning fedayeen—knew that operations against the British could hardly be considered militarily significant. The fedayeen were performing a ritual attack, the splendid gesture, and at some cost for eventually their losses numbered approximately six hundred. No matter what happened in Cairo, the British could not again take Egypt for granted.

By January, Egypt had slipped into a curiously ordered anarchy; everyone had power, and no one had. The British were determined to end the harassment, which according to the *Times* subjected the nerves of the soldiers to a harsh ordeal. British troops crept closer to Cairo and a final showdown. For the British, the fedayeen had become a matter of military security, the abrogation of the Treaty a typical, hardly splendid, Egyptian gesture, and the decay of political order no novelty.

On January 25 the British commander in Ismailia ordered Egyptian security forces to leave the town.[10] The British would maintain order. The Egyptian commander of the police station felt that such a withdrawal would compromise Egyptian honor. The Wafd Minister of the Interior, Fuad Serag el-Din, hesitated, realizing that excess honor was not practical in the situation, until the police commander indicated that in effect the decision had been made. The Minister agreed that there should be no withdrawal. The British opened fire as promised. For twelve hours the police held out, as rumors of massacre spread beyond Ismailia to Cairo and the Delta villages. The defense of the Ismailia police station cost fifty Egyptian lives. Honor was saved and the Egyptian people outraged. For all Egyptians conscious of politics, some sort of turning point had been reached.

On the following morning, Saturday, January 26, the country was gripped by a general strike. The streets of Cairo were clogged by demonstrators. They seemed the massed extras of a drama without director, without a script, without sponsor but surely with a message. Shortly after noon, small bands of adequately prepared arsonists began to break and to burn. The masses accepted the direction of the few. Shepheard's Hotel was burned; bars and nightclubs were put to the torch; Western cinemas were burned. Rioters broke into the Turf Club and slaughtered nine British subjects and the Canadian Trade Commissioner. The police could do nothing. The mobs burned out 750 establishments and did £4,000,000 of damage. The Constitution was suspended, a state of martial law declared, and a curfew imposed. The Egyptian army moved into the city. The British army burned a village in retaliation. The Minister of Interior hurriedly arrested several hundred suspects, mostly Communists and radicals—his candidates for the arsonists. The King the next day dismissed the Nahas Government—his choice as the guilty party. Everyone, in fact, had a candidate: the most popular was Ahmad Hussein and Young Egypt. Ahmad Hussein was tried, imprisoned, and later released by the Free Officers; the rest was rumor. Whoever, if anyone, was primarily responsible, the traditional temple of Egyptian politics, long rotten at the base, had been gutted. The fedayeen raids into the Zone ended and the militants waited for the next act. In the next six months four different Cabinets would flit across the scene, none capable of direction or program, each warped by the King's arbitrary interference. The sly money and the wise seemed equally divided between the ultimate success of the Brethren or a military coup.

In the six months after the fires of Cairo, Farouk seemed determined to play out his heavy hand without even passing regard for the consequences. He became more involved in manipulating a system that had lost all credibility. More dangerous for his throne, he ignored the signs of military unrest. The six months were used by the Free Officers to plot and plot again as Farouk gave them one excuse after another: the appointment of the incompetent; the disregard of the essential; the example of corruption. The Chairman of the Free Officers, Gamal Abdul Nasser, decided on August 5 as the date for the coup. On July 20 it became clear that the King, aware of the Army unrest, was closing in on the conspiracy. On the hectic night of July 23 the conspirators seized power. The Free Officers brought in General Mohammed Neguib, an elder statesman of reform, and set about contemplating what to do with the power won.

With the Free Officers in power, the British reviewed their position in the Canal Zone. First, the Anglo-Egyptian Treaty expired in 1956, so in any case there was a grace period of only four years. Second, a staging base in the Zone that could come under constant harassment by fedayeen was a costly means of maintaining a Middle Eastern presence. The price of keeping so many men behind barbed wire guarding stores seemed unduly high. Then, too, the continued presence of British troops in the Zone seemed to be a constant affront, not only to the Egyptians but also to the Arabs in general, exacerbating Britain's Middle Eastern position. If a deal could be made that would assure British strategic requirements, while reducing the cost of the Middle East presence and thereby Arab opposition to Britain, the long-standing Egyptian problem might be solved. The attractions of such an arrangement held only limited charms for many in the Conservative Party, but eventually it became clear that the only viable alternatives were a deal with the Free Officers or continued, costly confrontation. In the spring of 1953 negotiations were opened between the British Ambassador in Cairo, Sir Ralph Stevenson, and Nasser.

The first fruits came quickly. The Egyptians, in a move widely praised as wise and statesmanlike, agreed on February 12, 1953, to an Anglo-Egyptian Agreement guaranteeing self-determination to the Sudan. The British were delighted. The Sudanese were delighted. The Egyptians were resigned but hopeful that the Sudan might choose union. Negotiations on the problem of the Canal Zone continued. On July 27, 1954, a Suez Canal Agreement was initialled. It gave Nasser in time all that he would need: the evacuation of the British, albeit with conditions, by 1956. Nasser could claim that Egypt was to be free at last. The British felt that, partly to placate the Americans, they had given Nasser a great deal. In any event, the Egyptian issue was at last solved.

General Sir Charles Keightley, Commander in Chief of British land forces in the Middle East, defined the Agreement as an act of faith by both countries. Such an act of faith, the British anticipated, would bring specific advantages, not the least of which would be the normalization of Egyptian relations. Nasser too seemed to indicate that the future would be easier than the past: "The ugly page of Anglo-Egyptian relations has been turned and another page is being written. British prestige and position in the Middle East has been strengthened. There is now no reason why Britain and Egypt should not work constructively together."[11]

In two years it would become clear that there were other ugly pages in Anglo-Egyptian relations, but in 1954 the British assumed they had solved their Egyptian problem in the way they solved most of their Middle East problems—by negotiating a treaty. The Anglo-Egyptian Treaty had not, however, in any visible way been a result of the fedayeen raids into the Suez Canal Zone or even the burning of Cairo. The fedayeen "strategy," in reality a tactical display that undermined the existing, already decayed Egyptian power structure, had simply aided in bringing new actors onto the Egyptian stage. The Free Officers, who benefited from the fedayeen, negotiated the 1954 Treaty. The Treaty solution, however, differed from previous Middle East examples because the British relied on Egyptian good faith rather than their own military presence. As a strategy to accommodate imperial conflict, the 1954 agreement for Britain was by no means novel, except in that it would prove ineffective.

Commonwealth troops (New Zealanders) on patrol deep in the Malayan jungle, August 1957.

Five women MLRA members on the day of their surrender, 1953.

Detainees at a rehabilitation camp near Penang, Malaya, 1950.

Her Royal Highness the Duchess of Kent and Prime Minister Nkrumah dancing.

General George Grivas on his arrival at Athens airport.

Gamal Abdul Nasser addressing an Egyptian crowd.

6 Two Classical Confrontations: Containment of EOKA in Cyprus and Concession to the NLF in South Arabia

Are we not getting the old, old story? First, we do nothing because there is not a sufficient level of demand in the community with democratic means to express it, and then, of course, we cannot do anything because they have reverted to violence. Surely we are not going back to that? We had it over Ireland and over Egypt.

—R. T. Paget

If the national liberation strategies applied in Kenya and Egypt were badly flawed, and the struggles hardly recognizable as legitimate exercises in revolt, the same was not true for Britain's next experience. In Cyprus the British struggled through a complicated revolt that in many ways seemed similar to the original Irish experience. There proved to be crucial differences, but by the mid-fifties the similarities to Irish events or Irgun expectations or even Malayan tactics had become obvious. Cyprus offered an opportunity for both sides to apply the lessons learned. Britain knew the cost of maintaining the balance between strategic need, colonial self-determination, imperial responsibility, and the use of force. And the rebels assumed that they knew the British course record in the recent past.

The British never really thought Cyprus might produce a critical imperial challenge. For most of the years after 1878, when Britain took over control of the island from Turkey under terms of the Convention of Defensive Alliance, hardly anyone in the government or out paid the slightest attention to the island Disraeli had assured Queen Victoria was the key to Western Asia. Cyprus became and remained an orphan island, ruled quietly by a governor residing in a prefabricated, wooden bungalow originally destined for use in Ceylon. The inhabitants, mostly Greeks, who avidly professed their Hellenism, did not regard the British presence as permanent. In any case British authorities never were unduly worried about the Greek desire to be Greek or the Turkish minority's nostalgia for the mainland. The prospect of serious colonial unrest was largely ignored; there were too few Turks to count and no one took the Greeks very seriously.

Something of a heritage of Greek protest was embodied in the speeches of Archbishops and the emotional rhetoric of orators on Greek holidays urging ultimate union with the homeland, *Enosis*. A "national-ist" movement led by a clergy in strange costumes and using curious titles—the Archbishop was addressed as Your Beatitude and signed his name in red ink, a favor granted by a distant Byzantine emperor[1]— lacked for the British a sense of reality if not drama. Cypriot Hellenism had none of the rigor of Zionism or the commitment of Malayan com-munism. The 1931 riot was the only time the Cypriots had been trouble-some. During the next generation the British were bothered only by low-level Enosis agitation, apparently endemic but benign.[2]

Following World War II, when the tides of anticolonialism quick-ened, Greek Cypriot sentiment for Enosis resurfaced. A delegation went to London in 1946 and departed without attaining any satisfaction. No one seemed unduly worried about the future of Cyprus in London or even in Athens.[3] On March 12, 1947, the Colonial Secretary Arthur Creech Jones told the House of Commons that "no change in the status of the island is contemplated by His Majesty's Government."[4] And there the matter stood. At least the Turkish Cypriots were not displeased by the British presence. They feared that any future change in the island's status might open the door to Enosis—for them a disaster. The most desirable alternative for them was obviously a return to Turkish sover-eignty, but the major thrust of their protest was against Enosis. For every Greek demand there was a counter Turkish protest. When the Greek delegation arrived in London in 1946 so did a Turkish telegram. Because the Turks were a minority, 18 percent of the population, the Cypriot Greeks chose to ignore the potential Turkish complication and concentrate on the British. For them Creech Jones's statement was not the end of the matter.

The Greeks did not want a change in status or a new constitution, but only Enosis; at least, all Greeks but the Communist Party, AKEL, did. Accordingly, the Greek Church leadership turned down a more liberal constitution in 1948—Enosis or nothing. In August of the same year, the Governor, Lord Winster, again stated that no changes were contemplated. The following December the Colonial Office told the Cypriot Archbishop and the Ethnarchy Council, the shadow Church Cabinet, that discussion of Enosis was futile. In the Commons in June 1950, the subject was again closed: "It has been repeatedly made clear that no change in the sovereignty of the island is contemplated."[5] No one but the Greeks in Athens seemed to pay serious attention to the Cypriots. And the Greek regime was much too busy fighting a civil war against the communists. The war ended in October 1948, and with the homeland thus secure, Athens began to pay more attention to the prospects of Enosis. In London, however, Cyprus still remained very much a minor matter.

A significant development occurred in June 1948 when Michael Christodoulou Mouskos returned to Cyprus, after taking postgraduate work at Boston University, and became Bishop of Kitiun. The new Bishop, a shrewd and adamant nationalist, was determined that London be made to realize a Cyprus problem existed. Leadership of Cyprus had historically been in the hands of the Church, but the new priestly militancy assumed political forms. The Ethnarchy Council and the new Bishop of Kitiun decided to hold an "unofficial" plebiscite on Enosis. On January 15, 1949, of the 224,747 Greek Cypriots eligible to vote, 215,108 voted for Enosis, a percentage of 95.7. The Turkish response was a series of monster meetings during 1948 and 1949. Protest telegrams were sent to London. There were meetings in Ankara. Yet the British governor was unmoved by both displays. For him the subject of Enosis remained closed.

On October 18, 1949, at the age of thirty-seven, the Bishop of Kitiun became the Archbishop of Cyprus, Makarios III. On the day of his enthronement, two days later, he told the crowds in Nicosia, "I shall not rest for a moment in my efforts to see union with Greece achieved."[6] Greece' Parliament debated the Cypriot question and two hundred members signed a petition favoring Enosis. Prevailing Hellenic opinion was that the justice of Greek Cypriot self-determination, the long tradition of Anglo-Greek friendship, and the self-interest of Britain would coalesce in the concession of the inevitable.

Not all Greeks were sanguine about a British concession to sweet reasonableness. One in Athens was a retired Greek officer, Colonel

George Grivas, wartime leader of a royalist resistance organization called X. Cypriot-born, deeply devout, adamantly anti-communist and unswervingly patriotic, he had been upset by the repeated British refusals even to discuss Enosis. In 1948 he began discussions with a small circle of friends in Athens about practical means to achieve it. Tentative contacts were made within the Greek army and the political right. The direction of Grivas' thinking was known as well to the Cypriot Ethnarchy. His "conspiracy" moved only slowly beyond conversation and analysis. Not until May 1, 1951, at the Tsitsas Café in Athens did the central members, Savvas and Socrates Loizides, exiled Cypriot political figures, and George Stratos, former Greek War Minister, agree on an armed struggle. Finally Makarios, who was directing the political-propaganda strategy in Cyprus, would have a military arrow in his quiver.

Guided by Makarios, the major direction of the Enosis strategy during the next three years was to use the Greek regime as an advocate, backed by international opinion and expressions of Cypriot solidarity. For their part the British sought to play down this internal problem and depended on Greece, which needed security guarantees from the West, to moderate irredentist ambitions. So, in 1951, at the United Nations session in Paris, the Greek representative on the Political Committee mentioned for the second year in a row the principle of self-determination—but for the second year in a row neglected to mention Cyprus by name. At the same time Grivas visited Cyprus to check into the possibilities for a guerrilla war. However, he came away from his meeting with Makarios on August 3, 1951, with the impression that the Archbishop was skeptical about prospects for an armed struggle. Admittedly there were vast psychological and practical obstacles, but Grivas continued planning while Makarios played the diplomatic game.

Greek "hints" dropped in the United Nations led to an Anglo-Greek "discussion," at which Foreign Secretary Anthony Eden informed the Greek Undersecretary of Foreign Affairs Evangelos Averoff-Tossizza that a Cyprus question did not exist. Involved in negotiations to join the North Atlantic Treaty Organization, Athens could do little. Then, on November 12, 1952, in the Greek general elections Field Marshal Alexander Papagos' Greek Rally won an overwhelming 247 of the 300 seats in parliament. On December 17 Papagos, politically secure, included Cyprus in the official program declarations to parliament. Papagos still faced the same two problems: he was committed to the NATO alliance, and the British would not discuss Cyprus. On September 21, 1953, the Greeks raised the Cyprus issue in the General Assembly for the first time. The following day Eden, then in Athens, made it abundantly clear to Papagos that there was not and would not be a Cyprus "problem." That December, back in London, Eden refused again to discuss the matter. On

March 15, 1954, he reiterated his stand in the Commons. The best Papagos could do was to encourage Makarios' political approach by electing to approach the United Nations once again.

Papagos' hesitation, along with the difficulties of organizing "international opinion," persuaded Makarios that Grivas' mini-war plans were not the stuff of daydreams. If the British would not talk and the Greeks could not act, and after three years this seemed to be the case, it might be necessary to do more than talk. A few strategically placed bombs on the island might accelerate the Cypriot cause in the United Nations and more closely involve the Athens regime. Makarios by 1953 agreed to the efficacy of sabotage but not guerrilla warfare. In February 1954, he was persuaded, barely, to agree to the dispatch of a small caique filled with arms.

On March 2, 1954, the caique, carrying arms Grivas had salvaged from the disbanding of X and approximately £600 worth of other material, arrived at the village of Khlorakas. The arms were distributed by Grivas' agent Andreas Azinas, who also had been ordered to mark sabotage targets, locate army and police units, check on British agents, and select landing points for caiques. The first step was taken. A second caique arrived at Khlorakas without incident.

Then on July 28, before the House of Commons, the Minister of State for Colonies, Henry Hopkinson, implied that *never* could Cyprus be "independent." He obligingly "made it clear that there can be no question of any change of sovereignty in Cyprus."[7] This statement, particularly the indiscreet use of the word "never" in an ambiguous context, was snatched up by the Enosis propaganda mill and by Grivas. Although the Archbishop contemplated some form of action on Cyprus before the United Nations session met, he contented himself with advising Grivas to go to Cyprus, while he himself continued on to New York. Perhaps the "never" could be there exploited—a small island seeking self-determination—without Cypriot bombs.

Grivas arrived on November 10. His organization consisted of a tiny handful of trusted men with secondhand or surplus weapons in various conditions, plus some grenades and a considerable amount of explosives. The attempt to bring in a third caique, *Avios Georghios,* failed when on January 26, 1955, the British intercepted the shipment. The thirteen men involved were tried and convicted. Grivas' prospects were discouraging. Even if he had the capacity to act, his "allies" showed little enthusiasm for his methods or hope for his success.

Grivas actually had greater potential than appeared on the surface. The inner core of what in time became EOKA, Ethnike Organosis Kyprion Agoniston (National Organization of Cypriot Fighters)[8] had agreed with him that any attempt to create a broad organization before the armed struggle was foolhardy. No one trusted the naive and undisciplined Cypriot Greek community to keep a secret, nor were the EOKA people confident about the capacity of the Cypriots to bear the strain of a revolt. Grivas was certain that, in time, the Greeks would contribute to the struggle; but in the beginning, he wanted to hold EOKA down to a hard core, largely selected by himself on the recommendation of his agents in Cyprus. The recruits were to be young men who were pure nationalists, dedicated to Enosis, desperate for sacrifice, and uncontaminated by communism. They were chosen almost entirely from two youth movements, OHEN (Orthodox Christian Union of Youth) and PEON (Pan-Cyprian National Organization), formed into small groups, and trained in sabotage. The shortage of arms was no deterrent; more were expected. When they did not appear, EOKA fashioned substitutes. Given the size of Cyprus, EOKA could not have used many armed men either in the hills or on the streets.

As for the disapproval of Athens and the lack of enthusiasm on the part of Makarios, Grivas was reasonably certain that time and the direction of events would persuade the Archbishop that "a slave's freedom is gained with a slave's sword," not with words. And neither Greek honor nor Greek public opinion would allow Athens to abandon the Cypriots. In any case at last he was on the ground in command of his own creation about to enter battle, "not thinking about the chances of succeeding or not." Britain, under pressure on the ground and from world opinion, would reconsider and fashion "a solution that will be according to the desires of all the Greek nation," since the British obviously believed "in the ideals of a free people."[9]

Observers reported that British officialdom in Cyprus during 1953 and 1954 did not take Enosis agitation seriously. They were quoted as saying that the Greeks "do not really mean what they say. If they did, they would do the same as the Jews and the Egyptians." Another casually agreed that it was "all a paper agitation. There is no need for us to do anything about it. The Cypriots are terribly over-civilized people. They will never do anything violent or drastic. They do not really mean all this agitation about Enosis. Why, they have not even killed anyone yet. They have not even let off a bomb."[10] The idea of a revolt on Cyprus led by a short, obscure, retired colonel and a handful of young men creeping about the hills was ludicrous. And no one outside of Cyprus took Enosis seriously either. The Papagos initiative at the United Nations did not reach the agenda. Makarios, back from the humiliation in New York, at last agreed the time had come to let off a few bombs—launch the armed struggle and be taken seriously.

Despite the length of time Grivas had been preparing for the struggle and despite the subsequent acrimonious discussion concerning the degree of foresight involved, the revolt began with limited and perhaps contradictory intentions. There had been no rigorous analysis of what the immediate or long-range response to violence would be. What if the British were not converted by a few bombs? What would the Turks do or how would NATO pressure on Athens affect Greek policy? There was no clear idea of what, if anything, an armed struggle would accomplish.

On the evening of March 31, 1955, the EOKA cells moved into place to carry out a coordinated series of sabotage strikes. At 12:30 A.M. on April 1 the Archbishop in his palace and Grivas in his safe house heard the first explosions. The Government radio station in Nicosia was badly shattered by a group led by Markos Drakos. Bombs were tossed into the Secretariat and over the fence of Wolseley Barracks and exploded in Limassol and Larnaca. In Famagusta the attacks failed and the police were on the trail of Gregoris Afxentiou. Although some EOKA men were captured, on the whole, it was not a bad or expensive night's work for EOKA.

The bombings on April 1 should not have come as a total surprise to the British. Athens abounded with rumors and gossip. As early as August 1954, the British had picked up rumors of a new X organization building on an OHEN-base. In September there had been reports that Colonel Grivas was hiding in a Cypriot monastery plotting an insurrection. The capture of the caique *Ayios Georghios,* largely as a result of information supplied by British intelligence in Athens, indicated that the plotting had gone beyond the talking stage. In December 1954 for the first time the police in the Special Branch had been given a course in anti-insurgency and the structure of the CID reorganized. Still, most of the British establishment had *not* prepared themselves for bombs in the night. Intensive police work had turned up several names, including that of Afxentiou. The British claimed for a long while that the EOKA campaign was directed by a tiny handful of extremists and supported by few if any of the Greek Cypriot population. The latter, they felt, were basically loyal, passive, and law-abiding, moderate in approach, not deeply committed to Enosis, and uncooperative only because of intimidation, not conviction. Consequently, for too long a time the British response was to deprecate the seriousness of the incidents.

On June 19, 1955, a bomb in the Nicosia Divisional Police headquarters killed one man and wounded sixteen others. It then became clear in both London and Nicosia that EOKA was creating a new situation: there was now a Cyprus problem. As Grivas noted in his order of June 28, "our activity . . . cannot be wiped out no matter what measures the Government takes . . . In the face of our strength and persistence and the trouble they cause, it is very probable that the United Nations, through member countries who take an interest in Cyprus affairs, will seek to bring about a solution.''[11] Everything, give or take a few technical problems, had by mid-summer gone as planned by Grivas and Makarios. The British had been caught largely unaware; the EOKA campaign had not been killed in the egg; international attention had been attracted; Greece had played the part of a public advocate. Makarios now felt that another appeal to the United Nations would bear fruit.

For EOKA the British-directed police, those of them not yet co-opted or converted to EOKA, proved a serious challenge. These men knew the island, the family politics, the feuds, the major personalities, and the minor habits of everyone. For EOKA to operate, not simply freely but at all, the Greek police had to be smashed. EOKA warned the Greeks in the force. This led to resignations and a decline in police enthusiasm. It was still not enough for Grivas. More resignations and a steep decline in morale occurred in August, when the first attacks on loyal police by EOKA execution groups began. At the end of the month Michael Poullis of the Special Branch could be shot in broad daylight in the center of Nicosia in full view of hundreds of bystanders and the gunmen disappear untouched. Nor did extensive searches, curfews, and detentions by the reinforced army and police reduce EOKA pressure on informers.

On the diplomatic front Makarios found the British more wily, more flexible, and more successful than anticipated. The armed struggle had complicated his task. Once London had decided there was a Cyprus problem, the Cabinet announced that talks would be held in London with the Turkish and Greek governments on Middle Eastern matters, including Cyprus. To the horror of Makarios, the Greek government accepted the invitation. Two fatal, heretofore ignored weaknesses of the Cypriot strategy were revealed at one British blow: the Greek regime could sell out Enosis for other interests, and the Turks were formally involved. Something might be done about the Greek regime but the Turks were another matter. Turkish involvement was not an artificial British ploy, nor was it necessarily to British advantage, for a Turkish-Greek rivalry would complicate NATO ties and the Western alliance. Suddenly NATO, Ankara's intentions, and American priorities became significant. As the British pointed out, because EOKA was nothing but a hard-core murder gang and unless a moderate Cypriot spokesman appeared, decisions about Cyprus would be made elsewhere.

Makarios was in a nasty corner. Grivàs and EOKA wanted Enosis and nothing else. A substantial portion of the Greek Cypriot population, unorganized in April, had by autumn grown more adamant, more committed to EOKA and Enosis. Still, many wanted nothing but the quiet life, others profited by the British presence, and the communists of AKEL opposed incorporation in conservative Greece. But where the year before a show of British good will might have dampened the militants' ambitions, now aspirations had risen. With the benefit of hindsight and the appearance of international complications introduced by the British Makarios recognized that the old either/or attitude might no longer be viable. But his people had been led or prodded to the top of the hill and there had been shown Enosis; to try to lead them partway back down guaranteed that the most committed would refuse and the remainder fall into confusion. At some time they would *have* to be led to a compromise, and the longer the task was postponed the more difficult it would be. The Archbishop had opened a Pandora's box in April. The few bombs had led to an assassination campaign that angered and alienated the British without forcing concessions, a campaign that disturbed Western security and annoyed Washington, that brought in the Turks, and, worst of all, that had failed to commit the Greek government wholeheartedly to Enosis.

The Turks proved the most immediate threat. Trapped in a nasty financial crisis that had engendered vast popular discontent, the Turkish government was delighted to be distracted by the Cyprus issue. On September 6, 1955, almost simultaneously with Foreign Secretary Harold Macmillan's presentation of a British proposal sure to be rejected by Greece, an anti-Turkish bomb attack in Salonika was "reported" in Turkey. Demonstrations soon escalated beyond the government's needs. In Istanbul and Izmir crowds ran wild burning, looting and attacking foreign targets. Prime Minister Adnan Menderes had to call out the army to maintain order. Athens withdrew its NATO troops from Turkish soil, and the whole Western alliance system in the Eastern Mediterranean seemed in danger. Greek alienation and bitterness was not lessened when the American Secretary of State, John Foster Dulles, played a leading part in soliciting votes against inclusion of the Cyprus issue on the UN's General Assembly agenda. On the international level, Enosis had brought nothing but trouble for Greece and Greeks.

In Cyprus the British proved less successful and less flexible than in London or New York. On September 17, a demonstration in Nicosia turned into a riot led by rampaging schoolboys, who set fire to the British Institute and stoned army trucks. On September 23, in response to the adverse vote in the United Nations, there were demonstrations throughout the island and an effective twenty-four-hour general strike. To add the final humiliation, sixteen EOKA men broke out of the huge, maximum-security Kyrenia Castle where they had been detained. It was obvious that something had to be done. Just before midnight on September 25, London announced that Sir Robert Armitage would be replaced as governor by Field-Marshal Sir John Harding, former Chief of the Imperial General Staff.

At this stage, the Cabinet in London felt a corner might be turned. American support was firm, the Turkish card had been played, and

Papagos, to whom private and quite secret approaches had been made, recognized that Greek security needs outweighed Cypriot loyalties. On October 3, Harding arrived with a dual brief: to crush EOKA and offer the latest British proposals to Makarios. Harding could offer more than Hopkinson's "never," but not Enosis. The Imperial General Staff had concluded that only the entire island would satisfy British strategic needs. Bases could be at the mercy of some future Greek regime more than likely prey to ultranationalism or internal subversion. The necessity for a British presence had increased as a result of withdrawal from the Suez Canal Zone. Britain needed a stable aircraft carrier, a staging point and acclimatizing camp, and a place to plant the flag in the Near East. Cyprus fitted the bill almost exactly.

Grivas and EOKA did not foresee that Harding would come with a carrot as well as a stick. EOKA struck immediately, raiding the Lefkonico Police Station, carrying off the entire armory on the day Harding arrived. EOKA shot an RAF officer in Famagusta. Harding was incensed. A ten-day curfew was announced for Famagusta. More curfews followed. Harding's overtures to Makarios were evaded or rejected. Despite curfews and searches, EOKA continued to operate at an accelerated pace. On October 9 Grivas ordered attacks on intelligence agents and policemen. On October 28, "Oxi" Day, the Greek holiday marking the refusal to surrender to the Axis in 1940, banned demonstrations took place leading to bloody street battles. Hundreds of students screamed "Hang Harding" and threw stones at British soldiers, who in turn sprayed them with green dye for later identification.

On November 1 EOKA opened another operation with fifty bombs thrown in thirty attacks all over the island. By the end of the week the British admitted to five dead and dozens wounded. Several hundred acts of sabotage, raids, shootings, and ambushes had been carried out during the week. Guerrilla groups were operating full-time in the Pentadactylos, the Kyrenia range, and the Troodos. On November 26, 1955, Harding declared a State of Emergency. All the elaborate and by now familiar emergency powers were to hand to crush EOKA. The same night at the Caledonian Society's ball at the Ledra Palace Hotel two hand grenades were tossed into the room, injuring seven people.

But the governor refused to give up the contention that EOKA was unrepresentative of Cypriot opinion, a contention so devoutly held that Special Branch still numbered Greeks, some of whom reported to Grivas. All British spokesmen denied the attractions of EOKA so vividly expressed by Dr. Themistocles Dervis, Nicosia's mayor: "We are all EOKA!" All disinterested observers agreed that if the average citizen had any preference it was for Enosis, Makarios, and Grivas. Harding had to rely on coercion rather than conversions since the people were largely lost—no matter what his information officers told the press. His first, and in the long run most effective, move to counter EOKA was to reorganize the control structure under his command so that all military, security, and civilian services operated on a joint basis and followed a joint strategy with coordinated tactics. The police, reinforced by 300 new men, totaled 2,000 (and eventually, in 1958, 4,911) and were integrated into intelligence and army operations. The island was flooded with army troops. The entire security organization functioned directly under Harding and activities were made public by a single new information service intended to give coherence to British propaganda.

Harding did not intend to depend on coercion alone to restore order. On December 13, 1955, he proscribed the Cypriot Communist Party, AKEL, and all its front organizations, banned its paper, *Neos Demo-cratis,* and arrested 135 leaders. No one was more stunned than the AKEL members; for the Left had opposed EOKA and insisted that "the struggle of the Cypriot people had nothing in common with any kind of terrorist and extremist action."[12] Nicos Zachariades, the Secretary General of the Communist trade union KKE, had even publicly revealed that "Dighenis," the leader of EOKA, was Grivas. Thus, there were various and often ingenious explanations why the British had attacked their only potential Greek allies. Nevertheless, the anti-AKEL maneuver apparently had no impact on Cyprus, and Harding had to return to force to defeat EOKA.

EOKA Structure and Tactics

Just as Harding sought to weld the security forces into a single weapon, so Grivas prepared EOKA to continue the revolt. Despite its elaborate paper structure, EOKA was thoroughly centralized and authoritarian, an extension of the leader's will and personality. Strategy was beyond discussion except, and then rarely, between Grivas and Makarios. Almost all tactical military decisions were made by Grivas, with control maintained at every step. There was no delegating of authority, no questions, no positions other than those the leader indicated. To question Grivas was inconceivable; to argue heresy; to oppose treason. He was the core and the key to EOKA. Grivas shifted first from a village into Nicosia, then to the mountains, and then to Limassol, each time under pressure and each time with a loss of communication. EOKA was an army with one Field Marshal, a score of lieutenants, and the rest privates—and not too many privates.

EOKA was divided into twenty-one geographic sectors, each with town, village, guerrilla, and mixed guerrilla groups. Sectors controlled action groups assigned to carry out sabotage, raids, executions, and, later, anti-Turkish operations. Large urban areas like Nicosia had sub-groups: for example, one to carry out executions. Beyond the towns were the rural units, often without arms other than shotguns. Few of the sectors had many active EOKA men. The guerrilla bands in the mountains served as much as mobile "safe houses" for wanted men as military formations. The PEKA (Political Committee of Cyprus Struggle) harnessed and directed civilian energy, particularly through EAEM (United Unbroken National Front) into direct passive resistance. The key organization, however, was ANE (Young Stalwarts), a youth movement parallel to EOKA. As time passed, a major problem for EOKA was to use effectively the volunteers that flooded into ANE and EAEM in mass action that would not hamper the armed struggle—agitation and confrontation in the service of the armed struggle.

Not all Cypriots rushed into the struggle, certainly not the Turks and rarely members of AKEL. Grivas was more than willing to take AKEL defectors, but the communists remained national enemies.

> We were aware of the fact that all "leftists" do not agree with the attitude of AKEL towards our struggle and that most of them think patriotically as we do and acknowledge the fact that they have been misled by AKEL because of the false promises of its leadership. At this moment we address ourselves to the "honest leftists" *and not to AKEL in general,* and call upon them to sever their ties with the leadership of AKEL which has been proved as not serving the interests of the people of Cyprus. We summon these *honest* "leftists" to shake off Satan, that is to say AKEL, and to join the ranks of our national liberation movement.[13]

Grivas "had neither foreseen, nor suspected a dynamic reaction on the part of the Turks, especially when Turkey, according to the Pact of Lausanne, had given up all her rights to Cyprus."[14] More of a threat were those Greek Cypriots, relatively few in number but potentially extremely dangerous, who were lured by money or promises to cooperate with the British. One method of retaining the loyalty of the population, especially those of little courage or expensive habits, was delegated to the execution squads: organization by assassination.

Most of the usual problems of an armed struggle, particularly one on an isolated island against a determined and capable opponent, were solved in one way or another. Money proved fairly simple to acquire. EOKA was small, many members were not on the run, and those who were required minimal maintenance. Funds came through the Church or private sources and from the simple financial procedure of running up a million pounds of debts payable on victory. Logistically the paucity of arms and ammunition continued. The tiny shipments smuggled in barely kept ahead of campaign attrition. Arms were stolen from the British, or during the Suez crisis in 1956 bought from the French, or in the case of shotguns "donated" by civilians. In time, EOKA factories produced small automatic weapons. Because of the availability of explosives neither mines nor grenades were difficult to make. Again the capacity to use a vast supply of weapons against the British was limited, although once intercommunal violence began the lack of arms was sorely felt. EOKA also had to wage a propaganda war. The Greek government actively aided this through the broadcasts of Radio Athens, which were not jammed until March 1956. On Cyprus itself, EOKA published and distributed pamphlets and broadsheets and manipulated the news in the island papers through its agents.[15]

EOKA's tactics, like the organization itself, were divided into civil and military. The most visible, at least from a distance, were of course the most violent ones. In the mountains guerrilla bands not only occupied the maximum number of British troops but also gave credibility to the revolt. In the towns, and especially larger cities, a campaign of sabotage, bombs, and arson kept up the pressure. The most spectacular activity was that of the execution squads. The impact of the shooting in the streets—narrow, crowded Ledra Street cutting through the heart of the old city of Nicosia became Murder Mile—was immense. Along with urban terror and mountain guerrillas went almost ceaseless agitation and harassment. British troops and schoolchildren fought over the possession of Greek flags, over the defacing of English road signs, over slogans on walls, over banned demonstrations, until at times EOKA seemed a Children's Crusade.

All this activity led to harsher British repression, more extensive curfews, and more costly fines and thus to greater protest, larger demonstrations and fiercer riots, and no reduction in the number of grenades tossed or shots fired. After six weeks of proposals and counterproposals, suggested agendas, and special conditions, the time for Makarios and Harding to talk arrived.

On February 15, 1956, Grivas ordered the suspension of all EOKA attacks so that "no one could accuse me of barring the way to peace." He also sent to Archbishop Makarios his conditions for ending the struggle, conditions so extreme he had "scant hopes that they would fulfill these."[16] It was still really Death or Victory for Grivas. Makarios had the complex problem of maneuvering to moderate EOKA's posture, while at the same time urging militancy on Athens. Although a year earlier an interim agreement might have been possible, now Makarios had to have not only a substantive agreement but also a symbolic one—some sort of British "surrender" to satisfy the EOKA purists, who understood neither politics nor reality, only revolutionary rhetoric. Harding might manage the substantive agreement, but he too needed a "surrender" so that murder in the street would not go unpunished. The British felt if they had learned one thing from Palestine it was not to shirk their responsibilities and let chaos reign. Harding was willing to investigate any reasonable compromise, but both EOKA and the British felt accommodation, except on their own terms, unnecessary since time, not to mention justice, was on their side. Makarios, with time running out, hoped for a middle ground.

So the Makarios-Harding talks crept along point by point, ever so slowly but slightly closer to a satisfactory formula: Makarios would get something, Grivas nothing, and the Emergency would be over. Harding, however, grew uncertain of Makarios and about his own capacity, given his limited brief, to satisfy the Archbishop. Makarios, on the other hand, felt no sense of urgency, for progress was being made and the longer EOKA waited on politics instead of politics on EOKA, the more likely the eventual compromise could be sold to the people. Despite the fears of both sides, sufficient progress was actually made for the British Colonial Secretary, Alan Lennox-Boyd, to fly to Cyprus. On February 29, an hour before the Lennox-Boyd-Makarios-Harding meeting, Grivas allowed nineteen bombs to be exploded in Nicosia. EOKA was still a factor. Inside the negotiating room neither side seemed willing or able to take the final step. Lennox-Boyd flew off. Makarios felt the British had hardened their stand. Harding was almost convinced that Makarios wanted a pause rather than a compromise. Nothing happened. On March 5 the talks were suspended.

On March 9, just before Makarios' departure on a tour of "enlightenment," a British army unit arrived, removed the Archbishop, and disappeared with him. Later in the day the Government announced that the Archbishop, along with the Bishop of Kyrenia and two other clerics, had been exiled to the Seychelles in the Indian Ocean. Cyprus erupted in riots and demonstrations. EOKA redoubled efforts. A bomb was found under Harding's bed—a parting gift from his "loyal" Greek valet. In Athens the Karamanlis regime withdrew the Greek Ambassador from London.

In London the desire to settle politically with Makarios had diminished, for the balance of power in the Near East had shifted and Cyprus was more important to British security. The activities of the new Egyptian Free Officer regime had opened up the Middle East to Moscow. In September 1955 the Russians, the menace that the Northern Teir strategy and the ill-fated Baghdad Pact had sought to bar, slipped into the heart of the area, cloaked with the "Czech" arms deal. NATO's presence in the eastern Mediterranean was crucial to blunt the new Russian thrust and to contain Nasser, increasingly seen by Britain as a menace. It was no time to give up the Cyprus bases or make concessions to a small band of terrorists. Makarios in exile satisfied British morality, pragmatism, and patriotism. London's goal after March 1956 was to achieve a solution satisfactory first to Britain, then to Greece and Turkey, and consequently to NATO and Western interests, that could be imposed without reference to the Cypriots.

The situation in Cyprus decayed as the Turks, fearful of an unwanted accommodation, grew more militant. A curious organization, VOLKAN, appeared, issuing militant proclamations and filling a need felt by the Turks and the British for a counter-weight to EOKA. As a private army or even a defense militia, VOLKAN was a figment of the Anglo-Turkish imagination. There were some independent and ill-disciplined operations, often by self-appointed VOLKAN members, but no effective organization. The leaders of the Turkish community, Dr. Fazil Küchük and Rauf Denktash, could not even discover who controlled VOLKAN; in fact, there were many VOLKANS and none. The implications, however, were clear and made manifest on May 29 when a Turkish policeman was shot while chasing an EOKA man. The Turks poured into the Greek quarter of Nicosia; a factory was burned and an elderly caretaker killed. Nicosia was divided de facto into hostile quarters with British barricades running across the center of town. Greek property inside the Turkish quarter was burned or sequestered. The threat of further intercommunal violence became a permanent part of Cypriot life.

The British continued to think that the key to order was to eliminate EOKA. Early in June, with twenty-five thousand troops at hand, they mounted a vast sweep, concentrating ten thousand men in Operation Pepperpot. They almost captured Grivas, but he slipped away and arrived safely at the Trooditissa Monastery. Not only that, but the Troodos pine forest caught fire, killing twenty-one soldiers. On the diplomatic front, too, the British had difficulties. In Ankara, Menderes was not interested in Eden's suggestion of a tripartite alliance coupled to Cypriot self-government. In the Seychelles, Makarios was not interested in Harding's suggestion that he denounce terrorism and create a "new situation." In Cyprus, Harding refused to stay the execution of an EOKA man, even when Grivas released his British hostage; and there was another round of raids on military bases. Only the Greeks seemed willing to make a move and pressed Grivas for a ceasefire. Reluctantly on August 16 he issued a proclamation expressing willingness

> to suspend operations and await the response of Britain to the demands of the Cypriot people as set out for discussion by the Ethnarch, Archbishop Makarios. As proof of my unshakeable will

to press forward to that happy end, the completion of the work undertaken by Ethnarch Makarios, and to provide him with an opportunity to solve our national question.[17]

Not even Athens had much hope. During 1956 the island had been turned into a staging base for the Anglo-French attempt to smash Nasser, once more proving the worth of Cyprus to Britain. Anyway, a "solution" would have to involve Athens and Ankara; it would not come about as the result of a local truce. The best Harding could do was offer easy surrender terms valid until September 12.

On August 23 the Grivas proclamation "Victors Do Not Surrender!" appeared on village walls. On August 26 the British published sections of a captured Grivas diary which created despondence among Cypriot Greeks. Grivas admitted the loss of the diary was a blow. "The morale of the people has suffered a shock."[18] The British apparently knew the inner workings of EOKA. Forced to react, EOKA began operations the moment the self-imposed truce ended. Execution groups, in action again, shot down a British officer in the street. The British responded with an extensive campaign of sweeps in the mountains, arrests and detentions throughout the island, curfews, fines, searches, bans, raids, and a constant din of propaganda. This extreme British action from early September 1956 until mid-March 1957 did not receive much international attention because of the Russian occupation of Hungary and the Anglo-French descent on Suez. And, in London, the Suez issue occupied center stage. The consequent lack of interest in Harding's campaign was almost as great a loss to EOKA as their casualties in the field.

The only attempt to create a political option was a mission made at Eden's request to see if a compromise constitution could be constructed. Lord Radcliffe arrived on September 14, investigated the Cypriot scene, returned, and produced an elegant document that had no possibility of being accepted. In London the British suggested that more unpleasant alternatives could be *imposed.* Lennox-Boyd told the House of Commons on December 19, 1956, that self-determination worked both ways:

> the Turkish Cypriot community, no less than the Greek Cypriot community shall, in the special circumstance of Cyprus be given freedom to decide for themselves their future status . . . the exercise of self-determination in such a mixed population must include partition among the eventual options.[19]

The Turks snatched up the idea of partition (*Taxim*) and insisted that the only acceptable solution for Cyprus was double Enosis or Taxim. Nobody paid much attention to the difficulties of dividing a small island with an intermingled population into viable pieces. Double Enosis, no more than the Radcliffe Constitution, could extract Britain from the Cyprus impasse, and Harding's effort to smash EOKA for some time ran into heavy ground.

Between August 1956 and January 1957 the execution squad in Nicosia shot down twenty victims, most of them on Murder Mile and all of them with impunity. In November 1956—Black November—there were 416 EOKA incidents. By December the tide began to turn. There were new British tactics: tracker dogs, Cypriot agents imported from London, the weight of numbers, and information supplied by bribery or extracted by pressure. During December and January EOKA lost approximately half of its hard-core strength. Marcos Drakos, one of Grivas' key men, was killed on January 18, 1957. Three days later EOKA lost George Matsis in one place and Polycaropos Yorgadjis was captured in another; two guerrilla groups gone in a day. By mid-February there were few active hill guerrillas left. In Nicosia EOKA lost Andreas Chartas, the town commander; Nicos Sampson, the execution group leader; and Phidias Kareolemos, the head of the couriers. There was growing pressure from the Turks in late January. The worst blow of all came on March 3, when a British patrol acting on information found Gregoris Afxentiou's dugout. Hidden a half-mile down the side of the mountain from Makheras Monastery, at the three-thousand-foot level, he should have been safe; a wanted man since the very first operation on April 1 the year before, he had led a charmed life. Afxentiou refused to surrender and fought an epic eight-hour battle with the British forces that ended only when hundreds of gallons of gasoline were poured down the hillside into the dugout and ignited. Afxentiou's companion, Avgoustis Efstathiou, clothes and hair afire, rushed out to safety. Afxentiou did not.

Grivas felt EOKA could make good the losses and continue. Increasingly Athens felt continuing was a disaster. There was no help at the United Nations where a vague Indian resolution passed in February after it became clear that the Western alliance opposed Cypriot "self-determination." The new British Prime Minister Harold Macmillan seemed almost as intransigent as Eden. Once more Athens urged and once more, on March 14, Grivas reluctantly accepted a cease-fire. On March 20, in Athens, Karamanlis emphasized that the release of Makarios was essential before British-Cypriot negotiations could begin. The British were not really interested in talking to the Greeks on Cyprus; but when the Archbishop on March 22 urged Grivas to suspend operation, the Cabinet, not without debate, announced that Makarios might return to Athens, though not Nicosia. For the first time in a year there seemed to be a break in the stalemate.

On April 2 the Greek Consul in Nicosia wrote to Grivas noting that Athens was waiting to be consulted about his departure from Cyprus under the free passage of EOKA personnel announced by Britain when Makarios was released. Athens apparently anticipated that he would take advantage of the safe-conduct. Grivas was unwilling to abandon "the struggle without being given guarantees for a permanent solution." When Makarios arrived in Athens on April 17 his early communications with Grivas lacked militancy and only recapitulated "the arguments for peace at any price in return for an amnesty." Grivas' early fears of politicians appeared well founded. Not until May 17 did both Athens and Makarios give up hope that Grivas might be persuaded to return to Greece and accept a compromise solution. The island then entered a curious period of no-war and no-peace, a delicate balance between British security activities and occasional EOKA retaliation while everyone waited for diplomatic action.

An unexpected lethargy appeared in diplomatic circles. With the release of Makarios the British seemed to consider that further concessions were up to the Greeks or the Archbishop or someone. Finally, on May 28, Makarios urged bilateral negotiations on Prime Minister Macmillan. He was not interested. The diplomatic pause stretched on through the summer. Cyprus was quiet. In August, Emergency regulations were relaxed. In October, Grivas began a policy of limited reprisals. But the real news was that on October 22 Field-Marshal Sir John Harding resigned. Despite the recent attacks on the Cyprus Broadcasting System radio and the Nicosia RAF camp's electricity transformers, EOKA seemed to have been brought under control. There was little doubt that as a symbol of repression his departure would ease the situation locally. Grivas, none too sure that this would be to EOKA advantage, authorized more operations. The most impressive was the destruction of several British jets on the runway at the Akrotiri airbase on November 25, and the most ominous the attempted assassination of Superintendent E. N. Peirce of the Special Branch. These operations did not break the truce in Grivas' eyes; in fact, in an unusual show of moderation, when the new civilian Governor Sir Hugh Foot arrived on December 3, he formally granted him a "credit of time."

The new governor began his regime by traveling about the countryside shaking hands and listening to complaints. Many were impressed. In Athens there was hope that something might even come out of the United Nations debate on Cyprus or out of London or from Foot. Grivas was not impressed: "I continue to believe that the Governor is a cunning and dangerous diplomat who is trying to win the people over and estrange them from EOKA."[21]

The Turks were also concerned, but for a different reason: the new man might overlook their interests, now more protected by TMT (Turkish Defense Organization) organized by Denktash to replace the vague VOLKAN. There was indeed a Turkish "problem," when further rioting in Nicosia lasted for three days. At least the United Nations had accepted a resolution urging further negotiations with a view to applying the right of self-determination. Foot believed that an accommodation of all interests was a real possibility and prepared to fly to London. "By the end of December I was feeling pretty pleased with myself. I had a positive policy to take home to London. Locally I had at least shifted the logjam. The Press in England, and even in Cyprus, had been friendly."[22] The Foot Plan, based on a five- to seven-year pause, met immediately with a Turkish veto; the TMT motto on Cyprus *Ya takxim ya olum* (Partition or Death) was coined in Ankara.[23] When Foot and Foreign Secretary Selwyn Lloyd flew to Ankara, Foreign Minister Zorlu would not even read the Plan, tossing it contemptuously aside. In Cyprus, Turkish mobs screaming Taxim clashed with Greeks. In Athens, Makarios discovered that the British intentions were as unpalatable as Taxim. As Grivas noted: "The British did not put forward any concrete proposals; instead they stressed repeatedly that any plan for a solution was acceptable to them, if it also satisfied the Turks. They sounded us out on whether we would be willing to grant Turkey a base in Cyprus."[24]

The long truce, the United Nation's resolution, Harding's departure and Foot's arrival, the new proposals had all led back to square one: no war, no peace, no accommodation, no end.

By the end of February 1958 Grivas had lost all patience. Enosis was no closer. The only concessions that seemed to interest the British were those to be given the Turks. The Karamanlis regime was unwilling or unable to take a strong stand. Makarios had nothing to offer and no one to talk to. On March 4 EOKA launched a campaign of "passive resistance" which was to take the form of minor sabotage backed by a boycott of anything British, even street signs, with no killing except for reprisals. What gains Grivas expected from a return to even moderate violence is hard to discern. Outside of the closed ranks of EOKA, most of the thoughtful believed Enosis, even on the installment plan, was not possible. Athens would surely accept any seemingly "honorable" formula. The Turks had a veto and Ankara was not anxious for a solution. The British were determined to hold firm, a decision supported by the entire Western Alliance system. By 1958 EOKA, as the advocate of Enosis, was alone.

The "passive resistance" campaign was undertaken as much to mobilize and direct civilian energies as to penalize the British. It proved a success. British signs were painted out, British goods went unsold, and importers went broke. There were huge "banned" demonstrations, and a long series of sabotage commando strikes by EOKA units. A British interrogator was shot down in Famagusta. It was like the bad old days of the Emergency. Foot sent Grivas a letter urging a personal meeting. Grivas assumed it was a trick, but through a proclamation offered to open negotiations. The result, "far from being a cessation of hostilities, was an increase in searches, operations, ill-treatment of detainees, and the general terrorizing of the island." In reprisal for ill-treatment meted out in detention Camp K, EOKA shot two military policemen in Famagusta on May 4, 1958. Foot brought back Harding's Emergency Regulations. The Governor then flew to London for talks. Grivas responded by ordering on May 9 a complete suspension of activity except passive resistance and "once more deprived Britain of any complaint that EOKA was barring the way to peace."[25]

London's hope for peace, the Macmillan Plan, "An Adventure in Partnership," involved both the Greek and Turkish governments and appealed to neither. When the details leaked out, intercommunal riots began in Cyprus on June 7, 1958, and spread across the countryside. Massacre and arson, pillaging and slaughter were reported daily. In Turkey huge crowds shouted for war and Greek blood. In Athens the Greeks withdrew their staff from NATO headquarters in Ismir and threatened to appeal to the UN Security Council. To keep the peace in Cyprus, the British flew in Royal Marines and a brigade of troops, but without noticeable effect. In the midst of the chaos on the island and the near-collapse of NATO, the Macmillan Plan was formally unveiled. In Cyprus few had time to read the "monstrosity" amid the rising violence. EOKA increasingly had switched to Turkish targets in individual reprisals and to defend the boundary of Greek areas. In July thirty-five Turks were killed, compared to four the month before. EOKA attacks on the British, viewed as an ally of the Turks, were renewed. Soldiers were shot in the main street of Famagusta and the Teachers Training College in Nicosia went up in flames. By the end of July the death toll had passed one hundred and the British were as far from smashing EOKA as ever.

The countryside was dangerous to the British everywhere, to Greeks in Turkish areas, and to Turks away from their enclaves. No day was without incident and few were without fear. An appeal for peace came from the Greek, British, and Turkish Prime Ministers, endorsed by Archbishop Makarios and the Cypriot Turks. Grivas too moved to halt the slide into anarchy: "I have given orders for all action against British and Turkish alike to stop; but I declare that if provocation continues I shall consider myself free to order immediate action against both from the 10th of this month."[26] On August 6, TMT called for a cease-fire. This time everyone had been to the lip of the chasm. An intercommunal war might devastate the island and lead to a Greek-Turkish conflict that would leave NATO in shambles and the Western presence in the Near East in ruins. London accepted the fact that an alternative to the horror of the summer had to be found but considered that the Macmillan Plan offered the best foundation for accommodation.

It was becoming clearer in 1958 in London that British strategic interests in the area had shifted. In July a radical coup in Baghdad replaced an Anglophile regime and an old ally with men who took Iraq out of the Baghdad Pact. Only Jordan remained a close friend and there military intervention was necessary to counter a radical coup. The United States had taken up most of the slack and even intervened in Lebanon. Britian's position as the major regional power was over. It had been passing since the end of the Second World War; and, although Cyprus remained important, Britian had to act in the Eastern Mediterranean with greater circumspection. There was of course no intention of scuttling or of conceding vital British strategic interests to terrorists, but a more active effort to discover a satisfactory accommodation had begun. On August 11 Macmillan flew to Cyprus and offered a seven-year period of self-government before a decision was taken. Macmillan flew back to London. EOKA activity continued. There were gun battles in the streets. On September 1 Grivas informed Foot in a leaflet that "The British plan is dead and buried." The British knew better, for a vital shift had occurred to their advantage.

In a vast deal, arranged largely by the United States to prevent its loyal ally, Turkey, from disappearing under a sea of debts and popular discontent, Menderes received $359,000,000 in aid and credits. With all that money on hand, the Prime Minister no longer needed the Cypriots to distract his critics, and the Turks were delighted to accept the Macmillan Plan. The Adventure in Partnership was to begin on October 1, even if the Greek partner did not want to play a role. Makarios feared the British would go ahead in the absence of the Greeks and impose the Plan—de facto partition monitored by a permanent Turkish presence. There would be both Taxim and British sovereignty; there could never be Enosis, even on the installment plan, if the Macmillan Plan created such immutable "facts." With the chasm opening beneath his feet, Makarios felt some immediate *demarché* was necessary. On September 7 he privately indicated to the British government that independence as a goal might replace Enosis. On September 23 he informed the visiting Mrs. Barbara Castle of the Labour Party for publication that he did not exclude independence after a period of self-government. The British could have a Nkrumah if they wanted.

Grivas professed to being upset and shocked although the Archbishop's statement should not have come as a complete surprise. Athens had been filled with gossip and rumors for months. As early as May 25, 1958, a letter to Grivas from the Greek Consul General in Cyprus, G. Vlahos, indicated that the Archbishop was "oriented toward the solution of 'Independence.' "[27] With the Turkish acceptance of the Macmillan Plan, Makarios was no longer oriented toward independence but predisposed to it as the only alternative to disaster. With the shift, everything favored a compromise. The Turks did not need a Cypriot problem. The Greeks would be delighted to talk. The Americans were anxious to tidy up the Near East. But the British came to the rescue of Grivas and held firm to the Macmillan Plan.

In Cyprus the number of ambushes, bomb explosions, and gun battles increased. The British responded with searches and seizures, detentions, curfews and questionings. On October 1, the first day of the Adventure in Partnership, there was a general strike. The next day the first British civilian to be killed since January of the previous year was shot down. The following day in Famagusta, a Mrs. Catherine Cutliffe, mother of five children and wife of a Royal Artillery sergeant, was shot and killed outside a shop. Not unexpectedly, the British Army ran riot in the town smashing windows, roughing up Greeks, and dragging off hundreds of "suspects," many of whom ended in the hospital. The civilian death toll was four with over two hundred injured. Despite EOKA's formal denial of responsibility, British newspapers "knew" EOKA was guilty and largely ignored the subsequent British Army riot and reprisals. The Cutliffe murder became a sensation in Britain, and for the first time Cyprus crowded into the British consciousness. There was a demand for action.

A week later General Kenneth Darling arrived to take over the security forces, romping down the gangway of his plane crying "Where's Grivas?" Despite some novel anti-insurgency tactics, including unannounced searches at all hours and at any likely or unlikely spot, Darling found Grivas as elusive as had his predecessors. The helicopters were sent up and the dogs sent out, but the sweeps in the hills netted few EOKA guerrillas. During the first three weeks of October EOKA carried out fifty ambushes, leaving twenty-three people killed and three hundred wounded. On October 21 a Canberra jet bomber worth £ 900,000 was destroyed on the runway by a time bomb. On October 25 a mine in a storm sewer went off just as two trucks stopped in front of the Yiallousa police station, destroying one, damaging the other, and causing nearly twenty casualties. A few days later another bomb went off as a Comet jet was loading for England; ten servicemen were injured. On November 19 the army net finally closed on Kyriakos Matsis, Kyrenian guerrilla leader, who, like most of the EOKA leaders lost, had been betrayed. He refused to surrender and was killed by grenades tossed down into his hideout. It was "revealed" by the British that, since 1955, of the fifty EOKA sector leaders all but six had been killed or captured. Darling announced, "we've got the bastards on the run."[28] A bomb exploded in a sofa of a canteen, killing two airmen. Foot dismissed five thousand Greek employees from the Army camps.

In Britain the Gallup Poll announced that the British public for the first time felt Cyprus was the major problem facing the government. And in his office the Turkish Representative in Cyprus under the Macmillan Plan sat alone with British guards at the door and a machinegun post on the roof. Grivas might not be able to impose his own solution but he could prevent the British from imposing An Adventure in Partnership. In Athens both Makarios and Averoff-Tossizza felt that Grivas had made his point; perhaps now the British might talk. In fact there had been subtle approaches that might mean something and there was always the hope that the coming United Nations debate on the Cypriot question would produce a thaw. It was again time for a truce. Grivas, who again opposed the idea for all the old familiar political reasons, agreed "to smooth the way for the United Nations appeal." On November 22, after six weeks of "trouncing the enemy without respite,"[29] he issued a declaration that EOKA would confine its action to retaliations.

The United Nations appeal proved as barren as in the past for Cypriot hopes. But, although nothing happened in the UN, something vital occurred *at* the United Nations. Foreign Minister Averoff-Tossizza met privately with Zorlu on December 5, after the defeat of the Greek resolution in the General Assembly. There was a largely unspoken realization that a deal could be made. The Turks were willing to talk to the Greeks and Athens was avid for such a conversation. Theoretically the two countries were discussing the territory of a third, but the British in maneuvering everyone into a convenient stalemate had left the door open for the "impossible" solution: a Greek-Turkish bilateral agreement. More important, the British attitude toward Cyprus had changed. The General Staff had at last become convinced that bases on the island rather than the island as a base would suit just as well. (Who knew, the Cabinet might give up both island and bases.) Thus an accommodation that satisfied both the Greeks and Turks and the British General Staff had become a real possibility.

The Greek-Turkish talks moved to Paris where NATO was meeting. By the end of January 1960 there was sufficient agreement to move to a higher level. On February 5 Karamanlis and Menderes arrived in Zurich to join the two foreign ministers. In six days the two sides hammered out a highly complicated formula based on Cypriot independence, guarantees for the Turkish minority, and the presence of the British bases. On February 10, while British troops were still combing the mountains of Cyprus, the Miracle of Zurich was announced. On February 17 a tripartite conference opened at Lancaster House in London to legalize the Zurich agreements. The two Cypriot representatives, Makarios and Küchük, were brought to London to legitimize the agreements but not to alter them. Makarios had known of the Greek intentions, had been consulted beforehand, but had not been involved in the details of negotiation. The Greeks knew that the Greek Cypriots had agreed to the basic before Zurich.[30] Makarios could not be more Hellenic than the Hellenes. He made his peace and signed.

Grivas was a different matter. He had signed nothing, had not made his peace, and believed that EOKA was stronger than ever and able to continue the struggle. British suppression of EOKA was impossible. Withdrawal of Greek support would mean little tactically. It was not simply Greek support that would go of course but the symbolic presence of Makarios, the recognized leader of not only the Church but also the people. If Makarios advocated a policy of "Let Us Finish"—and he did so—a continued struggle would raise the nightmare prospect of civil war. Grivas had no choice and knew it. His long silence on being informed of the London agreement was symbolic rather than ominous. "In the end I decided with a heavy heart that I must call a final cease-fire, leaving the Archbishop and his friends to implement the agreement as best they could in the absence of my approval."[31]

On March 17, 1960, Grivas arrived in Greece. En route to Athens he answered a telegram from Karamanlis by declaring that "the hard fighting of the Cypriot people have borne its fruits"—though not the ones he had so long sought. The King confered upon him the Grand Cross of the Order of George I With Swords. The Parliament voted him the rank of Lieutenant-General. The crowds along his route cheered him as a hero. And as a military tactician he undoubtedly deserved each. But he received them with a heavy heart: he and EOKA had been outmaneuvered by the politicians; their sacrifices, if not fully wasted, were not truly realized.

A Failed Revolt

A tactical success, EOKA's struggle of national liberation failed of its ultimate goal and even created conditions and agreements likely to inhibit progress toward Enosis. Like Zionism, Cypriot Hellenism evolved from a long, emotional longing; unlike Zionism, for many the aspiration lacked urgency and even primacy. In attempting to transform a centuries-old dream into political reality, neither Makarios nor Grivas displayed more than parochial vision. Both realized that the long train of British "nevers" irritated and insulted the Greek Cypriots, both assumed the cause was worth fighting for and both believed that the anti-imperial tides of current history and their interpretation of British self-interest would shortly produce conditions congenial to Enosis.

Grivas felt that the British should be coerced into taking action on Greek demands; but, no matter how he later explained his expectations of British reaction, he made only the most minimal preparations for the campaign and accumulated Spartan stores indeed. More was possible and more would certainly have eased EOKA's problems over the ensuing years. Grivas' urgency was related less to political expediency than to the lack of enthusiasm of the Archbishop and the Athenian government. He wanted to begin his war and let the future sort itself out. Makarios had no interest in the charms of an armed struggle. He imagined an effort—as had the Haganah in Palestine—that would demonstrate a degree of seriousness to the British, attract attention, lever a way open to a dialogue. He misunderstood both Grivas, who wanted an armed struggle, and the nature of irregular war directed by a commander without rigorous political restraint. Makarios wanted a campaign of agitation and confrontation that would lead to concession; Grivas wanted to wage a war of attrition that would force concession. In practice, the parallel strategies canceled each other out.

By the time EOKA began killing policemen, Makarios knew that the British, even if they began to talk, were going to concede far less than he had hoped, so little in fact that such an "agreement" would never placate EOKA and would guarantee a continued armed struggle that would prevent further concessions. Even then, if the question of Enosis had been solely insular—a true struggle of national liberation rather than a question of Greek irredentism—Makarios would have been able to agree that a viable strategy was to allow Grivas to continue in the hope that the British would overstep themselves or pay to end the harassment. The limitations on guerrilla activity, the size of the island, isolation, limited arms, and the skilled British response made such a prospect unlikely but not impossible.

Three major factors prevented any such isolated struggle. First, the Turks had a vested interest in the island and the capacity to prevent a Greek solution uncongenial to Ankara. No one working to achieve Enosis had paid enough attention to the Turks; during much of the Emergency the Cypriot Greeks continued to act as if the British had invented the Turks. It was obvious that on all levels, from the first tripartite talks in London down to the encouragement of VOLKAN, the British exploited a natural Turkish response to Cypriot events—although this response would have occurred no matter what. Second, the British strategic interests and those of the Western alliance played a paramount role in Cypriot events. Shifts and realignments in the Middle East, the arrival of the Russians, and NATO's needs made Cyprus crucial. Consequently, the NATO powers, particularly the United States, tended to blame EOKA for disrupting the alliance in the Eastern Mediterranean, dividing Greece and Turkey, and causing trouble. The result was a lack of Western sympathy for Enosis and pressure for a solution that would eliminate the problem, and of course deny Enosis. Third, and most crucial of all was the refusal of the Greek government to place Enosis above the security of the mainland. Once again neither Makarios nor Grivas had anticipated such "dishonor," although Greek national survival as interpreted by Athens always had been given priority over Enosis. Makarios and Grivas had followed the devices and desires of their own hearts.

The London agreement produced almost exactly what the British wanted: permanent possession of the bases, a presence on the island supported by all Cypriot factions except AKEL, and an end to the emergency. Turkey was satisfied: no Enosis and the minority protected. Greece was satisfied: no Turkish threat, no break with NATO, no Enosis but still an independent "Greek" Cyprus. Makarios moved to the President's Palace. And, after nearly five years of pursuing the tactics of national liberation in strategic isolation, EOKA dissolved. Grivas went into exile in Athens, having liberated a nation for which he had not fought. Seldom has a guerrilla leader won so great a *success d'estime* on the ground, against such geographic and statistical odds, and yet with so limited an effect on the ultimate peace.

With the Zurich and London agreements the structure of the new Commonwealth underwent severe changes. A few years earlier, wisdom and financial prudence indicated that certain areas within the Empire might never anticipate independence, now Cyprus, a small island with limited resources and a bitterly divided population, entered the Commonwealth. There could no longer be barriers as a result of size, economic viability, domestic tranquility, or even, if proper provisions were made, the requirements of British security. The almost imperceptible Cyprus concession—the end of "never"—could be traced directly, if haltingly, to the trauma of the 1956 Suez Crisis.

When Nasser nationalized the Suez Canal Company and humiliated the British, revealing the pretensions of imperial Middle Eastern hegemony, the wound to Conservative advocates of Empire had been deep indeed. Until then, the Commonwealth Strategy in India and the Treaty Strategy in the Middle East had been accepted by the imperialists as a mutual accommodation made possible by British concession to the just aspirations of the imperial peoples. Nasser revealed that Britain had been acting out of weakness not strength, had disguised the decline in the Empire's relative power with the trappings of mutual accommodation. When the Cabinet sought to deny this by attempting to reimpose the vanished hegemony by force in Egypt, the international indignation, limitations on independent British action, and domestic distaste for such adventures revealed in a traumatic month the end of Empire.

Macmillan's new government wasted little time on recrimination, but began a masterly disengagement from the Egyptian adventure. The relatively brief span between the descent of the Anglo-French expedition on Egypt in November 1956 and the Zurich Agreements in February 1960 saw the almost complete reversal of attitudes that had persisted for a century. The key period occurred between the release of Makarios in March 1957 and the appointment of Iain Macleod as Colonial Secretary on October 19, 1959, with instructions from Prime Minister Macmillan to accelerate colonial self-determination. The intention of holding strategic counters, the fortress bases of Cyprus or Aden or Gibraltar, remained—as did the British presence East of Suez. The Empire was not discarded on a given day. What did occur was a gradual acceptance that British strategic and commercial interests could be served without the necessity of the existing colonial structure.

As a result, the winds of change whistled through the Treaty Empire in the Middle East where, despite Suez, Britain's security and economic interests were still capable of coexisting with the aspirations of the Arab nationalists. With the birth of the United Arab Republic in 1958 and the rapid spread of Nasserism throughout the Middle East, the British had to consider the strategic implications of the changes. The Russians clearly were willing to exploit Arab innocence for Soviet gain. The NATO powers buttressed the western reaches of the Middle East and the CEATO alliance the eastern, but the Arab south was soft and open to penetration. The immediate British response after 1957-58 could be adequately fashioned with the existing imperial legacy: Cyprus must be maintained at one corner, Aden in South Arabia at another, and the Gulf bases as the final apex of the Mideast triangle. The basis of the British position was no longer hegemony but rather a limited military capacity to protect the northwest reaches of the Indian Ocean and the vast Arabian oil reserves.

Revolt in South Arabia

At the very end of Empire, the final revolt occurred in South Arabia as once again Britain misjudged the Arabs. There the whole violent ritual of imperial revolt would once more be played out in the usual detail of muddle, blunder, and murder in the streets. Almost free of the imperial burden at last, the British stumbled and tumbled once more down the sandy Arab slopes as if nothing had been learned in a generation. South Arabia evolved into some fearful anachronism of Empire, a revolt rerun at half speed when much of the audience had turned to leave the imperial theater.

On a map of South Arabia the British position seemed quite clear: the dot of Aden and the smooth expanse of imperial red running into the highlands south of Yemen and along the coast below the Empty Quarter to the boundary of Muscat and Oman—a great, clean coastal slice of Arabia. On the ground, however, little was clear: "South Arabia" covered a whole spectrum of arrangements, treaties, disputed boundaries, and nomadic inhabitants. Some of the sultans and emirs had advisers, and on occasion even accepted advice; others had none. All were protected by the Crown, but often some were in exile or active rebellion. Outside of Aden the British were few on the ground. Most of the Protectorate states, Eastern or Western, resembled Normandy during a particularly fluid period of the Hundred Years War. Authority depended on a swift sword, bribery, and the ties of blood. Tribal society had, except in the matter of firearms, scarcely changed in centuries. A Sultan might live comfortably in a multistoried, fortified castle, a warlord of the wadi, while his subjects lived like goats. Some of the sultans were shrewd if untutored barons, others mad and depraved, a few knights without fear or reproach, and a few more without visible virtue. Life was raw, crude, cut to the bare essentials and often even deeper. Up-country with its exotic blue-dyed tribesmen in cotton kilts waving ancient rifles was still the stuff of romance, but Aden, a great, black, dead volcano that had created one of the finest natural harbors in the Indian Ocean, was the reason for British presence.

Aden had been snapped up in January 1839 and attached to the Bombay Presidency as a small but useful counter. [33] After the completion of the Suez Canal in 1869, the value of Aden increased as an entrepôt and bunkering port. If not exactly the Gibraltar of the East, as Lord Valentia had suggested in 1803, it was a vital link in the chain of British imperial communications. The only immediate threat came from up-country, where unruly tribes might fall under the influence of a competitor, either the Ottoman Turks or later the ambitious Imam of Yemen. As a result a series of protectorate treaties had leisurely been negotiated. For the most part Aden Colony slumbered, with only an occasional glance north toward Taiz and San'a in Yemen. In 1944 four Adenese were finally elected to the Legislative Council by a most limited suffrage. Politics had not really arrived; Arabic was not even an official language in the Council. Aden seemed less an Arab city than a polyglot multinational entrepôt that could have existed anywhere on the Indian Ocean littoral.

The rising tide of Arab nationalism, stirred by the Palestine debacle of 1948 and whipped to a series of crests by events in Egypt, began to show up by the mid-fifties in Adenese ripples. The Arab middle class of the Aden Association, as much a social and economic club as a political organization, felt that some British gesture to Arab opinion might not be amiss. There were, most admitted freely, great advantages in the British presence, not all of them financial, but the lack of self-government irked the Arabs. Beneath the quiet conversations and odd newspaper editorial of the elegant Arabs, a striking change had begun to transform the city's population. By 1954 British Petroleum had completed a huge new refinery across the harbor in Little Aden. During the postwar years a variety of economic factors combined to produce an expanding Adenese economy. From the north a steady stream of Yemeni poured into Aden to be absorbed into the booming economy. By 1955 40,000 of Aden's 104,000 inhabitants were Yemeni Arab "transients"; only 37,000 were Arab Adenese. The refinery, the Yemeni work force, and the growing sophistication of the economy created an ideal medium for the growth of a politically active trade union movement. In 1953 there were two trade unions. Three years later there were twenty-five united in the Arab Trade Union Conference (TUC) under the leadership of Abdullah al-Asnag. Even in Lahej, outside Aden, the Sultan in 1951 formed the South Arabian League (SAL), a "progressive" movement of uncertain ideo-logical posture but increasingly revealed as anti-British in intention. Arab politics had come to Aden even before the Suez debacle.

British Arabists found the change unappetizing. The previous Arab generation in Aden had been charming and loyal, polite Arabs of the Old School. The young men, however, listened to Nasser and had ideas beyond their station and aspirations that could not be easily accommo-dated with elegant conversation. The comfortable days of the Aden Crown Colony, a tiny, isolated world, abutting the unadministered Pro-tectorates, had about run out. Aden could not be left to the mercy of radicals. There had to be progress to channel the agitation into con-structive activity. But, the size of Aden limited full development unless somehow the Protectorates could be attached. Something might be done to rationalize the Protectorate structure, to encourage constitutional development in the more advanced Aden Colony and move South Arabia out of the vulnerable backwaters. The only novel suggestion had been an earlier federation proposal for the Protectorates, an administrative measure actually, rather than a response to radical pressure. In any case in 1954, the Sultans, suspicious of British intentions, spurned it. There was no sense of urgency in London to fashion a more satisfactory future.

Lord Lloyd, Undersecretary of State for Colonies, arrived in Aden and, on May 19, 1956, informed the Aden Legislative Council that further constitutional developments could be anticipated "in due course," but that there were limits.

> I should like you to understand that for the foreseeable future it would not be reasonable or sensible, or indeed in the interests of the Colony's inhabitants, for them to aspire to any aim beyond that of a considerable degree of internal self-government. Therefore, whilst I have indicated the type of constitutional advance to which the people in this Colony may legitimately aspire, Her Majesty's Government wish to make it clear that the importance of Aden both strategically and economically within the Commonwealth is such that they cannot foresee the possibility of any fundamental relaxation of their responsibilities for the Colony. I feel that this assurance will be welcome to you and to the vast majority of the Colony.[34]

This assurance came five months after the abrupt dismissal of Pasha Glubb by King Hussein of Jordan in 1955 and nine months after the Soviet-Egyptian "Czech" arms deal of September 1955.

In London the Cabinet apparently still assumed that the distance from Cairo to Aden protected South Arabia from subversion, that all the disagreeable young workers did not understand the implications of Nasser's ambitions and aspirations. In Aden, with Radio Cairo blaring throughout every café, Cairo was no distance at all and Nasser both mentor and idol. At least the British had one advantage in that the Yemeni aspiration to unite South Arabia with Yemen in a radical Arab state faced ideological complications. This aspiration meant that not only would the British have to be forced out but also the old feudal Imam would have to go as well. Any Nasserist faced two opponents without a safe base. In both London and Aden the conventional wisdom remained that there was time to effect adequate constitutional advance to accommodate legitimate Arab aspirations—no need for a radical Yemen Republic. In fact, at the very moment of Lloyd's visit, the British were again piecing together a new federal strategy that included concessions to Aden.

The construction of any satisfactory political institution for South Arabia faced incredible obstacles. Few of the rulers actually ruled, and a federal system in theory would not bestow additional power on the states but rather absorb it at the center. To base change on the rulers, who had the most to lose by it, was not an auspicious beginning. There seemed, however, no alternatives, and the advocates of federalism insisted that federation was the best solution and might do if certain conditions could be met: "the cession of British sovereignty over Aden, the rationalization of the federal constitution, a British guarantee of defence against the

Egyptian threat from the Yemen and the provision of additional finance for development.''[35] Opponents said that nothing the British could do would float a federal boat loaded with the dead weight of the sultans and presumably captained by the Adenese, who wanted to abandon ship even before it sailed.

The first step was to create a nucleus of federated states that would attract the more reluctant rulers and, possibly, could be wedded to Aden. The Imam was opposed and "allied" himself with Nasser. As a result border trouble broke out, as tribal dissidents fed on Egyptian funds and Yemeni encouragement, and there were bomb incidents in Aden. Eventually, on July 16, 1958, the British announced agreement in principle by six founder federal states. On February 11, 1959, Alan Lennox-Boyd represented the Crown at the inauguration of the Federation of the Amirates of the South.

> This Federation poses a threat to no one and no country. It has come into existence by the will of the people acting through their traditional tribal leaders and it has come into existence so that together the Amirates of this territory can give expression to their desire to pool their resources, to live without fear of subversion or attack, and to give their people greater security and prosperity.[36]

A new constitution came into effect in Aden in January 1959, opposed by the Yemeni population and the TUC, who boycotted the elections. Still, the Federation had picked up momentum; the time to merge Aden and the Protectorates neared—or so thought the British, and so they urged.

Federalism was regarded by the Arabs as a Machiavellian, British maneuver to prop up the medieval sultans and deny democracy to the Adenese Arabs, a formula that would allow the British to continue to sit in their great base, to continue to use Aden, to continue to pull the political strings. The British, with few options and growing reason to buttress their presence in the area, persisted. London felt the Yemen-Egypt-Russian axis had dangerous connotations for Britain and the Western alliance in the Middle East, and Aden grew more important. So, on September 26, 1962, the Aden Legislative Council, after nearly three days of debate, passed the federal agreement. Acceptance was probably a minor miracle. On September 27, the day after passage, the announcement came that a revolution had taken place in Yemen and a Republic declared. The radicals were ecstatic: one-half of the necessary South Arabian revolution had taken place. If the news had arrived before the vote, almost certainly the federal supporters in the Council would have been sufficiently intimidated to have killed the plan.

The Arab opposition hardened. In November 1962, the *Economist* saw the pieces falling into a wearily familiar pattern: Russia-Egypt-Progress on one side and on the other Britain-Monarchies-Reaction. So far, the latter alliance had shown limited success and the radical Arabs in South Arabia assumed that their own victory was sure. The drama thus began to unfold without surprises. On January 18, 1963, Aden officially joined the Federation as the twelfth member. In February the new Yemeni Republican government ordered the British to close their mission in Taiz. In June four members of the British army were killed in a border incident. Militant Arab nationalists drifted across the frontier into Yemen to find an enthusiastic welcome. Radio Cairo and Radios Taiz and San'a kept inciting revolt against British imperialism. There were rumors of tribal trouble instigated from Yemen. There was rumor of Adenese trouble.

The most articulate opposition to the British-sponsored Federation was al-Asnag's new People's Socialist Party, partially Yemeni in leadership and substantially so in membership, the PSP was a Southern Arabian reflection of Nasser's vision of Arab Socialism, vague but keen. The program was unequivocal: British evacuation, elimination of the Federation, independence, and union with Yemen in an Arab Socialist Republic. The British considered al-Asnag's party little more than a stalking horse for Soviet and Egyptian aspirations. As the Socialist-Camp-Third World-Anti-Imperialist machine was again cranked up, the expected resolution appeared at the United Nations. Those responsible for British colonial policy felt the Western "liberals" and Labour Left were suggesting the tried and pink solution for an area about which they knew little or nothing.

On October 14, 1963, an almost unknown party in Yemen, the National Liberation Front (NLF), announced that the long-anticipated armed struggle had begun in the Radfan mountains of Dhala. In 1962 uniformed rebels describing themselves as NLF had appeared in the area but withdrew within ten days as a result of RAF attacks on tribal herds of goats and flocks of sheep. Little had been discovered about the 1962 NLF and little was known of the 1963 model. There was no doubt that in Dhala, eighty miles north of Aden alongside the only track into Yemen, the tribes had resorted to the tactics of their ancestors. Whether for fun or profit or out of conviction, the snipings and ambushes began once more.

The details of the formation of this new National Front for the Liberation of the Occupied Yemeni South remained vague in Aden, where the British had long grown blasé on one Arab "organization" succeeded another. Only much later did the origin of the NLF become somewhat clearer. For many of the early key NLF members, the dominant intellectual current that had first attracted their interest in revolutionary nationalism was the Arab National Movement (ANM) founded in Beirut by George Habash. [37] Ideas of Arab unity, freedom, and socialism, not unlike those of the more popular Arab Ba'athists, were introduced into South Arabia by four teachers. Their students, the mother cell of revolution, had contacts up-country where Radio Cairo had long prepared the tribesmen for the arrival of the future.

Like-minded nationalists belonging to several small and ephemeral Arab movements in Aden gradually coalesced into an elusive group. The key men believed that the advent of the Yemen Arab Republic and the Aden Federation merger opened the door to revolution. They doubted al-Asnag's intentions and the willingness of the PSP to take up arms. The leader of the group was Qahatan Ashaabi, who had defected from the Sultan of Lahej's SAL. Using Yemen as a base, the leadership organized an NLF executive of seven members dominated by the ANM ideology. Preparations for armed struggle were begun. The Executive was later restructured into a General Command, of fifteen members, then twenty-two, and finally forty-one. With Egyptian and Yemeni help, men were trained to slip into South Arabia, particularly the tribesmen of Dhala, and to maintain contact with cells in Aden. Qahatan Ashaabi left for Cairo where at the center of the Arab revolutionary world he would announce the purpose and direction of the NLF.

On the morning of December 10, 1963, an official British party waited on the tarmac of Khormakhsar airport for the departure of the High Commissioner Sir Kennedy Trevaskis, several Federal Ministers, and various aides for a London Conference that might accelerate progress toward South Arabian independence. A smoking, green hand grenade, apparently out of nowhere, spluttered into the group. Trevaskis was forced away from the grenade by his aide, George Henderson. Within seconds the grenade detonated, killing an Indian woman; Henderson died a fortnight later. Fifty-three people were wounded, including the High Commissioner and several of the Ministers. British opinion was appalled—by the casualties and the skill of the attackers. The Federal Government immediately declared a state of emergency and closed the border with Yemen. In Aden the High Commissioner declared an emergency, deported 280 Yemeni, and arrested 57 members of the PSP. A groundswell of protest welled up in the Arab world, from the ranks of the European Left, and at the General Assembly of the United Nations, where a resolution passed demanding an end to the state of emergency, the release of the detainees, and an election forthwith as a step to immediate independence.

The situation in Dhala deteriorated. Any attempt to win the hearts and minds of the tribes through a civil action strategy might take years to prove effective, since to date no one had invested much thought in Dhala. This left military action. On January 1, 1964, the British army launched Operation Nutcracker as the first stage of a cleansing operation that had by March defeated the dissidents.[38] By April, in addition to border incidents, Egyptian-Yemeni planes had raided inside the Federation. Nasser made an emotional speech in San'a, promising to expel the British from all parts of the Arab world. And there was more trouble in Dhala the moment the British slackened their pressure. In the wild mountains, with temperatures of 110 or 120 degrees, without roads or proper intelligence, the British undertook another cleansing operation in April. By June 11, Radforce cleared most of the guerrilla infestation from Dhala. Further operations took place into August against the small guerrilla bands of ten or twelve still filtering across the Yemen frontier. In Aden at least, the grenade explosion was not followed by a terror campaign. In the first four months of 1964, there were no incidents at all, then thirteen in May, and another pause until three October incidents.

In February 1964 Trevaskis flew to London to find that Colonial Secretary Duncan Sandys had grave doubts about promising the Federation independence, even with guarantees for the British base. The Cabinet and the Defense Staff felt such a maneuver would smack of "weakness"; both wanted to be firm. Thus the British army pursued the Radfan campaign. The High Commissioner could do little to offer a case against that of Cairo: "a nationalist rebellion with British troops embattled in defense of federal puppets." In May, Sandys flew in to hear urgent pleas by the Federal Ministers for an independence date. He agreed to hold a conference the next month. By then the journalists could see al-Asnag's rise to power à la Nkrumah. The Federation would be sure to crumble and al-Asnag would move in. The Federalists also saw their position decaying: "You British always betray your friends! . . . You have done it everywhere. We should have listened to Nasser in the first place, when he warned us about what hypocrites you are."[39]

On October 14 the Labour Party won the general election. There was a new Colonial Secretary, Anthony Greenwood. Two days later the Aden elections produced confusing but embarrassing results. The PSP claimed a majority and demanded the release of a former air company official charged with the murders at the airport and his appointment as Chief Minister. Almost all of the Legislative councillors signed a petition to Trevaskis and Greenwood demanding Khalifa's release. The High Commissioner was opposed but the Colonial Secretary was not, and Khalifa was released. A new government was formed under the moderate Seyid Zein Baharoon. The new Labour Government, profoundly anti-imperialist and sympathetic to trade union men, foresaw no Egyptian obstacle to broadening the Aden political base. London wanted swift action to prepare a Commonwealth solution. British socialism would speak directly to Arab socialists. Furthermore, in September 1964, Nasser and King Faisal of Saudi Arabia had agreed to "work for peace in Yemen" so the Egyptians might soon withdraw from Arabia.

Things began to go wrong almost immediately. The Yemeni civil war did not end. Nasser did not give up his interest in South Arabia—"Occupied South Yemen." Al-Asnag did not act like Nkrumah. And the British army efforts in Dhala did not end the NLF's armed struggle. Until far too late, British intelligence forces misjudged the NLF, long thought to be little more than a handful of Egyptian agents carrying out Nasser's assassinations. With no visible political structure like al-Asnag's PSP, with instead small cells of young men with no record or reputation, the NLF conspiracy was never penetrated. Much of the politicizing in the name of the Arab National Movement up-country went unnoticed. In Aden NLF activities began to attract serious notice, but there was no way of proving that an officer in the Federal Army or a clerk at Besse and Company was a member of the organization unless he was caught in an illegal act. The Federal Ministers demanded the dismissal, if not the arrest, of NLF suspects. One, Fadhl Ahmed Salami, was Permanent Secretary to the Minister of Defense, with access to classified material. London, however, sternly discouraged arrests on suspicion alone, so security forces soldiered along in conventional ways with negligible results.

To a degree, then, for months the NLF General Command sent five-men cells into Aden after training in Yemen without attracting the interest of security forces.[40] Agents and liaison people organized up-country where there were few British eyes watching. Long before the airport incident the NLF had 150 men in place in Aden. Even during the most active period of Adenese terrorism, there were no more than 250 full-time NLF men in the city. The Aden commander from October 1963 until May 1965 was Abdullah Fattah Ismail, who then went to Cairo and was replaced by Ali Abdul Alim.[41] And Aden was to be the key to the NLF effort. The Aden state, Crater or Steamer Point or Little Aden, was administratively divided up into local units united under the Aden commander with his four- to seven-man council with a Special Intelligence Section, under Alim until November 1965, and commando units, under Saleh Abdullah Bakais, "Hag Saleh," until the spring of 1967. Outside this closed circle of cells, supplied by contacts in Yemen and through theft and bribery, lay broadening circles of supporters and accomplices. Essentially, however, until nearly the last days of the insurrection, the NLF was a hard core of about two hundred men, replaced if arrested or killed but not enlarged.

Analysis of the strategy of the NLF General Command at the beginning of 1965 shows that its leaders thought the British would not depart unless forced to and in order to stay would attempt to make a deal with anyone. And no one in South Arabia except the NLF could be trusted to spurn such an offer. Al-Asnag and his party were not true socialists. All others, the federal ministers or the sultans or the Aden intellectuals, were pawns in the British game. The General Command believed Britain was vulnerable, a decaying imperial power, that the anticolonial tides ran with them, that Nasser was the wave of the future. There was no real intention to lever the British out by making use of British virtues—although then and later the NLF was delighted to have the British as an opponent—but rather to open the armed struggle and wait for imperial withdrawal. And, from the point of view of the NLF, why not? The British had been withdrawing for a generation. So there were no vast geopolitical considerations, no closely reasoned analysis of Aden and the British posture East of Suez, no real second thoughts: to begin would accelerate an inevitable evacuation, would produce an Arab victory and ease a century of humiliation; in fact, Arab competitors were a greater danger than British imperialists.

Terror increased in the last three months of 1964, with twenty-three incidents in Aden. There were five in January 1965, eleven in February, and twenty-five in March. The long Ma'alla road, with the ugly, pastel concrete boxes on either side, housing British dependents, became, like Ledra Street in Nicosia, Murder Mile. And so it began again: the old familiar paraphenalia of cordon-and-search, road blocks and detention, thuds in the night, and new plane loads of correspondents rushing from Khormakhsar Airport to the bar at the Crystal Palace for word of the latest bomb. During 1965, two hundred and eighty-six incidents cost the lives of fifteen members of the security forces and twenty civilians. With inadequate intelligence, a Special Branch soon decimated by assassination, an Arab-speaking population, and a small, tightly organized opponent capable of fading into the *suq,* the British were badly hampered. No one got around to appointing a single director of intelligence—a step proven vital in Malaya, Cyprus, and Kenya—for twelve months. Conditions in Aden grew worrisome, irritating, occasionally dangerous. As violence there increased, the Labour Government embarked on a "new" policy. Because the Cabinet hoped to reduce the military establishment, eliminate an East-of-Suez role, and concentrate on domestic matters, London did not want a South Arabian "problem" but a swift, progressive solution. Sir Kennedy Trevaskis was replaced by Sir Richard Turnbull, who as Governor of Tanganyika had done a marvelous job during the transition to independence—an inspired application of the Commonwealth Strategy in Labour eyes. Every effort was to be made to find an accommodation between the existing Federal structure and the nationalist opinion represented by al-Asnag, who seemed the key man.

In February, however, al-Asnag had formed the Organization for the Liberation of the Occupied South (OLOS). The British were aggrieved by the refusal of al-Asnag to play the game by Commonwealth rules. Everything the government in London tried, no matter how well intended, crumbled because of inexplicable Middle East reasons. A try at a March Conference in London collapsed in recriminations that left as Prime Minister of the Aden government Abdel Qauwee Mackawee, dedicated to exactly the same program as al-Asnag: an end to the State of Emergency, the release of detainees, full suffrage, swift independence, and negotiations over the military base.[42] Labour ministers came in relays: Denis Healey, Defense Minister, in June, Greenwood arrived again in July. The NLF exploded bombs to welcome him. A London conference in August was attended by an NLF informant so that any Arab concession could lead swiftly to revenge; it collapsed on August 7. In September two constitutional experts, Sir Ralph Home and Sir Gawain Bell, arrived. There were committees and commissions. Lord Bewick emphasized to the Adenese that Labour did not support feudal chieftains. The sultans were incensed. The OLOS was unconvinced. The NLF remained active. In August British Superintendent of Police Harry Barrie and Speaker of the State Legislative Assembly Sir Arthur Charles were assassinated. Two members of the National Assembly urged negotiations with the NLF. Prime Minister Mackawee supported them. On September 25, 1965, the High Commissioner suspended the Aden Constitution.

Mackawee departed for Cairo to join al-Asnag. Neither would play the British game nor would Nasser; nor of course would the NLF, and increasingly Arabs who had done so began to reconsider. In February 1966 Lord Bewick, by then a minister in the Colonial Office, informed the Federal Ministers that Britain would abandon the Aden base in 1968. South Arabia would be independent without the British base, without a defense agreement, and without much prospect of repelling the radical borders hovering in Yemen.

Egypt began to prepare for an expanded terror operation in Aden. The first step was to force a merger of OLOS with the NLF. The Egyptians as well as the British has assumed that the NLF, dependent on Cairo for funds, access to Radio Cairo, training and arms, and certification as a legitimate Arab liberation movement, would be amenable to Nasser's wishes. The Egyptian leadership notified the NLF General Command of its intentions. Scattered from Cairo to Aden, members of the General

Command (in almost every case) reacted with horror. Merger would mean sooner or later the abandonment of the armed revolutionary struggle to Egypt's advantage and to al-Asnag's or to Mackawee's, and the end of revolution in South Arabia.

The NLF had reached the sticking point. For the leadership on the General Command, Nasser's advice had always been paramount. The Egyptians were adamant: merge or face excommunication and an end to aid. Several important NLF leaders, including Taha Muqbil and Ali al-Sallami, felt they had no choice. Emotionally they shrank from denying Nasser; practically they doubted their capacity without Egyptian funds and materiel. Aid from Algeria and Iraq might sift through, but this was doubtful. Several leaders narrowed their sights and went into the new Front for the Liberation of South Yemen (FLOSY). When there was no immediate decision by the General Command commiting the entire movement, the Egyptians lost patience, cut off funds, and restricted NLF people in Cairo. In response the NLF decided to call a party conference.

While these inner-party deliberations were going on, very little revolutionary activity took place and the armed struggle sputtered to a halt. There were only seven operations in Aden during February 1966. The arrest of forty-five NLF people in December 1965 hampered operations, but the main deterrent was the news from Cairo. Finally, Faisal Latif, one of the most important members of the General Command, managed to leave Cairo, reach Beirut, and make his way to South Arabia. In June under his direction, the NLF was partly reorganized. The long-delayed NLF conference was held at Geblah in August 1966. The NLF decided to pursue the revolutionary struggle in its own way, and an NLF memo to that effect was sent to Cairo. The Egyptians continued to back only FLOSY. Radio Cairo and Radio San'a made quite clear the disapproval of the orthodox Arab revolutionary world. There was no diplomatic aid or comfort, no secret flow of arms and funds, no kind words, but, except for the restriction of NLF people in Cairo, no open repression.

The strains between al-Asnag and the General Command in Aden had split the ATUC by the end of 1965. On January 10-12, 1966, several NLF people held a series of discussions with al-Asnag. All were later detained by the British. (Informers—toads in black bags stalking down the lines of suspects—soon became an accepted part of the British security operation.) On January 16 the Popular Organization of Revolutionary Forces (PORF) appeared on the scene. Under the leadership of Mohammed Maj'ali, later killed in a car accident, PORF was very much an Egyptian-made counterpart to the NLF, less a creature of al-Asnag and FLOSY than a well-armed, well-trained commando unit operating for Egyptian purposes. During much of 1966, with the trauma of excommunication gradually easing, the NLF and PORF concentrated on British and Arab "informers" rather than each other. Once the Defense White Paper on February 22, 1966, appeared—"South Arabia is due to become independent by 1968, and we do not think it appropriate that we should maintain defense facilities there after that happens"—[43] FLOSY-PORF and the NLF recognized that the crucial period had begun and that the other was as great a threat as the British. An open break was postponed month by month during 1966 in an atmosphere thick with suspicion.

The NLF continued to direct the armed struggle down two complementary paths. In Aden the cells pushed the terror campaign: parcel bombs were mailed, explosive charges went off indiscriminately, rocket launchers and mortars permitted long distance attacks, Land Rovers were ambushed. The most chilling NLF weapon, however, was simple murder. Special targets were British army personnel and Special Branch police but others were cut down as well. During 1966, the sum total of victims killed, seventeen, was, given all, a short butcher's bill; but the impact of murder in the morning mail or through an open window poisoned the atmosphere. Up-country during 1966 the NLF raised the stakes slightly, but tribal dissidence was still at a low level. While actual incidents were down from 1,372 to 868, British casualty figures were up from 71 to 111. Those loyal to the sultans were often too incompetent or too prudent to match the dissidents. The British had to take up the slack. On July 28 in Mukalla, Colonel J. W. G. Grey, Commander of the Hadrami Bedouin Legion of the Eastern Arab Protectorate, was shot and mortally wounded by one of his own men. It was a troubling omen.

The logic of abandoning the sultans, old promises aside, began to be accepted in many British quarters. The albatross of an alliance with feudalism was particularly objectionable to the Labour Party. And the sultans seemed unwilling or unable to defend themselves and their interests. London felt there must be a more reasonable base for a future government. But efforts to lure either al-Asnag or Mackawee into preprogrammed Commonwealth roles had foundered. In February 1966 the Cabinet had made it clear that Britain would evacuate in 1968 and had no interest in the base. Apparently there was some hope that this self-denial would prod the Arab nationalists toward an accommodation, but none of them felt much would be gained from it. The sultans began to make their own arrangements. Federal institutions suffered a crisis of morale. The High Commissioner's position grew increasingly more difficult. Every opening proposed by the British or by the Federal authorities brought an emphatic veto from the exiled Mackawee. Mackawee, a late convert to radicalism, was supposedly the moderate nationalist, but in December he even opposed the United Nations Trusteeship Committee decision to send a mission to South Arabia. FLOSY wanted immediate evacuation of the British and immediate recognition of its own position as the legitimate government.

By the end of 1966 the Federal government was little more than a caretaker administration going through the motions in an atmosphere of rising anxiety. There was only a little hope that the South Arabian Army would hold firm. Nearly everyone suspected the officers' loyalty to the Federation. No one knew what the soldiers thought; no one knew what the British would do next. But clearly something had to be done. And somehow there was still some hope in London. Foreign Minister George Brown seemed to feel that the United Nations mission offered a means to bring the exiled nationalists back into a political dialogue. If a direct Commonwealth strategy had aborted, there was still hope for a compromise of sorts. After all, in Palestine the UN had rescued British policy.

There never was a chance. Egypt announced that FLOSY was the sole representative of the people of South Arabia. The NLF denied both this and the legitimacy of the Federal government. The Federal government charged that the three-man UN mission was packed in favor of the radicals. The mission arrived in the midst of a general strike and a continuing terror compaign that produced seventy incidents the first day, and its three diplomats became involved in misunderstandings and displays of temper. Back at the United Nations, they blamed their troubles on the British, who thus received nothing but a bad name from this last hope of compromise.

The rivalry between FLOSY and the NLF finally became open war. On January 19, 1967, the annual general strike against the British occupation, though opposed by Radio Cairo, Radio San'a, and FLOSY, was ordered by the NLF. Its success revealed how serious a competitor the NLF had become, even in FLOSY's core areas. A little civil war began that by April had cost FLOSY forty-one men and the NLF ten, according to General Command estimates. In February three of Mackawee's four children were killed by a "warning" time-bomb detonated at his house by still unknown assassins. On the last day of the month, a bomb exploded in a flat in Ma'alla during a dinner party, killing two British women and wounding other guests. The High Commissioner suggested that children should not come out to Aden for the Easter holidays. Small arms fire formed a background to conversation in Crater, and the toll of assassinations picked up during March. The NLF escalated the war of attrition against FLOSY until an April truce. The British could do less and less on the spot. George Brown sent out Lord Shackleton, Minister without Portfolio, who arrived on April 12. He would talk with anyone;

but no one would talk. Lord Shackleton recommended only that Sir Richard Turnbull be replaced. At last Labour recognized that their ideological inclinations had led them astray. South Arabia was not the Gold Coast or Tanganyika.

Labour's Miscalculations

The Labour Cabinet had intended to play out the Gold Coast scenario in South Arabia. There was, London felt, no overwhelming strategic reason to remain in Aden since the entire East-of-Suez establishment was to be dismantled. An independent, if radical, Arab government in South Arabia would not necessarily be opposed to Western interests. The alternative possibilities, Egyptian-Russian forces in Aden or revolution on the edge of the Gulf, would not present a problem if the Gold Coast approach worked. Those with serious interests in the area—the Saudis, the Gulf sultans, the Americans, and the oil companies, not to mention the South Arabian sultans—were alarmed at the prospect, but Labour was determined and confident. Seldom has a relatively complex historical analogy proven so inept.

The Labour analogy assumed that the various actors in South Arabia could be labeled in British terms and assigned British motives. Trade unions were good, sultans were bad. Arab socialists, however, were not British socialists, and the Middle East was not subject to easy ideological explanation. The first basic factor glossed over was that after 1956 no Arab wanted any accommodation with the Treaty Empire unless it was a crucial matter of self-preservation: the British touch tainted. Only those sufficiently incompetent, obviously unfashionable, and temptingly wealthy needed the British to defend their interests. The radical Arabs wanted the British out and South Arabia restructured economically, politically, and socially. And they wanted this done on a foundation built on a British humiliation. Any segment of Arab nationalist opinion advocating a policy less militant than Egypt, the revolutionary bellwether, would be excommunicated as a puppet of imperialism. The NLF could be *more* extreme, but only those who had no alternative but to cast their lot with the British could be less militant. The supposedly magical wand of legitimacy that had touched Nehru, Nkrumah, and the others, the whole band of former felons and former terrorists, would in the Arab case kill the supposed beneficiary. Those who attempted to explain Arab reality to the new government had dossiers that failed to impress Labour, imperialists, Arabists, specialists of the wrong sort. The analysis accepted by the Cabinet was based on ideological premises and definitions that were not only naive but inapplicable. Sir Richard Turnbull was sent to do the impossible and was allowed to do nothing else.

Once it was shown that "ideology" had led Labour astray, he was replaced by a new man sent in with pragmatic instructions: cut Britain's South Arabian losses, talk to anyone, make any arrangement, but get Britain out.

The Labour Party could not be faulted for the Federal structure for that was fashioned by the Arabists of the Aden Secretariat and bought and expanded by their superiors in London. Nor could the good will and reasonableness of the Labour Cabinet be questioned in their efforts to find a middle ground between the Federation and Arab nationalist opinion. To be told that no such site existed and to make the discovery are quite different matters. Nor was Labour's hope that a traditional Commonwealth strategy would prove effective in what appeared to be a traditional colonial problem unreasonable—except in the Middle East of the sixties. The game played by the Arab nationalists *required* an Arab victory and a British humiliation. Neither the NLF nor FLOSY-Cairo wanted an easy transition from Treaty Empire to independence. Thus, each British offer spurned was recorded as an Arab tactical victory bestowing credits recognized by every Arab in every Middle East *suq* where Radio Cairo blared forth the latest news from occupied South Yemen. If the federal solution was too little and too late, it had been based, properly or improperly, on certain South Arabian realities and historical commitments. The Labour approach had made incorrect assumptions. There were no reasonable Arab moderates to play the Commonwealth game. Gresham's Law of Arab Politics guaranteed that the radicals would force out the moderates, at gunpoint if need be. The only question was who among the competitors was the most revolutionary and effective. So, in 1966 and 1967 Arab politics became a competition in assassination to gain faith and credit through anti-imperial deeds. And, then, since revolutions are not won on faith and credit alone, the assassins turned on one another to assure that triumph would not go to the "wrong" revolutionary.

With the sound of gunfire rattling offstage, Sir Humphrey Trevelyan arrived in Aden on May 20, 1967, to take up his duties as High Commissioner, surely one of the least attractive offices within the gift of the Crown. Harold Macmillan had indicated as much a few days before: "Poor man, poor man." The poor man had a simple brief:

> My task was to evacuate the British forces and their stores in peace, including the large Middle East Headquarters, and, if possible, leave behind an independent Government which could assure peace and stability in the tiny country of South Arabia . . . The British had had such good intentions, but things had gone badly wrong. . . . In May

1967 it was a mistake to look back. . . . Our job was somehow to untie the knot and release ourselves without disaster.[44]

The new High Commissioner's arrival was recognized by FLOSY and the NLF for exactly what it was, the beginning of the end, but neither believed the British would be gone by January. The NLF felt it was time to call in some of the up-country credit that had been three years in the organizing. Hag Saleh left Aden and slipped into the Hadhramaut. The NLF did not want to allow the British or the sultans an opportunity of detaching the Eastern Protectorates from the successor state. Other NLF people in the Western Protectorates, and particularly Lahej, also prepared for the moment when British disengagement would be far enough along for them to pounce. The major opponent to NLF ambitions, once the British were beyond call, would be the Federal Army. On June 1 it had merged with the Federal Guard to form the South Arabian Army; but both the new Army and the South Arabian Armed Police were rent with tribal dissidence and had been penetrated by the NLF. NLF agents up-country watched army politics for signs of shifts; the unfriendly Aulaqui made up a third of the army and might go for FLOSY or even defend the Federation. In the meantime, the war with FLOSY in the streets of Crater and Ma'alla was renewed.

News of the Israeli victory in the Six Day War in June 1967 stunned all Arabs. Frustrated and bitter, certain of British collusion, they sought a victim. There were strikes and demonstrations. Jewish property was looted and burned. The Indians and Somalis began to leave the city. On June 20 the new South Arabian Army mutinied over what appeared to be disciplinary action taken against four insubordinate colonels. The mutiny was the result of tribal jealousies and NLF connivance.[45] The NLF, fearful that the expelled men might signal a sweep against men loyal to their party, urged violence on the army and police. Given the tense atmosphere, neither needed much encouragement. Police mutineers seized arms and turned them on a detachment of the Royal Corps of Transportation driving past, killing eight British soldiers and wounding eight more. Rumors spread that the entire Army was rising against the British. The Armed Police detachment in the nearby Federal capital of al-Ittihad ran amok, smashing windows and tearing down flags. A mutinous battalion was reported moving on Aden.

The most disastrous event occurred in Crater. British patrols sent into the area without proper warning were ambushed by policemen under the impression that they were to be attacked. Only one man in the two British Land Rovers escaped alive. A rescue mission reached the site of the ambush but withdrew. The British soldiers who had stayed in the area were attacked and killed. A Sioux helicopter was shot down. FLOSY and

NLF men piled into the streets carrying weapons, Molotov cocktails, and party flags. The NLF men under Abdul Nabi Madram and Ali Salim Yaffi sought not only to keep the British out but also to intimidate the FLOSY forces. Another British column of three armored vehicles was forced to withdraw under heavy fire. A third attempt to reach the bodies and the ambush site also failed.

All British forces withdrew from Crater, leaving the Arabs the town and the bodies of thirteen British officers and men. The British army wanted to go directly back into Crater. Such a course of action might have disastrous repercussions up-country where British civilians still worked, at least so assumed those farther from the firing. The decision was to wait. The Federal Army waited as well, since its officers refused to move into Crater. If the South Arabian Army reoccupied Crater on behalf of the British—"which it could easily do—it would lose its popularity and disintegrate. Better to say to the British, 'It is beyond our capacity to re-capture Crater, beyond the capability of the entire Aden Police and South Arabian Army. Despite the fact that we shall have to rule it eventually *you* will have to capture it.' "[46] So NLF flags flew unchallenged over Crater.

The control was not achieved without cost. Madram, credited with thirty-eight "hits" in the campaign of attrition by assassination, grew too confident or too careless. According to NLF reports, he walked into a FLOSY group under Fuad Khalifa near a Crater hotel late on the evening of June 20 and was gunned down. His death did not reverse the tide, despite FLOSY strength in the Armed Police and stockpiles of arms, ammunition, and Russian grenades. The NLF kept control of the streets. Old scores against FLOSY men were paid off. Business ceased. The Armed Police maintained order by remaining in their barracks. Watching from the lip of Main Pass down into Crater, the British army could do no more than exchange shots with the besieged, flag-decked city.

Finally on the evening of July 3, the Argyll and Sutherlander Highlanders, under Lieutenant-Colonel Colin Mitchell, soon to be known to the press as Mad Mitch, in Operation Sterling Castle reoccupied Crater so efficiently that there was almost no organized opposition. At dawn on July 4 Crater awoke to Reveille by the Pipes and Drums on the roof of the Educational Institute. One Arab was shot for refusing to halt. The next night the Argylls assumed complete control of the town. Colonel Mitchell intended such control to be firm: "They know if they start any trouble, we will blow their bloody heads off."[47] The real trouble could not be cured so easily. The Armed Police could not be punished without destroying the force, so en masse they were forgiven. The South Arabian Army could not be reorganized or the mutineers punished without destroying the last prop. Apologies were accepted and in theory everything returned to normal.

Trevelyan tried to let Hassan Ali Bayoomi attempt to form a broad-based government, but it collapsed in recriminations and resignations. Trevelyan then flew to New York in hopes that the United Nations mission might be used as a go-between. The only light in the gloom was the NLF agreement on July 25 to discuss matters with the UN mission. What the NLF wanted was legitimization as the successor to the federal structure. When it became clear that the UN mission and the British still had illusions about a broad-base, the NLF withdrew its offer. On August 1 at 5 P.M. NLF commandos opened a new offensive in Aden with a two-inch mortar bomb attack on the Argyll's command post in the Charter Bank.

By August even the Auluquis in the South Arabian Army were re-evaluating their interests. The NLF victory in the Crater siege had concentrated many minds. The continued Crater offensive during August that resulted in five Argylls killed and eighteen wounded proved growing NLF strength. By September 1 Mad Mitch and the Argylls felt they had the situation well in hand: six weeks until mid-October without a single incident. The NLF began playing the up-country cards one after another. In June FLOSY had tried to move its Liberation Army out of Yemen; but both the NLF and the South Arabian Army for contradictory purposes had opposed that intrusion. Once the British began pulling out on June 30, the NLF moved in to replace them. The South Arabian Army by then was determined to take absolutely no stand on any point until the ultimate victor could be determined.

One after another the Federation's towns fell to local military garrisons, whose officers turned them over to waiting NLF agents. The NLF flag—black, white, and red with a blue triangle—was raised, the sultan and his relatives departed for Saudi Arabia or Yemen, and the local cadres moved on to the next target.[48] By the end of August the NLF controlled twelve federal states and sat on the boundary of Aden State. The shell of the Federal Government collapsed; and on September 3, after a hurried flight to London, Trevelyan announced that he was ready to negotiate directly with the nationalists. The NLF were more concerned with taking over the Eastern Protectorates before the British could devise some separatist solution. By October the NLF were in control of the entire area and the Eastern sultans, like the Western, had fled.

By then a great deal had changed elsewhere. The British began reducing the military establishment on August 25. The announced schedule was full withdrawal by January 9, 1968. This meant, Trevelyan's appeal of September 5 aside, that the NLF General Command had four months to liquidate FLOSY strength in Aden. Until the last, the

NLF suspected that, despite quiet advice to the contrary, the British would make a deal with FLOSY. On September 2, twenty-five miles up the coast at Zinjibar, capital of the Fadhli state, Qahatan Ashaabi announced at a press conference that the NLF was willing to talk about the means of taking power and nothing more. And this appeared all that was left to do: except mop up FLOSY. Where possible, as in Little Aden on September 12, the NLF simply moved in when the British Army evacuated. Some areas, however, were disputed ground. The fighting began as the NLF cadres, supported by tribal formations eager for the kill, moved south from Lahej into FLOSY positions at Sheikh Othman and Mansoura. Unlike the sultans, the FLOSY men could not flee, and many still hoped a military victory might turn the NLF tide. This was an illusion. PORF men began to defect. The South Arabian Army intervened where necessary on the side of the NLF. Finally some Army leaders urged a cease-fire. For tactical reasons the NLF accepted the truce in Sheikh Othman.

Under pressure from Cairo and within the Army, the NLF reluctantly agreed to send a delegation to Egypt to discuss ending the feud with FLOSY. On October 7 Qahatan Ashaabi and Faisal Latif arrived in Cairo. For a month, the three-cornered discussions continued without results. In Aden assassins barred from Crater and allowed free run of the Arab sections of Steamer Point picked off any "targets" foolish enough to stray outside the control line. Essentially the NLF was stalling in Cairo, where an impending agreement was reported, until the time for the final dash into Aden. The NLF General Command *was* willing to make a deal, to please Nasser, but the conditions were too stiff for FLOSY. The Cairo talks kept influential "neutral" officers in the South Arabian Army in line and lulled the FLOSY men. On November 2 George Brown announced in the Commons that the evacuation schedule had been altered and British troops would be out by the end of the month. The NLF General Command felt that "by the end of the month" meant the time for talking had ended. In any case the PORF commandos, acting independently of FLOSY, were again firing on NLF people.

The next day NLF command units began moving into FLOSY-PORF-controlled areas. The assassination teams were out in force. In two days fifty bodies were picked up in the streets, and hundreds were wounded. Gunmen, often with list in hand, went from door to door. Arab police officers were kidnapped and killed, and the force withdrew into inactivity. The South Arabian Army was no longer neutral. Army Saladin armored cars fired .76mm rounds into FLOSY gun positions and Army units rounded up FLOSY men. Within another twenty-four hours, it was apparent that FLOSY was smashed. Several hundred were killed or wounded. The NLF had over one thousand in detention and the Army another seven hundred. On November 7 George Brown told the Commons that the NLF had won. Its General Command was ready at last to talk to the British. On November 14 Lord Shackleton was designated as the chief of the British delegation that would open talks with the NLF in Geneva on November 21.

The Geneva talks in no way resembled that final ritual of the colonial rites of passage. There was no glow of mutual self-congratulations, a combination of end of term and the passing of the torch. There would be no joint ritual on the lawn with lowered flags and Scot pipers. The atmosphere at Geneva was correct but less than cordial. The Arabs on the other side of the conference table had ordered assassination attacks on British forces less than a week before. Yet, at last, a conference worked. Most of the outstanding problems were solved by November 29. This last-minute agreement in Geneva meant that someone would be in Aden to take over. On November 30 Qahatan Ashaabi flew into Khormaksar just in time to be on hand at midnight when the People's Republic of Southern Yemen was born.

Why the NLF Succeeded

The NLF armed struggle, declared in October 1963 and recognized by the British with the declaration of the Emergency on December 10, was over. The British were gone. FLOSY's cadres were dead, in prison, or in exile, and al-Asnag's prospects of future power were dim. The sultans were gone. The old politicians of the Federation were gone. Mackawee was gone. The Adenese elite were sullen and ineffectual. There was no competitor but anarchy, no problem but penury. Neither would prove as amenable to NLF strategy as had the party's revolutionary competitors or colonial opponents but neither was a new enemy in South Arabia. In December 1967 the NLF was euphoric over the victory, the struggle that would become legend, subject of ballad and fantasy, memorialized in postage stamps and street names. It was a victory that none could deny.

Not surprisingly, the British did deny any such "victory" by the NLF. The idea that a revolt resulting in the death of only fifty-seven members of the British security forces and an additional eighteen British civilians in the key Aden battle area could force a major power to accept the rebels' aspirations was ludicrous. In retrospect the whole South Arabian Emergency seemed minor league indeed: in Aden only 2,096 killed and wounded from December 1963 through October 1967, including all the victims of the FLOSY-NLF clashes; and up-country British forces lost only 57 killed and 235 wounded. This was hardly a major revolt, not even an effective terror campaign: "In Aden the thugs were hardly worthy of the name terrorist and most of their energies were devoted to intimidating the civilian Arab population."⁴⁹ Whitehall knew quite well that the British evacuation had not been forced by the NLF but was a matter of high strategy and low sterling balances.

No one of any great importance credited the NLF with more than creating a background noise of flak and stringing together a record of brutal murders. This was not quite true. From the first, and certainly after the decision not to merge with FLOSY, the NLF prevented any solution but one on their terms. They anticipated that it might take a decade of harassment before the British withdrew. Harassment alone would not win the war, but the NLF General Command was confident that they had the capacity to wage such an armed struggle for a decade. During that decade the Arab national revolution would arrive in South Arabia as the era of imperialism ebbed. Then, as they had elsewhere, the British would, for good British reasons, withdraw, NLF strategy was to reinforce the rise of extreme Arab nationalism, even at the risk of civil war, and to harass the British. In pursuit of the former, their revolutionary rhetoric tended to give the British reason to stay rather than go. Nasser, at least in 1954, indicated that Anglo-Arab relations would blossom after evacuation of the Suez Canal Zone, but in South Arabia the NLF insisted that there could be no satisfactory relations between the Arab masses and the imperialists. There could be no face-saving Commonwealth compromise or a deal on the base or even promises for the future. The NLF could not and did not want to show that it was to British advantage to go, only that it was disadvantageously expensive to stay and suffer.

The British faced, as they had in Malaya, in Palestine, and seemingly for so long in Cyprus, an opponent who wanted to leave the system, that proposed an alternative regime endangering British security and British prestige. The NLF could only be beaten down, not absorbed or coopted. Its containment if not eradication was within British capacities as a military venture. Such an exercise, divorced from a parallel political effort, would be open-ended, unless there was to be another Miracle of Zurich. The federal structure was not a viable alternative and no representative Arabs could risk a British alignment. Still, if Aden were needed it could have been kept, the harassment tolerated, and general Arab distaste ignored. Yet to send in the army, when the army was supposedly being cut in size, to invest large sums of money, when sterling was under pressure, and to maintain a major presence East of Suez, when Britain's future lay in Europe, seemed unreasonable options to the Labour government.

The NLF had nothing to do with these British options but a great deal to do with putting a price on the South Arabian position that Britain increasingly was only willing to maintain either on credit or on the cheap. For the British, South Arabia was no longer worth even the small price asked by the NLF. That it was really a low price and that those who balked did so for reasons far removed from South Arabia does not deny that it *was* asked. And, for the NLF and South Arabia, in the long run that was all that mattered. The British might not have been driven into the sea literally; but after November 30, 1967, they were nowhere to be found except in the Embassy accredited to the People's Republic of Southern Yemen.

PART THREE

On Revolt: Matrix, Models, and a Template

Britain has nothing to learn from anybody about the task of bringing progress, freedom, and self-government to the emerging people.
                    —The Times, *October 3, 1956*

Anti-British banners held aloft by angry Egyptians in Ismailia Square during a demonstration,
November 16, 1951.

7 A Generation of Violent Dialogue: The Evolving British Matrix

The supremely important fact about the history of the last years of the British Empire is that freedom, independence, self-government, membership of the United Nations, were granted to six hundred and fifty million people in twenty-six different countries without a shot being fired.
—Rt. Hon. Philip Noel-Baker, M.P.,
14 July 1969

When the next generation passes, the memory of Murder Mile and the Acre gallows will fade back into the small print of imperial history books, recalled in Britain by memorial plaques in parish churches and by old soldiers. What will remain remarkable about the generation of imperial dissolution, the great watershed of devolution, will almost certainly be that nothing so became the Empire as its passing. Millions upon millions of people passed through the ritual of the Commonwealth solution; colony after colony, ready or not, lowered the old flag and raised a new banner emblazoned with the devices of the future. Mostly the generation was splendid; mostly, for there had been those rebels against the Crown who could not be coopted or manipulated by the strategy of devolution, who would not play the Commonwealth game, who did fire shots.

That the Commonwealth Strategy did not work everywhere was mainly, the British assumed, because the imperial power was responsible either for adjusting conflicting claims, those of the Arabs and the Jews or the Greeks and Turks, or for eliminating unrepresentative claimants, the Communists in Malaya or the Mau Mau in Kenya. An imperial responsibility, no less than devolution, required that there be no retreat before the violent ambitions of a minority or in the face of an illicit effort by the few to grab what could not be granted. This responsibility was more keenly felt when British strategic interest might be at stake as well. Those gunmen and terrorists who sought power outside the Commonwealth route were without legitimacy. Thus, for the British a revolt opens not with bombs but with the surfacing of a conflict over legitimacy, a conflict that in most cases has had a long troubled history, a history cherished by the rebel and ignored or denied by the British.

The reaction to the rebel's aspirations, no matter what the circumstances, is outraged indignation. The rebel is an alien and evil man, motivated by personal ambitions and often deluded by an imported ideology, who uses terror to acquire support, a man outside the law, outside common decency. The full majesty of historically recognized, internationally accepted, *legitimate* authority is turned on the little band of assassins. In the long run legitimacy for rebels can be won only by force or by concession. Some of the illegitimate claimants could be coopted by means of the Commonwealth Strategy as had the Irish in 1921; but for other rebels there was nothing but repression.

Regularly after 1944, in some foreign corner or another, Britain pursued an anti-insurgency campaign. Colonial officials, career officers, and policemen might, and if they were keen usually did, serve in several emergencies. Like spirits of revolts past, some appear in each new campaign, a little grayer, a little wiser, a little further up the ladder. The British knew of, and continued to have their knowledge reinforced by, the dangers and costs of revolts and the means to avoid such conflicts. From experience they learned the tactics of anti-insurgency, the cost of an emergency, the importance of political concessions, and the means to manipulate the Commonwealth Strategy. The Cabinet discovered the cost of staying or getting out. And yet, every time a revolt began, the British were taken by surprise, were shocked, outraged, indignant.

Only rarely did the authorities, either on the spot or in London, foresee the possibility of an armed revolt. Conditions the potential rebels found intolerable, that created deep frustration and that could not be ameliorated except through violence, did not appear so to the British. The latter often could not conceive of aspirations different from their own.

In Palestine the British simply did not understand the impact of the holocaust and the depth of Jewish agony nor could they accept the charge made against them of collusion with genocide. In the Gold Coast the motive of the mob, political power, went far beyond the everyday issues of colonial politics. The British had not dreamed that such a demon would be raised in the colony for decades. In Malaya the MCP revolt was launched not from the depths of despair but from the high ground of ideological certainty. Native Chinese ambition there was emboldened with a vision of a communist future. In this case the British were more surprised that the MCP dared to revolt than that they had aspirations. In Kenya European settlers and local observers feared a revolt but had not anticipated one. Thus, although after mid-1952 following policies that almost insured that a Kikuyu "revolt" would take place, there was still surprise in Nairobi at the extent of Kikuyu alienation, and in London the new emergency was entirely unanticipated. In Egypt no one feared a "revolt" and few were surprised by the fedayeen forays, nor was the accommodation, another treaty, novel. What came as a bitter surprise was the Suez humiliation, but that fell largely outside colonial considerations. Long after the Cypriot Emergency was over, British spokesmen insisted that Enosis was and always had been an artificial issue exploited by agitators. By refusing even to consider the matter, the British, knowing what the Greeks really wanted, set a boundary to nationalism that someone sooner or later would cross, as Grivas did. By the time of the South Arabian misadventures, Britain should have been beyond surprise at the ambitions of radical Arabs. But, although Radio Cairo reached into the hills of Dhala, the British continued to hope that the old ways and old forms would work with the new Arabs and were indignant when they did not.

In some cases the potential rebel intended to revolt no matter what accommodation was offered; but there at least the British might have been fore-armed. Even if the rebels represented alien strains within the Empire, the possibility remains that a more perceptive eye would have uncovered the frustration and suggested an alternative to repression. To be fair, it is difficult to see how London, heeding Cassandra, could or would have acted differently in most cases. The rebels usually felt impelled to revolt; a nonviolent dialogue no longer offered them anything. In Palestine the whole direction of British Middle East policies since 1939 precluded undue concessions to the Zionists; and for the men of the Irgun no concession, however generous, would do. In Malaya the MCP's conviction that victory was certain would probably have been unshaken and the British would have been able to do little to convince them to draw back. In Kenya some realization of the nature of the most immediate Kikuyu grievances might have allowed time for a Gold Coast to evolve; but again, given the settlers' attitudes, perhaps the necessary concessions were out of the question. In Cyprus the British might have taken Enosis seriously enough to point out publicly the international complications that might ensue and the requirements of British security. But would the patriots have listened? And no concession would have swerved the Arabs in Cairo and Aden from their course. Almost nowhere, then, except perhaps in Kenya, would a dash of prescience have greatly altered the situation, for the rebels wanted to rise in arms for purposes quite beyond the capacity of the British to concede.

Usually the closer the individual was to the scene of action on the eve of trouble, the more likely the chance of error, the failure to perceive change. Those who knew most, often saw least. The Man Who Knew the Natives often missed the impact of modernization or the influence of new ideas. Often he had learned his job and about the natives on the spot, learning the rare and esoteric languages of the bush, acquiring detailed and extensive anthropological data, fashioning a career on extended tours. But the "natives" in Tel Aviv or Nicosia were quite different. And elsewhere the attractions of education and the appeal of Western technology wrought swift changes, stirred "unnative" ambitions, and tilted the familiar into new and not always visible patterns without ever showing the British on the spot a new face. And when the face did appear above ill-fitting white collar and obscure school tie, few realized just how profound the change and how limited the old means of control. Even when that control crumbled, there was only limited understanding of what had gone wrong.

> In Aden the thugs were hardly worthy of the name terrorist and most of their energies were devoted to intimidating the civilian Arab population. This led to riots, strikes, go-slows, non-co-operating, civil disobedience and general bloody-mindedness. Their role was to bring the Federal Government into disrepute, frustrate progress towards a stable South Arabia, create a void for later foreign influence (Egyptian and Russian), give the impression that the British were being 'driven out' of Aden by superior forces and generally undermine what was left of our reputation in the Persian Gulf. Upcountry, where the rural dissident could well be brave and resourceful, it was a different picture, perhaps more reminiscent of the Pathan on the old North-West Frontier of India.[1]

And yet those thugs in Aden did "drive out" the British for reasons that a decade before few who knew the natives would have credited.

In carrying on the imperial dialogue the British often talked without listening, looked at events without seeing. As the years passed, potential rebels turned to a more lethal dialogue. Mass nonviolence, the politics of confrontation, and the tactics of direct action, first in Asia and then in Africa, not only caught the British by surprise, but also finally caught their attention. The British monologue died down and the new native voices of the Gold Coast or Egypt could be heard. If the means of interrupting the monologue was illegitimate, Mau Mau oathings or Grivas' bombs, or the time to attract attention too short, Palestine in 1944, or if the rebels did not care to talk, usually the case, Britain was surprised at the new form of communication: a revolt in the hands of natives no one ever knew.

Surprise at the lethal dialogue was followed by shock that rebels had turned to violence when means of accommodation abounded, when grievances were not legitimate, when the mass of decent people disapproved. Without exception, the first analysis on the spot and then in London was that the revolt was the work of a tiny disgruntled minority, dependent on support achieved by coercion or intimidation or violence.

This British analysis was almost always in part correct. Revolts, certainly at the beginning, *are* the work of a tiny handful of men acting in the name of the masses, who of course cannot be polled. The Irgun, EOKA, the Egyptian fedayeen, and the NLF were small numerically and remained so until the end. But the British believed that because the revolutionary organization was small it was unrepresentative. And this was usually true. The Emergency in Kenya was as much a Kikuyu civil war as an armed insurrection; the Irgun were a self-confessed minority in a Jewish community that in turn was a minority in Palestine; the Communists in the jungles of Malaya were supported by less than a majority of the Chinese, another minority. Most revolutionary movements, where reasonable estimate is possible, have been led by a tiny minority and actively, or passively, supported by less than a substantial majority. Often the rebels must coerce or eliminate the loyalists. In South Arabia, for example, more Arabs were killed by the rebels than by British security forces. So the British were quite right: the rebels were a minority with limited active support and probably limited support of any kind. Still, from the first the British recognized that some, and usually vital, support did exist, that information and intelligence about the rebels was difficult to acquire, and that public expressions of gratitude toward the British were limited.

The obvious conclusion was that the minority was intimidating the majority. But, that rebel support results from intimidation does not logically follow. Many Jews in Palestine disapproved of the Irgun's campaign but did not oppose it. Many wanted to be neither informer nor advocate. Much the same was true of the Greek Cypriots, where many "average" men who were not organized into EOKA and did not advocate violence to achieve Enosis avoided active loyalist roles. Much if not all the mass seems to prefer the quiet life. This neutrality, even a slightly benign neutrality, however, is all a rebel needs. A government needs more: if the rebel continues to exist, he wins; but a government must govern, must win. The challenge for the government is to woo the vast apolitical audience only marginally interested in "politics." Yet their passivity is a British loss and a rebel gain. Not only has the dialogue been broken by violence but also the medium of order—the acquiescence of the mass—becomes suspect.

The British, denied the active support of the majority they had long assumed they possessed, accepted the fact that only through force could the rebels achieve toleration; force, therefore, would have to be a rebel weapon of mobilization. This often was the case. Neither EOKA nor the MCP nor the Kikuyu bothered to pretend that they were not executing traitors and informers; rather they spread the word. In British eyes such groups were merely gangs using terror to coerce public support. "Everyone is EOKA" is no more than a cruel and crude bit of propaganda, "a mafia-like vendetta by a fascist gang of murderers who managed to gain the support only of the toughs and the young."[2]

What many observers in Cyprus, and elsewhere during colonial troubles, failed to realize is that this British attitude is not counterpropaganda, but an article of faith. The British believe and so act. Trust in the "real" people is maintained and outrageous risks are taken because of it. The valet's slipping the bomb in Lord Harding's bed was by no means a unique betrayal of that trust. There were repeated betrayals. Yet everywhere, from Malaya to Aden, potentially disloyal servants were kept, often to the last day and the ultimate betrayal. Even the frantic settlers in Kenya wanted "to kill every Kikuyu but ours." Because British authority is legitimate, all good men and true will rally about in opposition to the illicit pretenders, unless so prevented by violence.

The British of course had to stand for something more than just being against sin. The simple legitimacy of previous possession of power is insufficient once the old dialogue has broken down and the violence begun. To stand behind the banners of imperialism and the primacy of British interests was not a very satisfactory posture. So the British stood for order, decency, fair play, good government, civilization, justice and law, and occasionally Christianity if appropriate. What Britain did not stand for was immediate independence and the placing of native interests over those of Britain. This was the nationalist program and it had great charm. For the British to insist that immediate independence would be disastrous and that Britain could do more for the natives than they could do for themselves did not have the same appeal. The rebels had to be shown as men who would use proud slogans for low purposes or wave the national banner and sell the nation abroad.

British Misperceptions

Thus, instead of nationalists the rebels are illegitimate pretenders to power that they intend to misuse, men who have gone beyond foolishness into criminal knavery. If the revolt is absolutely illegitimate, totally without moral justification, led by men without scruple or decency, then obviously it is easier to oppose naked evil and more difficult to take tea with a terrorist or accept a criminal into the palace. Much more important, it is far easier to seek out and destroy evil. So, from the start the leadership of the revolt is defined simply as evil, as well as alien. And the more effective the label, the more likely that the establishment of order will be pursued with maximum force. The "cause," as perceived by the British, that led to open revolt must also be alien, spurious. While some nationalists required the slow process of institution-building within the Empire and accepted the British national model, whether appropriate or not, having no other, the rebels did not. They felt no need for British models and found little value in a Commonwealth dialogue in British terms. Some of the non-British models proved of marginal utility, some had been influenced by the British example, but all—Zionism, Communism, or Hellenism—were alien to Empire.

The most alien of all enemies of Empire were the Mau Mau, an atavistic descent into savagery, absolutely illegitimate in political terms. The toll of Mau Mau killed, the mass detentions, resettlements, and imprisonments could more easily be undertaken in light of the horror of the oath and the brutality of the massacres. No one seemed particularly surprised that over a thousand Mau Mau were executed in comparison to only eight Irgun members during the Palestine Emergency. No matter what the provocation, it was hard for the British to kill Jews. Much the same was true in Cyprus, where the British were fond of the Greeks and frustrated that EOKA could not see where their struggle for Enosis was leading. The British were not fond of the Communist Chinese in Malaya. They believed that an international communist conspiracy led by Chinese and threatening British security and the future of Malayan development was illegitimate. The Chinese were not mad, as were the Mau Mau, but they had been converted to an alien ideology. So, too, in Malaya there was maximum force: detentions and arrests, deprogramming camps, wholesale movement of population, and a huge toll of dead terrorists, executed or killed in the forest and jungle sweeps. The more effective the British were in defining the rebel as alien, the more easily the authorities could see a polarized conflict without solution—and without a need for excess compassion.

Once this policy of repression begins to show results, any reversal to permit accommodation becomes difficult. In the Gold Coast, after the disturbances of 1948, the Watson Commission produced a report that depicted Nkrumah as "imbued with a Communist ideology which only political experience had blurred."[3] A red knave with a black skin obviously was not the man for the future. There was, however, in the Gold Coast sufficient leeway for Nkrumah to apply the Indian Strategy; more important, there were British officials in Accra and London who recognized what he was doing. In Kenya, even in 1960, Kenyatta was the leader to darkness and death, according to Governor Sir Patrick Renison. In two more years he would be a senior minister serving in an African administration presided over by the same Governor. The process of turning a man "definitely guilty" of leadership in a murder cult into the doyen of the new African statesmen took not only time but also the pressure of expediency. But it was done. Nor if al-Asnag or Mackawee had played in South Arabia is there any doubt that the Arab terrorists, thugs and pawns of Egypt, could have been transmuted. It is not a process without pain, for many persist in seeing yesterday's villain behind today's glory. Through practice and experience, however, the British could reverse the policy of alienation.

British Strategy and Tactics

At the time of the revolt, if the rebel is alien, the alternatives appear exacting: crush the revolt or evacuate. Both the Mau Mau and the MCP were crushed; in many British minds the latter remain puppets of international communism and the former primitive tribesmen. In South Arabia the British evacuated, leaving, in the words of Sir Kennedy Trevaskis, "a long line of Arab friends who I, and others, had led up the garden path."[4] The British managed only a semblance of devolution in the last-minute Geneva Agreement with NLF leaders who were a week away from an assassin's role. In Cyprus the Commonwealth Strategy finally came to the rescue. In Egypt a typical Treaty solution in 1954 led only to 1956 and the last violent hurrah of Empire.

Even facing what seemed alien, unrepresentative, and illegitimate power-grabs, the British did not rely on coercion alone. Experience had revealed that terror could best be countered by political maneuvers. Thus, if the rebels were not *too* alien, Irgun or EOKA or FLOSY, the British sought a political option to involve the forces concerned. Such a political strategy might exclude compromise with the rebels but produce an accommodation they would accept. This was the case with the Zurich and London Agreements for Cyprus. In Malaya and Kenya parallel political programs were launched to erode the support of the rebels, although such support was officially denied. It was of course easier to reach an accommodation, no matter what sort, when the perceived level of rebel violence was low. The Mau Mau violence level was seen as frightful, which in pure numbers it was not, while the fedayeen attacks and the burning of Cairo was labeled traditional Egyptian troublemaking, easily discounted at the bargaining table. Alien rebel or no, the British almost always sought a small bit of uneven middle ground, even when the aspirations of the rebels endangered crucial British interests or seemed beyond any rational accommodation.

Military tactics in the field, refined over a generation by officers and men experienced in counterinsurgency, could be learned, could be applied, and could in the long run be effective; but only if used in a cunningly prescribed political formula. British military tactics were, therefore, of little use unless political conditions were factored into the formula, and these conditions were usually very special. Consequently the ultimate formula adjusted to the various regional unknowns differed for each revolt.

British political tactics in pursuing a strategy of devolution, even in the midst of open revolt, varied vastly and could be quite flexible. A basic principle was to isolate and, if possible, ignore the rebels. This meant keeping out international investigators, ignoring United Nations resolutions, and turning back efforts to "broaden" the crisis. If there was advantage, however, the British had not the slightest compunction in switching gears. Until Grivas' bombs went off, Cyprus was an internal matter. Right after the reverberation of EOKA bombs there was a Tripartite Conference: Cyprus had become an international problem. Palestine in time became an "international" problem, although the British withdrew rather than effect an international solution to their advantage. And when all internal efforts failed in South Arabia, London snatched at the United Nations straw, one more mission, in the hope that something might result from the trip. There were few hard and fast rules for the use of political tactics.

The British continued to devise a variety of approaches to each crisis that might support a return to order. Constitutions, commissions, royal visits, aid and development, promises, and programs were used as part of the dialogue. Some of the offers might appear to be positive steps, some might actually be so, some might lead to further devolution, and all played a vital role in forcing the peace. The Macmillan Plan would not have worked in Cyprus, but it did save face in Athens; it made a point that was well and quickly taken. And so, year in and year out, the British did divide and conquer. They also united and ruled, found old ways out of new corners—and the reverse. Tactically, the political initiatives in colonial matters were inventive, creative, often effective. That there were so few revolts, and that they so often led to accommodation is witness to British political acumen. On occasion they stumbled, but there remained enough of that graceful swiftness of foot, so admired and so feared by the lesser peoples, to give evidence that there was life left yet in Perfidious Albion.

Devolution

There were often problems, because devolution was not always a first priority. In some areas British strategic, although seldom economic, interests were paramount. Colonial authorities often had to maintain possession of the odd bit of real estate the generals needed, unite the impossible to defend the bounds of the undigestible. Perhaps the granting of sovereignty would have saved the South Arabian Federation. The men in Aden had so hoped, but the generals would not go along. Perhaps the prospect of independence soon could have charmed Makarios early on, but the military would not accept the proposition. The military laid down the rule that the cost of maintaining a strategic position was worth the price in colonial turmoil. As long as the cabinet accepted the premise, the ground to maneuver politically was limited. The criticism that turmoil negated was the strategic value of the colony in question went unheeded. Whether or not Britain really needed Aden in 1965, Cyprus in 1957, or the Suez Canal Zone in 1952 was quite a different matter. What is clear is that the cost of repression, high or low, can pay strategic dividends. By the use of sufficient power the British occupier could put down or contain resistance and continue to use any base, as the British proved in Cyprus in 1956.

The review of value received as the generation of devolution progressed indicated that strategic considerations were often less vital than the generals assumed and room for political maneuver was broader. Even outright evacuation was not necessarily a strategic disaster. Much of the Empire had existed to protect or expedite communications with India. When Disraeli acquired Cyprus, he revealed to the House of Lords the true direction of his interests: "In taking Cyprus the movement is not Mediterranean, it is Indian: we have taken a step there which we think necessary for the maintenance of our Empire and for its preservation in peace."[5] With India gone, there was less need for these forts and ports that had acquired a patina of glamour and glory not easily lost.

Economic factors did not unduly complicate the process of devolution. Only in the Gulf was the presence of British troops at the wells thought necessary in order to ensure an ample supply of oil. And Labour was not even convinced of this. The government and most of the businesses involved felt that an independent nation would not necessarily undermine the local British economic position. Some capitalists had their doubts, but few wanted to stand up and be counted as opponents of devolution because profits might suffer. Many British capitalists saw positive economic advantages in devolution. Right or wrong, the capitalists, private or government-sponsored, felt not that they were taking their last gasp as Empire faded but were awakening to a new breeze of trans-international economic expansion.

In sum, within the process of devolution, the basic British responses to revolt, honed by experience not always properly absorbed, remained about the same. Surprise was followed by shock and the processes of defining the rebels as a minority of evil men using force to garner support from the basically loyal people. If the rebels were beyond compromise or had taken up arms openly, the army pursued an anti-insurgency campaign in sure and certain knowledge that their efforts in the field could succeed only if a political formula were found and supported by London. The means of fashioning such a formula might, however, be limited by the needs of the military, thereby protracting and complicating the problems of suppression. Seldom were economic factors the overreaching concerns, even when they were important, as in Malaya or India or the Gulf. In large part the British managed to avoid open revolts and, if that was not possible, devised solutions other than absolute suppression or evacuation.

Given the number of "natives" involved, the opportunity for misunderstanding, the international interference from various self-styled friends and avowed enemies, the dialogue of devolution seldom broke down. When it did, and the lethal dialogue of armed struggle was substituted, the British often responded appropriately to the violent message units, recognized the intent of the bombs or assassinations. Such response—internationalizing the Cypriot dispute or bringing the United Nations into Palestine or defining the Mau Mau as mad—was not always what the rebel strategists had anticipated and often removed the possibility of accommodation from them.

The British had a major asset in that no revolt threatened the dismemberment of the United Kingdom or a rebel victory in London. Ireland aside, the nation the rebels sought to liberate was distant and inchoate, perhaps a threat to British strategic or economic interests, but not to the survival of the nation. And because of the rapidly expanding Commonwealth, Britain would lose little grandeur: pride did not go before the fall of Empire but blossomed in the Commonwealth's triumph. Only the trauma of Suez revealed the narrow limits of British power and the actual nature of devolution. And even then a future in Europe and a swift, pragmatic end of the colonial heritage let the British down more easily.

Consequently, they proved flexible and at times accommodating opponents, adamant against the alien as long as there was need, capable, if necessary, of withdrawing without condition or staying and paying the price. And over a generation the price paid by the British in blood and pride was remarkably low. Few of the rebels won in battle the grail they sought; some gained much, some little, many death, a few dishonor. They rose against an Empire many admired and some cherished. In British eyes these rebels were violent exceptions in one of the greatest and most peaceful transfers of power in modern history.

Qahatan Ashaabi, leader of the National Liberation Front, 1967.

British soldiers stand guard over a suspect in Aden, March 1967.

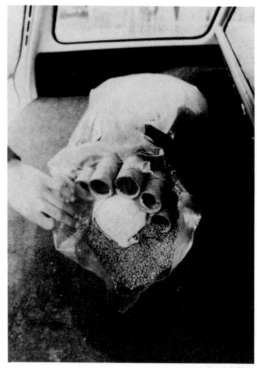

The first car bomb being constructed in Derry, Northern Ireland, March 1972.

A bomb being concealed by a Provisional IRA volunteer in a woman's cosmetic case.

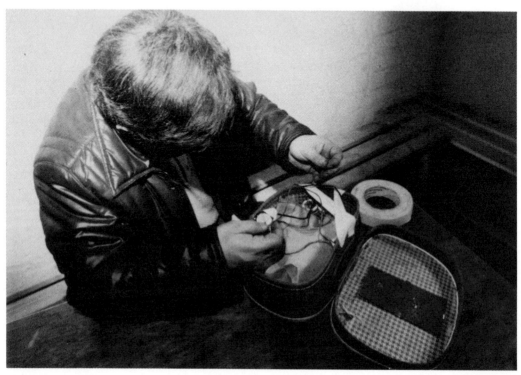

David Gifford

A camouflaged British soldier in Northern Ireland.

An Arab Fedayeen on the balcony of the captured Israeli team quarters at the Munich Olympic Village, September 5, 1972.

A BOAC VC-10 dynamited by the PFLP at Dawson Field, Jordan, September 12, 1970.

8   The Rebel Models

Deny them this participation of freedom and you break the sole band which originally made, and must still preserve the unity of Empire.

—*Edmund Burke, 1775*

In analyzing revolt there has been a tendency to list the variable factors, preconditions, that lead to a revolt and to detail the geographical, political, and socioeconomic aspects that favor or hinder the rebels. This trend reflects a belief that the rules of the game and the size of the playing field are more important than the players. On their side, the rebels have tended to stress that the motivation of the player, the rebel, and the structure of his analysis, his ideology, are far more important than the site of the campaign or the opponents' assets. The rebels seem to have the weight of evidence on their side.

A revolt does not begin because of optimum conditions. What makes it possible is not the chance of success or failure but the simple commitment by individual men to victory or defeat. What makes a rebel can be quite complicated, or so academic analysis has indicated: relative deprivation or aggression as a result of frustration or societal mimicry of neighboring patterns. On the other hand, those who view complex issues in terms of Liberty or Death feel little need to explain their motivation in waging what they consider a struggle against institutionalized evil in the name of the future. The world abounds in institutionalized evil and demonstrable oppression, and for over a generation overt imperialism has been so characterized, fairly or unfairly, by a considerable portion of informed opinion. Thus for the rebels against the British Crown the crucial question was not why they revolted—that was obvious—but how they fashioned their armed struggles.

If a small, renewable core of true-believers can be organized, willing to sacrifice their lives for a cause professed by a reasonable portion of the population and possible of realization, then, in spite of the obstacles, real or imagined, an armed struggle can be launched. The rebel cause need not be fully understood or completely accepted by those for whom they struggle, and it certainly need not have majority support, even if the rebels are certain that they represent the masses. Their tactics may be determined or limited by terrain and their operations narrowed by repression or geographic isolation, but their persistence can continue as long as casualties are replaced and there is hope.

Commitment

The essence of a revolt is commitment to a cause beyond the capacity of the system to coopt or absorb. No cause is perfect, and those of the rebels against the Crown were flawed in some manner: atavistic tribal customs in Kenya, ethnic communism in Malaya, a deviant minority strain of Zionism in Palestine. Yet George Washington no more than Mao Tse-tung or Grivas began with a democratic vote of confidence or represented more than a substantial if militant minority. Rare is the rebel without a flawed cause or who has all the pieces in hand at the start of the game. However, no matter how great or small the technical assets, what must exist is an indigenously felt degradation and humiliation, frustration long endured, that has produced conditions that to many seem almost, and to a few absolutely, insufferable.

The reasons that inspire the little group of men to take up arms in the face of common sense and often self-interest, to lay down their lives for the cause, are both very complicated and quite simple. Their opponents' explanations suggesting that revolt results from gross ambition or thwarted greed or a love of violence may in part be true. The mini-devil theory often explains some of the rebels' motives some of the time. It is equally apparent that most rebels do not live by greed and ambition alone. The risks, initially at least, were greater than any reward. It is not sinecures that prove attractive but power to change the future. In the case of the Irgun, for example, it was obvious from the start that the political beneficiaries of the revolt would not be the rebels. It is the commitment, strong or weak, to change the future because the present is insufferable that is the stuff of revolt, the ethos of the rebel.

To the potential rebel existing conditions build a frustration and an anxiety, a deep abiding rage, that cannot easily, or at all, be altered by words, by the slow pace of reform, by the sure promise of tomorrow. In many cases he wants to change the past, to rewrite history by force of arms, to erase humiliation as much as to end oppression. He may be driven by hidden hungers or raw avarice, be of unsound mind or warped by personal slights, but if this alone were true, he will find few colleagues and little tolerance among the people he professes to "free." There is most assuredly, however, a *need* to strike out. Even when in the Gold Coast the nationalists did not want to take up arms, did not need to and realized it, the struggle for liberty was carved in a vocabulary of martyrs and patriots, sacrifice and hero worship, that turned a relatively painless political process into a sublimated revolutionary war. In the Gold Coast, too, the need to strike out, even against honest paternalism if not vicious repression, was very great. Throughout the Empire the long litany of small snubs and offhand slights were the grains that often became the pearls of nationalist ideology. In Central Africa to receive dirty meat thrust from the back window of a butcher shop in Ndola was far more painful than to watch the long trains loaded with copper moving out. In Cyprus patriotic aspirations were treated with amused contempt: if they were *so* serious why didn't they set off a bomb! Nothing is more telling than the necessity to include in the Anglo-Egyptian Agreement of 1954 a provision that the British Embassy would give up part of the lawn so that the Nile Cornice—a long planned embankment—could be completed. Given a choice between allowing the Egyptians access to the river under the visionary scheme of the new government and the comfort of the Embassy staff, the British heretofore had chosen the latter. After all it was their lawn. The distance from the Cornice in 1954 and the Canal in 1956 was not great. Humiliation built rage and a sounder base for revolt would be hard to find.

Revolt within the Empire was engendered because aspirations could not be contained in the imperial structure—a Communist Malaya in Chinese hands, a Zionist Palestine, The People's Republic of South Yemen, a Black White Highlands, Cyprus as a province of Greece—nor could those dedicated to such change afford to wait any longer. Most important, the rebels' aspirations, however outrageous and illegitimate in British eyes, appeared possible of realization. Without some hope of success the potential rebel remains a private person suffering outrage but limited to sullen resistance and futile conspiracy. Few men, however humiliated, will rise in consort knowing that they will die and their cause fail and there will be none to begin again. Splendid gestures and blood sacrifices are rare and usually undertaken to fertilize future fields.

Perhaps only the Irgun accepted the possibility of failure, but the Jews would have fought rather than gone meekly into the dismal future: Never Again. In Palestine the "vain" sacrifice of the Warsaw Ghetto, a witness against evil, was transmuted and became a rich heritage rather than a futile gesture of the doomed. In Kenya the Mau Mau "revolt" was so stunted and warped by early British repression and the removal of almost all the KAU leadership that little can be known with certainty about rebel expectations. Apparently the KAU hoped for an Indian strategy of agitation and assumed that the militant Mau Mau could be controlled or exploited to advantage. In Malaya the MCP wanted what the ideological writ and their own experience indicated was possible: a communist victory over a decadent imperialist power, followed by a communist state.

In South Arabia the NLF wanted a revolutionary Arab state built on a British defeat. In Cyprus, EOKA wanted absorption in Greece, flimsily disguised as self-determination for the island. None of these ideological goals were unreasonable, unlikely perhaps but not impossible in an age of decaying imperialism. National liberation was an irreversible force in recent history, and Britain's power to reverse or stem the tide was increasingly limited. Even in 1944 the implications of Congress' success in India and the Japanese at Singapore were clear. So, the Irgun aside, the prospect of achieving the avowed goal was great, the need to do so overpowering—yet the rebels seldom rushed into battle at the first opportunity.

The revolt almost always came at the end of a slowly unwinding political process that, no matter how extreme the ultimate goal or compelling the immediate pressures, proved that armed struggle was often the final rather than the first choice. In Palestine, despite the impact of the holocaust, nearly the entire year 1943 was devoted to a long agony of analysis and uncertainty. One thing that made Begin's advent so welcome was an end to the strain. In Malaya even the MCP, assured of the inevitable direction of history, hesitated. Marxist-Leninist ideology insists that a mature revolutionary situation must exist before an armed struggle is launched; but no matter how fine the tools of analysis are honed, the final proof cannot be found until the day of victory. Even if conditions in Malaya seemed ripe, even if surprise were certain and support from the international movement assumed, the MCP still delayed. In Kenya no one listened to Kenyatta, or they listened and heard other voices. Whether or not the KAU and Kenyatta lost patience, many Kikuyu did, and brought in the killing oath—but not until years after the first mild oaths. For over a half-century agitation for Enosis in some form elicited only negative responses from London. The Egyptian fedayeen, like EOKA and the Mau Mau, resulted from years of "Never." The evolution of Arab nationalism began in 1948, and even Qahatan Ashaabi had first belonged to the conservative South Arabian League before opting for the NLF. In every instance, if there had not actually been a long train of abuses, there most assuredly was a long history of uncertainty and delay, procrastination disguised as analysis, behind each revolt.

The American experience resembled that of the rebels against the Crown. Those rebels in 1776 also had agitated for a generation and, for a time, sought an accommodation. When the sticking point came, the chances of opposing the British in the field, though not good, were far from hopeless. When the choice was between Liberty and Death, a small group of radicals sought to create a Republic of Reason, a fair goal for the time, by means of an armed struggle they would have preferred to avoid.

The Irish experience, as always, was different; there rebels had struggled against the power of the Crown for eight hundred years with a remarkable lack of success. In the nineteenth century the British had nearly killed Irish nationalism with kindness, conceding on everything but the national issue. In 1916 the rebels felt it was their last chance to achieve freedom before the island sank into a West Briton province. And even then this particular set of rebels had been organizing and delaying for years. With time slipping away, they still did not rush to the barricades. On the very eve of the Rising, there were those who opposed the final act—and some who tried to cancel it. The Irish rebels, however, were rising within Great Britain and sought to dismember the home islands rather than turn an overseas province into an independent nation.

Substructures for Revolt

In order to effect a strategy of national liberation the rebels needed a revolutionary structure. The Americans declared independence, established a government, and sought to defend political institutions with conventional military forms and procedures. The Irish in 1916 declared a Republic and failed to defend it in the streets of Dublin with the Irish Volunteers, a militia transformed into the Irish Republican Army. Thereafter the IRA remained the core of the Irish underground revolutionary movement, despite attempts to create other political structures. For the rebel generation after 1944 the factors that actually effected the structure of each specific revolutionary organization were a combination of necessity and previous theory. The greater the basic ideology taken into the armed struggle and the longer the parent organization had existed, the greater the effort to make the battle environment adjust to the existing revolutionary structure.

The movement with the scantest ideology, the most recently created formal structure, and the least organizational talent was the Mau Mau. It was governed almost entirely by geography and the charisma of individuals. By trial and error the Kikuyu during 1953 were forced into small bands by the forest and British security searches. These bands could be maintained as cohesive units only so long as the leader through oathing and the force of his personality created a band-bond. The longer such a bond existed, the fewer the contacts with other bands, and the more tolerable the forest life, the faster the options for dissolution declined. These bands were linked with other bands through an informal net of communications and intelligence that included not only regional alliances but, initially, joint operations. There was never a unified Mau Mau command nor, after 1954, any effective unity except the exchange of information. The Mau Mau forest organization was created in response to British imposed conditions rather than as a means to effect a strategy of national liberation.

The MCP took into the Malayan jungle a dual structure: the Party based on an idealized Moscow model somewhat altered by Malayan Chinese practice and aspirations; and the Army refashioned on the original anti-Japanese model that itself had been influenced by orthodox communist structures. Neither Party nor Army had been organized for a jungle campaign against the British. The Party had a hard core of full-time agitators skilled in subversion, conspiracy, cell mechanics, and urban coercion, and intimate with the litany of Marxist-Leninist analysis, a more than adequate instrument to control and mold the Army. It created and maintained a support wing, actually an illicit parallel political front. Yet the Party was often at a loss in directing an armed struggle. In theory revolutionary war might be revolutionary politics by other means, but the cadres often found it quite different. The Army too had problems. The British were not the Japanese, nor was the goal of the new army that of the original one, nor would the leadership recognize that the previous jungle experience was not the same as an aggressive war of national liberation. The strictures of ideology indicated, however, that no organizational change was desirable, much less necessary. So, for Party reasons, usually of control and discipline, the jungle army was organized into large rather than small units. In the jungle the MCP preferred to maintain as a revolutionary organization their own faulty version of orthodoxy rather than adapt to the task at hand. For twelve years of declining effectiveness, the MCP held to the orthodox forms, eschewing experimentation for doctrinal purity.

In no other revolt did the organization depend so much on ideological strictures, alien or indigenous, as that of Malaya or as much on the environment, physical and military, as in Kenya. In both Palestine and Cyprus, the Irgun and EOKA fashioned what was essentially a military resistance movement, largely aboveground, allied to legal political structures, and dependent on the talents of particular men and the geopolitical structure of the area of combat. Each had a small commando group, rapid and efficient communications within the organization, regional commands, and very few full-time people. The Irgun was a military organization with a long history of activity, a husk in 1943, filled by 1948 as a result of new volunteers. Grivas, on the other hand, started with nothing and built on dedicated volunteers, using his experience in the Greek resistance with the X organization. The Irgun and EOKA resembled European resistance movements in many ways. A singular difference between the two was the nature of power and decision. Though first among equals, Begin was open to challenge. Grivas had absolute authority. Given the size of Cyprus, the inexperience of the young volunteers, and the psychological comfort of a dominant figure during a time of uncertainty, his complete control had great attraction. If the Irgun was a band of brothers, most younger of course, then EOKA was a patriarchal, authoritative family. The quality of leadership and the talents of the volunteers determined the operational structure of both organizations.

In South Arabia the institutional problem of the NLF was multifaceted. The organization began as an alliance of conspirators with no sure base. Radical opponents controlled the labor unions. The Aden middle class was too conservative. The up-country tribes appeared to be poor revolutionary material. As a result the NLF had to create not only a revolutionary organization but also a revolutionary constituency. In Aden it offered a more violent revolutionary option to those who went unrewarded by al-Asnag or to those who admired the violence of the General Command's tactics or to those with an eye for future gain. Up-country, the NLF focused on traditional areas of discontent and in the name of the future prodded tribesmen into a relapse into the historical pleasures of pillage. There the sultans rarely could maintain the loyalty of their subjects without sacrifice, a course they found uncongenial, while the NLF promised much and much that was promised in no way contradicted the strictures of ideological purity. Finally NLF agents corrupted or converted key members of the South Arabian Army, a tactic perhaps even more vital than maintaining the momentum of the armed struggle against the British. In Aden the NLF resembled EOKA or the Irgun; up-country the General Command followed traditional paths familiar to the old feudal imams of Yemen and within the South Arabian Army not unknown techniques of subversion were exploited. The NLF was a mix of radical ideology, Arabian conspiracy, tribal ties, urban guerrillas, personal and national ambition, and ruthless dedication. It would not go on a form-and-function chart at all but in South Arabia it worked.

In the case of the Egyptian fedayeen, there was almost no necessity to create a special revolutionary organization, for existing political structures undertook the training of self-selected enthusiasts. The size of the operational bands depended on their mission, the nature of the opposition, and contingency. The fedayeen resembled the militant youth wing of an activist political party, which was in part what they were. In the old days of Cairo politics, renting a mob to perform on cue was a traditional technique, extrapolated in 1951 with the fedayeen option: the politics of gesture. Once the nature of the British response became clear and the cost of the gesture apparent, the fedayeen organizations of the various parties disintegrated. The police in Ismailia rather than the fedayeen tipped the balance. Cairo was burned not by fedayeen but by a tiny band of arsonists and the enthusiasm of the masses. After that the fedayeen disappeared.

The structure of each revolutionary organization is as likely to determine the choice of a strategy of national liberation as to be determined by it. The same is true in part of the nature of the cause, the timing of the revolt, and the ideological considerations of the rebels. No one really starts with a clean slate, and few rebels have time or inclination to parse out a strategy in detail. Most theories on how to carry out a revolt are developed from the experience of the retired or the theories of committed intellectuals. Despite the delay of potential rebels, few had a firm grasp on their assets and liabilities, few tried to see far ahead. To a degree many of the rebels recognized that they were opening a lethal dialogue, negotiation by means of violence. To a greater degree all perceived the British opponent as a special case. This was true even in Malaya, where Britain was not only a typical representative of the capitalist-imperialists but also a special Paper Tiger, proved fragile at Singapore. In South Arabia the NLF assumed that the day of Empire had passed and so soon would the British. The Irgun, on the other hand, assumed that the British could be levered out, while EOKA in the beginning accepted that Britain would not discard "Never" unless pressed.

In every case the anticipation of the rebels was limited by their desire to begin, by optimism, and by faith in the future. The MCP really believed that they could compress Mao's experience of two decades into a few months, Makarios that a few bombs would make the difference, the Egyptians that snatch-and-grab raids would effect imperial priorities. Considerably more accurate was the assumption by all but the MCP that the British response would be limited by the British character and the British judicial system. In opening a campaign against a fair opponent, the rebels could use certain tactics that might have had unpleasant repercussions in a struggle against a different imperial power or at a different imperial period. They need not anticipate torture, reprisals, violent retaliation, counter-terror, judicial executions, the murder of hostages, or the detention of the innocent—unless the British erred and lost patience, which would be even more to rebel advantage. They proved to be largely justified in their expectations. The bounds of coercion varied considerably—the more alien the rebel the more vulnerable—but in retrospect few would have exchanged the British for another opponent.

The British were often outraged by rebel charges of torture or murder. But the rebel cry of horror was not simply hypocrisy. Many knew the British were, given the provocation, being fair; but they wanted the British to be absolutely fair. This would not really have been to rebel advantage; for it was the gray and dangerous neutral zone between minimum force and open vengeance, between an honest execution and judicial murder, that alarmed and concerned the British public. In a strategy of leverage, if the British could be persuaded that repression was hateful, then the prospect of compromise or evacuation appeared reasonable. The Irgun and EOKA assumed such a victory was possible. The NLF foresaw the impact of world public opinion on the British government rather than British opinion. In Kenya, the Canal Zone, and originally in Cyprus the expectation was that the immediate response to violence would be a new dialogue. The NLF and the Irgun foresaw a longer and more serious struggle. The MCP wanted neither a dialogue nor to lever out the British, but to grow rapidly from strength to strength as had Mao and as the perceived British weakness would permit.

No matter what the anticipation of the rebels, few recognized that their strategic options had been narrowed even before the armed struggle began. The professed goal, the limits of ideology, the nature of the revolutionary organization, the talents of the leadership, and the nature of popular support all restricted the rebels' selection of options. Most rebel strategists at best fashioned a simple scenario based on the need to begin, the British character, technical limitations, and the odd assumption concerning the length and course of the struggle. The prime activity, the real rebel problem, was to fashion tactical means to pursue either a strategy of leverage or of incremental gain. Only the Irgun and the MCP had a closely reasoned analysis of assets and liabilities and the ensuing prospects. The Irgun's proved to be remarkably accurate and MCP's excessively optimistic.

A common failing of all revolutionary organizations except the Irgun was the assumption that the British would react to challenge without flexibility or originality. The rebels, therefore, concentrated on tactics to keep the armed struggle going. These military forays were limited by their ideological bias; none could operate as pure opportunists. All the movements came out of a complicated and limiting historical background. The communist ideology of the MCP may have allowed the broadest tactical leeway, but its insistence on Party structures largely negated whatever advantages might have accrued from opportunism. Whatever the theoretical limitations on violence, to the British under the gun there seemed few in practice. The rebels seemed to use violence indiscriminately: murder, torture, massacre, brutalities beyond measure in the name of high cause. Mau Mau massacres, the assassinations along Murder Mile in Nicosia or Aden, men shot down in church or in bed, Mackawee's children, the two sergeants in Palestine and Mrs. Cutliffe in Cyprus make, whatever the motive or subsequent rationalizations or denials, sorry reading. The fact remains that revolt is a brutal and violent business, often intentionally so. The stress of the campaign and murder in the streets often seemed to belie the high purposes of the movement. The success of the armed struggle depends in part on the horror of the tactical means; the impact of terror must be terrible to be effective. Yet the rebels often made every effort to be a legitimate military organization, a rival army not a band of assassins. Begin much later wrote in the London *Times* of April 14, 1971, that the Irgun had fought the good fight—and fought more cleanly than most and fought as an army:

> we battled, few against many. Our men were hunted, captured, tortured, imprisoned, deported, flogged, hanged, . . . They struck just like commandos . . . They waged fair battles . . . Our men were always instructed to avoid civilian casualties . . . When our soldiers fell in battle, it was never a cause for retribution. Our fight, we said, is for liberation not for revenge.

Rebel Tactic Options

Although tactical means varied, almost all the revolts have been called guerrilla campaigns. The presence of traditional guerrilla bands, however, is not really significant. In Palestine the Irgun had no full-time guerrillas but ran an urban-suburban campaign of sabotage and terror with aboveground men who did not need to be supported or supplied. In Malaya there was a jungle guerrilla army, although terror tactics played a significant role. In Kenya, after the early days of vengeance raids and murder, there were only fleeing bands of rural fugitives. The fedayeen raids into the Canal Zone were carried out by "commandos" seconded from conventional parties. In areas such as Cyprus it was impossible to maintain more than a few guerrillas in the mountains; their operations had to be very limited yet give the British the impression of being a serious threat. In South Arabia the guerrilla load was determined solely by British pressure. Most of the tribes could be considered part-time guerrillas in any case and some had literally tens of thousands of available rifles; but once the British arrived, the tribal "units" melted under pressure. The British could at any of several points clear the ground, but the NLF could then switch the area of concentration. These tribal "guerrillas" were supposed to attract British interest away from Aden, where only a very few NLF cadres operated full time. In any attrition campaign, particularly one applying a strategy of leverage, the escalation of the number of British troops was crucial. Whether guerrillas were included or excluded was not really significant. In some cases, although their ideological effect was important, their contribution was far less than that of the assassinations in the streets. The major intent of all the rebels was to cause as much disorder as possible, using guerrillas only if feasible. The methods of revolutionary-guerrilla war permeated discussions of tactics—flexibility, mobility, quicksilver on the hills, fish in a friendly ocean—but, except for Malaya, the traditional guerrilla seldom played a vital part. In fact, the rebels stole the rural guerrillas' clothes, broadened his role, and introduced irregular war to the cities.

The second major tactical option in the armed struggles was terror: urban "guerrilla" operations particularly assassination. In general the use of terror to create "disorder" is dependent for effectiveness on whether the operation is intended to eliminate a victim or intimidate a target. If the latter, the victim must be chosen with great care, for the target may be elusive. The Irgun shot and killed the officer in charge of police activities that included "forceful" interrogation. The impact was great. The care with which the Irgun used violence to make specific points—in the case of flogging and hanging—meant, however brutal it was, relatively few deaths resulted. If on the other hand the victim is the target, an informer or a police agent, assassination can soon be a common technique, with whole groups as victims. In Cyprus and South Arabia, the rebels attempted to eliminate the police, particularly the Special Branch, severely hampering them in both cases. Widespread elimination of collaborators can cripple an administration, but the awe, the terror of the crime, is lost in the welter of blood. To shock, the level of horror had to be raised.

The use of terror as an offensive weapon—for example, the selection of Lord Harding or Sir Richard Turnbull as the victim, with the target British opinion—was one of the two offensive tactics used everywhere and often quite effectively. The ambush of Sir Henry Gurney, High Commissioner of Malaya, on October 6, 1951, devastated British morale and started a slide into despair that might have been fatal. In Palestine the death of the sergeants played a major part in forcing the British Cabinet to choose between ruling by repression or finding a way to withdraw. The impact brings the revolt onto the English breakfast table in horror headlines: the King David Hotel, Murder Mile, Assassins in London. Most movements have also engineered spectaculars, operations that succeed despite the odds and British pretensions: jail breaks from impregnable castles in Acre or Kyrenia, bombs on airliners, bank raids. There are as well the day-to-day explosions, fires, shots in the night, riots controlled from a distance. The offensive point was to disrupt the system and hold on until the British or the United Nations noticed the turmoil. Only in Malaya did the MCP foresee the escalation of these tactics, a slide uphill to conventional war. The most other rebels could hope for was the capacity to continue their end of the lethal dialogue until the British will eroded, or history came to their rescue, or both.

A serious problem for the rebels was that, once launched, the armed struggle could not easily be turned on or off and that as time passed the British continued to receive the same violent message. Thus, one of the vital necessities in organizing a revolt was the construction of a political apparatus that could carry on a dialogue on several levels. What was needed was a political form with two faces: an external one that would negotiate with the world, including perhaps the British; and an internal one that would fashion a civilian resistance-and-support organization to complement the military forces and underscore the message of violence. In Palestine the established institution performed diplomatic functions, for its own purposes rather than those of the Irgun. In the Kenya forest there was a War Council and a Parliament, but they were largely illusionary and, with the KAU banned, no one performed diplomatic functions and no messages could be sent by African national opinion until years later. The fedayeen in Egypt evolved out of traditional political organizations, which had used them to send a message the British did not care to receive. The NLF of South Arabia let Arab institutions and individuals elsewhere transmit their message and found no difficulty in adapting the general command to play a diplomatic role in Geneva in November 1967 or as a government subsequently. In Cyprus, EOKA expected Makarios to speak for them, not anticipating that the British would fail to distinguish between his voice and that of EOKA. In Malaya, not until the very end with defeat looming, did the MCP feel the need to open a diplomatic dialogue. Grivas, who for varying reasons had to adjust his military coat to Athenian measures, announced unilateral truces, ignored by the British, who recognized his dilemma as a sign of political if not military weakness. In Cairo the old politicians called off their new fedayeen through fear of chaos and revolution. The rebels, accordingly, found that once under way, dedicated to Victory or Death and dependent largely on the armed struggle, negotiations became the very process of armed rebellion. Most were content to keep up the level of din; there rarely was opportunity to adjust the original strategic assumption, shift the direction or purpose of the struggle, or respond to new conditions. What could be managed from time to time was escalation, more operations, more officials assassinated, new boycotts, or expanded student riots—more varied and effective tactics, not a new strategy. Only twice did the original strategy prove effective, in Palestine and in South Arabia because again at least in part the rebels had been proven correct in their estimation of the ultimate British response and of the direction of history.

Every rebel leader has from the first insisted that *his* revolt is special. And it is true that all revolts are special; but some are more special than others and none is unique. Those rebels against the British Crown shared certain problems, devised on occasion similar solutions, tended to evade or avoid certain potentially unpleasant realities in fashioning their struggles for national liberation. At the moment of decision, a moment not easily recognizable as the rebels move closer to the barricade, a special heritage, the strictures of ideology, the limitations of the organization, or the uncertainty of the political-diplomatic voice narrowly confined any potential strategy of revolt.

Recognizing this to a degree, real rather than idealized rebels tended to base their strategy on a very few factors: their military capacity, the need to begin, the international climate, that is, the direction of history, and a brief analysis of British reaction limned for the most part in ideological terms. They usually concentrated on getting underway and keeping up the pressure. Once the killing began there was little opportunity to readjust the basic assumptions, or for that matter the desire. Begin was right about the British in Palestine and the NLF about Britain's future course in the Middle East. The others missed to some degree, except of course those who grasped the possibilities of the Indian Strategy and the example of Nkrumah. And to a certain extent the prospects of the politics of agitation had been considerably enhanced by the British experience with open revolt, their previous failures to initiate a dialogue until too late.

The rebels with the most subtle and complex analysis, with organizations fashioned for special purposes, with a grasp of reality unhampered by theoretical considerations, and most of all with a reasonable if not rigorous estimation of British assets and liabilities fared best. The simple, the short-sighted, the ideologically bound, the theorists, and the gunmen did less well; but even then the cost to the British to close down the flawed revolts was considerable. The rebels can claim today that their revolts added to a universal revolutionary heritage, hastened the end of Empire, and, successful or not, transformed the world in a way the advocates of devolution and the apologists for Britain do not care to admit.

9 An Irish Template

What a bloody awful place!
—Reginald Maulding,
returning from Northern
Ireland, 1970

By 1968 there was no doubt that the end of Empire had come. Little remained but the odd rock and a small colonial residue the Labour government intended to encourage, ready or no, into independence. With the end of Empire one might also have expected an end to the long series of imperial revolts, leaving the British Army free to concentrate on conventional war on the European continent. Yet, within a year civil disturbances severe enough to require the army occurred, not in some distant imperial backwater but in the home islands, in the province of Northern Ireland. The army's peacekeeping mission—separating the Protestant majority from the Catholic minority—gradually shifted between 1969 and 1971 to an exercise in irregular war. Britain in 1971 once more faced a revolt, this time within the United Kingdom, directed by the Provisional Irish Republican Army, an organization that had not even existed two years before.

As always this revolt was unique, but events in Ulster, maneuvers out of London, and the essence of the lethal dialogue between rebel and ruler were not unlike previous imperial experience. The problems facing the IRA, neither surmounted nor solved, were as complex and special as those facing any rebel, the difficulties of fashioning a relevant and effective strategy if anything greater, and the ultimate level of violence if anything higher. Most important, the rebel experience in Northern Ireland, although peculiarly Irish, also reflected the experience of earlier rebels against the Crown. The Irish template might not fit everywhere exactly; but even a revolt within the United Kingdom rather than on the edge of Empire was not alien to distant observers, old rebels, experienced journalists, or military officers who saw, if uncertainly, the analogy.

Background to Escalation

Although in London staunch Tories were wont from the comfort of their clubs to insist that Northern Ireland was as British as Kent, and as dear, this was not true. In fact, few in Britain really knew very much about the province, its people, or its problems. It was a strange sort of place stitched together during the Irish Troubles, inhabited by dour and difficult people involved in old and irrelevant quarrels. There was good fishing, scenery, run-down industry, high unemployment, and primitive politics. In 1921 Lloyd George and his advisers managed to separate six of the nine counties of historic Ulster from the rest of Ireland and establish the Province of Northern Ireland with a regional government at the huge marble hall at Stormont outside Belfast. Ulster thus was maintained as an integral part of Britain, while the remaining twenty-six Irish counties became the Irish Free State, drifted out of the Commonwealth, and in 1948 evolved into the Irish Republic. In Dublin the Irish leaders with varying degrees of intensity claimed all thirty-two counties. In the north the loyal Unionists, Protestant almost to a man, did not want all of Ulster, which would be difficult to control, but only the six counties in the northeast where a two-to-one majority over the Catholics would guarantee "their way of life" protected by the assembly at Stormont.

Suspecting Catholic disloyalty and fearing the ambitions of the Papist Irish Free State to the south, the majority maintained the symbols of their loyalty to Britain and flaunted their domination every year in a series of provocative parades and demonstrations usually led by the massed militants of the Orange Masonic lodges. The Catholic minority responded in kind where possible, organizing commemorations in honor of Republican patriots and martyrs. From time to time various Catholic-Nationalist politicians attempted to work within the Stormont system, but to little avail. Injustice became institutionalized in gerrymandered election districts, in housing allotments, in weighted ballots, in council employment. Privately, the two communities led lives of self-imposed isolation, attended different schools, sang different songs, played different games on different days, and knew little of the other but in caricature. The two tribes were distinguished by religious labels. Only rarely could a common interest, such as mutual poverty or community loyalty, breach the wall of suspicion and distrust.

In the south the militant IRA, defeated in the civil war in 1923, went underground determined to create a united Republic. Defections began. Eamon De Valera took with him those who preferred a political solution; others lost hope as the years passed. Still the IRA persisted in opposing both regimes in Dublin and at Stormont, clung to the means of physical force to break the British connection, and launched raids, detonated bombs, and shot policemen. Their ranks became fewer. The last guerrilla campaign sputtered to an end in 1962. Ireland seemed to have lost interest in the gun in politics. The two Irish prime ministers even exchanged visits—to the mutual horror of militant Orangemen and the Republicans.

Northern Ireland had for fifty years been organized as a siege state under potential attack by the forces of Catholicism. The secular claims of the IRA were ignored by those who knew what a thirty-two-county Ireland would mean: the victory of Papism. Consequently, the IRA, even when condemned by the Roman bishops, was regarded as a threat to the Stormont regime and the Protestant way of life. In case of need, the typical defenses used in any colonial emergency existed on a standby basis: extensive and draconian security legislation, a paramilitary police force (the Royal Ulster Constabulary, RUC), an almost entirely Protestant police militia (the B-Specials), and a considerable intelligence network. When there was trouble, and often there had been, Stormont's response was to come down hard with the boot. Not only did the IRA face an adamant, prepared opponent but also, claims of nonsectarianism aside, it depended for support on a Catholic minority who doubted the prosspects of unity achieved by physical force. Fearful of Protestant pogroms, a provincial habit of long standing, and suspicious of the RUC and B-Specials, Catholics were more than willing to look to the IRA as a neighborhood defense organization. A real campaign might spark Protestant violence unmonitored by the police and too great for the IRA to halt, too swift for London to intervene effectively, and too embarrassingly dangerous for Dublin to intervene.

After 1962 the gun was on the shelf and the volunteers faced left. The IRA drifted slowly into political agitation and a concern with social and economic issues. Ireland, north and south, seemed to be changing. There was a rising income level for some. More talent stayed home. More stayed in school longer. More hoped for something beyond frugal comfort. Isolation and ignorance eroded under the influence of television, a new generation, schooling, the impact of Pope John, and fresh possibilities. In the north some members of the new university generation felt the time had come to challenge the Stormont system. The rights and privileges of all Ulster citizens should be the same as elsewhere in the United Kingdom.

Civic disobedience in the name of civil rights was an effective means to mount a challenge. In 1967 and 1968 the civil rights campaign gradually escalated. Uncertain as to the appropriate response, Stormont vacillated. The militant Orangemen had no such hesitation, knew that "civil rights" was a code word for United Ireland, brushed aside "political" explanations, and attacked the demonstrators, apparently with the tacit approval of the RUC and the complicity of various B-Specials. The demonstrations grew larger, attracted attention in London, and provoked greater repression.

It became obvious that the protesters were not intimidated. Some of the more timorous in the Catholic community had joined the movement and most who stayed home had become involved. The regime would need to exert greater coercion than in the past. Moreover, the British public, long ignorant of Ulster matters, could watch the exercise carried out in their name and under a Union Jack every night on television. With a Labour government sympathetic to the legitimate grievances of the minority, gross repression would win few friends. By the 1969 season of Orange marches, the situation began to slip from Stormont's hands. The Protestants, frustrated and angered at the civil-rights provocation and lack of British understanding, were seething, suspicious of a Stormont sellout to London and fearful of a Papist victory. The Catholics and the civil rights people, scenting victory, pushed on determined to resist Orange "provocation." On August 12 an Orange parade in Derry provoked an escalating riot and the Catholics withdrew into their districts. Police charges into the Catholic areas were driven back. Rioting spread to Belfast as Protestant mobs sought to answer provocation by breaking into Catholic areas. It began to look as if the province would collapse into anarchy and sectarian war. Stormont was in the peculiar situation of being a police state without sufficient police. On August 15 the British Army arrived in Belfast and Derry, to the great relief of the fearful Catholic minority.

The Impact of August

For the IRA the August events proved traumatic. The shift to politics left the movement in disarray, particularly in the north. There was no longer an IRA to protect the Catholics. When IRA veterans rushed to Dublin for aid, they found GHQ without arms or resources. As a result, during the autumn of 1969 the IRA divided into a Provisional IRA, largely in the north, and supported by those who wanted a stronger military policy and an end to politics, and the Officials, who believed there was room for radical agitation as well as the gun. For a year following the arrival of the British army, both the Provos and the Officials pursued somewhat similar courses, organizing, collecting arms, and agitating. The Provos expanded their northern units, particularly in Belfast and Derry, created their own Sinn Féin political party, made contacts in America—created in fact an alternative Republican movement. The Officials, already organized, continued to concentrate on politics. Both foresaw continued sectarian trouble, both feared the Protestants would again run amok, and neither had much faith in the ultimate neutrality of the army. Neither had any intention of launching a revolt. Eight hundred years of Irish history indicated, if nothing more, that such a revolt would occur in the fullness of time, and much sooner than anyone would have credited a year before.

Between July 1970 and January 1971 Provo strength in Belfast alone grew from a few hundred, often self-selected, volunteers to a thousand. There were arms, often ill-matched and insufficient, explosives, often primitive and unstable, and vast enthusiasm; but not yet a direction other than area defense. Belfast's religious segregation meant that Catholic areas were safe ground, organized by local men and protected by their neighbors, who were in turn protected by the local IRA company. The city was divided into three battalion areas and commanded by a brigade staff, directed in general terms by the seven-man Army Council and the GHQ Staff in Dublin. There was a large unit in Derry and smaller groups scattered about the province, but the key was Belfast. There, until January 1971, the British army was still tolerated, though not welcomed as it had been a year before, and some Provo units even cooperated informally in keeping the peace. By that time, however, there had been a largely unnoticed change in Northern Ireland; the Provo potential, husbanded by the leadership, was about to be revealed.

The British army that had "saved" the Catholics in August 1969 had gradually and not unexpectedly been alienated from the minority, a minority with different symbols, one which suspected or opposed "legitimate" local authority and never was convinced that Ulster was British. The activities of the British Army were a prime cause for the shift. With a generation of experience in peacekeeping and low-level violence, the British army saw, and was allowed to see, its mission as the imposition of order. The doctrine was available and, with Aden only a couple of years in the past, so, for many, was the experience. This Irish mission, in spite of some institutional and political restrictions, was pursued with a vigor that seemed disproportionate to those most often gassed or beaten, the minority Catholics. The British army was perceived as biased, acting for Stormont, rushing in CS gas and Saracen armored cars to beat down a few lads tossing rocks at an Orange parade. The security forces insisted that they were merely getting on top of the situation, preventing worse trouble.

The British commanders in Belfast knew that although it might be possible to get on top of trouble for a while, without parallel political maneuvers the trouble would get worse. And it did. Yet in London this all but predictable decay of the new military order was ignored. There, Labour Home Secretary James Callaghan had finally come to recognize that there was a limit to order imposed by the army in the face of legitimate political grievances. He had even contemplated radical steps; but in

June 1970 the Conservatives unexpectedly won the general election. The new Home Secretary, Reginald Maulding, innocent of Irish matters, moved even more slowly into an area long dominated by the Conservatives' Orange allies. Matters drifted on, and by the end of the year a Provo "revolt" was inevitable.

In January 1971, during riots and the inevitable clumsy house-to-house sweep through the Ballymurphy housing estate in Belfast, a British soldier was shot and wounded by a Provo sniper. Early in February eight British soldiers were shot during rioting in Clonard. On February 6 the first British soldier was killed. The next morning the Stormont Prime Minister announced on television that Northern Ireland was at war with the Irish Republican Army Provisionals. Within a month Provo defensive sniping had given way to gunmen seeking targets of opportunity. Then the bomb was introduced: thirty-seven explosions in April; forty-seven in May; fifty in June. Between April and August 1971, four British soldiers were killed and twenty-nine wounded and over one-hundred civilians had been injured. The Provo leadership from the first had realized that their posture as Catholic Defender offered a base for a *real* campaign. The British heavy response to provocation, often cunningly fashioned by the IRA, restored order quickly at little visible cost but alienated the Catholic population. The process was accelerated, particularly after June 1970. The British Army became the enemy, the IRA the defender. The threatened minority could not disown the Provos and be left defenseless, and the Provos contended that the best defense was a strong offense.

Provo operations reached such a grave point by midsummer 1971 that the British cabinet acceded to the wishes of the Stormont government and introduced internment. What Stormont wanted was a sweep of known agitators and traitors, that is, visible Catholic troublemakers, to humiliate the truculent minority—and incidentally hamper the IRA. What the British security forces wanted and what they told London they could not get was an effective sweep that would break the IRA. What the Cabinet in London wanted apparently was an easy answer to the Irish question. After a year of doing nothing, the Cabinet erred in doing something. Internment was a disaster. The Catholic minority would not be humiliated. Most withdrew their consent to be governed and began rent and rate strikes. Internment failed to deter the two IRAs. Open urban guerrilla war erupted and was supported by the outraged minority. British Army spokesmen tried to explain how the IRA had been "virtually destroyed," while at the same time, a few blocks away, the Provo O/C of Belfast held an open press conference. Journalists began flocking to the newest emergency. The bombing and sniping escalated. There was rumor and then evidence of British torture and beatings. Large areas of Belfast

and Derry became IRA No-Go zones, beyond the reach of security
forces. On a single day in December the Provos mounted over thirty
bombing operations throughout the province—a level of violence far
more intense than those glory days of the Tan War back in 1921. At the
end of the month Maulding, on a flying visit to Belfast, admitted that the
IRA could not be defeated or completely eliminated, but only have their
violence reduced to an acceptable level. The Provos had their *real* campaign at last, thanks to the efficiency of the British Army, delay in London, and their own historic reaction to opportunity.

Bloody Sunday in Derry

In an effort to maintain the pressure on Britain, both the
civil rights people and the Republicans staged a series of demonstrations.
The result was violent confrontation. Then in Derry on Sunday, January
30, British paratroopers fired into the crowd and killed thirteen persons.
Subsequent, not very convincing, British explanations and investigations
of Bloody Sunday could not transform what in Catholic eyes was a massacre. The British Embassy in Dublin was burned by a mob. The Irish
government, no friend of the IRA, was gravely embarrassed. In London
at last came realization that "something must be done" in response to
Catholic grievances rather than in opposition to the IRA. Meanwhile,
Protestant militancy was rising. Paramilitary groups appeared, bigotry
under a suave exterior disappeared, and raw hatred could be heard from
Protestant platforms. In March the British finally terminated their long
deliberation and announced the promulgation of the Stormont assembly.
There would be direct rule from Britain. A year before the ground would
have been swept out from under the Provos, but in March 1972 the volunteers were in no mood to quit. The British were on the run. Stormont
was gone. The Protestants lacked the will and capacity to launch a fatal
sectarian civil war. There had been a brief truce in mid-March and now
after the end of Stormont the Provos were willing to talk, but about an
all-Ireland solution not a patched-up assembly. The bombs continued.
By mid-1972 Belfast and Derry were cities under siege. Large areas
were demolished by bombs, British roadblocks faced those of the IRA,
there was armor in the streets and constant sniping. The car bomb was
introduced in March and more shops and offices were turned into rubble.
Constant ambushes in the country and a border war drew British forces
away from the urban areas. There was no peace with or without justice,
and more observers began to feel that the Provos just might bomb their
way to a place at some ultimate bargaining table. And in fact they did. In
July 1972 the new British Cabinet Minister in charge of Ireland finally
met secretly in London with leading members of the Provos. As a first

step a truce was negotiated. The distance between the Provos—release all internees and prisoners, amnesty for all, British withdrawal from Ulster, and an Irish solution—and the British was vast. After all, Northern Ireland was an integral part of the United Kingdom whose inhabitants had by large majorities repeatedly declared their loyalty to the Crown and whose future was protected by parliamentary legislation. Still the impossible had happened and the Provos were in London to talk to the Cabinet. For rebels, most of whom had been retired, often for decades, or who were not involved in politics two years before, they had come a long way.

They were, it turned out, still a long way from the end of the road. The truce collapsed. The London talks were revealed by the Provos. The British Cabinet, outraged, decided to shift tactics once again. That a truce would lead to a formal accommodation had been a dubious prospect at best but worth attempting. The British in Operation Motorman moved troops into the No-Go zones, undefended by the Provos. There were more bomb blasts in Belfast. More voices called for a pause, including even those of the Official IRA. The Provos paid no attention and settled down to a campaign of attrition. After the brief emotion of the Derry deaths receded in the south, the Dublin government took increasingly hostile steps to limit IRA activities: arrests, new security legislation, internment, and harassment. Repression, north and south, the British determination to stick it out, the criticism of all types of Irish political opinion including the Official Republican Movement, the decline of international interest, the erosion of support by the exhausted minority, and the risks of renewed sectarian violence in no way diminished the determination of the Army Council to pursue the revolt.

The "Formula" British Response

Between the first great burst of sectarian violence in August 1969 and the campaign of attrition in 1973 the British response to Irish events, despite the special nature of Ulster, followed a pattern remarkably similar to those of the previous generation of imperial dissolution. It may be possible to say, and a good many Irishmen have done so, that this is so for an obvious reason: Britain's relation to Ireland has always been that of a colonial power. Although this might be a simplistic analysis of eight hundred years of very complicated history, a pattern emerges nevertheless. First, the British were surprised at the sectarian violence of August 1969, surprised at the rapid decay of the situation in 1971, surprised at the depth of hatred and the repeated recourse to violence, and perhaps it should be pointed out horrified as well. Maulding's comment after his first investigatory trip to Ulster was an appalled "what a bloody awful place!'' The initial tendency was to blame the new troubles on both Green and Orange bigots, but increasingly British animosity focused on the IRA. Indignation replaced horror at the tiny Republican minority's violent operations against the British army performing legitimate peacekeeping duties for the benefit of all. Clearly the IRA maintained support by intimidation, since most Catholics surely wanted only decent reforms and peace. The IRA, then, was illegitimate, outlawed in the north and south, composed of dreadful bombers who killed innocent civilians in an effort to force the loyalist majority into an alien state against their interests, in opposition to the promises of the London government, to the inclinations of the Dublin government, and perhaps even to the wishes of the Catholic minority, beneficiary of all sorts of British welfare programs.

These Irish Republican terrorists, unlike the Chinese communists in Malaya or the Mau Mau murderers in Kenya, were not all that alien to the British; but the aspirations of a secret army so disreputable as to be disowned even by the Irish Republican government in Dublin, not to mention most respectable opinion elsewhere, were alien enough. Thus, by 1971 British attitudes differed little from what they had been elsewhere in the Empire: surprise, shock, outraged indignation, a public determination not to deal with a small, illegitimate gang of violent men who used terror to garner support for a mistaken and flawed cause. In February 1971, when security forces slipped from peacekeeping into anti-insurgency, the typical two-pronged British attack on the problem began: military and security operations in the service of political initiatives that sought to erode rebel support by creating parallel options. Even the fact that the political option had been so haltingly deployed was not novel and much ground had already been covered before March 1972 by committees and investigations and consultations, as well as pressure on Stormont to do something more for the minority. The promulgation of Stormont was seen in part as a means to open up the road to a regional solution by devolution that would wean the minority from an all-Ireland solution. The Provo-Cabinet meeting in London probably resulted in large part from British hopes that a truce would work to British advantage by reducing the role of the gunmen and giving the minority a taste for the quiet life; whatever the ulterior motive, it revealed once more British flexibility. London had officially, if secretly, talked to the terrorists, just as they had talked to nearly everyone. In the year since internment, Britain had kept on throwing out lines and floating balloons.

The Ulster Emergency is peculiar in that no longer are important British security interests involved. (There never were serious economic considerations since the province absorbs far more funds than it returns.) However, it concerns the future of a part of the United Kingdom inhabited by those who, despite their professions of loyalty, are cherished by few in Britain. In 1921 Britain managed to cope with far more unusual and complicated Irish challenges; now London appears set on enduring the difficulties in the name of moral responsibility—to evacuate would insure sectarian civil war. Since the Conservatives, and now Labour, refuse to withdraw and have not found a formula to defuse the IRA, the Emergency may drag on for some time. All that an uneasy unilateral truce has accomplished is a decline in military casualties and a rise in sectarian murder.

The Irish as Rebels

The Irish rebels have remarkable similarities with their immediate imperial predecessors. The men, that hard core of dedicated and zealous men who came into the streets of Belfast in 1969 to defend their people, represented a movement, an attitude, a response fashioned by a heritage and an experience stretching back almost into the Celtic twilight. But Irish Republicanism, the specific political movement, sprang from Wolfe Tone and the French Revolution. Their cause, a united Ireland, free and Gaelic without religious distinction, had regularly attracted the idealistic and dedicated, often from a background neither Catholic nor Celtic. For two centuries the means had been the same: the use of physical force to break the British connection, the source of all Irish ills. Coupled with their long Republican heritage, the men in Belfast had lived their lives humiliated and oppressed in what should have been their own country by the institutionalized injustice of the Stormont system.

As often was the case, the Irish Republican cause in Ulster was flawed; no matter how the province of Northern Ireland had been created, or why, it was inhabited by a million Protestants who abhorred the idea of a united Ireland. For them there were two Irelands. Their wishes had been respected in the legislation of the British parliament, in the gradual and graceless acquisition to this fact by the Dublin government, and even by long toleration of individuals and institutions of the minority. The enlightened in the majority accepted that discrimination and oppression might have to go, but would accept neither need nor legitimacy in any all-Ireland solution. Irish Republicans contended that the Protestant minority had no right to stand in the path of a nation; that the "majority" had been manipulated for British interests and that once the connection was broken it would be absorbed to great advantage in a new Ireland; and that in any case there could be no justice for the Ulster Catholics outside a united Ireland.

Thus, in 1969 a small group of zealots had a cause, flawed or not, a remedy for the existing intolerable troubles, and a heritage of revolt. They knew what was wrong and how to cure it. During the autumn and winter of 1969-1970 the Provisionals created an alternative IRA and absorbed some units, north and south, or built up new ones. They did not alter the old form. Because of the habits of the past and the limited number of arms, the Provos remained a conspiracy of rebels tied into local neighborhoods, a structure guaranteeing an urban guerrilla strategy. No one really considered novel structures; the old structures would do, were comfortable, and reflected the reality of the situation in the north. Unlike other rebels once the organization was set and to a degree armed, there was no sense that time was running out, that someone must strike soon, nor any feeling that victory must be grasped immediately. Delay was for specific purposes since all were confident that sooner or later a revolt would occur. Between 1969 and 1971, the Provos concentrated on transforming themselves from Catholic Defenders to Rebels Against the Crown, without losing the support of the people. This point was reached by February 1971, when sufficient arms had been acquired. Internment in August simply made the shift more obvious.

The IRA did not create long-range scenarios. Its prime concern was to manipulate conditions so the revolt could begin. When that point was reached, the Army Council assumed that escalating operations in Northern Ireland would make the province ungovernable, destroy the Stormont regime, and coerce the British into withdrawing. Few recognized that because of a long heritage of attitudes and previous experience, tactical options would be limited unless seriously reappraised. Whole categories of tactics or techniques fell outside intended Provo practice: assassination, operations in either Britain or southern Ireland, spectacular "stunts," or calculated casualties in large operations in the north. The Official IRA was more flexible, but it fell along the wayside, abandoning most military activities for political ones. Also, Provo tactics, although they created great sound and fury, were not carefully orchestrated for effect or cunningly directed at a target rather than the victim. The Ulster campaign did not become an intolerable burden to Britain in funds, pride, or lives, although normal life collapsed under the detonating bombs. Therefore, as time passed Provo hopes shifted from coercing the British into leaving to the prolonged effect of violent attrition. There was *some* hope that leverage might work, perhaps within the Labour Party, but centuries of exposure to British hyprocrisy had convinced the Irish that London would rule without shame. And the official reports and explanations concerning outrages in Ireland—whether torture or Bloody Sunday or internment—underlined the lessons of the past. Unlike Palestine, Ireland was not a glass house, the Provos had no prominent friends, and the British public would support their army's exercises against the

Irish terrorists most of the time. The only hope was that the British would tire of defending "a bloody awful place" and withdraw under some face-saving formula. Accordingly, the same tactics, improved or elaborated, were continued: commercial sabotage by means of bombs, sniping, mass confrontations, and ambushes in the countryside. There was some improvement in techniques and more sophisticated weapons were introduced, but, with one or two exceptions, no novel tactical innovations were attempted.

As always, the armed struggle dominated the revolt and absorbed the interest and talent of the most committed; also, as always, it managed to send out but one message unit. Provo efforts to devise a political face with a political party, Sinn Féin, and support of a nine-county Ulster assembly, were largely ignored. (Sinn Féin traditionally ran candidates who would not take their seats in the "puppet" regimes in Dublin, Belfast, or at Westminster.) In spite of unilateral truces, massed demonstrations, and the rent and rate strikes, it appeared obvious that if conventional politics prevailed the Provos would be a small minority. Not unlike the dilemma that faced Begin in Palestine, they were in a position of bombing their political opponents into positions of power once the campaign ended and the ballot returned. The Army Council, reluctant to recognize this fact, hoped that once the British connection was broken the political scene, north and south, would be transformed. Thus, the Irish rebels against the Crown concentrated on military operations in the north, determined to wait it out, convinced that this time the connection would be broken and Ireland free at last.

Lethal Dialogues

If the British in Ireland followed the script without much editing and the Provos nearly so, the nature of their lethal dialogue hews even more closely to previous experience. No matter how complex and sophisticated the overt strategy of revolt may be, the basic essential for the rebels is to send a single, violent message unit, loud, persistant, adamant, and, if possible, only interrupted to rebel advantage. This effort in communication ordinarily absorbs almost all the movement's available talent and energies. And it does in Ireland. Subsidiary activities, civic disobedience or strikes or demonstrations, all those aspects of the strategies of agitation and confrontation, would be inappropriate and futile unless orchestrated with the armed struggle. In addition, much "political" activity is aimed at supporting the military: money, men, weapons, communications, intelligence, and propaganda maneuvered by the men behind the guns. Much legitimate agitation—demonstrations of mass support, riotous meetings, boycotts, displays, and gestures—is a means to increase the din of the armed struggle and erode the assets of the opponent.

The key for the rebel is armed violence. Once that is controlled as in Malaya or Kenya or Egypt by security operations, all is lost. A deaf British ear can be turned from the fainter and fainter message unit of violence. The rebel may be defeated by a combination of factors beyond the scope of his message unit, as was Grivas, or succeed because of decisions equally beyond his capacity to alter, as was the case in Aden, but as long as the message can be sent at volume he has not lost. Consequently, a movement must be so shaped and so directed that the message unit can be sent even under severe pressure. After that other messages taking other forms—a unilateral truce, a United Nations resolution, a petition to the Commons, or the intervention of friends—may be devised; but the overwhelmingly important question remains how to persist and perhaps to escalate the most effective means of communication.

There were not in Ireland or elsewhere a great many strategic options considered nor detailed expectations. Armed revolt is a crude and costly means of communication, and rebel analysis tends to reflect this. The strategy of most of the movements against the British can be set out in slogans: (1) Begin before it is too late, because we must (2) Keep up the pressure, without risking too many of our people (3) Because of the winds of history and the righteousness of the cause in time, willingly or no, the British, being British, will concede. Whether in Belfast or Aden the rebel arrives at the sticking point with all but one of the big questions answered: how to devise tactics that will amplify the single message unit.

Rebels concentrate on techniques and tactics, not strategic scenarios: which operations are possible; which will be effective in humiliating or damaging the British, especially, often solely, their security forces. And, as in Ireland, the possible has already been determined by the limitations of ideology, by the attitudes and values of the rebel and his people, by the structure of the organization, by the limitations of the campaign site, and by the assumed response of the British. No matter what the conditions or the situation at the moment the struggle begins, usually only a few tactical options remain to open the lethal dialogue.

Once under way, a rebel movement can rarely draw back; even a truce carries great dangers permitting decay of caution, guaranteeing exposure of the hidden, and encouraging a decline in militant support. In a real sense the rebel is doomed to his original either/or proposition. His only really effective means is violent; the protest and agitation often engendered by the armed struggle would fade away in normal negotiations —or so the rebel fears. Except in the realm of violence the British opponent, legitimate, replete with talent and funds, and practiced in diplomacy, has all the assets. This was a major factor in engendering the revolt in the first place; the British would not engage in a decent dialogue with alien spokesmen. All that remained was armed struggle or bitter resignation. In Ireland, more than anyplace, a heritage reflecting this analysis had been handed down through the generations. For Wolfe Tone, as for every Irish Republican since, the only effective means to free the country has been physical force. Others may place their hope in conciliation or confrontation, in agitation in the streets or election to parliament, boycott or general strike, but not the zealous and adamant Irish rebel. He knows from his reading of the past centuries that regarding Irish matters Britain listens to but one message, physical force. And few of his distant peers in Aden or Malaya or Cairo would disagree. If, then, the Irish template is placed over the entire recent British imperial experience, the fit is more than adequate. The British response to the revolt in Northern Ireland coincided to a remarkable degree to those of the generation of imperial dissolution.

PART FOUR

The Rebel Vocation

*The tree of liberty must be refreshed from
time to time with the blood of patriots and
tyrants.*

　　　　　　　　　　　　—Thomas Jefferson

A Palestinian Fedayeen at the Munich Olympics.

10 The Lethal Dialogue

Insurrection is a calculus with very indefinite magnitudes, the value of which may change every day.

—*Karl Marx*

Out of the long generation of imperial insurrection that stretched from Bevingrad in Jerusalem to the Bogside in Derry has come a wealth of lessons for the astute, a patchwork of myths and legends, tried techniques for the security forces, encouragement for other rebels—raw ore for future analysis. In the world of the rebel, no matter how distant from British imperial concerns or strange the banner of defiance, the long litany—the King David, Murder Mile, Mt. Kenya, Grivas and Begin and Kenyatta, and as always the IRA—has a special place. And that place is most special, for the dialogue between the rebel and the forces of the Crown, like all such lethal dialogues, has been special, unwieldy in comparison, fascinating, but often without application. British response to provocation often seemed to bear only slight resemblance to that of the Russians or Japanese. If, after 1944, an observer could watch British colonial history appear to repeat itself as each new rebel reached the barricades, it was because those rebels against the Crown had special assets, a particular opponent, and struck within a unique context. Rebels elsewhere had other assets, liabilities, and expectations—and a different opponent.

Imperial Revolts: Similarities

Similarities between Grivas and Castro or Begin and Ben Bella can, nevertheless, be recognized. The rebel's vocation apparently imposed similar disciplines and restraints, afforded similar rewards and risks. Techniques, indigenous or borrowed, of both participants in the lethal dialogue, the tactics of revolt if not the strategy, proved similar to those used in Kenya or Cyprus: assassination squads, tracker dogs, internment, ambushes, robbery for the cause, and guerrillas in the hills. Except for technological advances, the guerrillas of the Napoleonic Wars or the terrorists of Narodnaya Volya in Tsarist Russia would have found little alien. Techniques and tactics are relatively simple to learn and to apply, so British experience was exploited easily. The broad strategic concepts of the British imperial rebel, when they existed, seemed irrelevant to others or, if promising, difficult of application in an alien context. Few bothered to investigate the complex middle ground where the rebel against the Crown must fashion relatively well-known techniques into a tactical thrust for strategic purpose; the ensuing strategies were usually considered so specifically oriented to the British opponent as to be elsewhere inapplicable.

In a generation that witnessed the collapse of historic empires and the emergence of a new world of new nations, broad anti-imperial strategies were devised by rebels with similar aspirations, emboldened by similar assumptions. In the East Indies, the Dutch, accepting their limited resources, withdrew under pressure without even the benefit of a Commonwealth Strategy to soften the exodus. In Madagascar and Indochina the French refused to accept the end of empire. The humiliation of Dien Bien Phu in 1954 only strengthened their resolve in Algeria. Yet by 1960 all had changed, particularly in Paris where Gallic genius transformed an empire of discontent into a community of friends. In the Congo in 1960 the Belgians evacuated, leaving anarchy tempered by mercenaries. By then the British process of devolution was proceeding apace. Only the Portuguese, lacking other assets or the restraint of public dissent, clung to their colonial heritage for another decade, and so added to the litany of revolt the struggles in Angola, Mozambique, and Guinea-Bissau. Elsewhere, without exception, the early rebels' grand strategy had been appropriate and the wave of the future flowed over the old empires. Even tiny atolls and obscure enclaves ran up national banners and appeared at the United Nations in a world transformed, and transformed in part by the strategies of the rebels against empire.

Imperial revolts followed the British model to some degree, if no more than the rebel assumption that a tide in the affairs of man was about to crest. Certainly the motives, the aspirations, and the initiatives of the rebels appeared similar: all had been to some degree humiliated by their colonial condition; all sought to liberate a nation, whether historic or new; and few made their way directly to the barricades. In Indochina, Ho Chi Minh hoped first that the French would concede the inevitable and second that conventional military means could win the future. In Portuguese Africa the nationalists hoped for concession and, until the evidence proved to the contrary, that open revolt would be unnecessary; in fact the revolt in Angola swept up the conspirators with their plots incomplete. In their own way the rebels' opponents also seemed to respond in character, if not as had the British then at least as their tradition and heritage dictated. Rebel triumphs in Indochina and Algeria were not won entirely by military means; in large part the victory came in Paris out of the clash of logic, pride, rationality, and morality that sapped the French will to continue and permitted the construction of an effective and satisfactory alternative to empire. The Portuguese regime's dedication to historic responsibility and immunity from dissent permitted an uncompromising response that for a decade did not appear to parallel the British or French examples. In any case the rebels against empire were a special class, facing uncertain and irresolute opponents no longer in easy command of the big battalions or moral certainty.

At the end of the generation of imperial dissolution neither the techniques of revolt nor the strategies of the rebels could be discarded by advocates of national liberation or ignored by their opponents. Despite the victories conceded or won, the world was not satisfactorily transformed, even with the Portuguese collapse into "revolution" in 1974. The overt imperialism bested in Kenya or Algeria appeared to many to be but one facet of oppression, only the most obvious and visible opponent in an unsatisfactory world dominated and exploited by arrogant, greedy power centers. After the disappearance of colonies, there remained frustrated nationalists, zealots in causes others considered irrelevant or dangerous, utopian or flawed, as well as aspirations that created indignation and repression. Nevertheless, rebels rose to transform a world by means familiar to the imperial rebel, and, like him, aware of the necessity to rise against a foreign oppressor or domestic tyrant and end the humiliations of the past.

Whether the revolt is urban or rural, communist or not, separatist or irredentist, guerrilla-revolution or urban terror, most of the rebels involved feel that they struggle, whatever the tactics and whatever the ultimate form of their triumph, to liberate the nation. The opponent is as alien as would be a colonial oppressor, a minority regime supported or imposed from abroad or a tyrant enslaving the people for criminal purposes. The rebel opposes those who would bury the inchoate nation or the wiles of neo-imperialism, struggles against all those powers and dominations that have so far prohibited the emergence of a world of free men and free nations. He almost inevitably defines his struggle in terms of the opponent, the oppressor.

Dialogue in the British Empire concerned a legitimacy, on the one hand recognized by law, habit, and custom, and denied on the other with recourse to history and the supposedly demonstrable evil of colonialism, an alien occupier. To the rebel in Ulster or Oman or Rhodesia the opponent is illegitimate and alien: an imperial presence imposed by force oppressing the march of an Irish nation; a puppet regime created for imperialist purposes and overtly supported by foreign forces for alien purposes as in Oman; or a blatantly unrepresentative regime established for minority purposes, tolerated or supported by external and alien aid as in Rhodesia. In nearly all cases the rebel sees, often quite properly, that this alien opponent is but one facet of a vast, world structure of oppression. The Budapest revolt in 1956 opposed not simply a puppet Hungarian regime but, as swift Soviet intervention indicated, Russian control of Eastern Europe. Ché Guevara in the foco in Bolivia anticipated correctly that in some form the power and influence of the United States would be brought to bear against him. This rebel analysis of the opponent's illegitimacy, of being a pawn in the hands of distant, powerful oppressors, gives comfort during a difficult and protracted struggle. The foe is as evil as the old imperialists, as alien and as illegitimate, and is difficult to defeat because of the world system of oppression.

The need for an omnipotent opponent arose in the last generation partly as a result of the long litany of rebel failure. Apart from the struggles against open colonialism in Algeria or Palestine or Indochina, few revolts have been able to triumph over the forces at the center. China, a most special case, has everywhere been the example par excellence, followed by Cuba. There are few other relevant examples, only many continuing claimants to power. And power often changes hands with bewildering rapidity as a violent form of musical chairs produces one new regime after another. The Third World is wracked with coups that change little. The nation remains unliberated; only the faces in the limousines change.

In a generation the number of frustrated revolts, even those extended beyond symbolic bombs or conspiracy to open armed struggle, boggle the imagination. Almost no Latin American nation has been without its groups of rebels, but only Castro has grasped power. In Venezuela during President Rómulo Betancourt's five-year regime, one that ended with a unique democratic transfer of power, fifty-six attempts to seize power were recorded. For years there was violence, uncertainty, plots, and riots. Chaos became conventional. And yet Betancourt survived. In Latin America power might change hands illicitly within the oligarchy or be snatched by the military, but the rebels remain in the hills or university basements. In Africa attempts to bring down the minority regimes in Rhodesia and South Africa foundered, as did attempts to set up new nations in Biafra and Katanga. Some rebels, those in the southern Sudan, for example, compromised and found an accommodation with the center; some in Zaire or Eritrea have persisted with varying degrees of success; but none like Castro have swept into the capital and power after a successful campaign in the bush except those engaged in an overt anti-imperialist struggle—and that is won in Paris or Lisbon not the bush. In Europe no separatist or irredentist movement, including ETA in the Basque country and the IRA in Northern Ireland, has managed to do more than persist. To the east Russian intervention in Prague in 1968 again revealed the effective brutality of the socialist camp as directed by Moscow. In Asia, after twenty-five years and millions dead, the rebels in Indochina at last arrived in Saigon. Along with the triumph of the Khmer Rouge in Cambodia and the assumption of control by the Pathet Lao in Laos, Ho Chi Minh's dream became reality. Elsewhere in Asia, however, communist rebels have yet to find the road to power out of the bush and into the capital.

It is a comfort in troubled times for the rebel to view his immediate opponent as but the tip of a vast and powerful lance. How else to explain effectively the long and so far futile record of failure, the frustration in achieving a goal sanctioned by history? If such an oppressive, transnational system is seen to exist and always successfully exerts massive power against those who would resist, then there is no hope and none but those deluded by fantasies would rebel. This is not the case, for the rebel assumes that the oppressive system is ultimately vulnerable and believes that protracted resistance will result in the creation of rebel assets that will assure ultimate triumph. If this were not true, the rebel's goal would become, not the search for political power through armed struggle, but merely a symbolic flourish taken at great risk, a pointless, futile gesture of defiance. A protracted campaign, far from being a romantic excursion, a refusal to recognize reality, can be a carefully constructed exercise in nation-building and character transformation. Those previously humiliated and exploited, the wretched of the earth, through battle are transformed into the inheritors of a new nation also born out of the armed struggle through a catharsis of violence.

Despite the interim virtues of a protracted revolt, most rebels feel not only that success is the most important objective but that it can be achieved because the opponent *is* vulnerable as well as powerful. The Marxist-Leninists describe their opponents as paper tigers, vast and outwardly impressive but rent with hidden contradictions, vulnerable to the inevitable clash of classes, doomed by history. Even less ideologically rigorous rebels are convinced that the tides of history flow in their direction. The rebel, even if premature, opposes an inwardly fragile enemy and can exploit the hidden flaw by means of a varying but generally applicable formula of revolutionary activity. The alien regimes, unable to frustrate the rebels, will collapse not so much as a result of the armed struggle but as a consequence of the mass transformation the struggle will produce. In other words, the foco will begin a chain reaction that will sweep the people into power. In more modest terms, the advocates of the long guerrilla campaigns in southern Africa contend that the example of the armed struggle coupled with the discipline of the movement over the years will build new men and new nations on the ruins of imperialism and minority rule. Everywhere the communists await the disintegration of the capitalist-imperialist ruling class. No matter what the ideological assumptions, the contemporary rebel, if facing an adamant and powerful system of oppression, also possesses the sure and certain knowledge that the opponent's power is almost always flawed.

In certain cases, however, the rebels face an apparently insurmountable challenge. Outside the rhetoric of distant radicals or desperate dreamers, certain potential opponents seem immune to revolt. Defining them as capitalist-imperialists or alien oppressors appears to have no effect, for all revolts against them are abortive or none succeed. When threatened, efficient and determined authoritarian regimes have deployed their big battalions quickly, effectively, and without compunction, as rebels in Budapest and Tibet and Prague discovered. In Budapest a revolt sprang spontaneously from a people gripped for the moment by the delirium of the bold. With the arrival of Soviet armor their aspirations receded in despair and repression. Equally true, efficient and dedicated democratic regimes proved capable of accommodating almost all legitimate grievance, if not quickly or without trauma, at least within the system. Only when the national issue appeared as a challenge to the regime, as in Quebec or Northern Ireland, did agitation evolve into a serious challenge and at least in part because the rebel aspirations for a Republic of Quebec or a united Ireland had a foundation in reality that the dreams of the Black Panthers in the United States or the Baader-Meinhof Group in Germany lacked. The capacity of either the authoritarian or democratic center to repress or conciliate the rebel might well decay under the pressure of a strained economy, the defeat of the army, or the rise of novel challenges opening the door to revolt. A threatened authoritarian regime may grow more brutal but inefficient, permitting an expanding pool of unpunished discontent that might shelter rebel fish, as occurred in Tsarist Russia. A democratic regime grown incompetent and ineffectual may be unable to adapt to changed demands or respond to legitimate grievance, thereby emboldening the impatient and ambitious, as recently happened in Uruguay and before that in Weimar Germany and the Kingdom of Italy.

The efficient totalitarian or accommodating democratic regimes aside, there has been ample opportunity for revolts against opponents the rebels see as vulnerable. Every rebel has faith in the future and believes that his cause is just and *therefore*, if right in the past has not made might under rebel direction, it will in the future. Even after eight hundred years, each generation of Irish rebels believes that this time is the last time. The rebel often accepts that being right and opposing evil may alone be an insufficient basis for launching an armed struggle; the world abounds in evil and institutionalized injustice successfully defended for years by the forces of oppression. The rebel must have more than a pure heart; so his strategists have sought evidence of his opponent's vulnerability: minority support, class schisms, artificial nationalism, growing inefficiency, self-destructive initiatives, the escalating alienation from the people. By and large, the rebel seeks flaws rather than virtues in an opponent. And it is comforting to know that Latin American dictators, white minority regimes, and reactionary Asian cliques are doomed not only by history but also by their own internal contradictions and hidden weaknesses. It is distressing for the rebel and his cause when these flaws do not produce the anticipated collapse. The rebel analysis of the enemy both hides and reveals reality, and defines away, at least in part, the opponent's assets. The rebel strikes from weakness and must perforce be emboldened in part by an analysis that reduces the odds against him.

All opponents, whether the British or Batista, in rebel eyes have certain common traits: they are alien, illegitimate oppressors, doomed by history; though outwardly powerful and often part of a vast transnational system of oppression, inwardly they are vulnerable. In devising a strategy of national liberation the potential rebel must try to determine how his enemy will respond. Some rebels assume that with the advent of armed struggle such a consideration will be of little import since within months the regime will collapse. Less sanguine rebels accept that there is nothing to do but begin. To some degree at least, most rebels anticipate that the opponent will respond within a special context; but few, like Begin in Palestine, fashion a strategy on that response. In anti-imperial struggles the rebels assumed that antiwar sentiment in the imperial capital would be a significant asset, so rebel tactics in the field often were shaped to encourage its growth. In Vietnam the Tet offensive of 1968 was targeted on the United States. And if the Americans did not respond exactly as had the French in 1954, or as the British or Portuguese might have, nevertheless, there was some response. Elsewhere, more often than not, the response came as a surprise to the rebel too content with optimistic generalizations or too sure of ultimate victory. Many rebels seem content to concentrate on tactics—guerrilla war or rural foco—overlooking the potential asset of anticipating the opponent's response to provocation. Even this may not be as dangerous for rebel purposes as anticipating that the opponent will respond as if the optimistic, self-serving analysis tered in Washington and an alien, artificial crusader state imposed in the Middle East for distant but anti-Arab purposes would save the Zionists. In the struggle against colonialism, racism, oppression, and exploitation, Israel was for the Arabs an ideal foe, not only evil but also uniquely vulnerable. This was, as intended, comforting to the fedayeen: Israel as a paper tiger; Israel vulnerable to guerrilla tactics; Israel the epitome of the doomed forces of colonialism. Those fedayeen who advocated Marxist-Leninist analysis in only slightly different language came to the same conclusions.

As time passed and the Israelis thwarted the guerrilla raids and maintained law and order in the occupied zones, an elaboration of the original analysis was made in the fedayeen camp. A few had always contended that the Israelis were but part of a much broader problem. The enemy was not just Israel, or even the West, but all who might oppose the revolutionary future in the name of the conventional present. And the most dangerous were the reactionary Arab regimes. In order to release the Arab masses, already inspired by the armed struggle, and sweep away the Zionist state, a revolution within the Arab world was necessary. Unable to exploit the Israelis' hidden flaws with guerrilla tactics, the fedayeen increasingly turned elsewhere for an opponent and an explanation of their growing frustration. This led in September 1970 to an intra-Arab war in Jordan, the expulsion of the fedayeen groups, and a serious reduction in the capacity of the Palestinian leadership to act on events. Carefully monitored in Syria, uneasily tolerated in Lebanon, publicly praised and secretly hampered by the Arab regimes, the fedayeen, no longer a serious threat to either Israel or the host regimes, struck out with the tactics of terror against any vulnerable opponent.

For a generation the Israeli response to provocation had followed a pattern visible to all but the blind: swift, brutal, often efficient retaliation. For over a generation the Israelis had constructed a military establishment honed to perfection, a society that despite unique difficulties had proven flexible and effective, and a dedication of its citizens to the continuing survival of the state, no matter what the cost nor how great the sacrifice. Zionism as a creed might be open to ideological attacks as a late romantic collection of odds and ends based on bad history and dubious sociology; but Israel was in 1967 a fact, with a reality that fedayeen analysis could only evade out of desperate need. So the Arabs, following their own vision, summoned up an artificially vulnerable Israel. In despair they turned to guerrilla tactics, claiming them to be the one true means of victory rather then the only hope left. No effort was made to describe a real Israel, or even one recognizable to the disinterested observer, only to depicting a fictitious opponent. No attempt was made to use Israeli assets as Arab virtues; the Israelis facing the guerrillas would *have* no assets.

So the Arabs launched their fedayeen against an unreal opponent. There was not even a real guerrilla campaign, only raids across the border. The Arab masses in the occupied zone did not rise, did not even organize to support the fedayeen, and only rarely aided the guerrillas. The leaders of the fedayeen month after month chose fantasy over reality, hewed to their own special version of reality, explained away disaster in the field as victory, insisted the fault lay not with them but with traitors elsewhere. In 1967 the fedayeen had been quite right that conventional means to oppose Israel had aborted and that, unless the Palestinian cause was to be discarded, unconventional means were the alternative. The fedayeen contention that irregular means *alone* would prove totally effective proved to be wishful thinking. Perhaps irregular means coupled with conventional resources and directed against an Israel that bore some relation to an objective reality and orchestrated to an anticipated reaction might have had more effect. The use of terror might have provoked the Israelis to self-defeating retaliation. Eventually there were those who hoped to force a massive Israeli retaliatory invasion but had little grasp of the means to this end. No matter what might have happened, the fedayeen defined Israel so that their own available option —guerrilla tactics—would alone be certain of victory. For a generation the Arabs had ample opportunity to dissect the reality of Israel; they preferred their plaster version. It was more important to them to define a hidden flaw than to discover how to manipulate revealed strength. And when the flaw remained hidden, the Arab masses quiescent, the fedayeen ineffectual, by then the initial optimism had wasted too many Arab resources, either a real resistance in the occupied zones or a carefully constructed campaign of terror and provocation were beyond the scope of the attenuated movement.

Israel's reaction, flexible, cunning, and rigorous, to the fedayeen strategy was similar to responses to earlier provocations. To a degree the campaign innoculated the Israelis to excessive outraged indignation followed by massive retaliation, but not so much that the subsequent Black September campaign of terror was countered by less than traditional, forthright methods. Whether raiding into Beirut or seizing in-flight airliners, the Israelis reacted as might have been anticipated. The general significance of the response to revolt is not so much the variances produced by diverse national characteristics, but that for the rebel to anticipate these is an advantage. A few strategists like Begin can make such anticipation an absolute advantage. Others can add to their meager assets.

The shrewd rebel also recognizes that his opponent not only will react in a special way but also will have available a considerable number of options when faced with a revolt. While the rebel must concentrate on his single message unit, the threatened regime may and usually does respond in a variety of ways. In fact dependence solely on a firm military response indicates a feeble and ineffectual revolt, a diminutive threat. For example, in September 1963 Jorge Masetti, convinced that Ché Guevara's concept of the foco strategy was valid, opened a front in northern Argentina. Isolated in the rough country without intelligence or adequate supplies, the guerrillas were a threat to no one but themselves. So obscure was Masetti's challenge that not until a radical newspaper, *Compañero,* in Buenos Aires announced their existence did the authorities realize that there was a "revolt." By February 1964 the foco was wracked by sickness, executions, and desertions without ever striking a blow. Eventually in March the Argentine army showed up and by April eliminated the foco. Masetti fled into the jungles of Yuto, never to return. The Argentine government under moderate President Arturo Illia simply had no reason to respond to Masetti with anything but effective force; for the foco represented no one, could inspire no one, and could neither vitalize the masses nor spread the gospel. Masetti had played out a deadly fantasy.

A rebel-regime dialogue is always asymmetrical, for the weak can seldom afford more than one line of communication and often must steal from all others—propaganda, intelligence, political demonstrations, foreign contacts—to continue the armed struggle. The regime, on the other hand, brutal or benevolent, tyrannical or representative, with a demonstrative capacity for survival possesses the conventional resources of a legitimate state and can respond in many ways. Only when sufficient power exists at the center, as was the case with Masetti in 1964 and in Budapest in 1956, is recourse to other options unnecessary. Usually revolts tend to be protracted and the regime resorts to the use of parallel initiatives: it isolates the rebels through international contacts or new agricultural policies; it punishes and rewards, promises or threatens. The mix of responses is often related to security matters aimed at repression rather than transforming the "unliberated" nation.

The Experience of the Palestine Fedayeen

On paper the fedayeen in 1967 appeared to have most of the textbook assets for a successful guerrilla revolt: safe bases; the overt support of several legitimate governments; access to arms, supplies, and money; enthusiastic volunteers; an ocean of friendly Arabs in the occupied zone; and a cause greatly admired in many quarters. The Arab

world extolled them and the international press swarmed around fedayeen headquarters. The Israeli response was hampered because any Arab
resistance had to be met by security forces, that is, continued repression.
Unlike a German or Russian response to active resistance movement, the
Israeli would be monitored by the world press. Even if the authorities
preferred brutality, which they did not, it would have been impossible.
And Israel apparently had no conventional parallel political initiatives
available to woo an Arab population long alienated by Zionist aggression. As the occupying power, it did, however, have certain resources
overlooked at the moment and fashioned a mix that proved more effective than the fedayeen's guerrilla forays.

After three humiliating defeats at the hands of Israel, many Arabs,
while they dreamed the same dreams as the fedayeen, had serious doubts
about the ultimate outcome of a guerrilla campaign and different, more
parochial priorities. The new enthusiasm and new guerrilla tactics did not
convince the vulnerable inhabitants of the occupied zone. The Arab population believed, correctly or not, that given sufficient provocation,
using one excuse or another, the Israelis would expel them from the
West Bank. Most Arabs remained convinced that the original Arab exodus in 1948 that had created the refugee problem resulted from specific
Israeli policies. And in the occupied zone the Israelis, by destroying
"guilty" villages or houses, sequestering "guilty" property, expelling the
suspected and their "guilty" relatives, had shown that even marginal
cooperation with the fedayeen would prove costly. To cooperate with
certain winners was one thing, but to aid the probable loser, even a loser
in the national cause, was a less appealing course. The Israelis could, and
did, reward and punish. Playing on fear and parochial interests, setting
one faction against another, opening economic opportunities to the
greedy, employing the fruits of long years of intelligence, they made the
creation of a real resistance movement difficult.

Simultaneously with the details of the security operations, two long-
range trends developed: the rapid incorporation of the occupied zones
into the Israeli orbit; and the slow but visible freezing of the status quo.
The Arabs clearly lacked the conventional military capacity to change
matters—the end of the Egyptian war of attrition indicated that—and no
Arab regime would make a conventional peace. A stalemate existed that
only the fedayeen offered to break, and yet could not. Each month the
Israeli presence was more permanent, and with it certain advantages such
as public works and a booming economy. The fedayeen offered only sacrifice. Only when the Israeli presence, briefly, was distant, as in the Gaza
Strip, did the fedayeen have an opportunity to punish as well as promise
rewards. While the public eye was focused on the guerrilla spectaculars
the Israelis continued to tighten their grip on the Arab communities,

spending discreetly and harvesting with violence. Israel became the accepted authority, recognized daily by the Arabs in a variety of small ways: forms signed, permits accepted, jobs sought. Thus Israel responded to the fedayeen campaign despite severe limitations and the Arab assets, a response made easier because the Arabs did not effect a sufficiently lethal message unit to disrupt the process.

The fedayeen analysis of evolving events proved less than useful, but for reasons other than their warped description of the Zionist opponent. In the case of the time scenarios, the fedayeen were not so much inaccurate as irrelevant. When al-Fatah organized the first fedayeen operation on December 31, 1964, blowing up a water pump at El Koton in Israel, there was none of what was to become "typical" Arab optimism. Early efforts at armed struggle were deplored by all segments of Arab opinion. Most governments advocated Nasser's opposition to adventures until it was possible to achieve sure victory. Even the Palestine Liberation Organization opposed premature moves. The radicals doubted that the road to the future lay through parochial Palestine nationalism. And everyone, including the Israelis, had little but scorn for the blundering fedayeen operations. In the first three months only seven raids could be mounted, and little damage was done except to al-Fatah credibility. At this stage the core of al-Fatah anticipated that the armed struggle would have a greater impact on the Arab mind than the existence of Israel. Even the most optimistic plans did not foresee impending military success over Israel. The goal was to raise the issue of Palestine for another generation, to save the country from the patience and prudence urged by Arab allies.

The June War changed everything. The conventional Arab regimes were disgraced, the new weapons wasted, and the old strategies discredited. The fedayeen insisted that the only remaining path to salvation was guerrilla war. Humiliated and shamed, the Arab world grasped the dream of the fedayeen as an alternative to accepting the reality of the June "setback." By the end of the year the dissenters had publicly recanted. Other Arab countries maneuvered to set up their own fedayeen movements, and the scornful radicals rushed to embrace the Palestinian revolution. In less than a year the fedayeen had been transformed from a little band of irresponsible zealots into new Saladins, Heroes of the Return. At the same time, not unexpectedly, their analysis of future prospects underwent considerable change.

By 1968 many fedayeen thought victory was imminent. The aspirations of 1964 had been achieved in much less time than anticipated: Palestine was a burning issue, the fedayeen the new heroes, the catalyst that would transform the Arab world by means of a guerrilla campaign, destroying Zionism and rewriting history. And, whether or not the masses were on the point of mobilization, Arab enthusiasm was real. The fedayeen had captured the imagination of the Arabs, provided an alternative to the disaster of 1967, and as a result had been flooded with aid and admiration. They were in a position to launch a serious guerrilla-resistance campaign to exploit their very considerable assets. The leadership anticipated a rising level of operations. After a battle at the village of Karameh on the East Bank of the Jordan, where the fedayeen refused to retreat, optimism grew by leaps and bounds. Thereafter the fedayeen grasp on reality began to weaken rapidly. Spokesmen continued to report operations no neutral observer noted, Israeli losses beyond belief, and fedayeen triumphs invisible to skeptical eyes. But even in the heady days of 1969, occasional cold touches of reality could be felt. There had been no large-scale resistance in the occupied zone—a matter of policy, according to spokesmen. There had been only a few operations within Israel—another matter of policy. There were serious fedayeen splits—a matter of adjustment. It was conceded, reluctantly, that victory, though inevitable, was not imminent. Still the leadership assumed that the scales would tip even more in their favor in a year or so.

This relative pessimism, in contrast to the wildly exaggerated claims and invisible victories, arose in part from the impact of guerrilla-revolutionary ideology. An armed struggle was supposed to be protracted, to allow for the creation of a new militant generation, over time to vitalize the masses. The fedayeen recognized that the masses were yet to be mobilized and did not foresee a victory over Israel that year or even the next. Still the prevailing mood was heady optimism.

The highly predictable civil war in Jordan that smashed the fedayeen's hold on the East Bank was a cruel blow. It gradually became apparent that because of escalating inter-Arab conflicts there would be very little time to fight the Israelis. A long series of incidents, first in Jordan and then in Lebanon, weakened the fedayeen capacity to act independently or often at all. Power dribbled away. The masses did not mobilize. Aid and comfort dried up. The foreign journalists drifted off. Faith in "guerrilla action" began to fade as the difficulties of launching operations became insurmountable. Increasingly there was a switch to the tactics of terror. The purpose was no longer to strike at the brittle Zionist state but simply to keep the Palestinian issue alive.

Since the first raid in 1964, the fedayeen have three times accepted scenarios for revolt. In 1964-1966, the fedayeen of al-Fatah, really an armed pressure group in an Arab ideological dispute, felt the need to begin an armed struggle and thus gave limited thought to what was assumed would be the long years ahead. Like many other rebels they saw no end to the struggle. In 1968-1969, the fedayeen movements assumed that victory was both certain and imminent. In 1971-1973, fedayeen aspirations had ebbed and only the need to persist remained; rigid timetables had no place in a terror campaign. Unlike many rebels, the fedayeen estimations concerning time related almost entirely to their own posture rather than to the capacities of the opponent: in 1964-1966, the enemy was Arab lethargy; in 1968-1969, the triumph would be the impending mobilization of the Arab masses; in 1971-1973, the enemy was potential Arab treachery and world imperialism. The scenarios were not unreasonable; others accepted the cycle of pessimism-with-potential, optimism-with-reason, and pessimism-with-persistence. After the Arab euphoria following the October War in 1973, more conventional fedayeen circles were willing to rely, for the time being, on the old weapons of diplomacy and boycott, spiced with an occasional taste of terror—almost a return to the pre-1967 years. What still had not been attempted was to devise a fedayeen timetable based at least in part on the reality of Israel.

The Response to Revolt and the Rebel

By necessity, not choice, the rebel elects armed struggle, usually by irregular means. Yet is is not simply in battle that the rebel is weak, but everywhere; in point of fact, usually *only* on the field of battle does he perform effectively, for that is where all resources must be concentrated. The rebel is seldom able to undertake a survey or appoint commissions, hold elections or pave roads, though where possible, he tries to usurp government functions. Frente de Libertação de Moçambique, FRELIMO, opened schools and clinics, marketed produce, dispensed justice, and played the role of a counter-state in Mozambique. In Ireland in 1920 there were courts in the attics and Cabinet meetings in basements. But whether in Africa or Dublin, everything still depends on the armed struggle, on guerrillas in the bush or in the hills of County Cork. Some rebels may establish a government in exile, as Roberto Holden did for Angola in 1962 with the Govêrno Revolucionáiro de Angola no Exílio or switch to conventional warfare, as Nicos Zakhariades did with the Democratic Army in Greece in November 1948. But unless the men in the field can protect the shadow institutions or operate as a regular army, they give up much of the advantage of the guerrilla. If the time is not ripe to begin a symmetrical dialogue, the new direction may turn out to be an exercise in publicity, as was the case in Angola, or a disastrous innovation, as in Greece. Almost until victory, the key to rebel success lies in effective armed struggle, no matter what the level. All other initiatives must be judged cautiously. The rebel must realize that the regime has not only the big battalions but also the resources to respond in ways beyond the capacity of the weak to equal.

Not only will the rebel's opponent respond within a particular historical and social context and in a variety of ways, he will also persist in opposing rebel ambitions. Some of the most splendid rebel triumphs have come only at the end of protracted and bloody campaigns. Mao Tse Tung persisted from the collapse of the Autumn Harvest rising of 1927 until final victory in 1949. Ho Chi Minh, who began the struggle against the French in 1946, died before the 1975 victory of his successors. In retrospect, a few revolts triumphed quite swiftly, Castro's, for example (1956-1959). Most, however, drag on year after year, even when the rebel's assets are wasting and hope is lost, or even when the regime concedes that at best only a tolerable degree of order can be imposed.

In opposing the Portuguese colonial presence in Mozambique, FRELIMO opened the armed struggle with a far more realistic time schedule than most rebel organizations. By the time its first operations began, on September 25, 1964, events over the previous decade abounded with pointers if not lessons. Nonviolence not only aborted but proved a poor foundation for open revolt. Then, after 1961, the Portuguese in Angola revealed the intention and capacity to resist nationalist aspirations. Lisbon had real assets: allies in Rhodesia and South Africa; a repressive regime beyond domestic criticism; a NATO connection; and profits from the exploitation of the African colonies. FRELIMO recognized that the struggle would be protracted, and depend on raising the level of violence and forcing Lisbon into compromise or concession. By nature and necessity it contended that each year victory is closer; but such an estimate was based on Portuguese reality, tempered by enthusiasm, and gave a certain rigor to rebel planning that did not exist in fedayeen analysis. In both cases, however different, there was understandable rebel reticence to contemplate analytically just how long the revolt would last. Lisbon held out for a decade, and a Palestinian triumph still seems elusive.

The lethal dialogue is often protracted simply because it *is* asymmetrical: the weak sending a single message that the strong by varying means attempt to muffle. Only a carefully orchestrated rebel campaign, with pitch and reverberation amplified by a careful mix of tactics, can shatter the center as Castro did in Cuba. Elsewhere the rebel usually discovers that the legitimate center has remarkable staying power and can concede this province or that jungle, tolerate assassins in the streets and bombs in the markets, and adjust to chaos yet still somehow collect taxes, repair utilities, appear at the United Nations, and denounce the terrorists—until the first rebel clambers over the wall of the presidential mansion. A recognized regime not only has conventional assets to counter the rebel message but also can depend on the remarkable capacity of a threatened society to adjust, adapt to bombs and sniping, and accept law even without order. Thus to be fully effective a regime must reestablish order—not to do so admits rebel capacity—but many Third World governments have never been fully effective; even the colonial powers seldom controlled the distant bush where guerrillas of one sort or another now lurk. So, at worst the regime can cut losses, discard the vulnerable, and persist, for the rewards of continued power have great attraction and, in contrast to the risks the rebels run, the price is low.

Three aspects of the response to revolt should and often are considered in fashioning a strategy of national liberation. First, the opponent is likely to respond within the bounds of a national character and a historical and social heritage. This response may be manipulated to advantage, as Begin did in Palestine, or ignored at risk, as the fedayeen eventually discovered in the Middle East. Second, the response to revolt, except in the cases where the regime can deploy overwhelming force, will be multifaceted, involving all the resources of a legitimate regime that can hardly be matched by the rebel on the run. A rebel attempt to match the regime with shadow institutions or liberated zones may prove dangerous, may weaken the armed struggle for secondary purpose. Third, threatened regimes, no matter how crude, have remarkable staying power. If a regime cannot be replaced with a certain dispatch, the rebel should recognize that the lethal dialogue he is about to enter may be extended. There is of course a limit on how realistic a rebel can be when contemplating the alien oppressor, the puppet tyrant, the imperialist pawn. If the weak dwell too long on the assets of the strong, high purpose and desperate urgency may erode in a search for more mature revolutionary conditions.

The Rebel Analyzed

On the rebel side of the barricade, those men driven by high purpose and desperate urgency are at first always few. All revolts are largely the work of a small band of zealots who furnish the impetus, the leadership, and the enthusiasm for the others, whether few or many. Even in the case of spontaneous revolts, Budapest in 1956 or Angola in 1961, unless some rush to the fore to control the violence and the enthusiasm, the rising will be a three-day wonder of chaos followed by repression. And in Budapest, the threatened regime had the Soviet Army, an asset beyond the power of the new men to match. Most revolts develop out of a long-lived conspiracy and begin small, rarely as small as did Castro with his decimated dozen hiding in the Sierra Maestra, but nevertheless small. These rebels have potential but insufficient assets to acquire power by conventional means. In Angola, although the conspirators were not quite ready in 1961, they rushed into the vacuum and gave the insurrection coherence and direction; they had long recognized the potential, the yeast of violence in the seemingly inert African mass. Everywhere rebel potential rests largely on reading of the aspirations of the many: a cause.

The rebel assumes that his cause is so valid, so appealing, that the inert mass will be politicized, will lay aside narrow priorities, will support fervently the struggle to liberate the nation. It is a case of right in time will make might, or the truth will set the people free. The flash point of critical mass will begin the chain reaction that will sweep the rebels into power and the alien oppressor into the boneyard of history. The great difficulty for the rebel is that his cause appears illicit in contrast to the legitimacy of the established regime. The rebels may indeed be right, may actually act for the nation, may be on the side of the angels; but they must adopt the tactics of the weak, use irregular means, skulk and hide, evade open confrontation, harry and flee, murder from the ditch, and thus appear illicit no matter how proud their army without banners or noble the proclamation of revolt pasted on the ghetto walls. And some rebels must explain or ignore even more serious flaws than failing to poll the people in whose name the revolt is launched or resorting to the tactics of terror. Sometimes the rising seeks to free those comfortable with the existing situation or to create nations few seem to want or to evade the opposition of a minority. In Ireland the IRA must explain the opposition of the Dublin government as well as the Northern Protestants; in Bolivia, Guevara the paucity of Bolivians in his foco; in Palestine the fedayeen the ultimate fate of unrepentant Zionists. While others may see the cause as flawed—a minority acting for a minority, like the Irgun, or romantics like the Croatians attempting to bring back a long dead world—the rebel does not. For him the cause is pure and sufficient and necessary.

Underlying the ideological explanation of the struggle, whether elegant and convincing or torturous and naive, there usually exists a raw emotion, product of the unpalatable present. Even the coldest of rebels builds his rigorous analysis on a base of indignation or despair. Just as the Irgun rose in response to the holocaust and the NLF in South Arabia to redress past humiliation, so other rebels were motivated by factors not found in proclamations or political programs. In Nigeria the Ibos, far from humiliated, feared that their ambitions and aspirations had endangered their future within Nigeria and believed that safety lay in the establishment of Biafra. In the Southern Sudan, the African population, alien to the Arab-Islamic North, feared for their future even as oppressed subjects of the regime and for seventeen years resisted control from Khartoum. In Malaya many of the rebels in the jungle considered their revolt as a means of self-improvement, a pass to a better and more comfortable future, a ladder to security rather than a struggle to create a Communist Malaya. In most cases, however, no matter what the motive, for the first few rebels, the band of zealots, there appears to be a necessity to revolt. And such a need may be beyond the reach of any accommodation but compelling force.

In time, through success or repeated failure, the vocation of the rebel may erode, for only very few can dedicate a lifetime to the struggle. Most revolts may be protracted, but most rebels are usually young. The passing of time permits the growth of alternatives for the man previously inflicted with tunnel vision, blind to other strategies, immune to the quiet life or personal priorities, driven and determined. Ambitious for power, molded by a warped past or a long train of abuse, incapable of tolerating an evil present, rebels rise out of a need engendered by the intolerable structure of a society they never made but intend to dismantle in the name of the people they have not polled and who might well disown them. It is their very intensity that makes possible a lethal dialogue with a regime seemingly so assured, so possessed of material assets and general recognition. The real rebel anticipates the sacrifices and most important his need to revolt can not be assuaged by conventional currency.

All rebels assume they will win, that history and the strength of their cause guarantee success; but few revolt from strength or assume a swift victory. Most, albeit reluctantly, recognize their limitations but can wait no longer; they often feel they have waited too long. Frequently the armed struggle is launched only after all other means to free the nation have foundered and in recognition that finally someone, someplace, must strike the first blow. With rare exceptions the decision for the armed struggle dominates rebel thinking rather than contemplation of the appropriate strategy for the revolt, the nature of the opponent, or the length of the struggle. It is all too obvious to most rebels that they have only the most limited tactical options—sabotage, assassination, raids, or arson—and that their ideology, organization, and heritage limit even these. What matters is whether to begin and when. The truly important questions are matters of timing; much of the remainder of the analysis can be filled in with a broad brush dipped in clichés and slogans. If the timing is right, the process of draining the center by alienating the people through a revolt maintained by the available tactical options eventually will result in victory. If the timing is wrong, the revolt will be killed in the egg or drag on pointlessly for years. The only way to discover if the time is ripe is to begin, to open the lethal dialogue.

In his analysis the rebel more often than not defines the opponent to his own advantage, no matter how menacing in reality. The innate vulnerability of the alien oppressor is accepted just as is the tide of history. Rebels by nature tend to be optimistic about the immediate future. Even the Irish after eight hundred years are convinced that this campaign will be the last. Although it is rationally accepted that a rural guerrilla conflict will be protracted, in Mozambique or Guatemala there was hope that the chain-reaction of disintegration at the center would soon begin. Consequently, rebel analysis often contains a reasonable estimation of the time the struggle may take, balanced by an unreasonable, ill-contained optimism. Many like Mikhail Bakunin constantly mistake the third month for the ninth. Many like the fedayeen create a fantasy opponent to fit other needs. Many hardly give a thought to the long-range effect of a few bombs in the street. Most concentrate on beginning.

Meanwhile the conspirators have constructed an organization or inherited one to give form to the beginning. The most effective organizations reflect the familiar and relate to the rebel's special heritage and the habits of a real society. The new volunteer may enter a world of unusual values and strange disciplines, and pursue a life of hardship and risk; yet at the same time his new world must relate to the old, may supply what was lacking there but in a comfortable form that relates to rebel function. This is not always a first priority, for some rebels choose the current revolutionary fashion or set priorities other than efficiency. Some rebels seeking legitimacy attempt to create recognizable institutions: underground armies or a liberation front touched with respectability, a seal of approval issued by Havana or Peking. Others, attracted by the guerrilla tactic, create forms irrelevant to operational possibilities. Rules and comfortable formulas do not exist. Even commitment to an "alien" ideology need not foreclose an effective indigenous organization.

As the NLF in South Arabia managed to adjust Arab socialism to the customs of the tribe, so Castro in the Sierra Maestra with his little band mimicked the bandit-peasant. Both devised forms from necessity and within a heritage, not as a result of doctrine; so too other effective rebels have molded without using an alien die. It is not the paper form of the organization that matters but the actual functioning of the movement: Begin's band of brothers or Grivas as *paterfamilias*. NLF success in Vietnam resulted not from an organizational chart but from its ability to maintain and strengthen certain attitudes and values within the movement. Those who prefer elegant imports or accept charts of authority may discover in a Guatemalan foco or the jungles of Malaya that somehow they have missed the real point. Several Southern African liberation movements for varying reasons chose to wage "guerrilla war" organized by the exiled remnants of mass political parties reflecting the Indian Congress Party. The result was a series of tactical disasters arising from an ignorance of the essence of guerrilla strategy. The fashionable form had been constructed with little regard for the reality across the Zambezi. These organizational conceits were often the more dangerous because they were believed, because they determined the course of the armed struggle. In nearly every case the form that reflects the reality of the struggle, no matter what the charts say about battalions or political commissars, functions more effectively. Quite often the form of the organization tends to limit, often narrowly, subsequent tactical options. This restriction may be a virtue, for it reflects reality rather than aspiration. No matter what his movement was called, Begin knew he was directing an underground conspiracy, not an army; but the Africans truly believed they directed a guerrilla-underground when they were often simply ordering vulnerable and innocent "commandos" into an alien land.

The rebel with his organization in place often adopts his "strategy," little more than the mix of possible tactics, under an appropriate ideological banner. Frequently, in the rush to begin, his strategy is determined by events or the opponent. Always the overriding intent is to drain the center through an armed struggle: to send a message unit violent enough to erode the capacity of the center to respond in kind; to maintain a facade of legitimacy; to hold the support of the people. Ideally this process could be initiated and concluded without resorting to violence. In a sense in Russia in 1917 the power and the legitimacy of the center had bled away when for varying motives most of the population no longer accepted the dictates of Petrograd and the regime could no longer impose order. The resulting fragmentation of control and the billowing chaos created for Lenin the prime opportunity to seize the husk at the center, fill it with his band of zealots, and move out in a "legitimate" restoration of order. In Vietnam in 1962 the NLF had gone far to subverting central control from Saigon over much of the rural areas with only limited, if crucial, reliance on guerrilla tactics. Almost always the armed struggle is crucial as a catalyst, the element that will coopt the neutral, steel the converted, and accelerate the decay of the center. In Mao's strategy the process will continue until the rebels are superior even in conventional armed forces; but usually the rebel anticipates not parity but the collapse of the center after the alienation of the people has become irreversible. At this point the will to resist, whether in Havana or London or Washington, vanishes and the rebels rush toward power.

During the course of the struggle efforts are often made to shift tactics, move to urban warfare, mobilize the people in direct action, strike at different targets, open new fronts, and institute boycotts. But the singular thrust of the revolt remains the same strategic message unit: a level of violence that can not be indefinitely tolerated by the center. The rebels may suggest that accommodation is possible, announce a truce, put forth expressions of goodwill, and woo the press and the people with soothing moderation in the midst of escalating violence. This can create severe strains in an organization filled with the advocates of liberty or death, not one inch, and no compromise. As every rebel recognizes, if he is to reach the bargaining table he must bomb his way there. All the subtle

questions—when, where, and how the bombs go off, the size and importance of the target, the horror of the moment—matter not at all if the
bombs do not go off. They are the rebel's key card and it must be played
over and over. How it is played is less important than when, the start of
the game, and how often, the level of violence. Most revolts seem to be
zero-sum games, with one winner and one loser, but the lethal dialogue
may have many outcomes, may even be simply a means of pressure in a
still larger game, the rebel as a violent pressure group. No matter, once
the rebel arrives at the barricade, the only problem is to send, by a variety
of tactical means, that single violent message to mobilize the masses and
chip away at the center. By then most strategic problems have long been
solved or shelved.

Over the long years of conspiracy, time is invested in polemics and
schism, ideological purity and personal vendetta, distinctions. There the
acid pen and retentive mind pay off. There mature conditions are parsed
and strategies proposed. Yet most rebels, in spite of their ideological
baggage, arrive at the barricades with relatively simple, often singularly
similar, scenarios. This may be as well, for lovingly fashioned revolts,
ideologically pure and rigorously defined, often abort in the face of the
contingent and unforeseen or collapse under the weight of reality. Very
few revolts, whatever the strategy, no matter how extensive the assets or
ruthless the rebels, no matter how indigenous the organization or feeble
the foe, have succeeded. Yet, each year new rebels rise, despite the odds.
Did not Castro begin with a handful and end in power?

The Experience of Castro in Cuba

Because so much evolved from so little, Cuba has become a
lodestone. Older examples have grown dimmer. The epic days of Zapata
and Villa and the rest somehow produced in Mexico a government of
clerks and lawyers acting in the name of a revolution far from complete.
In Ireland the idealism of the Black and Tan days appears to have evaporated. In Cuba, however, a little band of men in a brief time overthrew
a powerful, determined despot and used their power to transform their
country and to export their experience. What happened in Cuba and why
seem more relevant to the rebels of the Third World than the adventures
of Zapata, the experience of Lenin, or even the accomplishments of Mao
and Giap. Castro proved that revolt was possible, despite the odds, and
revealed that real revolution may result from triumph on the barricades.

There are nearly as many explanations of the Cuban revolt as there
are rebels, real or romantic, active or academic. Most of the facts are
relatively clear, though the meaning remains elusive. The events began,
as much as any event in history has a specific beginning, on July 26,

1953, in Santiago. There Fidel Castro led less than two hundred volunteers in a raid on Moncada Barracks that he hoped would topple General Fulgencio Batista, who had returned to power in a successful coup on March 10, 1952. The raid was a disaster. A sentry gave the alarm, the barracks was alerted, and, although only four of Castro's men were killed outright, sixty-eight were murdered during the next two days. Castro and a few others wandered in small groups in the hills until captured. The survivors began plotting the next step from a prison on the Isle of Pines. Released on May 15, 1955, Castro went to Mexico to prepare for his return. Money and arms were raised and volunteers were trained in guerrilla tactics by a former Spanish Republican officer, Alberto Bayo Giroud. On December 2, 1956, Castro and eighty-one men aboard the *Granma* reached the Cuban coast. Again disaster struck. The force was immediately attacked, the men killed or captured or isolated. Castro eventually reached the Sierra Maestra with fourteen men, including his brother Raúl and Ché Guevara, an Argentine physician-turned-revolutionary. Despite the peasants' initial suspicion, the foco grew; guerrillas by necessity, the men acquired field skills through practice. Batista's security forces proved inept in the hills and the foco flourished. Herbert Mathews of the *New York Times* came to interview the Cuban Robin Hood, and Castro's example inspired others in the cities to oppose the regime. Another front was opened. Batista's support began to erode. Washington seemed increasingly less interested in his fate, and the Cuban middle class were less careful to conceal their scorn for the little "sergeant" who had all but dominated Cuban politics for two decades. Resorting more and more to torture and brutality, the security forces lost credibility and alienated any lingering support for Batista. At the end of December, Castro and the *barbudos* (bearded ones) came down out of the hills into Havana. On January 1, 1959, Castro and his five hundred barbudos commanded Cuba. Batista, who had once commanded fifteen thousand men, had fled.

From the start the rebels had perceived Batista as a crude and brutal oppressor without real support, a pawn to the least savory American interests. Outwardly impressive, he was in fact vulnerable. The first attempt at Moncada Barracks was the traditional means of changing regimes in Latin America: the rally out of the barracks. Usually the rebels, ordinarily a dissident military unit, sensing their moment, "revolted" and dispatched a *pronunciamiento* (the rebel demands). The target regime then polled potential support, often by telephone, and decided whether or not to retire. In reality the process was a complicated coup by parade that began in the provinces and ended in the president's palace, a favorite goal of ambitious military officers. In spite of Bayo's guerrilla training, Castro apparently thought the landing from the *Granma* would initiate such a process, perhaps slower but no less inevitable. With the failure of the landing, he was left isolated in the hills with his amateur guerrillas, no visible net of support, and no hope of issuing an effective pronunciamiento.

There had of course been rural rebellions and rural guerrillas in Cuban history; but Castro's foco was the result of a defeat not an act of planning. He had a choice of surrendering or trying to survive. In the hills his only potential recruits were the local peasants. His only hope there was to avoid security forces and later attempt hit-and-run actions. Castro by necessity created a nexus of disorder fueled by peasant recruits who found the guerrilla-bandits comfortable figures out of their own experience. The Cuban army, incapable of crushing the revolt in the egg, was increasingly unwilling to take serious risks to restore order. The din and disorder increased. Batista's response was ideal for Castro: brutality softened by inefficiency. Widening repression created widening rebel support without limiting the revolt.

Fidel Castro continued to be everything to everyone: the romantic barbudo in the mountain; a defender of liberty and justice, acceptable to the United States and the Cuban middle class, and yet also to the Left; a friend of the peasant, yet a sound man; an example and a goad to all those rich or poor dissatisfied or disgusted with the regime. His charismatic figure was created out of the wishes and hopes of people who knew him not, only that he and his men were with arms doing something. Ultimately Batista recognized the inevitable and, as had so many others, left for exile. In a sense Castro had extended the march from the barracks to a trek from the Sierra Maestra, collecting support along the way, until Batista, as the game required and such a strategy predicted, withdrew. In another sense he had fed an intolerable din into the Cuban machine, creating noise so loud that Batista's effort to silence it destroyed even the repressive machinery. No matter how the strategy was analyzed, everyone agreed that Castro and his foco had won.

Although Marxist-Leninists stressed the peasant component, the most influential analysis came from Ché Guevara, who made three points. The people's forces could defeat a regular army. The rebel need not wait until all conditions are favorable. In underdeveloped American countries the battle should be in the countryside. Castro added the contention that the guerrilla was the nucleus of the revolutionary movement. None of this was very profound but it formed a theoretical foundation for the foco concept: guerrillas injected into the countryside will infect the body politic and convert the masses to resistance—and the time to begin is now. Almost at once, inspired revolutionary idealists attempted to export the Cuban experience to repeat the triumph of the barbudos. During the next decade these revolts reflected each stage of the Cuban experience, in isolation and often without serious consideration of local conditions. Without exception they failed.

The first attempts to export revolt during 1959-1961 were in effect new *Granma* expeditions, this time sponsored by Havana. In April 1959 Pedro Albizu's expedition to Panama lasted for only a few hours. A foco in Nicaragua managed to persist for several months. In June two landings were made in the Dominican Republic; both were crushed within hours. In August a landing made in Haiti lasted several days. And so it went. The strategy of the pronunciamiento required an initial blow of some strength or the revelation of considerable power. Castro had hoped at Moncada and with the *Granma* landing to inspire an escalating rising that would force the center to concede. But in neither case did he command force enough to make such a strategy effective. And in neither case was the center interested in conceding any more than would Castro when the same inapplicable and inept strategy was tried at the Bay of Pigs.

The second wave of attempts concentrated on organizing rural focos and politicizing the peasants. Instead of beginning with the landing, the rebels began with the band of escapees in the Sierra Maestra. These, more carefully constructed, attempts in Guatemala, Venezuela, and Peru fared no better; they only lasted longer. The most pitiful was probably Jorge Masetti's fantasy journey into northern Argentina in 1963, but the most influential, certainly the most famous, was Guevara's own foco in Bolivia in 1966 and 1967. As always many lessons were learned from the various failures. The most important was a reconsideration of the impact of a rural revolt. The concept of the pure foco—all that need be done is to begin in the country—no longer held any charm. Even the most determined idealist had long felt that a strategy so bare-boned held great danger for both the rebel and the revolt. Guevara, no matter how inspiring his gesture, made every mistake imaginable. More important, the very concept of a rual foco no longer held pride of place. Latin America had become urbanized. The power, the targets, the opportunities were in the city. São Paulo or Caracas or Buenas Aires might prove more fertile guerrilla ground than the cordillera of the Andes.

The third wave attempted to incorporate the urban-suburban guerrilla operations, overlooked in the Cuban experience, as the crucial component. Its most famous advocate probably was Carlos Marighella, who in his late fifties resigned from the orthodox Brazilian Communist Party and organized the Action for National Liberation. He rejected the rural foco as the key (all Brazilian efforts had foundered; one because a member contracted plague), though he assumed that there could be a rural front. The new battleground was to be the city; the first target, banks. In one year more than a half-million dollars (U.S.) was stolen from banks in São Paulo alone. Operations became more spectacular. On September 3,

1969, the United States Ambassador in Brazil, Charles Burke Elbrick, was kidnapped and exchanged for fifteen political prisoners. Despite further operations, including other diplomatic kidnappings, the Brazilian security forces proved utterly ruthless and highly effective. On November 4, 1969, Marighella was shot and killed by the police. Several other important associates were also captured or killed by early 1970, and the movement was severely strained. In Uruguay the Tupamaros, founded in 1962, managed effectively longer than any other urban-oriented guerrillas. Where in Brazil counter-terror and absolute repression by the state was the immediate reaction, Uruguay as a democracy tried to respond to the challenge in more conventional ways. Many saw the Tupamaros as urban Robin Hoods, who produced one spectacular after another and had a keen grasp of publicity. The democratic structure of the state was badly undermined. Seemingly incapable of solving the country's problems by conventional means, the establishment drifted and the center decayed. Ultimately the army was permitted to employ oppressive measures, and the urban guerrillas found themselves sorely pressed. By 1972 the early promise of the switch to the cities had faded. Swift and effective vengeance by the regime largely destroyed the rebels' organization without alienating the loyalists, even those who abhorred torture. And still no one had discovered Castro's secret.

For a decade rebels had sacrificed their lives and their aspirations because they had misread the Cuban experience and, more important, had sought in Cuba what they could not find at home. Although Cuba is part of Spanish America, the differences in style, temperament, heritage, systems, and attitudes are marked. A Cuban example may no more work for Marighella in Brazil, even if perfectly understood and cunningly adapted for local conditions, than Lenin's experience worked for Mao or Mao's for the MCP. Castro's revolt was Cuban, a child of special conditions and opportunities, open to analysis by Marxists but misinterpreted by rhetoricians, open to the enthusiasms of Guevara but not capable of simple export, open to examination by the next and future rebels but not as inviolate writ. And no one seemed to know what *had* occurred in Cuba. Each successive manipulation of the Cuban strategy exposed another facet of that experience, some fashioned by Castro, others by events or history or his opponents. Like all historical events the Cuban revolt was complex and tangled, subsequently made simple by the dedicated. They were driven to begin somewhere, somehow, even with a handful, even without mature conditions.

In retrospect certain aspects of the Cuban revolt seem clear. First, Castro did not choose a foco strategy; it was forced on him. He made do with what he had, cultivated as many friends as possible, made as few commitments as he could, and benefited from the daring of others in the cities and towns. The revolt was an often carelessly orchestrated collection of forces that produced escalating violence as a result of Castro's diplomatic ability, his grasp of the principles of publicity, his ambiguous but romantic image, and the ambitions and sacrifices of others. This very Cuban alliance of forces opposed a specific, not very talented, Cuban enemy: one crude, stupid, and unimaginative, living on brutally borrowed time, who, soon finding himself out of his depth, was willing to withdraw in a traditional manner. Dependent on ineffectual repression, facing a new Robin Hood of the Sierra Maestra, written off by Washington, despised by those who ordinarily sought the easy life and a reasonable return on investments, unwillingly served by an uneasy military, Batista opted out.

Other rebels could not count on this. Everywhere cheers for a few hundred barbudos awakened potential target regimes to the fact that in many ways Castro had won by some sort of violent sleight-of-hand. The scorned despots and puppet regimes parsed a great many more lessons from Cuba than did the idealistic rebels. Henceforth a romantic interview by a Mathews would not fool Washington nor a few bombs in the streets frighten the man in the president's palace. Henceforth if torture were to be used it would be both brutal and effective. Henceforth the dangers of permitting a foco to set up a din would be recognized. In fact legitimate regimes were forewarned enough so even a most ingenious indigenous movement, artfully maneuvering a variety of tactical approaches, would have far more problems than Castro had faced. And in many cases the rebels appeared to seek out additional problems rather than solve some of the vast number on hand. Guevara, for example, wanted to involve the United States, as part of a worldwide strategy to mire the imperialist center in a series of people's wars. This when he had a handful of men isolated in Bolivia.

The Cuban experience follows the same general pattern of other revolts. The little group of zealots, humiliated by the odious Batista, resentful of the predominant American influence on the island, indignant at long-standing injustices, rise as an end product of repeated radical efforts to transform Cuba. The Moncada scenario had to be discarded at the start, so Castro entered the Sierra Maestra without a strategy. One had to be determined by his very weakness. All that could be done was persist and hope to expand. His foco in time benefited from events elsewhere, beyond his control and expectations. And Castro, the dashing Robin Hood who alienated no one, tranquilized radicals and elite, proved successful, fell heir to the legacy of Cuban history.

The Rebel Vocation

Ideally the rebel arrives at the barricades possessed of maximum assets: a cause worthy of sacrifice, deeply appealing to those to be liberated; a clear grasp of the obstacles ahead and the nature of the opponent; a core of zealots possessing the textbook assets of space and materiel and strong friends; and, perhaps most important of all, the luck to rise at a moment when the contingent and unforeseen, the tide of history, favor change. The world is cluttered with the ruined husks of national liberation movements that overestimated their assets, missed the sure tide of events, and began what they could not finish. The odds on success for the little band of rebels in the Sierra Maestra or the hills of Samaria on the West Bank are formidable even when vast assets do exist: an incompetent tyrant, a sullen people enraged by an unfair fate, enthusiastic and powerful friends, and money in the bank. Mostly the center holds. The truly vulnerable imperialists have dismantled their empires, with the result that someone, someplace must strike not only the first blow but blow after blow. Not just the revolt is protracted but the impact of repeated revolts. The rebel can thus find comfort in the fact that his failed foco or disbanded guerrilla column has laid a foundation for a more effective lethal dialogue in the future.

All things seem to limit the rebel's options, to restrict his strategy to tactics. His organization, cause, scenarios, and expectations limit his prospects. Once the battle is opened, most of the intricate ideological disputations on aims and means, on the infantile Left or the unleashed masses, evaporate in the detonation of bombs. Though massive, revolutionary theory is often only tangential to practice. When the pure theory, honed of the knobs and gnarls of reality, is applied in the field, whether the field be the bush of northern Argentina or the escarpment of the Zambezi, disaster looms. When theory is laid aside and power picked up in the streets of Petrograd or accepted by the barbudos in Havana, the subsequent ideological explanations hang limply over the inner frame of pragmatism. If there is any hope at all in fashioning a revolt, seizing the opportune moment rather than the fashionable text, pragmatism is everything, the ultimate weapon available to the rebel. His cause, his anticipations, his organization, and his daily rounds must be natural and real, must relate to the past and fit comfortably with the present.

If nothing more, Cuba suggested that not only does pragmatism play a significant part in a successful strategy of national liberation but also that a rebel must act effectively within a historical context. The rare successful rebel often arrives in the seat of power by standing on the shoulders of his elders. Simply being practical and adapting to the native scenery is an insufficient basis for an effective strategy of national liberation. Foco advocates appear to be romantics dealing in imported strategic currency. The fedayeen dealt in fantasy in depicting a "brittle" Zionist opponent. Yet, just according to the law of averages, with so very many liberation fronts and so many tempting despotisms atop institutionalized injustice, the revolutionary record should not appear so bleak. The lethal dialogue instigated by the rebel has often proved an ineffectual means to power. Putting aside the feeble foe or the one who promises to withdraw in time, the few victories have often come because the challenged center must carry on dialogues other than that initiated by the rebel. Begin could concentrate on the armed struggle while the British also confronted the resources of world Zionism, the suspicions of the Russians and Americans, the disapproval of public opinion, and the doubts of an informed citizenry. The FLN in Algeria had many assets—other dialogues. In China, Chiang Kai-shek, if nothing else, had to face a Japanese invasion. Even then the center has a vast capacity to resist. Essentially, all rebels are weak and threatened regimes are strong; and the weak seldom best the strong. The rebel may grow into strength, as did Mao and Ho, or find a hidden flaw in the regime's armor, as did Begin, or benefit from unanticipated factors, as did Castro, but usually the center holds. Revolt is a deadly game, lethal for most rebel players, a dialogue of the desperate with the determined. The dialogue is deadly, brutal, cruel, warping the present in the name of the future—and often futile.

But the vocation of the rebel will persist. Against logic and prudence, rebels will continue to rise. Their all-but-certain failure ultimately will bear fruit for others, prove vital to the future. In the meantime, the need to act is assuaged, the heritage of humiliation denied, the frustrated longing for control of the future eased. For the reasonable man, however, one less tormented by the present and bruised by the past, one with fewer hopes for the future and without dread fears or whetted ambition, the vocation of the rebel offers no charm. The odds are too long, the results, if any, too difficult to control. The prudent man withdraws from politics or adjusts to the system. Sweet reasonableness, the logic of numbers, and the length of the odds have never yet deterred the brave, determined to strike the first blow. Such men often fashion their strategies of revolt to evade the reality of the weak, consider in haste the scenarios of the future, and march to the barricades to an air too shrill for the cautious. There on the other side waits the future, open to molding through a dialogue of violence. The time for analysis has passed, the dialogue begun, the caldron lit.

Sources
Notes
Index

Sources

A serious attempt to compile a selected or concise list of
printed sources would extend the length of the book beyond my editor's
patience. Much of the material is known to the specialist and would be of
little use to the mythical, common reader in search of "more," since the
focus of the study lies outside most of the traditional sources. There are
multivolume studies of the Empire and/or the Commonwealth replete
with all the scholarly apparatus and based on manuscript sources, official documents, and the wealth of secondary sources. Whole libraries of
books examine the economics of imperialism or the ideas of Empire
(George Bennett, *The Concept of Empire: Burke to Atlee, 1774-1947.*
New York: Barnes and Noble, 1962) or the nature of the Commonwealth
(Nicholas Mansergh, *The Commonwealth Experience.* London: Weidenfeld and Nicolson, 1969). There are general works on decolonization
(Rupert Emerson, *From Empire to Nation: The Rise to Self-Assertion
of Asian and African People.* Cambridge, Mass.: Harvard University
Press, 1960) or those of more narrow focus like Charles Jeffries, *Trans-
fer of Power: Problems of the Passage to Self-Government* (London:
Pall Mall, 1960), and fascinating, popular ones on *The Fall of the Empire,* by Colin Cross (New York: Coward-McMann, 1969), and *The Collapse of British Power* by Correlli Barnett (New York: Morrow, 1972).

There are those like Alan Burns, who write *In Defence of Colonies*
(London: Allen & Unwin, 1957), and those who do not (Donald Mac-
lean, *British Foreign Policy: The Years Since Suez* (New York: Stein and
Day, 1970). There are all the White Papers, Reports and Recommenda-
tions, Constitutions, and Commissions that tolled out the Empire:
Watson and Devlin and Radcliffe and the close columns of *Parliamentary Debates.* No finer introduction to the Empire can be found, nor to
its troubles. The memoirs too often tell what is known and conceal what
is wanted. The Prime Ministers are of little help: Churchill concentrated
on glory days; Eden took three volumes to reveal nothing; and Macmillan too showed great conservatism. Atlee wrote little, and it would
appear Wilson should not have followed suit. Still there are good
memoirs with meat on which to grind an axe—and even there too many

to list. And there are sound books more narrowly focused but even a list on the last days of the Raj or the end of the Palestine Mandate would be awesome.

Therefore, shirking the traditional scholarly duty—or rather evading the will-o'-the-wisp of omnipotence—beyond those sources listed in the notes only, I have included a judicious selection of the printed word for the open revolts against the Crown, and have not even there attempted to detail primary sources. These mini-bibliographies are for those who might like a basis for further reading and to give some indication of the collateral sources for the study. The basic source has been throughout a series of indeterminable interviews capped by long correspondence that is included after these more traditional listings.

Palestine

Zionism has engendered a veritable library, and no mean one at that. One of the best, if growing elderly, surveys of the Mandate, Jacob C. Hurewitz, *The Struggle for Palestine* (New York: Greenwood, 1968; originally printed in 1950), also includes a detailed bibliography; for additional items see the bibliography of my own *The Long War: Israel and the Arabs since 1946* (Englewood Cliffs, N.J.: Prentice-Hall, 1968). Excluding the relevant sections of British memoirs, the printed sources specifically for the Irgun are not great. The most vital are Menachem Begin, *The Revolt* (New York: Henry Schuman, 1951), and Samuel Katz, *Days of Fire: The Secret Story of the Making of Israel* (London: Allen, 1968). Yaacov Meridor, *Long Is the Road to Freedom* (Johannesburg: Newzo, 1955), largely chronicles events off the Palestine scene, and Doris Katz, *The Lady Was a Terrorist* (New York: Shiloni, 1953), is interesting if slight. Begin's four volumes of documents, David Niv's multivolume history of the Irgun, and Eliah Lankin's work on the *Altalena* have not been translated. Also still in Hebrew only is much of the material on Lehi, including the published documents and the work of Dr. Yisrael Eldad, Friedman Yellin-Mor, and Mattiyahu Shmulevitz, although Geula Cohen, *Women of Violence: Memoirs of a Young Terrorist, 1943-1948* (London: Hart-Davis, 1966) and the fictionalized *Memoirs of an Assassin* by "Avner" (London: Blond, 1959) give the flavor of the movement. Besides the ill-assorted, hard-to-find polemic literature, there is the small *The Conquest of Acre Fortress* by Jan Gitlin (Tel-Aviv: Hardar, 1962) on one side, and R. D. Wilson's *Cordon and Search* (Aldershot: Gale and Polden, 1949) on the other. One of the first efforts by orthodox Zionism to view the Irgun through scholarly spectacles is Yehuda Bauer's impressive *From Diplomacy to Resistance: A History of Jewish Palestine, 1939-1945* (Philadelphia: Jewish Publication

Society, 1970). The conventional British account can be found in *Great Britain and Palestine, 1915-1945* (London: Royal Institute of International Affairs, 1946) and *Survey of International Affairs, 1947-1948* (London: Royal Institute of International Affairs, 1952). For the interested the works of Jabotinsky are crucial as is Joseph B. Schechtman, *Rebel and Statesman: The Jabotinsky Story,* 2 vols. (New York: Yoseloff, 1956, 1961).

Malaya

Unlike most of the other revolts, the Malayan Emergency inspired several full-length, solid studies. The most famous is undoubtedly Robert Thompson's *Defeating Communist Insurgency: The Lessons of Malaya* (New York: Praeger, 1966), based on his service in Malaya and three years as head of the British Advisory Mission in Vietnam. (See his later *Revolutionary War in World Strategy* [New York: Taplinger, 1970].) More detailed studies are Richard Clutterbuck, *The Long, Long War: The Emergency in Malaya, 1948-1960* (London: Cassell, 1967), and Edgar O'Ballance, *Malaya: The Communist Insurgent War, 1948-1960* (Hamden, Conn.: Archon, 1966). See also Harry Miller, *The Communist Menace in Malaya* (London: George Harrap, 1954), and Gene Z. Hanrahan, *The Communist Struggle in Malaya* (New York: Institute of Pacific Relations, 1954), both of whom wrote before all the results were in, and Riley J. Sunderland, *The Communist Defeat in Malaya* (Santa Monica, Calif.: Rand, 1962), who summed up the results. Perhaps the most fruitful and influential study is Lucien Pye's *Guerrilla Communism in Malaya: Its Social and Political Meaning* (Princeton: Princeton University Press, 1956). There were as always several on the scene in the jungle or at the briefing session: Oliver Crawford, *The Door Marked Malaya* (London: Hart-Davis, 1958); Han Suyin, *And the Rain My Drink* (London: Jonathan Cape, 1956); M. C. A. Henniker, *Red Shadow over Malaya* (Edinburgh: Blackwood, 1955); Richard Miers, *Shoot to Kill* (London: Faber and Faber, 1959); J. W. G. Moran, *Spearhead in Malaya* (London: Peter Davis, 1959); J. B. Oldfield, *The Green Howards in Malaya, 1949-1952* (Aldershot: Gale and Polden, 1953); Vernon Bartlett, *Report from Malaya* (London: Verschoyle, 1954). The Communists, having lost, retired into the odd pamphletic recrimination and did not carry on a battle of the books.

Kenya

The Kenya Emergency engendered a rather remarkable wave of books by journalists and participants that tended for some time to concentrate on anti-Mau Mau operations. The most famous, or per-haps notorious, of the genre was Fred Majdalany's *State of Emergency: The Full Story of Mau Mau* (London: Longmans, Green, 1962). See also: William Baldwin, *Mau Mau Manhunt* (New York: Dutton, 1957); Robert Buijtenhuijs, *Le Mouvement "Mau Mau": Une revolte paysanne et anti-coloniale en Afrique noir* (La Haye-Paris: Mouton, 1971): Ian Henderson and Philip Goodhart, *The Hunt for Kimathi* (London: Hamish Mailton, 1958); Dennis Holman, *Bwana Drum: The Unknown Story of the Secret War against the Mau Mau* (London: Allen, 1964); Frank Kitson, *Gangs and Counter-Gangs* (London: Barrie and Rockliff, 1960); L. S. B. Leakey, *Defeating Mau Mau* (London: Methuen, 1954); Ladislav Venys, *A History of the Mau Mau Movement* (Prague: Charles University, 1970).

On the psychology of Mau Mau, orthodox version, see F. D. Cor-field, *Historical Survey of the Origins and Growth of Mau Mau* (London: H.M.S.O., 1960) and J. C. Corothers, *The Psychology of Mau Mau and the Kikuyu* (London: Methuen, 1952). There is a great deal of scholarly material on the Kikuyu, Kenya tribes, and even the white set-tlers: see J. F. Lipscomb, *White Africans* (London: Faber and Faber, 1955), and most especially Elizabeth Huxley, *White Man's Country,* 2 vols. (London: Macmillan, 1935), for background. For liberal European opinion see Michael Blundell, *So Rough a Wind* (London: Weidenfeld & Nicholson, 1964), and for persistent paternalism J. F. Lipscomb, *We Built a Country* (London: Faber and Faber, 1956); opinion further to the Right can best be imagined. On the other side, there are various books on, about, or by Kenyatta, such as Jeremy Murray-Brown's *Kenyatta* (London: Allen & Unwin, 1973), Montagu Slater, *The Trial of Jomo Kenyatta* (London: Secker & Warburg, 1955), George Delf, *Jomo Ken-yatta: Towards Truth about "The Light of Kenya"* (London: Gollancz, 1961), and Kenyatta's *Facing Mount Kenya* (London: Secker & War-burg, 1938); all somehow fail to answer the more pressing questions. The other memoirs or collections of speeches of Kenya Africans (P. M. Koinange, Oginga Odinga, Tom Mboya) are about the politics of Kenya rather than the events of the Emergency.

Two most interesting books, however, by Africans *are* about the Emergency. Warhuhiu Itote (General China), *Mau Mau General* (Nairobi: East Africa Publishing House, 1967), and Josiah Mwangi Kariuki, *Mau Mau Detainee* (Oxford: Oxford University Press, 1963). One of the participants in the Revolt, Karai Njama, has his story related in Donald L. Barnett's *Mau Mau from Within: Analysis of Kenya's Peasant Revolt* (London: Macgibbon & Kee, 1966). An attempt to counter the orthodox version of the Emergency is Carl G. Rosberg and John Nottingham, *The Myth of 'Mau Mau' Nationalism in Kenya* (New

York: Praeger, 1966), which, if it does not convince the adamant, is most certainly based on extensive and previously unexamined sources. And yet, when all is said and done, intentions of the Kikuyu and the nature of Mau Mau remain elusive—which is perhaps as it should be.

Cyprus

The place to start is probably with General George Grivas' *Memoirs* (London: Longmans, 1964), an abbreviated edition of the Greek original, and *Guerrilla Warfare and EOKA's Struggle* (London: Longmans, 1964). For a more jaundiced view of EOKA see Dudley Barker, *Grivas: Portrait of a Terrorist* (London: Cresset, 1959), and W. Byford-Jones, *Grivas and the Story of EOKA* (London: Robert Hale, 1959). And in the same vein is Stanley Mayes, *Cyprus and Makarios* (London: Putnam, 1960). The official view can be found in *Terrorism in Cyprus: The Captured Documents of George Grivas* (London: H.M.S.O., 1956). This is the Cornfield Report of Cyprus; once Makarios was rehabilitated through the Commonwealth ritual it no longer was widely distributed—although in the case of Cyprus the documents were quite authentic. The most interesting, perhaps even the fairest, is the survey of EOKA and Cyprus by Charles Foley, Editor of the *Cyprus Times* at the time: *Island in Revolt* (London: Longmans, 1962), later rewritten and extended as *Legacy of Strife: Cyprus from Rebellion to Civil War* (Harmondsworth: Penguin, 1964). Another longer overview by the Foreign Editor of the *Observer,* Robert Stephens, is *Cyprus: A Place of Arms* (London: Pall Mall, 1966). And there is Leontios Ierodiakonous, *The Cyprus Question* (Stockholm: Almquist and Wiksell, 1971) and George Tenekcides, *Cypre: Histoire recente et perspectives d'avenir* (Paris: Nagel, 1964). A sympathetic view is Doros Alastos, *Cyprus Guerrilla, Grivas, Makarios, and the British* (London: Heinemann, 1960). There is no definitive work on the revolt as a revolt. Most scholars have, perhaps justifiably, been concerned with the international repercussions; see Stephen G. Xydis, *Cyprus Conflict and Conciliation, 1954-1958* (Columbus: Ohio State University Press, 1967), or the various monographs and journal articles concerned with conflict resolution or international law or NATO matters. Much of the work of Turks has been to prove Cyprus Turkish and of the Greeks to demonstrate the reverse. A few involved (G. I. Konidaris, Petros Stylianou, and Nikas Kranidiotis) have written in Greek, but seldom has EOKA been approached disinterestedly, separate from the continuing Cyprus crisis and the implication of Cypriot events for others. Several of the British on the island have written their recollections, the most famous being Lawrence Durrell, *Bitter Lemons* (London: Faber and Faber, 1947), and the most useful Hugh

Foot, *A Start in Freedom* (London: Hodder and Stoughton, 1964). See
also D.J.R. Radcliffe, "The Problem of Cyprus," *United Empire,* 44,
no. 1 (January-February 1958) and John Harding, "The Cyprus Problem in Relation to the Middle East," *International Affairs,* 34, no. 3
(April 1958), for high policy and Sylvia Foot, *Emergency Exit* (London:
Chatto and Windus, 1960), for a wife's view. While in all of this there is
a massive amount of Cypriot material, see, for example, the biblography
in Stanley Kyriakides, *Constitutionalism and Crisis Government* (Philadelphia: University of Pennsylvania Press, 1968), and some excellent
scholarly works, see, for example, T. W. Adams, *AKEL: The Communist Party of Cyprus* (Stanford: Hoover Institution Press, 1971), there
is no definitive study of EOKA.

South Arabia

The British fascination with Arabia has been continued
onto the printed page so that, with the exception of Sir Richard Turnbull,
an old Africa man in any case, all those who directed British policy have
in some form produced their version of events: Bernard Reilly, *Aden and
the Yemen* (London: H.M.S.O., 1960); Tom Hickinbotham, *Aden*
(London: Constable, 1958); Charles H. Johnston, *The View from
Steamer Point* (London: Collins, 1964); Kennedy Trevaskis, *Shades of
Amber: A South Arabian Episode* (London: Hutchinson, 1968);
Humphrey Trevelyan, *The Middle East in Revolution* (Boston: Gambit,
1971).

A view from the British side is found in Tom Little's *South Arabia:
Arena of Conflict* (London: Pall Mall, 1968); and a detailed account of
British military operations is given in Julian Paget, *Last Post: Aden,
1964-1967* (London: Faber and Faber, 1969). Much of the scholarly
writing on Federation in the journals is now an academic exercise; but the
flavor of South Arabia can be found in: James Lunt, *The Barren Rocks
of Aden* (London: Herbert Jenkins, 1966); David Holden, *Farewell to
Arabia* (London: Faber and Faber, 1966); Colin Mitchell, *Having Been a
Soldier* (London: Hamish Hamilton, 1970). There is nothing yet from the
Arab side except Qahtan Ashaabi's short work and an attempt by a
Beirut journalist that has pleased no one. In Cairo, Adhmed Atiah Al
Masari is at work on a detailed and authorized history of the NLF, but
the prospects of English translation are dim.

Ireland

The Ulster troubles have inspired innumerable publica-
tions, ranging from indifferent to the dreadful with the few noble excep-

tions. See J. Bowyer Bell, "The Chroniclers of Violence in Northern Ireland: The First Wave Interpreted," *The Review of Politics,* 34:147-157 (April 1972), and "The Chroniclers of Violence in Northern Ireland Revisited: The Analysis of Tragedy," *The Review of Politics,* 36:521-543 (October 1974); also *The Secret Army: The IRA, 1916-1974* (Cambridge, Mass.: M.I.T. Press, 1974) and "The Escalation of Insurgency: The Provisional Irish Republican Army's Experience, 1969-1971," *The Review of Politics,* 35: 398-411 (July 1973). A judicious selection of the available material follows: Liam de Paor, *Divided Ulster* (Harmondsworth: Penguin, 1970); Owen Dudley Edwards, *The Sins of Our Fathers: Roots of Conflict in Northern Ireland* (Dublin: Gill and Macmillan, 1970); Max Hastings, *Barricades in Belfast* (New York: Taninger, 1970); Henry Kelly, *How Stormont Fell* (Dublin: Gill and Macmillan, 1972); John MacGuffin, *Internment* (Tralee: Anvil, 1973); Richard Rose, *Governing without Consensus: An Irish Perspective* (Boston: Beacon, 1971); *Sunday Times* Insight Team, *Ulster* (Harmondsworth: Penguin, 1972).

General

As noted, the books listed are concerned only with specific areas of armed revolt and ignore the troubles of India or the Gold Coast, the breakup of the Central African Federation—and of course the Irish background and the American experience. Nor has any effort been made to include more general views of violence or politico-psychological analyses (see, however, Ted Robert Gurr, *Why Men Rebel* [Princeton: Princeton University Press, 1970]) nor even a sampling of the wealth of periodical literature. For those seriously concerned with insurrections, another source can be found in the pages of military journals. The United States governmen has sponsored a variety of studies of insurrection that should concern few but the morbid except for some interesting work done from time to time by Rand. There is an unbelievable wealth of more general material on guerrilla warfare, on counterinsurgency, on revolt and/or revolution, but even the effort to produce bibliographies of this material have aborted in the face of the churning printing presses; however, a most interesting study inspired by British experience is Frank Kitson, *Low Intensity Operation, Subversion, Insurgency, and Peacekeeping* (Harrisburg, Pa.: Stackpole, 1971).

Interviews

With a few rare exceptions where only a brief or informal discussion was possible, the great bulk of these interviews were of considerable length and often of sufficient depth to exhaust both sides. Usually only a few notes were taken during the course of the dialogue—recent revolution and present position being touchy matters—but the results were put down in detail as soon as possible. Room for error clearly remains, and only very rarely has an effort been made in the text to paraphrase an answer. In some cases written material was supplied and further details given in a subsequent interview. Several individuals proved more than kind and the hours they contributed to the project reached substantial totals. No effort has been made to include the more then a hundred individuals who contributed to my earlier book on Ireland, *The Secret Army: The IRA, 1916-1970* (London: Blond, 1970; New York: John Day, 1971; brought up to 1974, M.I.T. Press, Cambridge, Mass., 1974) but *their* efforts form an unseen foundation. All are listed under interview sites except Ireland; for clarification their area, if different, is included in parenthesis. The lack of consistency in Arab names is a concession to the individuals' preferences. Titles have been cut to the minimum for reasons of brevity, not malice.

Great Britain:

Lord Alport	Lord Radcliffe
Julian Amery	John Reddaway
Lord Chandos (Oliver Lyttelton)	Lord Samuel
Lord Colyton (Henry Hopkinson)	Lord Trevelyan
Lord Harding	Sir Richard Turnbull
Sir Evelyn Hone	Sir John Shaw
Tom Little	Kenneth Younger
Lord Lloyd	Nicos Agathocleous (Cyprus)

France:

Constantinos Karamanlis (Greece/Cyprus)

Greece (Cyprus):

George Grivas-Dighenis	Socrates Loizides
Savvas Loizides	Teferos Loizou

Cyprus:

Doros Alastos	Antonis Georgiades
Andreas Azinas	Dr. Kyriacas Hadjiannou
Sir Henry Blackall	Nicos Kossis
Costas Christodoulides	Constantinos Loizou
Glafkos Clerides	Elenitsa (Serafim) Loizou
Raul Denktash	Dr. Vassos Lyssarides

Archbishop Makarios, III
Ramiz N. Manyera
Yiannakis Matsis
Polyvios Nicolaan
Osman Orek
Christopolous
   Papachrysostomou

Tassos Papadopoulous
Pavlos Pavlakis
Nicos Sampson
Christoforos Seraphim
Fani Seraphim
Pavlos Z. Stokkos
Petros Stylianou

Israel:

Haim Adar
Bezalel Amizur
Menachem Begin
Arieh Ben-Eliezer
Dr. Yehuda Benari
Geula Cohen
Julie Elazar-Torenberg
Dr. Yisrael (Scheib) Eldad
Yaacov Heruti
Yitshak Izernitsky-Shamir
Dr. Meir (Marc) Kahan
Samuel Katz
Raphael Kotlovitz
Haim Landau
Eliahu Lankin
Yehuda Lapidot

Shlomo Levami
Eitan Livni
Yaacov Meridor
David Niv
Amihai Paglin
Jerachmiel Romm
Moshe Rosenberg
Mattiyahu Shmulevitz
Avraham Selman
Boris Senior
Anshuel Spilman
David Tahori
Dr. Ely Tavin
Avraham T'homi
Friedman Yellin-Mor

Lebanon:

Walid Khalidi
Kamal Nasser

Ibrahim Noori (Southern Yemen)
Dr. Youseff Sayegh (Palestine)

Jordan:

Emile El-Ghori
Hamad Farhan

Fahya Hammudeh

Egypt:

Dr. Louis Awad
Dr. Salah El-Akkad
Ahmad Bahaeddin
Tahseen M. Basheer

Mohammed Hashish
Dr. Hassan Sabri El Kholy
Khairy Hamad (Palestine)

Southern Yemen:

Abed Syed Ahmed Ali
Mohammed Abdo Ali
Ali Abdul Alim
Badr Amud
Mahmood Arasi
Ali Ba-Dib
Saleh Abdulla (Hag Saleh) Bakais
Anthony Besse
Abdull Rahman Omer Bulgong
Mohammad Abdel Wahad
   Chowdery
Obeid Furhan
Gawad M. A. Ghabary
Mohammed Saleh Ghazi
Muhammad Ali Haithem

Munawar Hazmi
Ahmad Khamis
Mohammed Ahmud Kordi
Faisal Abdul Latif
Farouq Luqman
Hemza Luqman
Nagwa Makawee
Ali Mubarak Muhawraq
Khalid Muheiraz
Ismail Al-Noman
Abdul Wasa K. Noman
Awad Nasser Sadaqa
Fouad Mohamed Saeed
Aida Yafai

Sudan:

Saddik El Mahdi

Ethiopia:

M. A. Sahnoun (Central Africa)

Kenya:

Jack Couldrey
A. Dalton
John Gachuhi
Stanley Ghersie
Oginga Odinga

Achiene Oneko
Oliver Salter
Sir Humphrey Slade
Victor-Cook

Tanzania (Central Africa):

O. O. Adesola
George Magombe
L. S. Oyaka
Dr. M. S. Sami
L. P. Chihota
Eduardo Mondlane

Noel Mukono
John Mutamba
Stephen Parirenyatwa
Alfred Tsikayi
Henry B. M. Chipembere

Malawi:

Dr. Malekebo

Zambia (Central Africa):

Mark Chona
Munu Sipalo
Herbert Chitepo
Simpson Mtambanangwe

Edward Ndlovu
Mukudzei Mudzi
George Silundika

Rhodesia:

Andrew M. Braes
Jack Brendon
Brian Chalk
P. M. Christie
Robert Cornell
M. W. Crabtree
T. C. Craeg
Paul Davis
Clifford W. Du Pont
Sir Athol Evans
Douglas Garner
Edward Idensohn

Desmond Lardner-Burke
M. J. McGuinness
S. D. O'Donnell
Noel Robinson
Harry Shine
A. E. Smith
Ian Smith
F. P. F. Sutcliffe
Trollope
Sir Roy Welensky
Major James Hughes (Kenya)
Michael Rowbotham (Kenya)

Ireland:

Rory Brady
Seán Brady
Vincent Brown (New York)
Dan Bryan
Mannus Canning (New York)
Denny Carmichael
Joe Clark
Seán Convery
Maurice Conway
Seán Cooney (New York)
Seán Cronin (New York)
Seán Daly
Frank Driver
Maira Drum
Paddy Duffy
Roger Fisher
Michael Flannery (New York)
Seán Garland
Tom Gill
Cathal Goulding

Jimmy Grahame
Fulvio Grimaldi
Seán Henderson (New York)
Seán Hopkins
Seán Og Keenan
John Kelly
Patrick Kennedy
Gerry Lalor
Stein Larsen
Des Long
Walter Lynch
Bob McCann (New York)
Tomás MacGiolla
Charles McGlade
Francis McGuigan
Clan McGuinness
Martin McGuinness
Maira McGuire
Malachy McGurran
Mark McLaughlin

Seán McManus (New York)

Peter McMullan

Seán MacStiofáin

Tony Meade

Martin Meehan

Tom Mitchell

Charles Murphy

Kevin B. Nowlan

Dave O'Connell

Donal O'Connor

Rita O'Hare

Owen O'Murchu

Seamus O Tuathail

Richard Rose

Rico Ross (Boston)

Tony Ruane

Mick Ryan

Packy Ryan

Myles Shevlin

Oliver Snoddy

Sister St. Hugh (New York)

Liam Sutcliffe (New York)

Antony Taylor

Eammon Thomas

Eammon Timmony (New York)

Seamus Twomey

Desmond Williams

(Not listed by name are members of Active Service Units in Belfast and Derry; staff members in Belfast, Derry, and Dublin; volunteers from Dublin; members of the GHQ Staff of the Provisional IRA; members of Cumann na mBan (Sinn Fein, Kevin Street), Derry and Dublin; and various Republican organizers in Ulster.)

United States:

Elias P. Demetracopoulos (Cyprus)

Mahmoud El Okdah (Egypt)

Amin Hilmy (Egypt)

Nicos Kossis (Cyprus)

Abdul Malek Ismail (Southern Yemen)

Kamal Mustafa (Sudan)

Andros Nicolaides (Cyprus)

Dr. Joseph B. Schectman (Palestine)

Fouad Sherif (Egypt)

Kenneth Towsey (Rhodesia)

Vamik D. Volkan (Cyprus)

Correspondence and Communications:

In the hope of clarification and criticism various parts of sundry drafts were dispatched for comment. In some cases this led to extended and detailed correspondence and/or the production of what were really minor White Papers. In some cases the burden of the correspondence was that I was writing nonsense or warping the past or sadly misinformed. In most cases, fortunately, details of my errors of fact or interpretation were included therefore giving aid if not comfort.

Great Britain:

Lord Caradon (Hugh Foot)   Lord Radcliffe
Lord Chandos (Oliver Lyttelton)   John Reddaway
Frank Kitson   Sir John Shaw
Lord Lloyd   Sir Richard Turnbull
Philip Noel-Baker

Greece:

Evangelos Averoff-Tossizza   General George Grivas

Israel:

Menachem Begin   Eitan Livni
Dr. Yehuda Benari   David Niv
Dr. Yisrael (Scheib) Eldad   Dr. Ely Tavin
Julie Elazar-Torenberg   Friedman Yellin-Mor
Samuel Katz

Rhodesia:

Douglas Garner

United States:

Andros Nicolaides   Henry B. M. Chipembere

Finally, under the auspices of the Center for International Affairs at Harvard University a Seminar on Political Violence made possible further discussions with several of those involved. Andros Nicolaides (Cyprus), Vamik D. Volkan (Cyprus), Henry B. M. Chipembere (Malawi), Sean Cronin (Ireland), Dr. Ely Tavin (Israel), Mahmoud El Okdah (Egypt), and Tahseen Basheer (Egypt); and Friedman Yellin-Mor came to Cambridge and discussed certain details.

Notes

Chapter 1. The Nature of Revolt

1. Hannah Arendt, *On Revolution* (New York: Viking, 1967), p. 41.

2. An official spokesman on May 24 underlined the potential for revolt: "Thank God the army moved quickly and acted ruthlessly otherwise the whole state would have gone up in flames" (*New York Times,* May 28, 1973). Reports from Lucknow used both terms revolt and rebellion.

3. The People's Revolutionary Army, a non-Peronist, Trotskyite, urban-guerrilla group, announced that their campaign would continue, although it was implied that a correct response on the part of the new government might cause them to reevaluate their position.

4. The definitive source for Angolan events is John Marcum, *The Angolan Revolution: The Anatomy of an Explosion (1950-1962)* (Cambridge, Mass., M.I.T. Press, 1969). The leadership of both liberation movements, MPLA and GRAE, subsequently claimed more control over the events of March 1961 than the evidence warrants.

5. J. Bowyer Bell, "The Escalation of Insurgency: The Provisional Irish Republican Army's Experience, 1969-1971," *Review of Politics,* 35:398-411 (July 1973).

6. Mutinies of course need not be narrow of scope. Some of the rebels aboard the French Black Sea Fleet sought to change the world not just their rum ration; often a mutiny may be an integral part of a wider plot.

7. Because this dialogue concerns the legitimacy of authority, those who pursue armed struggle in the name of an old and largely recognized legitimacy, rebels of resistance, lie outside present concern. The White generals who opposed Lenin did so in the name of a real and recent legitimacy, just as did the members of the *maquis* who opposed the German occupation of France. These "rebels" did not consider their campaigns revolts but as resistance to an illegitimate or alien authority. Often the legitimate regime lies so far in the past—the Hebrew kingdoms in Palestine or the Ireland of the Earls—that only the most devout would accept the concept of a millennium of resistance. The claims of the Zionists in 1946 or the Irish in 1916 may or may not have been legitimate, but the earlier institutional basis played a limited if comforting role.

8. The Provisional IRA scornfully uses the term "National Liberation Front" to refer to the rival Official IRA, a collection of "Communists" and not a real national movement. Grivas, on the other hand, would not give up the term just because the Left often adopted it.

9. Not all strategies of national liberation are based on revolt. The unification of Germany rested on the attraction of the Prussian core that, through the catalyst of foreign war, attracted all but the Austrians. In Italy Prussian meth-

ods, adapted to Piedmontese standards and combined with a series of risings with Garibaldi's republican expedition in the service of a monarchy, proved effective. Some submerged nations seek liberation through alliance with the strong: a Czech Legion fighting for the Allies in World War I, or the Zionist enthusiasm for the Balfour Declaration. Some depend on justice: the supplicants at Versailles in 1919. Some like Norway, because the dominant Swedes accepted in 1905 the logic of separation, arrive without birth pangs, as did so many of the old colonies after World War II. Many potential rebels prefer strategies of civil disobedience, mass confrontation, parliamentary politics, boycotts, or strikes. Others anticipate that revolt will be a single battle in a campaign dominated by a foreign liberator, as did the Poles in Warsaw in 1944 or to a degree the Arabs in 1917-1918.

10. For an elaboration of guerrilla-revolution see J. Bowyer Bell, *The Myth of the Guerrilla: Revolutionary Theory and Malpractice* (New York: Knopf, 1971).

11. Daniel Cohn-Bendit and Gabriel Cohn-Bendit, *Obsolete Communism: The Left-Wing Alternative,* tr. Arnold Pomerans (New York: McGraw-Hill, 1968), pp. 17, 252.

12. George Grivas, *Guerrilla Warfare and EOKA's Struggle* (London: Longmans, 1964), p. 4.

13. For an analysis of Debray see Leo Huberman and Paul M. Sweezy, eds., *Regis Debray and the Latin American Revolution* (New York and London: Monthly Review Press, 1968).

14. Ferhat Abbas, "Editorial" from *Realites Algeriennes et Marxisme,* in William J. Pomery, ed., *Guerrilla Warfare and Marxism* (New York: International, 1968), p. 20.

Chapter 2. The British Imperial Stage

1. P. N. S. Mansergh, "Commonwealth Membership," *Commonwealth Perspectives* (Cambridge: Cambridge University Press, 1958), p. 19.

2. The Montagu-Chelmsford Report of 1918 on Indian constitutional reforms suggested that placid contentment and British-directed law and order was poor ground for fostering Indian nationhood. In the interwar period the only substantial concession that satisfied nationalist demands was made to Ceylon, where the 1931 Constitution provided for a Parliament with unrestricted franchise, only seven years after the introduction of such a system in Britain—and sixteen years before its introduction in India.

Chapter 3. The Palestinian Archetype: Irgun and the Strategy of Leverage

1. Great Britain, *Parliamentary Papers,* Cmd. 6019, "Palestine Statement of Policy," May 17, 1939.

2. [Lord] Chandos, *Memoirs of Lord Chandos* (London: Bodley Head, 1962), p. 222.

3. Great Britain, *Parliamentary Debates,* Commons, vol. 385, col. 2083.

4. Henry Maitland Wilson, *Despatch* ii, "Operations in the Middle East From 16th February, 1932 to 8th January, 1944" (supplement to *London Gazette,* 12 November 1940, no. 37786), paragraph 323.

5. In private conversation Begin was charming, sincere, iron-hard in his convictions but committed to persuasion and reason rather than force of delivery.

Although in public his oratory is more elaborate and more adamant, even shrill to the unconvinced ear, some consider him Israel's greatest orator—and others Israel's greatest demagogue. During the revolt, however, there were no opportunities for platform appearances.

6. There was very little theoretical analysis before the revolt. The only examples of armed uprising against the British were the American, too distant in time to be particularly relevant, and the Irish, which was studied as closely as available sources permitted. The civil disobedience tactics of the Indian National Congress were also examined, but the opportunity to make use of Gandhi's techniques never arose. The only really theoretical work that interested the Irgun was Katherine Chorley's, *Armies and the Art of Revolution* (London: Faber, 1943), which suggested that orthodox armies would not easily tolerate "irregular" attacks.

7. Menachem Begin, *The Revolt: Story of the Irgun* (New York: Henry Schuman, 1951), p. 56.

8. The basic position for the Irgun was that there need not be a conflict between Zionist and Arab aspirations, unless the British instigated one. "We told the Arabs that we had no desire to fight or harm them; that we were anxious to see them as peaceful citizens of the Jewish State-to-be. . . . We warned them that it was the object of the British officiality to enflame them against us and to get us to fight each other" (Begin, *Revolt,* p. 49). If, however, for whatever reasons Arab aspirations did come into conflict with those of Zionism, then the latter should have precedence. "Of course the Arabs have rights; but our rights, and far more important our needs override theirs" (*The Sentinal* [Jerusalem], vol. 1, no. 10, April 7, 1939).

9. The largest single "contribution" to the Irgun war chest, quite late in the struggle, was £38,000 from a raid on a guarded train carrying the monthly pay of the Palestine railways. A similar sum was taken in diamonds in 1945 during a raid on the Post Office parcel dispatches office.

10. There were also a number of "incidents" of varying degrees of severity. Increasingly within the Mandate all sorts of violence was credited to the various undergrounds, often justly, and the distinction between political violence and criminal violence often became lost in the growing disorder that gave independent operators a freer hand to ply their trade or avenge wrongs.

11. Begin, *Revolt,* p. 84.

12. Ibid., p. 90.

13. The Irgun African prisoners, joined from time to time by late arrivals, created a saga of hardship and escapes, including several spectacular ones, for one of the Irgun's policies was to continue the struggle from inside prison—to the despair of their British captors who, for example, recaptured Meridor seven times before he finally made it all the way. See Ya'acov Meridor, *Long is the Road to Freedom* (Johannesburg: Newzo, 1955).

14. Begin, *Revolt,* p. 143. The Irgun was seriously concerned about the use of the word "liquidate" by Agency spokesmen because it had unpleasant overtones beyond adamant opposition to the revolt.

15. Great Britain, *Parliamentary Debates,* Commons, vol. 404, col. 2242.

16. Begin, *Revolt,* p. 152.

17. Great Britain, *Parliamentary Papers,* Cmd. 6873, "Palestine Statement of Information Relating to Acts of Violence," p. 4.

18. Remarkably successful efforts were made by the non-Revisionists in Israel

to bury the Season. Few, otherwise solid studies made mention of the period. For example, the second (1949) edition of the excellent ESCO Foundation's *Palestine* (New Haven: Yale University Press, 1949) still credited the decline in terrorism after the Moyne assassination as much to psychological revulsion as to measures taken by British or Jewish authorities. As the years passed and other works were published, the Season faded from view, at least among those who would have liked it forgotten entirely. Today in Israel some in responsible positions are honestly capable of denying that Jew informed on Jew. Only in the past few years, particularly after Begin entered the government in 1967, has there been revisionist history written by non-Revisionists who treat the period fairly.

19. For example, in July 1946 a special recruiting campaign was undertaken in Britain for the Palestine police that included the publication of a colored booklet entitled "Palestine Police as a Career." Charles Jeffries, *The Colonial Police* (London: Max Parrish, 1952), p. 158.

20. When the revolt began, in January 1944, no one could see an end to it. Not until 1946 did some of the more optimistic members of the High Command see light at the end of the tunnel; and then their analysis was based on the continuation of the united resistance, a continuation that Begin for one did not take for granted, given the nature of the leadership of the Jewish Agency. By the winter of 1946-1947, the corner had, to the Irgun High Command at least, been turned; but not until the actual declaration of Israel in May 1948 could it be taken as *certain* that the state would exist. A week before the declaration of the state on May 15, the Irgun felt compelled to warn: "if . . . a declaration of shameful surrender is published . . . we shall rebel." Samuel Katz, *Days of Fire: The Secret Story of the Making of Israel* (London: W. H. Allen, 1968), p. 225.

21. The exact number of British forces, army, police, and other, has been repeatedly exaggerated for effect; in any case there were sufficient. Jeffries, in *The Colonial Police,* gives the police total for 1946, the last year figures were issued, as 8,923. Even if reinforcements were added to the total, and wardens and guards from the prison service were included, the figure was unlikely to be as high as some Zionist propaganda indicated. The Irgun of course knew exactly the list strength of the British Army units: 6th Airborne Division, 4th and 7th Armoured Divisions, a Highlanders infantry regiment, the Indian and Cypriot troops, as well as the Air and Naval units, and could estimate police strength.

22. R. D. Wilson, *Cordon and Search: With 6th Airborne in Palestine* (Aldershot: Gale and Polden, 1949), p. 47.

23. British intelligence had been in the process of collecting documentation that tied the Agency to the Haganah operations, later published as a Command Paper 6873, "Palestine Statement of Information Relating to Acts of Violence, July 1946." Even without specific evidence, the British knew the Haganah was not an "independent" underground but integrated into the Jewish institutions. Therefore, disclaimers to the contrary, the Agency was specifically and directly responsible. A repeated reaction of the British authorities to the Irgun attacks was to withdraw into isolation as a means of protection, a means demonstrably ineffective, doing little more than clumping men in "secure" and therefore challenging targets. Cut off from local intelligence, gossip, old friends and normal daily life, the British dependent on barbed-wire ghettos, Tegart towers, and armored convoys left the Palestinian ocean free for the underground fish.

24. Jon Kimche, *Seven Fallen Pillars: The Middle East, 1945-1952* (New York: Praeger, 1953), pp. 42-43.

25. There was never much of an Irgun organization in England, and at times

none at all. Both Irgun and the Stern Group did, however, undertake assassinations. The Irgun objective, General Barker, escaped because of the usual contingent and unforeseen complications that dogged so many of the assassination operations of both Lehi and the Irgun.

26. Great Britain, *Parliamentary Debates,* Commons, vol. 433, col. 2007.

27. Jorge García-Granados, *The Birth of Israel* (New York: Knopf, 1949), pp. 191-192.

28. Great Britain, *Parliamentary Debates,* Commons, vol. 441, col. 636.

29. Included in a collection of pamphlets and writings of the period, *This Is the Way,* p. 10.

30. Given the impact of the troubles in Palestine on Britain and the world, and the impression, not always unjustified, that 100,000 British troops were fighting if not a war then a substantial battle, the number of casualties inflicted and suffered by the Irgun was remarkably small. Official figures are often difficult to sort out by both appropriate dates and in relation to Irgun operations. The Irgun, however, lost twenty-seven killed in action, and eight were executed from January 1944 until the end of the Mandate. After the beginning of the irregular war in December 1947, there was of course a substantial rise in casualties: the Irgun total killed was three hundred and twenty-two.

Chapter 4. Two Alternative Strategies: Agitation in the Gold Coast and Communism in Malaya

1. David E. Apter, *Ghana in Transition* (New York: Atheneum, 1968), p. 201.

2. Kwame Nkrumah, *Autobiography* (London: Nelson, 1965), p. 92.

3. Arthur Creech Jones, "The Labour Part and Colonial Policy, 1945-1951," *New Fabian Colonial Essays* (New York: Praeger, 1959), p. 36.

4. Ibid., pp. 28-29.

5. Almost every British spokesman of note in London or Malaya in Parliamentary debate or press conference indicated that the MCP was acting under Moscow's orders, and coordinating the revolt with similar attempts throughout Asia. The Malaya Emergency was, to the British, the outcome of outside communist agitators' continent-wide strategy of revolution.

6. By no means the majority of the jungle guerrillas were Party members, although at first the percentage was considerable. Maximum Party membership for all of Malaya in and out of the jungle was three thousand (see Lucien Pye, *Guerrilla Communism in Malaya* [Princeton: Princeton University Press, 1956], p. 51). Approximately 10 percent of the Army, no matter at what date, consisted of women, and, judging from casualties, something over 90 percent was Chinese.

7. Robert Thompson, *Defeating Communist Insurgency: The Lessons of Malaya* (New York: Praeger, 1966), p. 40. Edgar O'Ballance, *Malaya: The Communist Insurgent War, 1948-1960* (Hamden, Conn.: Archon, 1966), p. 112.

8. Lord Chandos, *Memoirs* (London: Bodley Head, 1962), p. 367.

9. O'Ballance, *Malaya,* pp. 177-178.

Chapter 5. Two Flawed Strategies: The Mau Mau in Kenya and the Egyptian Fedayeen in the Suez Canal Zone

1. Philip E. Mitchell, *African Afterthoughts* (London: Hutchinson, 1954).

2. There is still no consensus on an orthodox interpretation of Kenyan

events, especially the role of the Mau Mau. The forest bands did not evolve in the national tradition into liberators—although the KAU and Kenyatta did—perhaps because most of their victims were Kikuyu and perhaps because their oathing and techniques in the light of independence appeared too crude.

3. The total of executions during the Emergency was 1,104, contrasted with, for example, 8 members of the Irgun executed in Palestine and 9 EOKA men in Cyprus. During the Emergency, only 26 Asian and 32 European civilians were killed by the Mau Mau, in contrast in 1,819 Africans; the security forces lost 167 killed and the Mau Mau 11,503. The number of unrecorded Mau Mau and African deaths in the forests and reserves must have been quite high indeed; but the visibility for settlers of those 32 European deaths, 19 of whom were women or children or old people, loomed far larger.

4. Chandos, *Memoirs,* pp. 394-395.

5. After the Ruck incident the settlers' demand for instant action had been in part met by creating zones where anyone but members of the security forces would be shot on sight, the forests, and others where the suspect must be challenged before shot, the Reserves.

6. Tom Mboya, *Freedom and After* (London: Deutsch, 1963).

7. Anouar Abdel-Malek, *Egypt: Military Society, The Army Regime, the Left, and Social Change under Nasser* (New York: Random House, 1968), pp. 15-16.

8. Even the normally apolitical Copts cooperated with the national movement.

9. In retrospect, some Egyptian Marxists recall that the Communists led the fedayeen movement, while the Brethren or the Wafd held back.

10. The ultimatum had a stringent time limit that gave the Egyptians very little time to maneuver. If the British had wanted an incident, it would have been an excellent ploy; more likely, however, out of habit the British army took little interest in Egyptian feelings.

11. Tom Little, *Modern Egypt* (London: Benn, 1967), p. 157.

Chapter 6. Two Classical Confrontations: Containment of EOKA in Cyprus
and Concession to the NLF in South Arabia

1. "This right which was taken away by the Christian Venetians, was given to the Church by the firman of the Turkish Sultans. To this day, this firman, which re-established the autocephalous position of the Church is used to Courts whenever its authority is challenged." Raul Denktash, "Letter," Nicosia, February 4, 1971.

2. Greek Prime Minister Elegtherios Venizelos, whose regime was the intended beneficiary of Enosis, refused to alienate Britain by championing the Cyprus cause.

3. In 1946 Prime Minister Constantin Tsaldaris declared that "the question of Cyprus is not a demand and it should not be posed in a vindictive manner; it only concerns Greece and her friend Great Britain." Constantin Tsoucalas, *The Greek Tragedy* (Baltimore: Penguin, 1969), p. 157.

4. Great Britain, *Parliamentary Debates,* Commons, vol. 434, col. 1318.

5. Great Britain, *Parliamentary Debates,* Commons, vol. 476, col. 1279.

6. Stanley Mayes, *Cyprus and Makarios* (London: Putnam, 1960), p. 21.

7. Great Britain, *Parliamentary Debates,* Commons, vol. 531, col. 507. Hop-

kinson, later Lord Colyton, has been enshrined in Cypriot history as The-Man-Who-Said-Never and thereby precipitated EOKA's armed struggle. In point of fact, as British spokesmen were keen to point out, he did not use "never" in a specific reference to Cyprus, only to "some territories"—although the word was employed in a debate specifically on the Cypriot question; anyway, everyone *knew* what he meant. In any case, Cypriot plans were by then well in hand and no Cypriot needed one last "never," for they had been so informed regularly for a generation.

8. During most of the movement's conspiratorial period the name was EMAK (Ethniko Metopon Apeleftheroseos), National Front for the Liberation of Cyprus. The name shifted to EOKA at Grivas' suggestion not long before the beginning of the armed struggle.

9. General George Grivas-Dighenis, "Private Communication," Athens, July 16, 1969 (in Greek).

10. Great Britain, *Parliamentary Debates,* Commons, vol. 540, col. 1950 (R. H. S. Crossman reporting attitudes in Cyprus in January 1955); col. 1962 (John Strachey on attitudes in 1954).

11. George Grivas, *Memoirs* (London: Longmans, 1964), pp. 37-38.

12. *Neos Democratis,* April 2, 1955; quoted by Andros A. Nicolaides in his Master's thesis (University of Maryland, 1970) on Communism in Cyprus.

13. ((George Grivas-Dighenis), "To the 'Leftists' of Cyprus," Nicosia, EOKA Proclamation, May 15, 1956.

14. Grivas, "Communication," July 16, 1969.

15. Andros A. Nicolaides, "Guerrilla Warfare in Cyprus" (unpublished paper at University of Maryland, Spring 1969), p. 18.

16. Grivas, *Memoirs,* p. 64.

17. Ibid., p. 87.

18. Ibid., p. 90.

19. Great Britain, *Parliamentary Debates,* Commons, vol. 562, col. 1268.

20. Grivas, *Memoirs,* pp. 116, 118.

21. Ibid., p. 131.

22. Hugh Foot, *A Start in Freedom* (London: Hodder and Stoughton, 1964), p. 162.

23. Grivas believes Turkish interest in the possibilities of Cyprus was attracted by Küchük, who acted on the encouragement of Lennox-Boyd ("Communication," July 16, 1969); however, other evidence indicates that Turkish Cypriots obeyed on Ankara's orders, than in effect Küchük and Denktash from the first were on tight rein.

24. Grivas, *Memoirs,* p. 132.

25. Ibid., p. 140.

26. Ibid., p. 151.

27. Grivas, "Communication," July 16, 1969.

28. Charles Foley, *Legacy of Strife: Cyprus from Rebellion to Civil War* (Harmondsworth: Penguin, 1964), p. 143.

29. Grivas, *Memoirs,* pp. 181, 180.

30. With the shift in the fashions, at a later date, Makarios indicated that he had not been in full agreement. "They told me: 'If you refuse, you will be responsible for all the repercussions in Cyprus. The world has put its hope on the success of the conference, and you will be responsible for its failure. I was sure that, if I did not sign the agreement, there might be partition. Cyprus would be divided

as a colony and should not be able to raise the question again. The less bad thing was to sign.' '' Robert Stephens, *Cyprus: A Place of Arms* (London: Pall Mall, 1966), p. 166.

31. Grivas, ''Communication,'' July 16, 1969. The largest shipment of arms EOKA received had arrived in Cyprus while the Zurich talks were taking place. There were indications, however, that the British knew of Grivas' safe house and held off so as not to upset a diplomatic solution. Without Grivas EOKA, arms or no, would *not* have been stronger than ever.

32. Grivas, *Memoirs,* p. 199.

33. As early as 1799 a British force had occupied, if briefly, the obscure but advantageously located island of Perim in the narrow strait between the Red Sea and the Gulf of Aden. Although the French menace in Egypt soon disappeared, Britain in 1856 annexed the island not out of ''need'' but to remove from the board a piece that may attract a competitor.

34. Bernard Reilly, *Aden and the Yemen* (London: H.M.S.O., 1960), pp. 44-45.

35. Kennedy Trevaskis, *Shades of Amber: A South Arabian Episode* (London: Hutchinson, 1968), p. 230.

36. Tom Little, *South Arabia: Arena of Conflict* (London: Pall Mall, 1968), p. 59.

37. The Arab National Movement, as fashioned by George Habash, had attracted certain Arab intellectuals, particularly Palestinians and American University (Beirut) graduates, but had far less appeal than the Ba'ath ideology that has in one form or another dominated Syrian and Iraqi political discussions. There was no ANM party of any importance until the founding of the Popular Front for the Liberation of Palestine after June 1967. The NLF belonged to a direction, a current, rather than an international political structure, and could freely adapt the ideas of Beirut to the reality of southern Arabia. From the beginning, however, the ideology of Habash rather than that of Nasser dominated the NLF. Nasser was the example par excellence but, if anything, the NLF considered their movement to be more revolutionary and their vision of a socialist future in southern Yemen more rigorous than the Egyptian direction.

Qahatan Ashaabi, in his *British Colonialism and Our Arab Battle in Southern Yemen* (Arabic), indicates that the basis of the NLF could be found in the decision by seven organizations to send telegrams requesting the end of Arab recognition of the South Arabian League. The seven were the Aden Trade Union Conference (al-Asnag); the Greater Yemeni Confederation (Mohammed Ali al Aswadi); the Cultural Club (Taha Mugbil); Mohammedan Youth (A. R. Na'Rug); the Crescent Sports Club (Nassir Urriqi); the United Youth Club (Mohammed Uthman); and the Tawahi Youth and Islamic Union (Mohammed Abdullah Aldahab). Within the ensuing, short-lived Committee-of-Seven the strongest units were the ATUC, the Yemeni Confederation, the Ba'athists, and the ANM. In addition to the Movement of Arab Nationalism in the Occupied Yemeni South, other smaller groups were absorbed into the new National Front for the Liberation of Occupied Yemeni South: The Nasserite Front; the Secret Organization of Free Officers and Soldiers; the Yafi Front for Reform and Peace; and the Revolutionary Organization of Free Men of Occupied Southern Yemen. Just *how* organized these groups were, particularly the officers, and how broad their memberships were remains clouded. Soon after the formation of the NLF three other groups joined: The Organization of the Vanguards of the Revolution in Aden; the Organization of Young Men of Mahra; and The Revolutionary Organization for the Young Men of the Occupied Yemeni South. The two key groups, however, were the ANM, the intellectual-leadership base, and what were called the Tribal Formations, the up-country support. The NLF General Command was formed by those of the ANM associated with the Committee of Seven as well as other ANM people mainly in Yemen.

38. A most detailed account of the British Army's up-country operations is found in Julian Paget, *Last Post: Aden, 1954-1967* (London: Faber and Faber, 1969).

39. Trevaskis, *Shades of Amber,* pp. 208, 218.

40. Perhaps as many as five thousand Arabs from the south were trained and fought in the army of the Yemen Arab Republic; some formed the basic NLF cadres.

41. After Alim's arrest by the British on October 31, 1965, he was replaced first by Abdull Fattah on his return from Cairo after an illness and later by Ahmed Saleh Asha'er.

42. The NLF also let Mackawee know that he could be held accountable for his actions by dropping off admonishing letters—hand delivered by police guards —from time to time.

43. Great Britain, *Parliamentary Papers,* Cmd. 2901, "Defense White Paper," February 22, 1966.

44. Humphrey Trevelyan, *The Middle East in Revolution* (Boston: Gambit, 1971), pp. 211, 215.

45. During 1967 it became increasingly difficult to determine who was responsible for what since the ultimate success of the NLF necessitated the rewriting of history in order to save lives and reputations and ensure preferment. The NLF claimed to have managed the mutiny, and certainly after November 1967 those involved would not deny such a claim. Similarly, many men might have fired shots in the name of FLOSY but later remembered them as NLF actions. Until very near the end, everyone in the South Arabian Army tried to keep open all possible options.

46. Colin Mitchell, *Having Been a Soldier* (London: Hamish Hamilton, 1970), p. 171.

47. Paget, *Last Post,* p. 229.

48. Several of the sultans were away for one reason or another, including one more meeting with the UN Mission in Geneva, and with few exceptions none had prepared for the NLF coup. The British had to shepherd their families out into exile. The Ruler of the Wahidi state tried to return in a British helicopter; two British escorts in the helicopter were killed and the Ruler "removed." The Eastern sultans got as far as the port of Mukalla before deciding not to disembark and meet the NLF welcoming committee; they sailed off again to Saudi Arabia. Only the Auluqui resisted, if briefly with the help of FLOSY, the NLF takeover. Because of the strong Auluqui position in the South Arabian Army, the NLF did not want to alienate the entire area and so delayed moving in. Soon FLOSY was accusing the British and the NLF of arming the Auluqui.

49. Mitchell, *Having Been a Soldier,* p. 151.

Chapter 7. A Generation of Violent Dialogue: The Evolving British Matrix

1. Mitchell, *Having Been a Soldier,* p. 151.

2. Peter Paris, *The Impartial Knife: A Doctor in Cyprus* (London: Hutchinson, 1961), p. 203.

3. Great Britain, *Report of the Commission of Enquiry into Disturbances in the Gold Coast, 1948,* Colonial no. 231 (London: H.M.S.O., 1948).

4. Trevaskis, *Shades of Amber,* p. 238.

5. *Hansard Parliamentary Debates,* vol. 241, col. 1773, July 18, 1878 (London: Hansard, 1878).

Chapter 10. The Lethal Dialogue

1. Walter Laqueur, *The Road to War: The Origin and Aftermath of the Arab-Israeli Conflict, 1967-8* (Baltimore, Penguin, 1968), p. 116.

Index

Abaza, Wagih, 109
Abdullah, Emir, 56, 65
Acre prison, raid at, 64, 69, 167
Aden. *See* South Arabia
Aden Association, 143
African independence, concept of, 93
Afxentiou, Gregoris, 121, 131
AKEL (Cypriot Communist Party), 117, 122, 125, 126, 140
Albizu, Pedro, 233
Algeria, 16, 210, 211, 212, 237
Alim, Ali Abdul, 149
American Revolution, 25, 182-183
ANE (Young Stalwarts; Cyprus), 126
Anglo-Egyptian Treaty: (1936), 108, 113; (1954), 113-114, 181
Anglo-Irish Treaty (1921), 24, 27, 29
Angola, 6-7, 210, 223, 225-226
Arab National Movement (ANM), 147, 149
Arab Trade Union Conference (ATUC), 143, 145, 152
Arden-Clarke, Sir Charles Noble, 75
Argentina, 6, 219, 233
Armitage, Sir Robert, 123
Ashaabi, Qahatan, 147, 160, 161, 182
Asia Youth Conference, 82
Asnag, Abdullah al-, 143, 148, 161, 174, 185; and People's Socialist Party, 146, 147, 149, 150; and revolt in South Arabia, 151, 152-153
Assassination, as technique of revolt, 15, 189
Attlee, Clement, 42, 53, 108
Autumn Harvest Uprising, 11, 224
Averoff-Tossizza, Evangelos, 118, 137
Azinas, Andreas, 119

B-Specials, 194
Baharoon, Seyid Zein, 148
Bakais, Saleh Abdullah, 149
Bakunin, Mikhail, 4, 9, 228
Balfour Declaration, 33

Banah, Hassan el-, 106
Bangladesh, 9
Baring, Sir Evelyn, 97
Barker, Sir Evelyn, 60
Barrie, Harry, 151
Batista, Fulgencio, 231, 232, 235
Bay of Pigs, 233
Bayo Giroud, Alberto, 231
Bayoomi, Hassan Ali, 159
Begin, Menachem: mentioned, 33, 53, 91, 182, 185, 191, 218, 225, 228, 229, 237; and the Irgun, 38, 40; and Betar expedition, 39; his strategy of leverage, 40-45, 67-69; and negotiations over revolt against Britain, 47, 49; and Haganah versus the Irgun, 51; and Ben Gurion, 55; analysis of his role in revolt of the Irgun, 67-70; use of moral pressure by, 78; on Irgun's fight, 188; similarity between Ben Bella and, 209
Bell, Sir Gawain, 151
Ben Bella, Mohammed, 209
Ben Gurion, David, 59, 66, 68, 91, 94; and Jabotinsky, 39; and the Jewish Agency, 43; and Begin, 47, 55; and the Irgun, 60, 61
Ben-Yosef (Irgun member), 39
Benson, Arthur Christopher, 19
Betancourt, Rómulo, 212
Betar (Polish youth movement), 38, 39
Bevin, Ernest, 42, 53, 54-55, 108
Bewick, Lord, 151
Biafra, 9, 212, 226
Bitker, Robert, 39
Blundell, Michael, 97
Bolivia, 9, 11, 212, 226, 233, 235
Brazil, 233-234
Britain: 1916 Irish uprising against, 14; use of repressive measures by, in Ireland, 16; revolts against, 17-18; growth of Empire of, 19-23; and Indian struggle for independence, 22-25;

and Irish struggle for independence, 25-27; and Communist Strategy, 27-28; postwar changes necessary in, 29-30; reaction of, to revolts, 167-172; misperceptions by, 172-174; strategy and tactics used by, 174-175; and strategy of devolution, 176-178
British Petroleum, 143
Brown, George, 154, 160-161
Burke, Edmund, 179
Burma, 23, 72

Callaghan, James, 196
Cambodia, 213
Cassel, A. F. H., 59
Castle, Mrs. Barbara, 135
Castro, Fidel, 209, 212, 225, 228, 237; experience of, in Cuba, 9, 11, 224, 230-235
Castro, Raúl, 231
Ceylon, 21, 72
Charles, Sir Arthur, 151
Chartas, Andreas, 131
Chiang Kai-shek, 11, 237
Chilembwe, John, 25
Chin Peng, 82, 83, 85, 86, 89
China, 11, 212, 237
Churchill, Winston, 53, 63; on Gandhi, 20-21; on Indian independence, 23; his advocacy of Zionism, 33, 48; and assassination of Lord Moyne, 50-51; and Egyptian problem, 106
Cohn-Bendit, Daniel, 11
Collins, Major, 62
Communism, communists, 8; in Egypt, 106, 107, 109, 110; in Cyprus, 117, 122, 125, 126, 140. *See also* Malayan Communist Party
Communist Strategy, 27-28
Compañero, 219
Congo, 210
Congress Party (India), 23, 228
Conservatives (Britain), 92-93; policy of, for East Africa, 95; and IRA, 201
Convention Peoples' Party (Gold Coast), 71, 75, 78; formation of, 74
Cooper, Nev, 98
Coussey Commission, 74
Creech Jones, Arthur, 63, 65, 79; on British policy on Cyprus, 116-117
Cripps, Sir Stafford, 22, 24, 29
Cuba, 9, 11, 212, 224, 236. *See also* Castro, Fidel
Cunningham, Sir Alan Gordon, 58, 64
Cutliffe, Mrs. Catherine, 136, 187

Cyprus, 9, 12, 141; 1931 disorders in, 22, 116; British policy concerning, 115-117; preparations for armed struggle in, 118-121; revolt by EOKA in, 121-125; EOKA's structure and tactics in, 125-138, 184-185; failure of revolt in, 138-140; British reaction to revolt in, 169, 171-172, 173; Commonwealth Strategy used in, 174, 176; impact of EOKA bombings on situation in, 175; commitment of rebels in, 181, 182; rebel tactical options in, 188, 189, 190

Danquah, Joseph B., 73, 76
Darling, Kenneth, 136-137
Davar, 35, 48
Dayan, Moshe, 62
De Valera, Eamon, 193
Debray, Regis, *Revolution in the Revolution,* 14-15
Denktash, Rauf, 129, 133
Dervis, Themistocles, 124
Devolution. *See under* Strategies of national liberation
Din, Faud Serag el-, 107, 108, 111
Disraeli, Benjamin, 116, 176
Dobie, David, 98
Dominican Republic, 233
Drakos, Markos, 121, 131
Dulles, John Foster, 123
Durham, Lord, 20

EAEM (United Unbroken National Front; Cyprus), 126
East Indies, 210
Economist, 146
Eden, Anthony, 118-119, 129, 130, 131
Efstathiou, Avgoustis, 131
Egypt, 169; revolt by fedayeen guerrillas in, 106-114
Elbrick, Charles Burke, 234
Elizabeth (Queen of England), 97
Enosis, 138-140; Cypriot Greeks' desire for, 116-117; British attitude toward, 118, 169, 171, 182; agitation for, 119-124; EOKA as advocate of, 133
EOKA (Ethnike Organosis Kyprion Agoniston; National Organization of Cypriot Fighters), 12, 119-120, 123, 190; bombings by, 121, 175; attacks on police by, 122; British efforts to crush, 124-125; structure and tactics of, 125-138, 184-185, 187; suspension of attacks by, for peace talks, 127-

128; and VOLKAN, 129; success and failure of revolt by, 138-140; dissolving of, 140; British reaction to revolt by, 171, 172, 173; British strategy and tactics with, 174; ideological goal of, 182

Eritrea, 9, 212

Erskine, Sir George, 101

ETA (Basque movement), 213

Ethiopia, 93

Exodus 1947, 64, 65

Faisal, King, 149

Fanon, Frantz, 12

Farouk (King of Egypt), 110-111, 112

Fatah, al-, 221, 222

Fedayeen: revolt by, in Suez Canal Zone, 106-114; British reaction to, 171; structure of, 185-186; evolution of, 190; failure of, 216-218; experience of, 219-223

Fellows, Ronnie, 104

FLN (Algeria), 16, 237

FLOSY. *See* Front for the Liberation of South Yemen

Foot, Sir Hugh, 132-133, 134, 135

France Soir, 60

Free Officers (Egypt), 7, 13, 109, 128; seizing of power by, 112-113; negotiation of treaty by, 114

Frente de Libertação de Moçambique (FRELIMO), 223, 224

Front for the Liberation of South Yemen (FLOSY), 162; and revolt in South Arabia, 152-160 *passim;* smashing of, 160, 161; British strategy and tactics with, 174

Gandhi, Mahatma, 20-21, 93; and struggle for Indian independence, 22-24; his strategy of nonviolence, 24, 78

Gent, Sir Edward, 83, 85

Germany, 14, 15, 214

Ghana. *See* Gold Coast

Giap, Vo Nguyen, 10, 11, 16-17, 230

Glubb, Pasha, 144

Gold Coast (later Ghana), 23, 106, 168-169; agitation for independence in, 72-77; becomes Ghana, 76; strategy of agitation used in, 77-79; British reaction to revolt in, 168-169, 170, 173-174; commitment of rebels in, 180-181

Golomb, Eliahu, 47, 49, 52

Gort, Lord, 50, 58

Government of India Act (1935), 21, 23, 24, 29

Granma, 231, 233

Greece, 22, 223

Green Shirts of Young Egypt (later Socialist Party), 107, 109

Greenwood, Anthony, 148, 151

Grey, J. W. G., 153

Griffiths, James, 75, 95

Grivas, George, 9, 169, 175, 180, 190, 209, 228; and EOKA, 12, 119-120; preparations for armed struggle in Cyprus by, 117-121; and revolt by EOKA, 121-125; and EOKA structure and tactics, 125-138 *passim,* 184-185; suspension of EOKA attacks by, 127; success and failure of his revolt, 139-140

Gruener, Dov, 62, 63-64

Guatemala, 228, 233

Guerrilla warfare, as technique of revolt, 15-16, 188-189

Guevara, Ché, 9, 12, 15, 212, 219, 226; myth of, 11; his experience with Castro, 231, 232, 233, 234, 235

Guinea-Bissau, 210

Gurney, Sir Henry, 87, 189

Ha'aretz, 64

Habash, George, 12, 147

Haganah, 36, 70; versus the Irgun, 49-55; and United Resistance Movement, 55-60; concentration on "illegals" of, 60; and destruction of King David Hotel, 61

Haiti, 3, 233

Harding, Sir John, 123-125, 189; his talks with Makarios, 127-128; bomb found under bed of, 128, 172; refusal of, to stay execution, 129; resignation of, 132, 133; his Emergency Regulations, 134

Hawatmeh, Naref, 12

Healey, Denis, 151

Henderson, George, 147

Hilmy, Amin, 109

Hitler, Adolf, 15, 34, 35, 39, 40, 41, 67

Ho Chi Minh, 11, 14, 210, 213, 224, 237

Holden, Roberto, 223

Home, Sir Ralph, 151

Hopkinson, Henry, 119, 124

Hungary, 225; Russian occupation of, 130, 212

Huseini, al-Hajj Amin al- (Mufti of Jerusalem), 25, 28

Hussein, Ahmad, 107, 109, 112

Hussein (King of Jordan), 144

Illia, Arturo, 219
India, 20-21, 228; struggle for independence in, 22-25, 72
Indochina, 11, 210, 211, 212, 213
Inner Zionist Council, 49
IRA. *See* Irish Republican Army
Ireland, 193, 223, 230; relationship of IRA and Irish nationalists in, 7; 1916 Easter Rising in, 14-15, 183; British security forces' repressive measures in, 16; struggle of, for independence, 25-27; Palestine revolt contrasted with example of, 68; Cyprus revolt contrasted with events in, 115; commitment of rebels in, 183. *See also* Irish Republican Army; Northern Ireland
Irgun (Palestine): emergence of, 36-40; and Begin's strategy of leverage, 41-45; structure of, 43-44, 184-185, 187; Proclamation of Revolt by, 45-49; Haganah versus, 49-55; and United Resistance Movement, 55-60; further pursuit of revolt by, 60-67; analysis of revolt by, 67-70; impact of, on creation of Ghana, 78; and Malayan Communist Party, 90-91; British strategy and tactics with, 174; commitment of rebels in, 180, 181, 182; Begin on fight by, 188; tactical options of, 188, 189, 190
Irish Republican Army (IRA), 27, 68, 183, 209, 213, 226; and riot in Derry, Northern Ireland, 6; relation with Irish nationalists, 7; on united Ireland, 9; terror campaign of, 26; and revolt against Britain, 192; tactics and strategy of, 193-194, 202-203; division of, into Provisional IRA and Officials, 195; impact of events of August 1969 on, 195-198; and Bloody Sunday in Derry, 198; negotiations between London and, 198-199; British response to, 200, 201
Ismail, Abdullah Fattah, 149
Israel, and Palestinian fedayeen, 216-218, 220-223
Italy, 93, 214

Jabotinsky, Vladimir, 35, 37, 38-39, 40
Jefferson, Thomas, 5, 9, 12, 207
Jewish Agency, 36, 37, 43, 53, 68, 69; and the Irgun, 38, 39, 50-52; and Proclamation of Revolt, 46-49; and United Resistance Movement, 55; and violence in Palestine, 58, 59; and propaganda, 60

Jewish National Home, British support for, 33, 35, 36
Jewry, extermination of, 35, 36
John, Pope, 194
Jordan, 217, 222
Joseph, Dov, 46

Karamanlis, Constantinos, 128, 131, 133, 137, 138
Kareolemos, Phidias, 131
Katanga, 9, 212
Keightley, Sir Charles, 113
Kenya: African nationalism in, 93-94; emergency in, 94-98; Kikuyu and Mau Mau in, 98-106; British reaction to revolt in, 169, 170, 171, 172; and British view of Kenyatta, 174; British strategy and tactics in, 174; commitment of rebels in, 180, 181, 182; rebel tactical options in, 188, 190
Kenya African Union (KAU), 94-98, 100, 104, 105, 181, 182, 190
Kenya Land and Freedom Army, 102, 103, 105
Kenyatta, Jomo, 92, 98, 182; and KAU, 94, 95, 96, 97, 105; on Mau Mau, 97; arrest and detention of, 100, 104; British view of, 174
Kikuyu tribe, 94-98; and Mau Mau, 98-106; British reaction to, 169, 171, 172
Kimathi, Dedan, 102, 103
Kimchi, Binyamin, 61
King David Hotel (Jerusalem), 59-60, 61, 69, 189, 209
KKE (Communist trade union), 125
Kol Israel, 56
Küchük, Fazil, 129

La Rochefoucauld-Liancourt, Duc de, 3, 4
Labour Party (Britain), 71-72; and 1945 general elections, 29, 53; and Palestine revolt, 30; Zionist policy of, 48-49, 53-54; policies of, toward Africa, 78-79; and revolt in South Arabia, 148, 150, 153; miscalculations of, in South Arabia, 155-161; and Northern Ireland, 201, 202
Lahej, Sultan of, 143, 147
Lai Teck, 82. 84
Lankin, Eliahu, 47, 49
Laos, 213
Lari, Kenya, massacre at, 100
Latif, Faisal, 152, 160
Lau Yew, 83, 85
Lebanon, 217, 222

Lenin, V. I., 5, 106, 229, 230; acquisition of power by, 7; ideological strategy of, 9-10; and Communist Strategy, 27-28
Lennox-Boyd, Alan, 128, 130, 145
Libya, 12
Lloyd, Lord, 143-144
Lloyd, Selwyn, 133
Lloyd George, David, 26-27, 42, 193
Loizides, Savvas and Socrates, 118
Louis XVI (King of France), 3, 4
L'Ouverture, Toussaint, 3, 10
Lyttleton, Oliver, 34, 87-88; and emergency in Kenya, 98, 99, 102, 105

MacDonald, Malcolm, 83
Mackawee, Abdel Qauwee, 151-152, 153, 161, 174; murder of children of, 154, 187
Macleod, Iain, 141
Macmillan, Harold, 123, 131, 132, 141; his Plan for Cyprus, 134-137, 175; on Sir Humphrey Trevelyan, 156
Mad Mullah, 25
Madagascar, 210
Madram, Abdul Nabi, 158
Maher, Ahmed, 106
Maj'ali, Mohammed, 152
Makarios III (Archbishop of Cyprus), 117, 139-140, 176, 186, 190; and preparations for armed struggle, 118-120; and revolt by EOKA, 121-124; and EOKA structure and tactics, 125-138 *passim;* his talks with Harding, 127-128; exile of, 128, 129; release of, 131-132, 141
Malaya, 23; revolt against British crown in, 80-90; revolt by MCP in, compared with Palestine revolt, 90-91; British reaction to revolt in, 169, 171, 172; British strategy and tactics in, 174; commitment of rebels in, 180, 181, 182; tactics of guerrilla army in, 188, 189
Malayan Communist Party (MCP), 190; revolt against British crown by, 80-90; Irgun and, 90-91; British reaction to revolt by, 169, 171, 172, 173; crushing of, 174; ideological goal of, 181; hesitation of, 182; structure of, 184, 186, 187
Malayan People's Anti-British Army (MPABA), 82-83, 85-86
Malayan People's Anti-Japanese Army (MPAJA), 81-82, 83
Malayan Races' Liberation Army

(MRLA), 86-90
Mao Tse-tung: ideological strategy of, 9-13, 16; compared with Washington, 13; incremental strategy of, 14; and Communist Strategy, 27, 28; mentioned, 80, 180, 186, 187, 224, 229, 230, 237; his principles of guerrilla warfare, 83; application of his strategy to Malaya, 84-85, 90
Maraghi, Mortada el-, 110
Marighella, Carlos, 233-234
Martin, Sergeant, 64-65
Marx, Karl, 4, 9-10, 27-28, 106, 209
Masai, 94
Masetti, Jorge, 219, 233
Mathews, Herbert, 231, 235
Matsis, George, 131
Matsis, Kyriakos, 136-137
Mau Mau, 96-98, 182, 187; Kikuyu and, 98-106; British reaction to, 173, 174, 177, 181; ideology, structure, and organization of, 183-184
Maulding, Reginald, 197, 198; on Northern Ireland, 192, 199-200
Mazzini, Giuseppe, 4, 8, 9
MCP. *See* Malayan Communist Party
Menderes, Adnan, 123, 129, 135, 137
Meridor, Yaakov, 40, 41
Mexico, 230, 231
Min Yuen (People's Movement), 82-83, 86, 87, 88
Mitchell, Colin (Mad Mitch), 158, 159
Mitchell, Sir Philip, 96, 99
Mouskos, Michael Christodoulou. *See* Makarios III (Archbishop of Cyprus)
Moyne, Lord, 15, 50-51
Mozambique, 210, 223, 224, 228
Muqbil, Taha, 152
Murder Mile, 127, 131, 167, 189, 209
Muslim Brothers (Egypt), 106, 107, 110

Nahas, Mustafa el-, 106
Nasser, Gamal Abdul, 13, 112, 113, 129, 130, 150; nationalizing of Suez Canal Company by, 140; and revolt in South Arabia, 143, 144, 145, 148, 149, 151-152, 160; his vision of Arab socialism, 146
National liberation, 3, 8-9; ideological models for, 9-13; nonideological models for, 13-17
National Liberation Front (NLF; Yemen), 191, 228; origin of, 146-147; and revolt in South Arabia, 149-161 *passim;* reasons for success of, 161-163; British reaction to revolt by, 171,

174; ideological goal of, 182; structure of, 185, 186, 187; rebel tactical options of, 188, 190
Neguib, Mohammed, 112
Nehru, Jawaharlal, 20, 72
Neos Democratis, 125
New York Times, 231
New Zionist Organization, 39
Nigeria, 226
Nkrumah, Kwame, 80, 93, 135, 191; and Gold Coast's agitation for independence, 73-77; use of strategy of agitation by, 78; British view of, 173-174
NLF. *See* National Liberation Front
Noel-Baker, Philip, 167
Nokrashy, Mahmud Fahmi, 106
Nonviolence, Gandhi's strategy of, 24
North Atlantic Treaty Organization (NATO), 118, 121, 122, 128-129, 140
Northern Ireland, 6, 18, 201-205; revolt against Britain in, 192; background to escalation in, 193-195; impact of events of August 1969 on situation in, 195-198; impact of Bloody Sunday in Derry, 198-199; British response to situation in, 199-201
Nyasaland, 24-25

OHEN (Orthodox Christian Union of Youth; Cyprus), 120, 121
Operation Anvil (Kenya), 103
Organization for the Liberation of the Occupied South (OLOS), 151

Paget, R. T., 115
Paglin, Amihai "Gideon," 59
Paice, Sergeant, 64-65
Pakistan, 72
Palestine, 30, 212; Arab revolt in (1936-39), 22, 25, 28-29; British intentions in, 33-36; Irgun in, 36-40, 184-185; Begin's strategy of leverage for, 40-45; and 1944 Proclamation of Revolt, 45-49; and Haganah versus the Irgun, 49-55; United Resistance Movement in, 55-60; persistence of revolt in, 60-62, 64-67; referral to United Nations of problem of, 62-64, 65-66; analysis of revolt in, 67-70; British reaction to revolt in, 168, 169, 170, 171; British strategy and tactics in, 175; commitment of rebels in, 180, 181, 182; rebel tactical options in, 190
Palestine Liberation Organization, 221

Palestine Post, 66
Papagos, Alexander, 118-119, 120, 124
Paris "Revolution" (1968), 11
Peirce, E. N., 132
PEKA (Political Committee of Cyprus Struggle), 126
PEON (Pan-Cyprian National Organization), 120
People's Socialist Party (PSP; South Arabia), 146, 147, 149
Percival, Arthur, 22
Peru, 233
Popular Organization of Revolutionary Forces (PORF), 152-153, 160
Portugal, 224
Poullis, Michael, 122
Prague, Russian intervention in, 213

Qaddafi, Muammar el-, 12

Radcliffe, Lord, 130, 131
Rahman, Tengku Abdul, 89
Raziel, David, 39, 40, 62
Rebels, 8, 179-180, 209; commitment of, 180-183; revolutionary structures necessary for, 183-188; tactical options of, 188-191; Irish as, 201-203; and similarities in imperial revolts, 209-216; response to revolt and, 223-225; analysis of, 225-230; vocation of, 235-237
Renison, Sir Patrick, 174
Republicanism, Irish, 27, 201
Revisionist Party (Palestine), 46
Revolution: discussed, 3-5; contrasted with revolt, 5-9
Rhodesia, 212, 224
Rifaat, Kamal, 109
Roseberry, Lord, 20
Rosenberg, Moshe, 39
Rowbotham, Mike, 98
Royal Ulster Constabulary (RUC), 194
Ruck, Michael, massacre of, 100
Russia: collapse of (1917), 10, 229; opening of Middle East to, 128-129, 141; occupation of Hungary by, 130, 212; intervention in Prague by, 213

Sadat, Anwar el-, 92
Salami, Fadhl Ahmed, 149
Saleh, Hag, 157
Sallami, Ali al-, 152
Sampson, Nicos, 131
Sandstrom, Justice, 64

Sandys, Duncan, 148
Season (anti-Irgun campaign), 49-52, 53, 55, 66
Shackleton, Lord, 154-155, 161
Sillitoe, Sir Percy, 103
Singapore, 22, 29
Sneh, Moshe, 47, 49, 52, 55, 56
Somalia, 93
Somaliland, British, 93
Sorel, Georges, 9
South Africa, Union of, 20, 212, 224
South Arabia, 175, 176, 182, 228; revolt in, 141-155, 157-161; miscalculations by British Labour Party in, 155-157; British reaction to revolt in, 169, 170, 171; evacuation of British from, 174; structure of NLF in, 185; rebel tactical options in, 188, 189, 190
South Arabian League (SAL), 143, 147, 182
Srinagar, Kashmir, 6
S. S. Patria, 36
S. S. Struma, 36
Stalin, Joseph, 4, 8, 10, 80
Statute of Westminster, 20
Stern, Avraham, 36, 37, 40
Stern Group, 36-37, 48, 51; assassination of Lord Moyne by, 15, 50; and United Resistance Movement, 55-56, 58, 59
Stevenson, Sir Ralph, 113
Strategies of national liberation: ideological, 9-13; nonideological, 13-17; Commonwealth, of devolution, 19-20, 21, 30, 72, 79, 91, 106, 167-168, 176-178; Indian (nonviolence), 24, 28; Irish (guns), 24, 25-27, 28; Communist, 27-28; of leverage, Begin's, for Palestine, 40-45, 67-69; of agitation, in Gold Coast, 77-79
Stratos, George, 118
Sudan, 9, 93, 113, 212, 226
Suez Canal Agreement (1954), 113
Suez Canal Zone, 107, 176, 188; revolt by fedayeen guerrillas in, 108-114; Anglo-French descent on, 130; British reaction to revolt in, 169; and strategy of devolution, 177
Sunday Express, 63
Syria, 217

Taxim (partition), 130-131, 133
Templer, Sir Gerald, 88-89
Tenuat Hameri. *See* United Resistance Movement
Terror, use of, as tactical option in armed struggles, 189
T'homi, Avraham, 38, 39
Times (London), 111, 165, 188
TMT (Turkish Defense Organization), 133, 134
Tone, Wolfe, 27, 30, 201, 205
Trevaskis, Sir Kennedy, 147, 148, 150, 174
Trevelyan, Sir Humphrey, 156-157, 159
Trotsky, Leon, 8, 10-11
TUC. *See* Arab Trade Union Conference
Turks (in Cyprus), 139-140; involvement of, in Cyprus problem, 122, 123; attitude of, toward EOKA's armed struggle, 126; increasing militancy of, 129; and partition, 130-131; and Zurich agreements, 137-138
Turnbull, Sir Richard, 150, 155-156, 189

United Arab Republic, 141
United Gold Coast Convention Party, 73, 74
United Nations, 175; referral of Palestine problem to General Assembly of, 62-64, 65-66, 177; Special Committee on Palestine (UNSCOP), 64, 65; and independence for Somalia, 93; and Cyprus question, 118-119, 121-122, 123, 132, 133, 137; and revolt in South Arabia, 147, 153-154, 159
United Resistance Movement (Tenuat Hameri), 55-60
United States: Zionist policy of, 48, 49; and Anglo-American Committee, 54; 1776 rebels in, 182-183
UNSCOP (United Nations Special Committee on Palestine), 64
Uruguay, 214, 234
Uttar Pradesh, 6

Valentia, Lord, 142
Venezuela, 212, 233
Victoria (Queen of England), 116
Vietnam, 14, 215, 229
Violence: low intensity, 6; creative function of, 12
Vlahos, G., 136
VOLKAN (Cyprus), 129, 133, 139

Wafd Party (Egypt), 106, 107, 108, 110, 111

Warsaw Ghetto, rising in, 36
Waruhiu, Senior Chief, 97
Watson, A. A., Commision of, 74, 173
Weizmann, Chaim, 39, 40, 50
White Paper (1939), 22, 28, 29, 33, 35, 36, 40
Winster, Lord, 117
World Zionist Organization, 35, 39, 70
Wyndham, Ralph, 62

Yaffi, Ali Salim, 158
Yamashita, Tomoyuki, 22

Yemen, People's Republic of Southern, 161. *See also* South Arabia
Yishuv, defined, 35
Yorgadjis, Polycaropos, 131
Young Egypt movement, 106, 107, 109, 110, 112

Zachariades, Nicos, 125, 223
Zaïre, 212
Zaki, Selim, 106
Zorlu, Fatin Rustu, 133, 137